Training for Development

The Irwin-Dorsey Series in Behavioral Science

Training for

Development

ROLF P. LYNTON

and

UDAI PAREEK

University of North Carolina

Education is not for knowing more but for behaving differently.
RUSKIN

The world owes all its onward impulse to men ill at ease.
HAWTHORNE

1967 • RICHARD D. IRWIN, INC., and
THE DORSEY PRESS, Homewood, Illinois

To

STEPHEN M. COREY

and

FRITZ J. ROETHLISBERGER

*from whose courage to develop
themselves and others
we have directly profited*

Preface

IN A SHORT TWENTY YEARS, training has mushroomed into a large-scale activity. This is so the world over. In industrially developed countries training is a means to reduce obsolescence among people and organizations in the face of relentless technological innovation. The U.S.A. provides our examples for this group throughout the book. In developing countries, far away to the East and not so far away to the South, increased knowledge and skill—and application—are the latent resource that can be mobilized by training without heavy demands on scarce capital and scarcer foreign exchange. For these countries, India is our example. The concept, strategy, and method of training does not differ from the industrialized to the industrializing countries. But India's poverty and tradition, scale and stark need, make the bare bones of the task stick out and clarify the issues.

The immediate question is whether all this training activity, or even the greater part of it, can be justified by its results. Our answer is no, with honorable exceptions. The action question then is how it can be improved. This is what the book is about. Involved in answering the question in action are program directors and trainers now numbered by the thousands, as well as participants in training programs, and their organizations, who are entitled to receive good value for their investment in training.

A few sample figures can indicate the broad dimensions of what we are concerned about. American industry alone spends on the order of three billion dollars on formal training programs each year, that is, a sum about equivalent to all American foreign aid. Investment in skills acquired through systematic training now accounts for over half of the expenditure on all formal education in the country. Six hundred million dollars are spent on management development programs alone. Total annual expenditure on training of all kinds is above ten billion dollars. Professional membership of the American Society for Training and Development now exceeds 5,000. It was 15 in 1943.

India must have about 4,000 industrial training institutions alone and spend seventy-five to one hundred million dollars a year on them. If the wages of participants for the time spent in training are added, as they should be to get at the whole cost of training, the total doubles to 150–200 million dollars. Seventy to eighty percent of Indians who live in villages by farming are served by other training programs and institutions. Reports mention "training camps" each year for over 700,000 village leaders, for instance. Our estimate of expenditure on all kinds of training in India comes to about six billion dollars a year, that is, the equivalent of ten to fifteen percent of the Fourth Plan outlay.

These figures, great as they are, do not upset us. Training is indeed required on a vast scale. But it must yield results more or less commensurate with the expenditure, results in terms of more and better output of goods and services and satisfaction.

Increases in effectiveness and reductions in cost must be achieved, if at all, by individual training programs and training sessions. There can hardly be a training session that costs less than $200, overall, or a training day that costs less than $1,000. A one month's program is a $25,000 product, at least. Here then is the first question that "consumers" of training ought to ask themselves: is *this* $25,000 dollar product what they really want and need? Maybe they ought to get a new machine instead, or spend a similar amount toward reorganization. Do they need *this* training, not any other; for *this* person, not another? We simply cannot assume that this kind of question now gets raised.

If the answer to this question is affirmative, then quite simple costing makes another important point: The trainer's salary is a minor item in the total. The participants' time is the main expense. Table I sets out for

Table I

PARTICIPANTS' WAGES AND SALARIES DURING ONE TRAINING
SESSION, ONE OF 100 SESSIONS PER MONTH

	Dollars				
One participant's pay per month	200	400	600	800	1,000
One participant's pay per session	2	4	6	8	10
All participants' pay per session					
10 participants	20	40	60	80	100
20	40	80	120	160	200
30	60	120	180	240	300
40	80	160	240	320	400
50	100	200	300	400	500

easy reference the cost of that time for a session for participants earning various amounts, and training in groups of various sizes. Since the trainer's part is the key to the results of training, it is good business to attract top-class people to this profession, to pay them well, and to establish work loads that allow time for adequate preparation of any session. No effort or expense is excessive to help develop their skills further and to ensure an institutional climate favorable to their use. The development of more effective trainers, training programs, and training institutions restates the scope of this book.

The training and development themes overlap and intertwine throughout the book. Both are strongly contrapuntal: they call for new divergent elements to make a change—and also for convergent, unifying strengths to hold the social fabric together; they move people from the comforts of dependence to assertive independence, and must then move them beyond assertion to mature interdependence and collaboration. Big swings like these are difficult to contain within the same program and structure. We see training institutions as having this basic function of demonstrating societies in miniature, like a mirror reflecting development and also initiating and sustaining it. Only trainers who are great as people are suitable staff for such institutions.

Concept and Words

A word about the basic concept and the terminology we use throughout the book. *Training* as we see it aims at a lasting improvement "on the job." The kind of education we call training—more of this distinction later—is in truth "not for knowing more but for behaving differently." Training then is concerned with *people-on-jobs-in-organizations*—the whole of this unwieldy amalgam.

All people who plan and run training courses and sessions are designated in this book as trainers. In real life they may be called members of the faculty or of the training or directing staff, or instructors, and so forth. *Participants* describes the people who come for training and is here synonymous with trainee, member, intern, and the like. We use the word *organization* only for the place and program in which participants have jobs, and *institution* only for the place and program that offers training.

Structure of the Book

The book has five parts. Part I differentiates training from other instructional activities and then traces the contribution to the training process of two partners in it: the participants and the organizations in which they work and are to use their training.

In Parts II, III, and IV—the core of the book—we look at the training process from the point of view of the third partner, the trainers at work on a program in a training institution. The parts deal in turn with the three major phases in training: pretraining, training, and posttraining. It is significant that the pretraining part is by far the longest. For training to be well organized, every major activity has its roots in the pretraining phase, even follow-up services which have to go into operation only much later. In the pretraining phase trainers choose training strategies appropriate to the organization's training needs (Chapter 3), prepare the participants and their organizations for a program (Chapter 4), choose training methods to attain specified purposes (Chapter 5), and build them into a program design (Chapter 6).

Part III deals with the training phase; the transactions between trainers and participants, and among participants themselves. The fact that participants are in groups introduces social complexities and possibilities. Chapter 7 examines the trainer's attitudes and activities particularly in relation to the social processes that help or hinder learning. Many different training styles turn out to be effective—for different trainers. The trainer's personality comes into focus in Chapter 8 as a very important factor in choosing training methods and activities. Part IV, on the posttraining phase, examines the contact trainers maintain with participants and their organizations after the program is over, through personal support and services of many kinds (Chapter 9).

In Part V we raise our sights to encompass the training institution as a whole and the development of training as a profession—through research and action. To be effective over the long run, trainers need the support of colleagues and a favorable climate in which to work. The principal plays a key role in promoting both (Chapter 10). For training to progress beyond intuitive practice requires systematic review of experiences and planned research, not by experts primarily but by trainers themselves. Research, particularly action-research, can and must become second nature and properly organized as a major part of a trainer's work.

To make the book directly useful to the practicing trainer and principal, we have included many descriptions of experiences, ours and colleagues', in various institutions; research findings in summary; and additional readings. This material is set off from the continuing text in various ways. Descriptions that directly illustrate the main text and can be read as part of it are indented, for easy reference or omission, whichever the reader prefers. Numerical data are set out as "tables," diagrams and graphs as "figures." "Exhibits" contain conceptual material or sample forms and other aids that enable the reader to try out some idea mentioned in the text. Finally, there are two kinds of "readings." One kind consists of summarized research findings on some points. To avoid unbalancing the main text, they are set out in separate "boxes" and are only referred to in the text. The other readings are longer and follow the appropriate chapter. They go into more detail on various matters than we want to include in the text of this book. Some offer a different approach or point of view than ours.

To facilitate reference to these different kinds of data, each chapter has a detailed contents sheet.

The book is the product, most of all, of direct training experience. Before we became colleagues in 1963, one of us had been a trainer and a principal in local and international programs for industrial and community organizations, the other in programs for teachers and for farmers and rural development workers. Two years of wonderfully close collaboration followed at the Small Industry Extension Training Institute, where Pareek became Director of Extension Education, and Lynton was the Ford Foundation Consultant attached to that department and also team leader of the international consultant group attached to the Institute as a whole. Being new, Siet Institute offered unusual opportunities for thinking afresh about many key tasks that in other institutions were enveloped in traditions, and for getting our colleagues to join in. We are full of admiration for the efforts and achievements of many of them. Colleagues in several departments read and commented on parts of this book at various stages.

Colleagues elsewhere whom we have consulted are too numerous to mention individually here. The initial plans for the book went to forty people known to us in various parts of the world. Some have a reference or a reading in the body of the book.

The final readers must have special mention and warm thanks. They are five: Betty Mathews, then Ford Foundation Consultant in Public Health Education in India, now Professor of Public Health Education at the University of North Carolina; Goodwin Watson, Distinguished Service Professor and Director of the Laboratory of Applied Behavioral Science at Newark College, New Jersey; Shib Mitra, Director of the Department of Psychological Foundations of the National Council for Educational Research and Training, Delhi; Warren Bennis, Chairman of the Organization Studies Department at the Massachusetts Institute of Technology; and Harriet Ronken Lynton, one of our already long-suffering wives.

Some parts of the first three chapters of the book were initially used in an inter-institutional faculty program in 1965. The list of secretarial staff involved in typing successive drafts since that time is long: Dhun F. and Maharukh F. Mehta, Sundri Merchandani, Siloo Nakra, Joyce Pearson, H. N. Seethamma, V. Srinivasan, and, in the U.S.A., Charlotte Mansfield and Sandra Cameron. Only those who have at one time or another labored to decipher our handwriting and our propensity for using all available space on a sheet of paper for rectifications and insertions can really appreciate the contribution this staff has made to the book.

What has impressed us most throughout the process of consultation with colleagues and collection of data is the near unanimity of concern that training as now practiced needs to shift gears in a major way. The consensus seems to be that there is enough dissatisfaction and also enough competence and endeavor to make significant progress in practice.

Chapel Hill, N.C.   ROLF P. LYNTON
August, 1967   UDAI PAREEK

Table of Contents

List of Figures, Boxes, and Exhibits

FIGURES

BOXES

EXHIBITS

PART I

Training: Aims, Partners,

and Process

Chapter 1

rrrrrrrrrrrrrrrrrrrrrrrrrrrr

What Is Training?

ⲅⲅⲅⲅⲅⲅⲅⲅⲅⲅⲅⲅⲅⲅⲅⲅⲅⲅⲅⲅⲅⲅⲅⲅⲅⲅⲅⲅⲅⲅ

"Seek simplicity and distrust it."

—A. N. Whitehead

"Firstly, gradualness. About this most important condition of fruitful scientific work I never can speak without emotion. Gradualness, gradualness and gradualness. From the very beginning of your work, school yourselves to severe gradualness in the accumulation of knowledge."

—*Pavlov's Bequest to the Academic Youth of Soviet Russia*

"All 'graduations' in human development mean the abandonment of a familiar position, . . . all growth . . . must come to terms with this fact."

—Erik H. Erikson

POVERTY-STRICKEN India spends $6 billion on training each year, wealthy U.S.A. nearly twice as much. Expenditures of such magnitudes call for a periodic sharp look. Training needs this look extra much. For one thing, it is a new field and is still expanding fast. For another, controversy seems to envelop every attempt to find benefits commensurate with the costs of training.

No one doubts the contribution that training *can* make to development of all kinds. Training is essential, obviously so. The doubt comes over its contribution in practice. Complaints are growing about its ineffectiveness and waste. The training apparatus and its costs have multiplied but not the benefits. Many organizations feel obliged to fill the apparatus with people but do so with no enthusiasm. Training has become like a tax levied on willing and unwilling alike. The growing disillusionment shows in many ways: in reluctance to send the most promising people for training, for instance, and in the inadequate use often made of personnel after training. Yet training continues to be in fashion. No self-respecting country does without it. With this mounting disillusionment, training has entered a dangerous phase in its development.

Extreme swings of opinion, from loud acclamation to utter despair, denote impatience and a lack of skill, that is all. This is true in the case of training no less than in other endeavors. An inexperienced operator on a machine uses movements too large and tiring. A small child alternately runs or sits before it can "just" walk. A new teacher raises his voice or whispers before he settles down to an appropriate speaking volume. The extreme views on training have a similar basis. In sober fact, training is neither a panacea for all ills, nor is it a waste of time. What is required most of all is to use the divine sense of impatience to acquire more insight into what training can or cannot do and more skill in designing and carrying out training effectively and economically. In short, to take a good sharp look.

The searchlight of inquiry may make the task and its challenges stand out too starkly, too simply. The risk seems worth taking in order to achieve the greatest possible clarity. The reader's own experience will be the best guard against oversimplification. Using experience with training in India and other rapidly developing countries has this same advantage, too, at similar risk. The contribution that training can make to development is needed there so acutely and so obviously. At the same time, resources available to make this contribution are so terribly tight. The lines are then most sharply drawn: on the one hand, no promise can be ignored; on the other, no wastage can be allowed to continue.

The point about wastage may also help readers who are inclined to fret with impatience when clarification of an issue requires slow, meticulous attention. Why bother? First, of course, because all life is lived minute by minute, and the minutes in succession hold all the potential there is for good and ill. Second, when this feeling comes, it may also help to remember the high cost of training. One hundred dollars per training hour is common, even in poverty-stricken India. Clearly, the very best use of that hour is worth the most careful attention on this score alone.

ASSUMPTIONS FOR PREVAILING AND NEW CONCEPTS OF TRAINING

The way training is usually set up now is something like this: There is pressure to improve performance in some field, say medicare or agriculture. Policy decisions are taken to give existing staff "some" training and to add more staff. It is urgent. (In developing countries things are always behindhand by definition and hence urgent.) The first training course has to start without delay. Its length is "roughed out." The syllabus is developed quickly at a desk, discussed with other officers down the corridor. It ensures that the "subject" "gets covered." The "subject" fans out as its application is considered and as more and more people want to contribute to planning the course. Soon the syllabus is overfilled. Trainers are told to follow it strictly; otherwise they could not "get through it."

Agencies are asked to send staff to the first course. The notice may be short, but they feel obliged to send their quota of participants. Qualifications are minimal: a certain academic standard and so many years of experience. The experience qualification is loosened when necessary so that the course is sure to be full.

The course starts. Lecturing seems about the only way to "get through." Trainers console themselves with the thought that participants will at least be "exposed" to the subject that way, "oriented." As soon as the first "batch" leaves, the next batch comes. There are so many people to train and time is short. After the first round or two the syllabus is standardized. In this manner, a new training program has now been set up.

The assumptions underlying this kind of process are usually not stated. There is "no time." There is also little inclination to touch things that seem so unmanageable and may be upsetting, either to those who are responsible for the course or to those who will decide about sending people to it, or both. But these underlying assumptions can be stated and checked against experience. And more useful assumptions can be developed. We will start with this.

Exhibit 1.1 lists four assumptions that are implied by current training practices and, parallel, a second list of four other assumptions which look more useful. The first two are assumptions about individual learning. They lead on to the two others, which concern responsibility for training and action.

1. Knowledge and Action

Much training now proceeds as if knowledge and action were directly related. This is itself a striking illustration of the wide gulf that separates these two. Often the very same people who organize or countenance the imparting of knowledge under the heading of training are on

Exhibit 1.1

ASSUMPTIONS UNDERLYING TWO CONCEPTS OF TRAINING

The Prevailing Concept	*The New Concept*
1. The acquisition of subject matter knowledge by a participant leads to action.	1. Motivations and skills lead to action. Skills are acquired through practice.
2. The participant learns what the trainer teaches. Learning is a simple function of the capacity of the participant to learn and the ability of the trainer to teach.	2. Learning is a complex function of the motivation and capacity of the individual participant, the norms of the training group, the training methods and the behavior of the trainers, and the general climate of the institution. The participant's motivation is influenced by the climate of his work organization.
3. Individual action leads to improvement on the job.	3. Improvement on the job is a complex function of individual learning, the norms of the working group, and the general climate of the organization. Individual learning, unused, leads to frustration.
4. Training is the responsibility of the training institution. It begins and ends with the course.	4. Training is the responsibility of three partners: the participant's organization, the participant, and the training institution. It has a preparatory, pretraining, and a subsequent, posttraining, phase. All are of key importance to the success of training.

other occasions vociferously clear that knowledge is "no use." New graduates, even in agriculture and engineering, are of no use to them till they gain "experience"; and this experience is gained over many years of hard work and hard knocks. They *know* this. But they do not *act* on this knowledge when it comes to plans for training.

Indian tradition makes it difficult to use this distinction between knowledge and action or to accord it the basic importance it deserves. There is the traditional reverence for the man of knowledge, the sage, the guru. Trainers would be less than human if they were not tempted to enjoy this.

The trainer's personal memories of his own student days may also hold him back from change. The basic learning processes at school and in training may indeed be similar. But they head for different goals and strike different limits. On a continuum that has personal maturation and growth at one end and improvement in the performance of predetermined tasks at the other, education would be near the former end and training near the latter. Education is primarily concerned with opening out the world to the student so that he can choose his interests and mode of living, and also his career. Training, on the other hand, is primarily concerned with preparing the participant for certain lines of action which are delineated by technology and by the organization in which he works. Education helps the student choose and decide his activity. Training helps the participant improve his performance in it. Education deals mostly with knowledge and understanding. Training deals mostly with understanding and skill.

It seems urgent to nail down tightly the distinction between knowledge about something, on the one hand, and skill and experience, on the other. What to expect from training, how to design effective programs, and what training methods to use all depend on this distinction in the first place. Over a half century, William James and Elton Mayo labored to clarify this same distinction between cognitive learning, on the one hand, and internalizing a skill, on the other. It has been dealt with in poetry and philosophy, in the classics as well as in modern scholarship. We must now use this distinction for more effective training.

Focusing training on skill in action makes the task wide and complex. The "subject" widens so that enough of other disciplines gets included to make sense of action in the real world of people, things, and time. It embraces an understanding of the complex processes by which various factors that make up the actual situation interact. Presently, participants begin to practice new skills in situations resembling the complexities of real life—the pressures, the limited resources, the choices and uncertainties, the conflicting motives of people, including the participant's own. For many kinds of action, greater self-knowledge is a necessary part of training.

2. Training and Learning: Two Points of View

Learning is a kind of action, and like other kinds of action, it depends on many things. What is taught is only one of these. So the connection between what the trainer teaches and what the participant learns is at best indirect and partial. To assume that teaching and learning are related simply, as cause and effect, in fact has a basic defect: It equates the trainer's point of view—from which he teaches—with the participant's point of view—from which he learns. As trainer and participants work together, they may understand each other's viewpoints better and take them into account. But proceeding on the assumption that the viewpoints are the same in the first place is quite unrealistic.

When a patently unrealistic assumption persists, something more personal than an intellectual difficulty is usually involved. Indeed, trainers seem intellectually quite clear on the principle that training must start from "where the participants are." But they then take no action to find this starting place. Many trainers do not seem to want to establish it. Among them are those who later take credit for participants learning something intended by the trainer—but who refuse to accept responsibility for participants learning something different. The former "result," according to them, is due to the trainer's skill and devotion; but the latter is due to the participants' incapacity, laziness, or contrariness. Many trainers enjoy the idea that they can mold others in their own image. What most participants are likely to learn from such trainers is greater dependence or opposition, neither of them attitudes to be found in the objectives of training or useful on the job.

The implications of putting learning and the points of view of participants in the center of the training process, and of treating the trainer's activity as related to the participant's points of view, are far-reaching. On this basis the trainer's functions include stimulating and motivating participants to wish to acquire certain kinds of knowledge and understanding and to practice certain skills because they recognize that they need them. Training then comes to consist largely of well-organized opportunities for participants to acquire the necessary understanding and skill. The trainer appreciates that he is close to only some parts of the whole learning process and can in the final analysis hope to control only one: his own behavior. He is like a farmer who prepares the soil, plants good seed, and tends and nurtures the new growth. He does not harbor the illusion that he *makes* things grow or determines their ultimate size and shape.

3. Learning and Action: The Participant and His Organization

However well an individual has learned a useful skill, that in itself by no means guarantees action. Bitter experience in plenty ought to have taught us that. A participant returning from training often finds his new capacities ignored, even resented. He looks for support, finds instead indifference or opposition. Doubts assail him about the usefulness of his training. His enthusiasm wanes. Soon he accepts his colleague's advice to "forget it." And so another man has been trained only into disappointment and frustration. Next time he will know better than to invest so much of himself in new initiatives and developments.

The simple linking of individual training and effective action ignores the manifold problems of introducing and sustaining change in an organization. Putting individual skill to use depends on a number of people and often on additional resources. It calls for encouragement, support, and a receptive organization.

Taking an organizational approach means starting training off with a set of *organizational* questions. Instead of asking what X or Y needs to learn in order to carry out a new activity, the first training question needs to be addressed to all involved in the projected change. What do they, as interrelated workers, have to do differently, and what various things, therefore, do they have to learn anew and need training in? This question concerns those who collaborate directly on the job and also those who provide new services and organizational support. This very different assumption leads to a systems approach to training.

This approach often involves training minimum concentrations of staff at several levels of the organization, the provision of supporting follow-up services from the training institution later on, and the allocation of resources from within the working organization for various stages of the change in process. Instead of thinking in terms of someone's participation in this or that training course, it calls for training strategies that include pretraining and posttraining activities and sequences of training events related to career plans. For the longer term this approach tries to deal with the whole network of factors that determines an organization's readiness for development. For what is required under modern conditions is not an occasional change but change on a continuing basis, more or less, in interaction with a changing environment. In this continuing process, the organization is both a recipient and a contributor.

It is useful to be clear that a problem remains even with this approach, a real uncertainty. The gap between what the trainer teaches and what the participant learns leads to unintended consequences of training. These may work to the disadvantage of the organization, or its advantage.

As a problem, the unintended consequences hit a manager, for instance, when he finds his engineer asking to leave the organization soon after returning from training. He may in the course of his training have come across a more promising opening in another company. He may have used the course to think up a project of his own and may have decided to become his own employer. He may have reflected that it is time for him to make a move of some kind to try a different line of activity altogether. It is for reasons such as these that some organizations refuse to send staff for training outside. They are afraid to lose them or, as an alternative, to have them come back insisting on all sorts of unsettling changes for which their superiors are not ready. Timing training in relation to the organization's needs and opportunities, and taking care in choosing participants, are important ways of keeping individual growth and organizational needs in some balance. But they do not mesh automatically or necessarily. It is no use pretending they do.

Often managers take a more positive view of the gap. If a member of their staff gets something more out of training than they intended, so much the better. Personal growth is a good thing. These managers may or may not be aware that their generally positive attitude toward people and personal development itself tends to make the organization a good place in which to work. This attitude of theirs elicits initiative and free application from the staff and provides work satisfaction that staff members might lose through leaving. It makes for the kind of organization which, if some leave, others join.

The same positive policy can be deliberate. It can be derived from the changing nature of industry, the speed with which new technologies, management methods, markets, and so on, crowd in on the organization. Staff cannot realistically be trained for such changes one by one. Managers can see their tasks as developing employees who are generally inventive and receptive, aware and thoroughly alive, not just now and then, but as a normal condition. They can see training, unintended consequences included, as helping them do this.

4. Responsibility for Training

To invest the training institution with the whole responsibility for training is unrealistic if action in an organization is the aim. This type of misunderstanding now protects many institutions against the demands for more effective training that participants and their organizations could rightfully press on them; to confuse things further, it protects, in return, the organizations against demands that ought to come from the training institution for clear training goals, carefully selected participants, and organizational support for the improvements to be effected through training. It is a kind of collusion.

Participants, their organizations, and the institution are all partners in the training effort. To be effective, their collaboration starts with the definition of training goals and strategies. It continues after training with follow-up services from the institution and support for the innovation from within the organization.

ACTION THROUGH TRAINING OR ACTION THROUGH FORCE

Alongside the quartet of assumptions that inspires much current training we have set up a matching quartet. The new quartet takes account more adequately of experience to date and seems therefore a better basis on which to proceed. But it calls for much more thought and rigor than the first set and for the most careful consideration of expectations, needs, relationships, and costs. This initial investment of care and attention is very taxing. Organizations are entitled to ask whether training is worth that.

Is it even necessary? For instance, can similar purposes not also be achieved without training and achieved with greater expedition, certainty, and economy—through management "doing its job," through parents "doing their duty" by their children, teachers "teaching," community leaders "leading"? Maybe people in positions of authority need to exercise authority, that is all—see to it that their views are carried out. They are in positions to know what is necessary. They ought to insist—kindly, of course—listen to objections, make adjustments where possible, consult, "take people along," "get them to do" willingly what the authorities have decided, give people the impression that the decision is "really their own." The many phrases used to clothe this familiar line show that it is out of fashion and needs to be disowned; that it is nevertheless very much present; and, unmasked, is recognized as the argument of force. Its antecedents and personal implications deserve a closer look, briefly. Force is in fact the motive power of traditional relationships and often comes readily to hand even now. Its success has been monumental. The cathedrals and temples, the massive forts, the great old roads and water systems, even that timeless monument to a loving relationship, the Taj Mahal—they were all built by a few imposing their will on thousands by personal mixtures of kindness and cruelty. India at the height of her glory and power centuries ago was characterized by relationships of force. And so elsewhere. If this was productive then, why should force, authority, not serve now? Why not now train only a few masters to get work done through force exercised on servants by the thousands? That this is not merely a theoretical question we have already noted by the string of up-to-date phrases for the same phenomenon. Moreover, it requires only a look across some frontiers to see large-scale changes getting accomplished through force.

A look inside shows many impatient to advocate force and also using force, openly or camouflaged. In truth, the resort to force to achieve better action is close to hand for us all, in our heart of hearts. We may call it authority or some other nicer words. Perhaps embedded right here, deep down, is the real spring of genuine opposition to training for action. And facile approval, excessive expectations, and kind words for training are only the varied manifestations of this very same opposition.

The opposition, then, may be deep-rooted and stay with us. But it is founded neither in the relative efficacy of training and force as means for securing action, nor in their relative consonance with the requirements of modern developments. At best, force engenders action that is limited to the occasion, often limited to the actual presence of a powerful supervisor. Training, on the other hand, leads to action that can be repeated, to self-motivation and further improvement through onward practice. In short, though force may result in an action, and repeated force in repeated action, only training can lead to sustained, self-generating development. Training, not force, promises what is essential to modern technologies and economic systems: flexibility in action through understanding and confidence; inventiveness, initiative, and ability to make decisions; and also respect for the contributions of others and readiness for collaboration with others.

Training is therefore properly part of the grand march toward greater equality between people, toward more widely spread opportunities, participation, involvement, rising expectations. However stumbling the progress, these mark a quite definite direction in all spheres of new life. Those who prefer force do so quite understandably. They are among those who would apply force, not act under it; and their real opposition is not to training but to the kinds of development that training aims to foster. They would have to share power with others, for instance, or probably lose it, and to forgo their positions in society. From training for development, some people therefore stand to lose personally and immediately. Many more are afraid without reason. These are the people who really have nothing to lose but have to work themselves slowly toward a preference for a new kind of society, one that is developed and maintained through hard work in partnership with many others. Only after that can they discard the simple attractions of force. Others are caught in their histories in a different way again; these include the individual who buckled under his father's authority, waiting for his day when similar authority would be his to exercise in turn. The new society would cheat such individuals of a prospect in which they have invested much. And others, again, are willing to pay the price of force as long as it provides order, neatness, and predictability in their world in return. That they hang on to this promise when it is wearing thin by all indications, this shows the depth of their fears, fears of an unknown world ahead, with familiar landmarks gone and experiences to date perhaps irrelevant; blind, without rules or instruments; fears of other people whose trustworthiness is untrusted.

The case for training stands firm. It has deep roots and is broadly based. The present inadequacies of training may be glaring. But they can be examined and removed, and real progress made in action.

Chapter 2

The Training Process in Three Phases
  Some Conceptual Models
The Learning Spiral for the Participant
  1. Pretraining: Expectations and Motivation
  2. Training: Exposure to Opportunities for Learning
  3. Posttraining: Transferring Learning to the Back-Home Situation
The Training Process for the Participant's Organization
  1. Pretraining: Objectives, Selection, and Motivation
  2. Training: Removing Preoccupations and Communicating Interest
  3. Posttraining: Support and Organizational Adjustment
Figures
  2.1. Simple Model of the Training Process
  2.2. Elaborated Model of the Training Process
  2.3. Spiral Model of the Training Process

An Overview of the Training Process

╭╭╭╭╭╭╭╭╭╭╭╭╭╭╭╭╭╭╭╭╭╭╭╭╭╭╭╭╭╭╭╭╭

"We must lead men to the particulars themselves, and their series and order; while men on their side must force themselves for a while to lay their notions by and . . . familiarize themselves with facts."

—FRANCIS BACON

". . . any change in any of the factors, independent of the way in which it is brought about, will, by the aggregate weight of the cumulative effect running back and forth between them all, start the whole system moving . . . with a speed depending upon the original push and the functions of causal interrelation with the system."

—GUNNAR MYRDAL

THE FOCUS of training right at the very outset is on a person-on-the-job-in-the-organization—all of this whole amalgam. Wherever it moves during the training process, the same starting point becomes the focus again at the end, hopefully with a difference. The difference lies in what-the-person-has-learned-that-he-now-applies. That difference, in terms of actually more effective behavior, is the measure of the effectiveness of training. It is essential to insist on this starting point and goalpost, and on this measure. Complicated as it is, and much as we may wish to reject the complication, nothing less will do.

We will separate the process into three phases: pretraining, training, and posttraining. "Preparation," "training," and "follow-up" would be more graceful words to use. But they would hide the important fact that each phase has preparatory and follow-up parts, not the training phase alone.

THE TRAINING PROCESS IN THREE PHASES

Phase 1: Pretraining. The process starts with understanding the situation that calls for more effective behavior. A key aspect of that

15

situation is the job on which improved performance is to be achieved. Training therefore rightly begins with a description of the job which is to be changed by it. For this purpose standard job analyses that are largely limited to technical requirements will not be descriptive enough. An operational description is needed of the job as it actually gets carried out. This would cover, besides technical requirements, the kinds of personal contact the job calls upon the person to have with others, for example, colleagues, customers; the pressures on the job, such as quick decisions and heavy responsibilities; any wide variations in the quantity of work and the time required to complete it; and other salient features.

The second key aspect of the situation to be understood is the organization's receptivity to more effective behavior on the part of people to be trained. Who feels the need for this new behavior? The person involved? His immediate superior? A distant head office? These issues raise questions of motivation and relationships. They are personal to the possible participant, to others in the organization, and also to his wife and family. They will affect his capacity to learn and thus the effectiveness of his training.

Phase 2: Training.   The participant does not leave these questions behind when he goes for training, whether for a session, an evening course, or a residential program, although in the residential situation the back-home questions will tend to fade into the background for a while. That can have disadvantages as well as advantages. In an evening program, these questions will be immediate, since the participant is reminded of them by the daily reality of the work situation. Certain it is that he has the back-home questions on his mind as the training starts, as new impressions crowd in on him—new subject matter, new people, a new atmosphere.

Out of all these impressions, severally and in combination, the participant then focuses his attention on what seems to him useful, stimulating, engaging, and in line with others.

There is no knowing, perhaps not even by himself, how he weighs personal interest in relation to technical importance or acceptability by colleagues. Is something to be learned because it is needed? Fun? Promising? Promising what? Greater achievement or promotion? Is it acceptable to colleagues but not to the immediate superior? This is just a sample of the questions that play in and out of the participant's mind as he begins his training and selects what he wants to learn from the program just getting under way. There is no guarantee, of course, that the participant will in fact learn what he has chosen. His selection may have been an error. He may lack the necessary capacities or may be frustrated by inadequate or irrelevant training design, methodology, and relationships. But the main point remains: The participant explores in the training situation what interests him, and the training institution's basic task is to provide the necessary opportunities.

Having explored, the participant tries out some new behavior. Then either of two sequences takes over. If the participant finds the new behavior useful, he tries it again, checks it for effectiveness and satisfaction, tries it repeatedly, gets better at it. Finally, he incorporates the new item into his habitual behavior in the training situation. Or, he does not find it useful. So he discards it, tries some variant and/or discontinues learning in this direction. This intricate selection and testing-out process goes on continuously and more or less consciously.

Phase 3: Posttraining. With the end of training, the situation itself changes. The participant goes back to work, to his colleagues and his family. He goes prepared with some anticipations of these encounters. The people at home also have more or less definite expectations of him, changed or hardened while he was away. When he actually arrives, at best there begins a process of adjustment for everyone involved. For instance, the newly learned skills undergo modification to fit in with the work situation. The participant may find his organization encouraging, helping him use his training and offering him the additional support of continuing contact with the training institution. At worst, the colleagues, the organization, the family members, will let the returning participant know that they resented his absence and the extra burden it put on those who stayed behind, that his holiday is now over, and that he better get back to work to make up for lost time. In that case, contact with the training institution is broken off.

Some Conceptual Models

More effective behavior of a person-on-the-job-in-the-organization is the aim of the whole training process. At its simplest, the improvement is a dependent variable. The person and the organization are independent variables in the process. Figure 2.1 shows this model of training—the simplest.

But training is a more complex process than Figure 2.1 suggests. In the first place, the training agency itself needs to be added. It may be a temporary system, such as an occasional program, or a permanent institution, such as a training department. In either case, the trainers-in-the-institution also learn, through various opportunities of checking their own effectiveness, i.e., through some kind of feedback. From time

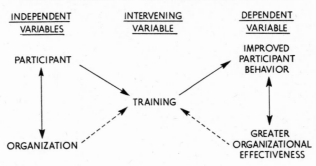

Figure 2.1

SIMPLE MODEL OF THE TRAINING PROCESS

to time the independent and intermediary variables, therefore, become dependent variables in turn. This elaboration is shown in Figure 2.2.

The process as a whole with its three partners and three stages is shown in Figure 2.3 This is a spiral model, overlapping at the person-on-the-job-in-the-organization. The spiral model is useful to visualize a training program as a whole and also each event and series of events which make up the program. For each session, for instance, there is a before and an after phase, and, in between, the phase of actual transmittal of new knowledge and skill.

The spiral itself shows the phases through which a participant passes as he learns and returns, with capacities enhanced, we hope, to his job. At various stages in the process the two other partners in the process make "inputs" to aid him. The inputs are shown as arrows: arrows originating inside the spiral for inputs of the work organization; arrows originating outside the spiral for inputs of the training organization. These are visual conveniences only. The large spiral itself is made of a continuous spiral feedback system.

We will use this spiral model to help us walk through the process,

Figure 2.2

ELABORATED MODEL OF THE TRAINING PROCESS

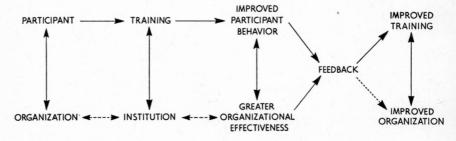

Figure 2.3

SPIRAL MODEL OF TRAINING PROCESS

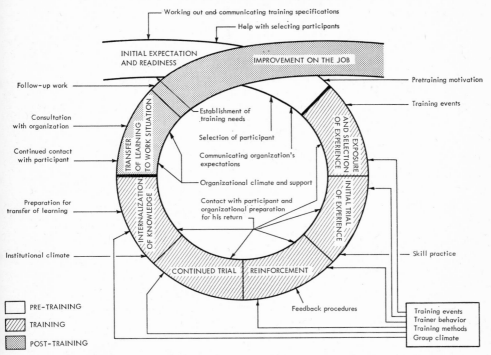

first with the participant, then with the work organization, and finally, for the remainder of the book, with the training institution.

THE LEARNING SPIRAL FOR THE PARTICIPANT

1. Pretraining: Expectations and Motivation

To start learning, a person needs to feel the need for it. That applies to any kind of learning. The need can be desperate, as for survival, even economic survival. More commonly, the participant needs more skill in a particular job so as to qualify for it, to understand particular things or events, to feel that he is continuing to grow as a person. Some people feel this latter need readily and take pride in their ability to develop new habits. Others reject it or play it down, because learning is to them akin to an admission that they are not already competent and are for that reason less significant people than they thought. Both kinds, and others, face the prospect of training with very different expectations and are right in thinking that they will derive very different experiences from the same training session or course. Here the essential point to hang on to is that the participant's motivation and point of view will determine his focus of attention and learning.

This basic fact holds good not only for the general overtone that the prospect of training has for a participant but for the details of the particular course he is considering. Does he regard it as suitable for himself? Does he feel qualified for it? Does he have the necessary background, neither too little nor too much? Is it suitably timed? If a participant has sickness in the family, a wedding to arrange (an Indian domestic crisis) or a new baby coming (an American one), that is hardly the time to send him far away for training. His mind will be preoccupied with domestic events and fantasies, when this same mind and other resources need to be focused on the training course.

Very importantly, the participant wonders what his going to this particular training course tells about him in comparison with others. How does it affect management's evaluation of him? For what level of person is the course intended? Does going mean that he is heading for a promotion or that he is the person most easily spared? Who are the other participants? That is, with what people is he being equated? What do others apparently think he stands in need of learning? The general reputation of the course and the institution running it, the ways people are selected for it, and its cost, all play into this personal calculation that each prospective participant makes for himself before he even goes for training. The Advanced Management Program at the Harvard Business School has come to stand for imminent promotion, valuable contacts, and high personal value to those selected to attend. Many other training programs, on the contrary, are regarded as a pretty meaningless chore. The organization's main reason for sending participants may be to ensure that its name figures in the attendance list. Participants know this, either way, and approach participation eagerly or reluctantly, inclined or disinclined to learn.

2. Training: Exposure to Opportunities for Learning

These expectations, whatever they are, the participant brings to the training program. The exposure to learning opportunities that training then offers him hopefully results in a series of five-stage sequences. Each sequence begins with the selection of an item to learn and finishes with making some new behavior into a habit. The participant keeps several sequences going at a time. They may well be interrelated.

(*i*) *Selection of Some Items for Learning.* With whatever motivation and degree of readiness he comes, the participant starts training and is exposed to its opportunities for learning. Out of the numerous new impressions that crowd in on him, he chooses some for attention: Those are the parts of subjects, people, and atmosphere that affect him more than other parts. They satisfy some of his needs and are, therefore, meaningful to him. Although the training program may be thorough and well planned, participants will learn different things from it for this reason. Each of them, not the trainer, "decides" where his attention will go and with what expectations. The quotation marks signal that many factors, not all conscious, go into the selection.

(*ii*) *Initial Trial of Experience.*   The participant now explores and uses the item which he has selected. He thinks about it, translates his interest into specific behavior. He tries it out. Does it fit into his way of thinking? Into other people's expectations? The purpose for him of this initial trial is to see its effect on his organized system of thinking, including the way he thinks of himself.

(*iii*) *Feedback from the Initial Trial.*   The participant's experiments may be rewarding or discouraging, or merely open to further trials. The possibilities are affected by his own reaction to the trial, the reactions of the fellow participants, the reaction of the trainers. If the feedback is positive and the item which he has tried "fits" him, he gets satisfaction. This is important as a step in the process of learning. The participant then *feels* he is learning.

(*iv*) *Reinforcement and Continued Practice.*   Satisfaction from a positive feedback reinforces the participant's new pattern of behavior. This amounts to practice. Repeated practice followed by repeated satisfaction will result in establishing the new pattern of behavior firmly.

(*v*) *Internalizing What He Has Learned.*   Learning based on repetition tends to be mechanical and barren till the participant ceases to be self-conscious about it and uses it routinely as a part of his habitual pattern of behavior. This process of digestion takes time. The new item, or the modification of an established habit, affects many parts of the participant as a person. It gets woven into his experiential texture, makes him a somewhat different person. In Erikson's[1] scheme of thinking about these things, the most important learning requires a period of "moratorium," a period of withdrawal from everyday pressures and expectations. At such a time a participant allows himself and his life to take on a new shape. It is like a honeymoon, away from friends and relatives. At a much lesser depth, all learning has this essentially reflective, withdrawn stage. It ends when self-consciousness with the new

---

[1] Erik H. Erikson, *Childhood and Society* (New York: W. W. Norton & Co., Inc., 1950).

ways has gone. The participant has then learned something new; he has made something new his own.

Some such sequence as this describes the learning by one participant of any one item. Hopefully the training program will engender not just the learning of a few discrete items but generally induce strength and an orientation toward new experience in which further learning is attractive. So there is an overall cycle in which learning becomes enjoyable as a process. The participant will then be more open to learning in the future.

3. Posttraining: Transferring Learning to the Back-Home Situation

The training session or program ends. The participant leaves for home with whatever he has learned. If things have gone well, he goes back to his own organization with a somewhat new pattern of behavior, as a somewhat changed person. With his motivation heightened and new enthusiasm from the satisfactions of learning, he is eager to use on his job what he has learned. When he does so, he in fact behaves differently from the way he used to before he went for training. Now he has to add one more dimension to his learning, the organizational one.

(*i*) *Organizational Support or Lack of It.* Once again the participant watches for feedback. How do others react to his new behavior? If his colleagues and superiors approve of it, he feels encouraged and will be inclined to continue to behave in the more effective way. If they ignore his return or any indication of change in him, and behave as if he had never been away, he will be discouraged from persisting with attempts to use what he has learned. Some anxiety will persist until the trend is reasonably clear.

(*ii*) *Improvement on the Job.* In the final analysis, training is successful if the participant's effectiveness at his job goes up as expected. Verbal support for more effective behavior will not suffice for this result. Other preconditions, such as adequate equipment, basic attitudes of colleagues, and organizational policy, have to line up with the change. Discrepancies mean that the participant gets frustrated at the very end, that is, when his expectations are at their highest. This final failure of training is all too well known to young people returning to India from training overseas. Others fear it so much that they do not return even to try. Alternatively, when conditions are favorable, changes actually take place. Permanently more important is the favorable outlook this success creates for further learning in the work situation itself. Training has then succeeded. The learning spiral can wind on.

The participant's learning depends on continuity. It must not break at any of the several stages. The risk of a break is highest at those stages when the usefulness of an item or its acceptability to others is in question: at the first trial stage, for instance, or on returning home. At these stages the process must be able to carry the accumulated burden of doubt and anxiety, or it will fail. These are the stages when the onward process becomes like a spiral staircase. Either each round supports the next, or even a momentary frustration makes morale plummet and prejudices further opportunities for learning—a vicious circle. At these crucial stages the participant needs support and needs to feel it.

THE TRAINING PROCESS FOR THE PARTICIPANT'S ORGANIZATION

Learning proceeds along the participant's point of view, training does not. Training has in the forefront the purposes of the work organization. The wishes of the participants and the training institution come only after that. So there are three points of view altogether, all different. Training has to relate all three. It does so by offering learning opportunities of such kinds and qualities, and so timed, that they support the participant's learning things important to his performance on the job. The rest of this chapter will outline the contributions to the training process required from the participant's work organization. The roles of trainers and training institutions will then occupy in detail the rest of the book.

The contributions of the participant's work organization to the training process are concentrated in the pretraining and posttraining phases, but they can be significant also while the participant is in training. The contributions of the training institution are concentrated in the training phase but are significant also in the other two phases. We will postpone to later chapters the detailed examination of the required collaboration between the work organization and the training institution at each stage: what they each need to do, and what they can do jointly. Here we will try to establish the objectives which the participant's organization needs to be concerned with at successive phases in order to ensure effective training.

1. Pretraining: Objectives, Selection, and Motivation

The organization's concerns before training are mostly in three areas: clarifying the precise objectives of training and the use the organization expects to make of the participant(s) after training; selection of suitable participants; and building up favorable expectations and motivation on the part of participants before they go for training.

(*i*) *Clarifying Objectives of Training and the Use of Trained Personnel.* This is where the rigor starts—and where it is almost everywhere now lacking. Few organizations have gone beyond generalized job descriptions calling for certain standard qualifications. For instance, from reading the job descriptions for salesmen or some kinds of extension officers, one could get the impression that contact with customers and other people is a marginal requirement, whereas it is in fact of the essence. If the omission means that those selected for these posts can be assumed to have the skills needed to deal with people already, this assumption is not borne out by experience. In order to specify training needs and go on from there to choose appropriate training opportunities for a participant, a full operational job description is most important. That means attention at least to job content, relationships, and time. Since prevailing organizational practices fall far short of desirable standards of job analyses, the training institution may have a special contribution to make in this connection. We will, therefore, return to this matter again in more detail in Chapter 4.

Once the job requirements are defined, the next step is to pinpoint those parts which can be met through training. In many cases, new material resources or different work assignments are also required. That the need is wider than training is a salutary recognition and will clarify the organizational support required later by the trained personnel. Finally, operational job descriptions and precise training objectives will give the first indication of how many people may need to be trained: some in the same fields and for the same purposes, others in fields which will be affected as the planned change gets underway.

(*ii*) *Selecting Suitable Participants.* This is a complicated matter. It involves not only an individual's suitability but also the organization's and individual's convenience at the time. It needs to avoid questions of popularity or reward for past services. Some organizations have clarified their operations sufficiently to pinpoint personnel for specific types of training according to career plans which fit into the organization's own plans for growth and diversification. The question of who is to be involved in the selection is also important. Ideally, selection becomes a joint responsibility which then carries through to helping the returned participant use his training. Certainly the candidate's immediate superiors need to be involved. So should his immediate colleagues who are affected by what happens during his absence and by what he will do differently after training. The people with whom he works know better than others the suitability, preferences, and prospects of candidates for training. Moreover, if they are not involved in the process at this phase they may express their resentment about it in unhelpful ways later, when their colleague returns after training.

(*iii*) *Building Up Favorable Expectations and Motivation in the Participant.* It is important that the selected participant leave for training assured that the organization regards his training as thoroughly worthwhile and is taking steps to enable him to use his new competence when he returns. This requirement is clear. The question is how to meet it.

It is a complex question for the same kind of reason that the relationship between training and learning is complex: two points of view are involved. What influences the participant's expectations and motivation is not organizational action or inaction as such but the view he takes of it. And this view is determined immediately by the context, relationships, and general atmosphere in the organization, and more particularly, by many personal and historical factors over which the organization has little or no control.

Two examples may help to make the distinction concrete and meaningful. To one participant his organization's check on departure details and smooth handing over of responsibilities may indicate high regard and personal care. By the same check another participant may feel belittled rather than elated: as if he could not be relied upon to look after such things by himself. Again, when the organization pays a large fee and goes out of its way to facilitate a participant's going, it clearly attaches importance to the occasion. But the effects of this signal of importance will vary according to the participant's preoccupations. At one time he may see the organization attaching most importance to his learning something important. At another time he may conclude that the organization wants him well out of the way to effect a reorganization that he has opposed.

This distinction between what the organization does and what the participant sees in the action may now be firmly fixed in the reader's mind. It is very important. We will see a similar distinction in our discussion of actions by trainers and institutions.

Perhaps the main objective of organizational action is to ensure that the participant's expectations are realistic as regards the nature of the training he will receive and also the possibilities of its application afterwards. For the first, the organization can secure necessary information, put the participant in direct touch with the institution, and encourage contact between him and others in the organization or locality who have participated earlier in similar training. The minimum condition for any of this is some preparatory time; this is only worth mentioning because participants do sometimes arrive for training having first heard about the training program and their going to it by telegram the previous day. For the second, the organization can associate the participant with the preparations for the changes to be facilitated by his training, or at least acquaint him with them.

2. Training: Removing Preoccupations and Communicating Interest

The second phase, which is to contain the participant's major new experience, is wide open to neglect by his organization. Having sent him off to training, it may turn its attention elsewhere. He is forgotten till the time approaches for his return. If the training is residential, the participant's physical absence makes this neglect particularly easy. But even when he takes part in an evening course or some other series of training events, little attention seems to be given to his progress during his training. It is as if, at best, the organization were interested only in some imaginary neat package labeled "end result" of training and could assume that achieving it was wholly the responsibility of the participant and the training institution.

It cannot be so. For instance, the participant could give the training session his attention better if he were sure that his family and personal affairs were taken care of during his absence. At least the organization better ensure that no distracting preoccupations occupy the participant during training or bedevil his anticipation of what comes afterwards. Organization contact during training can go beyond this to sustain interest and positive anticipation, which help the participant to learn. Lack of contact, to the contrary, makes the opposite communication of disinterest or even opposition. "No action" too is an action; that is, it has consequences. The context is very important. Unfamiliar amounts of contact may communicate a mechanical effort rather than real interest, or pressure on the participant to put into words what he has learned as a check on whether he is working hard.

In some way or other, whether it likes it or not, the organization contributes something important at various phases of the training process. The only questions each time are, first, at whom was the contribution aimed, and, second, was it effective.

3. Posttraining: Support and Organizational Adjustments

The participant is back from training and needs to be encouraged to use what useful things he has learned. It may help to allow time for him to "settle in again." Explicitly so; otherwise he will take the time surreptitiously and feel guilty about it. The opposite, for instance finding a desk overloaded with work held up till his return, will not help. That way signals how indispensable he is; it is a signal for him, maybe, though not for the organization. But piled-up work is also a clear indication that people expect him to get right back into the same old rut and were probably put out by his absence. Facilities to talk about the training experience with colleagues signal that the organization expects him to use his training and expects others to collaborate with him.

Without going into more detail the principle is clear. The organization started out with clear expectations of what the participant was to do when he returned, what he needed in order to do it, and how all this would affect his colleagues. The predictions and related adjustments became more accurate as the organization had contact with him during training, learned of his progress and also of what he anticipated about his return, and as it made other preparations for instituting changes. Now that he is back, all join up to make the changes which require the participant to use his training.

Thoughtfulness and application to this degree may seem to require a lot of trouble and cost. It is worth establishing carefully what is worth doing, considering the investment that training represents. Organizations will normally find that the expense of training was high, both in direct costs and in loss of work from the participants during their time of training. Training a young executive earning $1,200 a month in a three months' residential course costing $1,500 plus hotel expenses involves direct expenditure of the order of $8,000–$10,000. Other costs, maybe substantial ones, occurred in the organization in connection with making preparations for impending changes. The organization needs to decide how to make the most of this total expenditure. It will usually find that the additional trouble by which the returning participant is helped to use his training is thoroughly worthwhile.

Chapter 3

/ /

Training Strategy

((((((((((((((((((((((((((((((((((((((

"The object of . . . ideas as a whole is . . . to provide us with an instrument for finding our way about this world more easily."

—HANS VAIHINGER

"Everything is more important in time than anything else, of course, which is exactly what happens when people don't exhibit the right amount of fortitude in planning on a broad basis."

—DAVID E. LILIENTHAL

RIGOR in engaging resources only on projects for which training is a significant variable is one of the first professional responsibilities of a training institution. This includes a judgment of whether adequate conditions exist for its likely success. Contrary to the popular saying, something is often *not* better than nothing. "Something" may convey a mistaken sense of movement and progress toward a goal when in reality no ground will be gained.

Effective training calls, in the first place, for clarity of objectives and means. In that respect it is just like a manufacturing process. Both the ends and the means must be appropriate to the purpose. Relating them demands clear specifications for each part of the training task, including the resources of time, skill, and facilities required for it. Ensuring this is a responsibility of the first order for the training institution. Unless this task has been accomplished, a new training program is launched into a kind of void: to sail a predetermined course through an uncharted sea to an unknown goal.

To avert this futility, it is necessary to consider four strategic questions, which we shall examine in turn. The first and second are of external strategy: establishing training goals and defining training specifications. The importance of these questions has been greatly under-rated; they are two cornerstones of any program. The other two are outcomes of internal strategy: organizing the training inputs and improving the training institution.

EXTERNAL STRATEGY

External strategy is concerned with two kinds of questions: The first is, what are the training goals, that is, the changes to be effected? The second is, what are the number and kinds of people who therefore need to be trained and the resources of time, skill, and facilities required for this particular training—in short, the training specifications?

Much training fails right at this initial point. It is a failure from which there is no hope of recovery, whatever the mounting subsequent effort to make up for it.

The first failure is usually not the training institution's but the work organization's. The goals of change, for which training is supposed to be needed, are not defined with sufficient precision either to give the organization the criteria for measuring progress or the institution the guidelines within which particular training objectives and specifications can be worked out. Without these the consumer of training stands disarmed. At no point later can the organization say to the institution, "*This* is what we asked you to do and you agreed to do. It is not done. Why not? You owe us a reckoning." Without precise goals there is no telling whether *any* training program, course, or session was in fact worthwhile.

If this is the situation at the organization's end, it is ripe for the institution's own classic first error. This consists in going ahead as if the fundamental questions of goals did not matter or as if the institution could itself do the homework on which the organization has fallen down. The latter is an attractive illusion. It sets the trainers up as knowing best what is required at organizational, even national, levels. But it is an unpromising posture. Even if the trainers did know best, which is doubtful, by assuming the function of deciding and defining what it is that the organization needs they drastically limit or even eliminate the organization's commitment to the training. Later on, the organization can turn round and say, "We did not ask you to train our people for *this*. How could you dare to decide *our* training goals? We will support you no further." Then no amount of institutional protest, for example, that the organization failed to do its proper homework in the first place, will serve. The simple truth is that the institution ought not to have proceeded this far. It could have offered consultation, even collaboration, to work out goals, as we shall see. But that is essentially different from stepping into the organization's sphere of responsibility.

If it has in fact proceeded this far, the institution commonly reacts to the client's opposition and resentment with righteous indignation: "What were we to do? Nothing? Wait forever?" The threat lies in losing the client and in encountering a possible decline in the number of organizations and candidates that apply for training. This, in a developing society which has such vast needs for effective training, ought to be grounds enough for pause and review, with no holds barred. Institutions characteristically react differently; they proceed in the same barren direction with renewed determination and greater speed. They go out and beat the bushes for candidates for the same inadequate programs, "selling" training to the "conservative" or "traditionally-minded" organizations. They reduce minimum qualifications and fees till all places are more or less filled. It is as if they wanted to show the world outside: "See how wrong you are and how much *others* appreciate us." But this self-assertion has a hollow ring, not least to those who stage it. What Dorothy Sayers[1] calls the human trend to randomness reasserts itself. Activity may continue, but on sufferance. Training of this pattern has no more or less significance than most human activity.

Training to be worthwhile has to do better than that: it has to be a creative action. We will retrace our steps, therefore, to have a second look at the strategic tasks of establishing training goals and specifications.

1. Establishing Training Goals

The training institution does not set the goals of change. It is important to be quite clear about that. National and organizational policies set those goals. Trainers may contribute—as citizens. But the training institution does have the task of setting to work only on goals which training can help to reach and that are adequately backed by organizational contributions.

For instance, an Indian District Development Plan may call for 20 medium-sized cooperative farms to be in operation in three years. The institution does not question whether this general goal is desirable. It is directly concerned, however, with whether managers and other staff can be found and trained within that period and, if so, that other inputs required for these

---

[1] Dorothy L. Sayers, *The Mind of the Maker* (New York: Harcourt, Brace and Company, 1941).

developments, such as land acquisition, buildings, equipment, and finance, are likely to be organized to dovetail with training. The latter consideration leads to a procedure akin to a critical path analysis as it is used in industrial and construction operations: the various inputs are to join up as and when needed.

The first strategic question, then, on which the institution needs to satisfy itself concerns the reality of the goals already set. Are the goals realistic at all? Second, is the training input envisaged in the development also realistic? Or is training in danger of being misused? For instance, is it once again too little and too late?

With very few exceptions training institutions now concern themselves with these kinds of questions only when they consider the suitability of a particular applicant for a particular course, and then by general implication rather than careful consideration. For instance, Joe Blow is not sufficiently qualified, he lacks experience; let him apply again in two years. Bill Smith, on the other hand, has the requisite age and experience, and the educational qualifications; therefore, he can be accepted. A great deal of work has been done to provide institutions with tests to measure many aspects of an individual's capacity for learning. Institutions that use these regularly are among the best in every respect.

The main point here is different in any case. It is that the capacity of individual applicants to learn what a course offers is only the second question to ask about the usefulness of training. The first is whether the training program under consideration is realistic in the light of the needs of the particular organization and in the general context of development.

Perhaps the most striking example of the dangers of paying inadequate attention to this dimension is the cumulative residue in industrially advanced countries of newly trained managerial and technical personnel from overseas. In the last 20 years, 30,000 foreign engineers alone have remained in the United States after completing their training. That they are able to make a living in competition with native Americans confirms their individual competence. Even if many stayed on because of attractive living standards, others did so because they were trained "out" of their country in the same way that school in a less developed country such as India seems to educate young people "out of their villages." The training qualified them for settings and conditions that do not (yet) exist at home. This may be good for the individual, i.e., good education. As training, that is, for achieving development in their home organizations, such overseas training has obviously been unrealistic and unsuitable.

In fact, not two but three steps back are necessary before a training course can be properly set up. Let us go right back to the beginning and walk through systematically.

The first step, after a change has been decided upon, is to be sure that the change calls for training at all. What many organizations need is not training, certainly not in the first place, but lots of detailed, operational planning and implementation of plans. Training at this stage would be a disservice if it deprived the organization of skilled people currently needed for action.

The second step is to define the part that training can play in the change. What new competences does the organization require and what part of these can be systematically trained? We need not get lost in the abstract argument over whether or not managers and leaders can be trained. This feasts unendingly on fuzzy definitions of amorphous goals. Several key aspects of a manager's or leader's skills can surely be developed through suitable training, suitably timed, for suitable individuals suitably placed in organizations. Other aspects cannot be so developed. Training strategy determines which goals can reasonably be attempted by a training institution and which cannot.

More taxing and worthy of the most careful consideration are questions of quantities and levels of personnel to be trained, and of timing the training well. Only rarely is training of one person enough to achieve a change in an organization. While one person goes for a special program elsewhere, others need to be trained no less systematically. They may not leave the organization for this. Work with senior staff engaged in working out the change, staff meetings devoted to examining the implications, perhaps a week-end conference, may serve the purpose well. Whatever the methods—this is a later question—it is important to establish what minimum concentration of trained personnel of all kinds is required to achieve the change. If the training program as a whole does not reach this minimum, the effort amounts to treading water instead of progressing toward the goal. Or worse, it trains personnel into general frustration.

The principle of accurate timing is to have personnel return from training as and when the organization will be ready to use their new competence. The other inputs get scheduled for the same time: changes in technologies and supplies, the fresh climate of readiness for the change, and so on. Newly trained personnel will then be able to get on with their new jobs without delay. Only when plans for such detailed dovetailing have been worked out has the time arrived for the third step: the selection of particular courses and of suitable persons for them.

The responsibility for going ahead with each of these steps is the work organization's. The institution can assist if the organization wishes it. It can help, for instance, in defining the training inputs required for a contemplated change and in selecting personnel for training. But that is all. It must not assume responsibility for the steps themselves.

2. Defining Training Specifications

The responsibility is reversed when the time comes for defining training specifications. The organization has specified the new knowledge, understanding, and skill required for the change it has decided on. The institution in turn has helped pinpoint those which can be developed through systematic training. *How* this is to be done, that is, what training designs and methods to use, are strictly the business of the training institution. That is at the core of its job.

There are enough analogies to help us understand this division of functions. For instance, nobody would dream of drilling a $\frac{1}{16}$-inch hole with a $\frac{1}{2}$-inch tool, or of expecting delivery in two weeks of a finished product that takes two months to season. In the same way, training has its specifications. They tell, for instance, that a half day is not long enough to develop new attitudes or leadership skills and that training one person is not enough to initiate a change for which a company of like-minded people are required. For a work organization to try to tamper with such specifications is not economy but waste and throws doubt on its commitment to getting the job accomplished.

Here are two instances of training specifications:

> Learning a mechanical skill usually requires opportunities for supervised practice. Proper supervision calls for a small training group, say, not over 12 to 15. It requires careful preparation on the part of the supervisor; his work schedule has to be so constructed that it allows x hours for this preparation. Participants have to master the skill to y extent before they can usefully proceed to the next steps in training.
>
> Or, back to the hypothetical example of managers of cooperative farms: This job requires competence in a variety of farming subjects as well as in organizing and managing groups of farmers, keeping accounts, etc. Candidates can be selected for training who already are competent in some of these aspects of the new job. It is the other skills that they then have to learn. Experience has shown that some of these skills can be learned at work, others most efficiently in full-time training—in short bursts of, say, two weeks each.

By matching methods to requirements, the total timetable of training for the change can then also be established. The training requirements for the different parts are added together. Allowance is made for some wastage in training.

The sum may show that 14 months of systematic training is required before the manager can assume full responsibility for the farm. Six weeks may be required prior to that for finding candidates and selecting the future managers. If most of the candidates can be assumed to hold jobs that call for one month's notice to their present employers, this month too needs to be added, perhaps a calendar month, if that is the custom. The whole series of activities to provide key managerial manpower for this particular development has, therefore, to start at least 16½ months before the farms are to go into operation. This assumes that all else goes well. Perhaps it would be wiser to start 18 months before and then keep up the detailed schedule. If this advance calculation is correct, it would be no use to start the whole process even 12 months ahead and proceed with the same expectations.

Training specifications have to cover two further aspects. First, they need to state precisely the contributions to training that agencies other than the institution have to make. The provision of opportunities for field work placement is an example during the course, adequate support after participants return from training and start the new work is an example for later. The participant's organization will certainly be involved in this, but so also may agencies of various other kinds. It is the institution's responsibility to define the various contributions and to ensure that they get made when needed. Second, the training specifications need to take into account the minimum concentrations of trained personnel required to effect the change *at any stage.* These have been calculated earlier. The training strategy will embrace the plan as a whole.

For the training institution, external strategy then involves a sequence of five steps. Each step brings the institution into closer relationship with the work organization. The whole sequence is shown in Exhibit 3.1.

The training specifications worked out by the institution and agreed upon by the work organization include services and activities following the participants' return from their training. Some services will be carried out by the training institution. From time to time the institution may provide information and occasions for contact between former participants and the training staff. Other follow-up activities will be carried out by the organization. The organization may arrange staff conferences or develop various other ways of helping the participants relate their new skills to the general process of change. Still other services may

Exhibit 3.1

EXTERNAL STRATEGY: FIVE STEPS PRIOR TO TRAINING

The Institution	*The Work Organization*
	Decides on a change.
	Specifies inputs required, including ⟵ new knowledge, understanding, skills.
1. Responds by specifying which new knowledge, etc., can be acquired through training.	
	⟶ Studies who exactly is involved—numbers and levels—and when; all this in relation to other inputs, for example, technological, financial, ⟵ and organizational.
2. Offers help with working out minimum concentrations of trained personnel required for change.	
3. Works out and communicates training specifications, for example, kinds and duration of training for different people, sequences, follow-up services, and contributions required from the organization and other agencies.	
	⟶ Decides to go ahead.
4. Collaborates with the work organization in drawing-up a training plan for implementation.	⟷
5. Collaborates in selecting individuals for particular kinds of training.	⟷

draw both the institution and the organization into further collaboration.

At the follow-up stage, important information can flow back to the training institution. The organization feeds back to the institution information about the effectiveness of the training in practice, on the job. The training input can then be improved and made more economical on the basis of this practical experience.

INTERNAL STRATEGY

Let us assume that external strategy has been mapped out satisfactorily: the training goals make sense, and the training specifications are met. Internal strategy then addresses two further considerations. How to organize the various training inputs for maximum effectiveness and economy is the chief concern of the rest of Chapter 3. The other consideration, the improvement of the training institution, will at this stage only be mentioned in outline to complete the picture; Part III of the book is devoted to its further study.

3. Organizing the Training Inputs

The training institution's first task is to use to the best advantage its training resources, the skills of its trainees, and available time and facilities, as well as training resources and opportunities in the locality. The range for choice is wide, even for the humblest institution, and choosing is possible at any stage of the training process. The institution can make use of a wide variety of training settings: the participants' work organizations, a special small group setting, field work, individual learning, follow-up services, to mention just a few. And it has available a wide and expanding variety of methods and materials, the study of which, one by one, makes up the bulk of this part of the book.

Internal strategy combines various discrete resources into purposeful inputs. It goes on to relate these inputs in proper quantities and sequences so that they make up a training program that achieves real impact. For the individual participant the program as a whole then provides an integrated learning experience. For his organization it provides a comprehensive and consistent input of the new skills required for development. In such a system the impact of the training process will be highest and also most economical. Careful evaluation at critical stages can ensure continued impact and economy. All this can follow if training starts with a clear and sound internal training strategy.

Different Training Strategies. The conceptual scheme formulated by Kurt Lewin[2] for developmental activity of all kinds seems to us most useful. It describes development as a succession of three stages: "unfreezing," "moving," and "refreezing." Unfreezing is necessary because the participant, and at the back of him his organization, family, and locality, comes already replete with ingrained habits of feeling, thought, and action, the very opposite of a clean slate. To affect him through training, his normal habits have first to be questioned and disturbed, or unfrozen. Training can do this by focusing attention on needs that participants cannot satisfy by habitual behavior. Into this disturbed stage the trainer then introduces other events which allow participants

---

[2] Kurt Lewin, "Group Decision and Social Change" in T. Newcomb and E. Hartley (eds.) *Readings in Social Psychology* (New York: Holt, 1947).

to try new ways of behaving, that is, moving. If they find the new behavior more useful to meet the "new" needs, participants can then be helped to make it habitual in turn. Each individual then gains a new identity and personal continuity, which he again freezes. Matthew B. Miles conceptualizes this process as a "change-inducing temporary system." Box 3.1 summarizes his formulation.

Box 3.1

CHARACTERISTICS OF CHANGE-INDUCING TEMPORARY SYSTEMS

MATTHEW B. MILES

Temporary training systems are set up for inducing changes in the durable aspects of *persons,* changes in relationships, and changes in *action.* The changes result from decisions made by participants during the life of the temporary system. The characteristics of such temporary systems are:

INPUT CHARACTERISTICS

Time limits: the system terminates at a point in time.
Initial goal definition: it deals with a sharply focused range of content.
Boundary maintenance: it has clear and nonpermeable boundaries.
Physical and social isolation: it separates participants from their ordinary pursuits. This:

Removes barriers to change.
Reduces role conflicts.
Supplies a strong protective function.
Creates sense of a system.

Size and territoriality: it is usually small in size and has defined physical territory.

PROCESS CHARACTERISTICS

Time use: awareness of time limits results in:

Distorted perceptions of elapsed time.
Pacing effects.
Goal redefinition.

Procedures are a set of timed, specified activities of persons, aimed at accomplishing system goals.
Role definition as socialization: the system provides opportunities for role redefinition and refashioning of identity.
Communication and power structures: it provides new feedback loops.
Sentiments: it induces some salient states of feelings and group climate:

Defensiveness: initial uncertainty with respect to the goals of others.

Play: fluid, spontaneous, game-like behavior.

Interpersonal liking: acceptance of and intimacy with others.

Esprit de corps: a sense of group identity.

Involvement: engagement in the system's goals.

Norms: The system stimulates the development of regulatory norms which define and govern behavior:

Equalitarianism: an increased belief in the appropriateness of equal status relationships during the life of the system.

Authenticity: emphasis on importance of openness and trust among participants.

Inquiry: problem solving with use of available data.

Hypotheticality: valuing of experimental, provisional, tentative-until-the-facts-are-in approaches.

Newism: favoring novelty and innovation.

Effortfulness: valuing hard work, energy, and effort.

SOURCE: Matthew B. Miles, "Temporary Systems" in Matthew B. Miles (ed.), *Innovation in Education* (New York: Teachers College, Columbia University, 1964), chap. xix.

The guiding principles for working out training strategies lie in these dynamics of the development process and in the minimum critical concentration of the effort required at each stage of it. This basic process can be shown as a schematic model, as in Figure 3.1.

In different circumstances and, above all, to achieve different goals, the same paradigm leads to different training strategies and to different emphases at various stages of the training process. All take the same basic factors into account but relate them differently and give them different weights.

The differences occur along two axes. The first axis delineates the subject matter that participants are to learn. At one extreme it points toward learning about a specific task or piece of knowledge, such as the pros and cons of using power drills of various makes for a certain job, or the composition of the national income. We will call this kind of

Figure 3.1

SCHEMATIC MODEL OF TRAINING

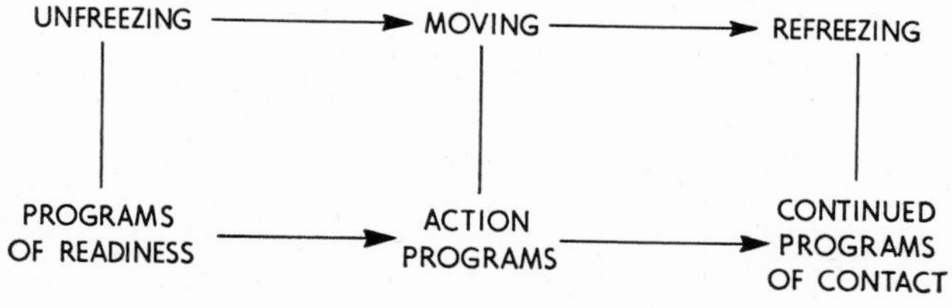

UNFREEZING ⟶ MOVING ⟶ REFREEZING

PROGRAMS OF READINESS ⟶ ACTION PROGRAMS ⟶ CONTINUED PROGRAMS OF CONTACT

knowledge "content." At the other extreme are general understanding and insight into how people and things function. We will call that kind of knowledge "process." To continue with the same examples for process examples, participants would learn how drilling machines work and how national income figures are collected, compiled, and calculated, and the principles that underly these functions. The first axis then has "content" for one extreme and "process" for the other.

Figure 3.2

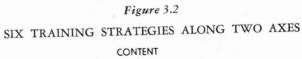

SIX TRAINING STRATEGIES ALONG TWO AXES

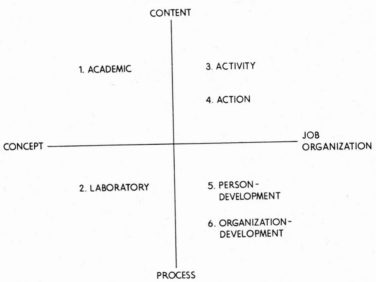

The second axis delineates the primary use that training is to be put to. Is it to be used for abstraction, for constructing new concepts and theory? That would be one extreme. We will call this "concept." Or is it to improve action directly, in the field and on the job? That extreme we will call "job."

Along these two axes, we can set out six major training strategies. They are as shown in Figure 3.2.

Before we go on to consider the six strategies in turn, we will pause for a reminder. The diagrammatic clarity of these distinctions is bought at the price of undue sharpness. The distinctions are not so sharp as they seem here, certainly not so exclusive. Which is after all just what we should expect from all such mental, man-made distinctions. They serve to put some complex and far-ranging affairs of life into pigeonholes in our minds, with each hole containing only as much data as we can manage to work on at one time. The question to ask of these six strategies, therefore, is not whether they occur so neatly in real life. The question is only whether the distinctions we draw between them are useful for our purpose here. This purpose is to throw into sharp relief different approaches to training. The different approaches result in different strategies. Therefore, they are worth distinguishing clearly. We understand that what looks sharp and uncompromising in exposition describes only trends and tendencies in practice, tendencies that can often be offset (or strengthened) by extra deliberation and care.

For greater comprehensiveness, we will here ignore the distinction we draw in the first chapter between education and training and encompass both in this exposition. We will, in fact, start with the most familiar: the *academic strategy*.

(*i*) *The academic strategy* gives pride of place to transmitting content and increasing conceptual understanding. Its characteristic methods are lectures, seminars, and individual reading and preparation. The goals are incorporated first in a syllabus which has to be "covered" and then in examinations which test the student's recall of the content and principles and his ability to "apply" them under simulated conditions.

The strategy makes two assumptions. One is that content and understanding can be "passed on" effectively from those who know— professors, writers—to those who are ignorant. The other is that the participants can translate the abstract generalizations into improving their actual performance in concrete real-life situations. Universities need not be concerned about the second assumption. But the use of the "academic strategy" is not confined to academic institutions. It is commonly used for many training activities, that is, where specific improvements are expected to take place on the job and in the organization. Many parts of teachers' training for instance, offer examples of academic training for action goals. In fact, it would not be too much to say that the academic strategy tends to be generally preferred in the training world. Program directors have to be argued out of it. It "comes naturally," apparently, and is used until something else takes its place. Its attractions include the special status accorded to the "educated" man irrespective of what he can *do,* the neatness and orderliness of the syllabus, and, more basically, the control that this strategy leaves firmly in the hands of the trainer.

(*ii*) *The laboratory strategy* is also distant from the job and organization in real life, hence its name. It has enjoyed prominence and respect for centuries from a variety of disciplines, for it provides an opportunity to gain insight and skill from the direct experience and manipulation of a limited number of elements under controlled conditions. It is real to that limited extent, and so can also provide enough distance from real life to permit both the freedom to experiment and the safety to learn from the consequences of trial. It is through laboratory training that the student of medicine discovers for himself the wonders of the human anatomy, the bacteriologist-to-be develops first-hand familiarity with pathogens, and the budding physicist discovers subtle applications of the law of gravity.

In recent years, the concept of the laboratory has found wider use, in language laboratories, for instance. We are here particularly interested in training laboratories for personal and organizational development. The laboratory strategy can be used for improving skills of social interaction that are essential for managers, supervisors, trainers, community workers, and a host of others who need to influence the quality of human interaction and human relationships in the work environment. For this purpose, the laboratory strategy gives weight to considerations of process, not content: *how* things do or do not get accomplished, not *what* is to be accomplished. This strategy is used to experience, and then to understand through this experience, how different people (real people—myself, my fellow trainers) think, act and react; how leadership and other roles are performed in a group; how people get involved in a task or reject it. Where this kind of training laboratory is given a subject heading, it is something in the area of human relations and organizational behavior.

Two assumptions underlie the laboratory strategy. The first is that it is useful and possible to help people pay attention to the reality inside each of us, the psychological reality, so that they can then better understand the springs of their own behavior and others' and become aware that all these are important factors in actual performance on the job. The second assumption is that people can themselves translate this experience and learning in the laboratory to actual life situations, including other learning and work situations.

This is not a common strategy. It is novel and difficult to handle well. It raises fears of intrusion into people's privacy. As it cannot replace, only supplement, strategies that lay stress on content, it seems an expensive extra. The more basic difficulties of giving this strategy the place appropriate to its purpose and its limits include its seeming disorder and unpredictable "coverage," the complexities involved in evaluating its effectiveness, and, above all, the different, nonauthoritarian relationship it calls for between the trainer and other participants.

(*iii*) *The activity strategy* emphasizes practice of a particular skill.

Clearly in view is improved individual performance on a specific job. The most elementary version of this strategy would be: try, try, and try again, until the participant can do the job. A skilled practitioner, particularly if he has the inclinations and skills of a trainer also, can greatly help this unprepared process along. This strategy has founded the long and honorable history of apprenticeship, understudy, and internship, and the "counterpart" function of international aid schemes. The advantage of leaving the learning process unaided and unsystematic to this extent is the opportunity for exploration it affords the participant by which he can "get the feel of the job," given sufficient time.

Since this strategy puts training "on the job," it avoids all problems of transfer from training to back home. Finally, it makes lighter demands on the work organization than other strategies.

Two assumptions underlie the activity strategy. The first is that the skill required by the organization is comprised within the ability to do this particular specified job plus whatever the participant can "pick up" as he goes along of the ways the surrounding organization operates. An alternative to the first assumption is that the participant will sufficiently conceptualize his activity for himself to be able to deal with any additional needs on the job. The second assumption is that production and training can be combined rather simply.

These are assumptions that may have been generally useful some time ago. Now they are useful for fewer and fewer jobs. Job requirements are in fact changing so fast and to such an extent that limited job training leads to repeated needs for retraining. The activity strategy leaves to chance questions of individual motivation and of collaboration between two or more people which are assuming increasing importance in modern conditions. The assumption that production and training can be readily combined is also no longer useful. Production goals tend to crowd out training goals, so that in many instances this strategy ends as all work and no training. On jobs that call for very little skill anyway, this may not matter. But the number of such unskilled jobs declines sharply as the economy develops. Finally, the activity strategy puts participants in danger of learning outdated or faulty methods of work. For the rapidly increasing number of jobs for which speed, precision, and adaptability are required, the activity strategy is in fact of little value and may do harm.

The limitations of the activity strategy have been belabored because of its prevalence. Many of the wide range of production-cum-training centers in India, for instance, really institutionalize this confusion. Though logically incontestable, the combination of production and training is in practice so difficult as to border on the impossible. When the centers concentrate on getting production out, as many do in order to satisfy their evaluators' itch for concreteness, then training becomes very costly. Often it is also ineffective because the skilled workmen, instead of instructing and supervising the participants, are put on direct production to augment the monthly production record. On the other hand, the centers' training function allows organizers to avoid responsibility for inefficiencies in production or other aspects of management.

Institutions that include field placements in their training program often encounter a variant of the activity strategy and its limitations. Often the training placement yields nothing beyond sheer activity. The participant is kept busy on a motley assortment of tasks that permanent staff members leave to him. Or he is ignored, hopefully to "make his own way." Either method represents no training.

The updated versions of the activity strategy avoid some of these pitfalls, but never all. As used by an increasing number of systematic training programs, in trade schools, for instance, it is based on rigorous detailed analyses of a particular skill. The skill is practiced in parts, often with the use of simple aids. When the participant has gained specific standards of accuracy and speed on the parts, he practices the parts together and attains accuracy and speed for the whole operation. In this way, training time can be greatly curtailed and wastage, for example, of spoiled materials, reduced. The "feel of the job" is not acquired even by this procedure, nor is the capacity for further learning should conditions change. These must come on the job, over time, or they will not come at all.

(*iv*) *The action-program strategy* is brother to the activity strategy. It does for a whole organization—a group, a town, or some other social system—what the activity strategy does for an individual. The training component of work camps and many other community action programs is based on this strategy. Its emphasis on action rests on the same assumptions and runs the same dangers for an organization that the activity strategy does for an individual. It too is focused on content, not on process. Its emphasis on the "practical" can become so strong that the training purpose gets lost. In the absence of renewal through training, action soon fails in quality, becomes discontinuous, and in many cases ceases. If action is called for above all else, as in disaster relief or in digging a common village well, these limitations need not concern us in this book. But if an action program is chosen as a training strategy, then action by itself is not enough. It ensures neither sound practice nor the understanding of working procedures required for further development.

The massive Indian program for rural community development has been beset by dilemmas which can be traced to an increasing reliance on action strategies. With heavy pressure for "concrete results," in terms of seed distributed, wells dug, roads and schools constructed, and the like, the program became all action by officials; and in this shift they lost their underlying purpose of stimulating participation, initiative, and collaboration by villagers. With that they were in a vicious circle in which secondary goals could be met only at the cost of primary goals.

With every round it became more difficult to revert to the original intent. By now, in many places, attention is so relentlessly concentrated on physical results that harassed officials have no time left even to think. And without time to think there can be no training—or learning. The result is that the basic resources of motivation and skill which the program was to multiply remain small, and the few participants can only achieve small physical results.

(*v*) *The person-development strategy* completes the range of strategies that aim to train an individual. This strategy gives weight to both the job requirements and to the processes by which these requirements are met. It consists basically of providing participants with alternating opportunities. For parts of the program, participants work on tasks and problems similar to those they face on their jobs. In between they analyze, elucidate, and understand the factors that underlie the experiences they have just had and the points of view with which they approached them. This strategy does not lead to improvements limited to a specific job or situation but to widening and deepening the participants' competence to understand and deal with many situations. *What* to think is taken to be a less potent learning than *how* to think. Action and discussion methods of training are characteristic of this strategy: field training, simulation methods, and the discussion of incidents and cases.

This strategy rests on two sets of assumptions. One set states that participants are already sufficiently familiar with work situations to be able to deal with any new job content or other details that can be expected to be required. Any additional knowledge they feel they need, they will be able and eager to secure for themselves. They are also already adept at analyzing their experiences and generalizing from them for the future. This assumption suggests that the person-development strategy is most appropriate for training professional personnel and that it will become widely appropriate also in India, as education spreads and improves and as more and more jobs call for the kind of aware use of oneself that this strategy fosters.

The second set of assumptions is one that all individual strategies share. It states that an individual will have the support of his organization to put his training to use. To leave the organizational factor to chance would lead to many heartaches and much wastage. This now happens when a competent, well-trained individual cannot use his training because his organization will not give him enough elbowroom to change his behavior. In other cases, the individual may be able to create a little elbowroom for himself and then to do his job more effectively and with greater satisfaction than before. But the effect of this is limited to his immediate surroundings. He is tolerated, no more. The wider organization remains unaffected and his innovations would die tomorrow if he left.

> Judging by the very high rate of mobility of competent engineers and administrators in India, experienced professional people in India are demanding more scope and leave organizations which deny them adequate work satisfaction. Attributing such losses to the general economic situation in the country is not convincing. As high personal taxes pare differences in net income very fine, opportunities for personal satisfaction and development count for more and more. People who refuse to get involved in this question are usually blind also to the wasted expenditure on training from which the organization gets no benefit. The policy some organizations have of not sending staff for outside training is at least more logical, and cheaper. But everyone recognizes it for what it is: a temporary expedient at best.

(vi) *The organization-development strategy* goes beyond the person-development strategy in just this, that it has organizational change as its explicit, central focus and sees the change of individuals through training as a means of organizational change. This strategy requires the closest collaboration between the training institution and the work organization. The institution acts in a consulting role prior to executing the core parts of the required training and often again after participants return to their jobs.

As a starting point, this strategy addresses the question, what does the organization need to learn to achieve a particular change. The next step is to assess the training needs in detail and relate them to other requirements of change. The organization then uses training to ensure that competent staff is available in such numbers, at levels and at times that the change can be accomplished. This strategy directly guides the selection of individuals for training and for jobs upon their return. Beyond accomplishing an immediate discrete change, it has the more general and lasting aim of developing the organization's own training function. This is basically not a matter of setting up (or not setting up) a training department. Rather it is a matter of fostering an attitude and allocating resources so that staff is developed further through the organization's normal operations. The aim is to achieve in the organization a pervasive sense of continuous development and a heightened receptivity and readiness for change.

The first of two assumptions that this training strategy makes is analogous to the first made by the person-development strategy: attention to organizational needs and to the processes by which they can be met will induce participants to acquire any additional knowledge required and also to enhance their ability to conceptualize developments for the future. The second assumption also covers parallel ground, but in reverse. The person-development strategy assumes that organizational change will follow individual learning. We know that this is not necessarily so. The organization-development strategy assumes that the individual will change as the organization changes and will change in line with organizational requirements. This is the specter of organization man. It also does not necessarily work out as assumed.

The organization-development strategy can incorporate two provisions to minimize possible discrepancies between individual and organizational interests. One is to associate individuals in advance with organizational changes that affect them and to give them opportunities to contribute toward shaping the changes. The second step is an open acknowledgment that such discrepancies can exist and may lead to some movement of staff within the organization and, if all else fails, to some loss of staff.

In the organization-development strategy, the training institution has the function of clarifying these issues and of insisting that the organization resolve them before it embarks upon a training program. To the many rapidly expanding organizations in a developing country like India, it can point out that they are in the most favorable position for providing opportunities for trained staff to change to jobs within the organization which promise continued personal satisfaction.

The use of the organization-development strategy is so new that a series of six examples in ascending order of complexity may help readers visualize it. The common simple mathematical extrapolations of staff needs at various levels to cope with new or expanding activities are only the bare beginnings of this kind of strategy.

1. Selecting participants in pairs or threes who work side by side or in functional interrelationship in an organization is a simple attempt at an organization-development strategy. The Small Industry Extension Training (Siet) Institute, Hyderabad, has tried to do this in its regular three-months'

industrial management and area development courses. It is a rough-and-ready rule, because two or three trained people of any level in the organization may not in fact be the minimum concentration required. When the basic idea is not understood by the organization, the two or three candidates put forward by the organization for training may not in fact work sufficiently closely together to provide the necessary support on the job.

2. Siet Institute used the strategy more massively when it recruited 60 potential entrepreneurs from one small town for a succession of four 10-day courses in entrepreneurial motivation. The majority of these participants formed themselves into an entrepreneur's association which could show tangible results three years later in terms of industrial units started and new investments.

3. To stimulate industrial development in a District, a largely rural area with a population of 1.5 million, the Institute decided to concentrate training on two or three District towns and offer them a sequence of training events and services. The first stage aimed at creating broadly based interest. It proceeded by locating in local factories the in-plant field work of a group of participants in one of Siet Institute's regular courses. The faculty required for this work could, at the same time, organize and run weekend courses for 60 or so local entrepreneurs and managers. The second stage consisted of short entrepreneurial motivation courses, again for 60 or so local people and organized locally. Out of these 60, some promising participants could then be selected for stage three, a succession of regular management training courses at Siet Institute.

4. In its three-tier management programs the Indian Institute of Management, Ahmedabad (IIMA), has attempted to take into account the hierarchical relationships in an organization and the support of changes needed from the chief executive. Each program has three stages. Participating organizations have to be represented in all three. The first, which lasts for six weeks, is for one or two members of middle management; the second (one week) is for a member of senior management; the last (three days) is for the top executive. The stages overlap. The idea is that each participant will be more effective after training for having the support of at least two others at different levels of the organization.

5. A more intensive three-tier program is run by the South India Textile Research Association (SITRA) for individual textile mills. Primarily for supervisory training, the program includes training also for the managers and the managing agent higher in the organization, and for the jobbers below. Short special courses and other in-service activities are also arranged for clerical and administrative staff. The training of each level is largely based on feedback about existing practices and suggestions from the next lower level in the organization. Each unit program is limited to 20 participants and lasts four weeks, excluding follow-up services. The Ahmedabad Textile Industry's Research Association (ATIRA) has another "unit program." Financed by

four mills and lasting several years, the program aims at training all firstline supervisors in those units and ensuring adequate organizational support for them. The program has grown out of collaborative action-research projects designed to elicit training and job requirements.

6. The Institute of Rural Health and Family Planning at Gandhigram in South India bases its training on service activities started at least a year in advance of any new training program. These activities, concentrated in six community development Blocks, are designed to involve the people themselves in planning and implementing health programs in their own communities. Health leaders, elected by the people, form a village health committee that gradually takes responsibility for more and more health activities. The Institute's service staff performs as staff members of the official government health centers at the Block level. The Primary Health Center staff participates in the program and evaluates its effectiveness.

In time, official health workers from other areas and other States come for training in the methods of work developed. Opportunities for developing similar skills are then provided through field assignments in the operating Blocks. A trainer is assigned to be a liaison with the staff in each Block and assumes responsibility for field activities for the participants.

Each of these examples of an organization-development strategy of training embodies the attempt to take care of the needs that actually arise in carrying out specific changes. It does this through planning in advance and then flexibility in operation. This is painstaking, hard work. It delays the start of training and demands expensive staff time, not just once, but continuously. The onward work is necessary to keep abreast of developments and to work away at paring down to the minimum the numbers of participants and time requirements of training. But as in building so in training this investment pays: it is wise to build extra strength into a program initially, and then pare down, rather than make it too slight. Once the program is under way, tighter specifications can greatly reduce the cost of mobilizing, moving, and sustaining an organization in development.

High cost is not likely to be the main obstacle to the wider application of the organization-development strategy of training. Properly carried out, it is cheaper in terms of results than the present costs of haphazard training for which organizations find the money. Two difficulties figure more prominently than costs. One that confronts all careful planning is the reluctance many executives feel to commit themselves and their organizations to a definite course of action over a significant period ahead. Uncertainties seem to loom too large, the estimates not being worth the paper on which they are written. Much of this hesitation cannot be logically justified. The vaguenesses occur at the fringes, not at the massive core of the calculations. Perhaps at the back of the hesitation may stand a more serious difficulty: the threat that careful planning and action may impose to senior executives. As a result of detailed studies of operations and requirements, strategic factors of resources become more widely known and discussed. But exclusive acquaintance with the determining factors has often been the weapon by which a senior executive thinks he can sustain his power or a company its competitive position. Thus in this connection also attitudes toward training may reveal a responsible person's general orientation.

Choosing the Appropriate Strategy.   It may be useful to summarize the main features of these six strategies side by side. This is done in Exhibit 3.2. The exhibit compares them in terms of their emphases, characteristic methods, assumptions, and action steps.

The selection of an appropriate strategy depends on a number of factors. One is the training goals. Once the training institution is clear about the goals, it can choose a strategy that leads to them.

> For example, the goal of developing individuals with sufficient skills to be able to perform more effectively on their jobs cannot be accomplished by the academic strategy of training. For that goal an activity or person-development strategy is more appropriate. The activity strategy will be appropriate if the job calls for limited skill and is not likely to change much in the near future. The person-development strategy is more appropriate if the job is complex and developing. If the main emphasis is on changes in the total organization, it is necessary to use the organization-development strategy.

The second consideration when choosing a strategy is the resources available for training. The resources include the faculty of the training institution in the first place, the extent to which it can draw on additional professional resources and community contacts, and the availability of various other facilities necessary for successfully using a particular strategy. Above all, so long as available trainers are not competent to operate a particular strategy, attempting it would only create a frustrating situation likely to lead to failure.

Time and money are often mentioned as factors that rule out otherwise desirable strategies. Programs are to be large and to start with minimum delay; and they must be cheap. Without gainsaying these values, it is difficult to be patient with these particular limitations. So very many people have already been "put through" so many repeated courses, all to so little effect. What could be more time wasting and expensive than that? Time is an acceptable limitation only if brevity can induce heightened intensity and rigor in the program, for example, by working with smaller training groups, with more and better faculty,

Exhibit 3.2

COMPARISON OF SIX TRAINING STRATEGIES

Strategy	Emphases	Characteristic Methods	Assumptions	Action Steps
1. Academic	Transmitting content and increasing conceptual understanding	Lecture Seminar Individual reading	1. Content and understanding can be passed on from those who know to those who are ignorant. 2. Such knowledge and understanding can be translated in practice.	Building a syllabus to be covered in the program Examination to test retained knowledge and understanding
2. Laboratory	Process of function and change Process of learning	Isolation Free exploration and discussion Experimentation	1. It is useful and possible to pay attention to psychological factors for separate attention. 2. Understanding of own and others' behavior helps in the performance of the jobs.	Unfreezing participants from their usual expectations and norms Helping participants see and help others see own behavior and develop new habits
3. Activity	Practice of specific skill	Work on the job under supervision Detailed job analysis and practice with aids	1. Improvement in particular skill leads to better performance on the job. 2. Production and training can be combined rather simply.	Analyzing skill and dividing it into parts Preparing practice tasks, standards, and aids

Exhibit 3.2 (Continued)

Strategy	Emphases	Characteristic Methods	Assumptions	Action Steps
4. Action	Sufficient skills to get organizational action	Field work, setting and achieving targets	1. Working in the field develops people. 2. Individual skills and organizational needs will fit together.	Preparation of field programs Participation according to schedule
5. Person-development	Improved individual competence in wide variety of tasks and situations	Field training, simulation methods, incident and case sessions, and syndicate discussion	1. Training in job requirements with emphasis on process will help a participant develop general skills and understanding. 2. Organization will support the individual in using understanding and skills acquired.	Identifying training needs Preparing simulated data
6. Organization-development	Organizational improvement	Study of organizational needs Work with small groups from the organization	1. Attention to organizational needs as process develops understanding. 2. Organizational change will result in individual's change.	Survey of organizational needs Determining strategic grouping for training Working on organizational requirements

with extra-careful training designs, and fewer gaps in time. But once the limit of substitution has been reached, as it will be reached sooner or later, then to go below the minimum specification of time and other resources would be irresponsible and damaging.

Rather similar dangers are incurred by requiring a training institution to scatter its efforts in an attempt to serve a large number of organizations, over the whole country and perhaps abroad as well. This cuts out its use of an organization-development strategy, for the institution cannot achieve the concentrations of participants and resources necessary for it. Action strategies may also be ruled out by this condition. We doubt the value of doing all over the place "something, whatever is possible." This something may simply be too little to make any useful difference and therefore all waste. The proper choice, surely, is to use appropriate strategies in as many places as possible, and not institute training where it cannot be done effectively—yet. The outcome of this kind of decision, difficult as it often must be to make it stick in the face of pressures of all kinds, is likely to be realistic and economical. Similar hardheaded choices do get taken and are accepted in other fields. There is nothing strange about recommending them for training.

The general conditions in developing countries in fact put a premium on just such hardheadedness. Rapid change and the urgent need for greater independence of action and for skills of collaboration on the part of individuals and organization all call for training strategies that emphasize attention on process and organizational dimensions, i.e., the four strategies of laboratory, action, person-development, and organization-development. If few institutions are competent yet to handle these strategies, that only calls for renewed emphasis on faculty and institutional development. That, not carrying on somehow, needs to command priority.

4. Improving the Training Institution

Internal training strategy has to provide for the growth and development of the training institution itself. Improving the training institution includes, as priority items, the development of its faculty, increasing the other resources within, developing close professional and working relations with other institutions and concerned agencies outside—in short, equipping the training institution in every way for performing even more effectively its primary roles. In the specific context of this chapter, institutional development means that the institution can with minimum delay choose and use those training strategies that would best meet the needs of the organizations which it serves. We will return to these questions at some length in Part III.

Reading 3.1

A LABORATORY STRATEGY OF TRAINING*
Leland P. Bradford

A training approach directed toward bringing about desirable changes in the way people work and relate to others must analyze five major areas. These are:

1. The aspects of individual learning necessary for change in the total individual.
2. The optimum condition under which change can be encouraged—the training plan.
3. The psychological atmosphere conducive to change.
4. The ways of handling the personal problems arising from efforts to change.
5. The support necessary to enable the individual to maintain the change.

The Training Design

The training plan or design which can reach this target requires certain basic parts.

(*a*) Opportunity to interact with others in a training group and to analyze the experience and gain insight into oneself and others.
(*b*) Opportunity to gain an awareness of inadequacy and of the potentiality for improvement.
(*c*) Opportunity to hypothesize about the consequences and effectiveness of new behavior and to test out the hypotheses in practice.
(*d*) Opportunity to practice new skills until security in their use is gained.
(*e*) Opportunity to foresee backhome resistances to new behavior and to plan and develop ways of overcoming such resistances and of maintaining the new behavior after it has been learned.

These conditions essentially add up to the following requirements for training:

---

* Abridged from Leland P. Bradford, "Human Relations Training," a paper partially based on *Explorations in Human Relations Training* (Washington, D.C.: National Training Laboratories, 1954).

(*a*) Creating experience-centered training groups in which curriculum content is derived from the behavior of the members. Essentially a feedback system is established in which the individuals and the group as a whole are collecting information about their own behavior in relation to their goals, bringing the information as input to create changes in the manner and direction of output.

Methods of appropriate and adequate observation and collection of perceptions and feelings, as well as methods of feeding back data so they will be received and not resisted, should comprise some of the skills of the trainer.

(*b*) Creating opportunities for the individual to test out hypotheses about changed behavior. The two basic principles of feedback and experimentation are adapted in a variety of ways to make up a training program.

Action and interaction, analysis, hypothesizing, testing and practicing compose an effective training program in human relations. Lectures, research reports, films, demonstrations provide the cognitive basis to provide more meaning and direction to experiential learning.

Two additional aspects of an effective training program are needed. Because much of leadership and membership in all areas of life—the work place, the trade union, the social organization and the home—takes place in group processes, group methods are needed. These can only be learned through participation in group situations under training conditions and analysis of the group experiences.

Secondly, the training group, if it has been helped to develop strength and sensitivity, can help its members along the rough and sometimes painful road of change.

Change, whether in behavior or in related knowledge or attitudes, does not usually come easily if the change has any depth or importance for the individual. New ideas and attitudes frequently upset old ideas and attitudes that had comfortably "explained" situations. The acceptance of new ideas and attitudes usually requires a reorganization of other ideas and attitudes and implies different approaches to planning and executing. Change in behavior is usually even more difficult, particularly in relationships among people. Change in behavior means that the individual will appear different from that which he has appeared to be to other people and this implies a host of anxieties the individual may have about the consequences of his being seen as different. He may not be successful. He may lose status with others, or may suffer ridicule. All of these factors may lower readiness for learning and change on the part of the individual.

Group influences can be strong in helping individuals develop readiness (overcome resistance) to learning and change. If the group is attractive to the individual, it can exert pressures on him to change as the other members of the group are changing. The fact that other group members face the same problems for which change is needed is comforting and reassuring. There is a lessening of feelings of guilt for having a problem and for needing to change old ways in order to solve it.

An Atmosphere Conducive to Change

Equally important to the creation of effective training groups using appropriate methods is the establishment of an atmosphere or climate that supports readiness for change and learning rather than resistance. Briefly, such an atmosphere includes the following ingredients: a standard of permissiveness to have problems; an expectation that everyone is changing and an acceptance of learning and changing as desirable, not as marks of previous ineptitude or failure; a realization that the process of learning and change may be difficult, but that it will not be punished by the group or other members; a group situation where individual members show concern for others, and give emotional reinforcement to them; healthy levels of aspiration as a group and as members; a standard of scientific objectivity in analyzing and interpreting group events and processes.

The task of creating a permissive atmosphere is not an easy one. Certainly permissiveness is not created by passivity, but by sensitive action upon the part of leaders. Permissiveness is not the same as *laissez faire* leadership in which leadership is abdicated.

In developing an atmosphere of permissiveness, the training leaders attempt to accomplish the following aims:

(*a*) To create an awareness of the similarity of the problems facing individual group members. A problem census collected by going around the table, or by sub-groups of two or three exploring problems among themselves and reporting them to the group is a means of discovering similarity among problems.

(*b*) To relate these problems to the set of forces producing them, including the actions of the individual trainee. However, when the trainee sees his behavior as only one among many forces, he may tend to have reduced feelings of guilt and defensiveness.

(*c*) To prevent, in early stages of discussion, quick answers or judgments from others about the importance of any individual's problems.

(*d*) To prevent interpersonal attacks under the guise of discussion of the problems, and efforts to gain status through lowering the position of others by ridiculing their problems.

(*e*) To establish objective methods of examining problems such as role-playing, careful examination of the problem as a case study, etc.

(*f*) To develop group concern for each individual and emotional support for the group member in the process of change. As the training leaders, in continuous interpretation of the process of the group, relate members' behavior to what the group is really requiring in terms of needed roles, there comes a greater tendency for the entire group to be concerned with each person and to provide support and reinforcement to him.

Permissiveness, obviously, will not be developed in a group where leadership is insensitive to the various needs and feelings of the group and its members, or is too concerned with problems of achieving status for the leaders.

Personal Problems Resulting from Change. Anxieties are easily aroused in people in a training situation. Anxieties about failure to measure up to the expectations of others or of one's self; rejection by the group or trainer; attacks from others; loss of status; uncovering one's self to ridicule or hurt; the consequences of changing when "I get back home"—these are anxieties which any or all trainees may develop and feel. Because change requires moving from a position of relative security—or at least familiarity—to a less familiar position, the process of changing is often perceived by the individual as opening him up to a variety of threatening experiences.

The degree of confidence the individual has in himself, his feelings of security in the training group or backhome groups, and the extent to which the area of change touches his sore spots and fears are important factors in determining the extent of the anxieties he will feel. Some people are more readily threatened and made anxious than are others, even though some anxiety will build up in everyone when there is a dimly perceived threat to security and safety. Effectively handling such problems presents one of the most crucial points in training and is one where the responsibility of the trainer most closely parallels that of the therapist.

Maintenance of Change Back on the Job

Change in a training situation does not imply that the change will be maintained back home. Many summer-school workshops, institutes, and courses have labored to produce change in teachers or other workers only to find that when the trainees returned to their several jobs, forces against the changes induced by training were so strong as to cause them to fall back into old ways of operating. Many supervisory training programs have failed because the boss or other workers back on the job made it difficult, if not impossible, for the trainee to apply his new learnings. It is one thing to create change in an individual's behavior in a training situation. It is usually more difficult to help him to transfer and maintain the change in other situations. Yet the responsibility of an effective training program is to help the individual plan ways of maintaining change on the job.

Increased thought is being given to how the training program can help increase the maintenance of change back on the job. Lippitt found that training teams of persons rather than single individuals resulted in more significant change per person back on the job.[1]

Conclusion

The research evidence indicates clearly that traditional methods of imparting knowledge, exhortatory efforts to change attitudes, or simple capsuled courses guaranteed to eliminate human relations problems do not change behavior back on the job. Even though foremen, supervisors, and executives may verbalize satisfaction with a course, there is no evidence that this satisfaction results in behavioral learning and change. In fact, satisfaction may indicate that the program has been pleasurably painless—that it in no way has touched the behavior of the individual but has dealt with a series of platitudes interpreted as supporting present behavior.

Bringing about improvement and change in flexibility to meet shifting conditions in turn requires a training program directed toward change in behavior of the trainee back on the job. Research and experiential results indicate that experience-centered training programs using adequate methods of analysis, utilizing feedback systems, and adapting experimental concepts to learning can be effective in producing changed behavior.

On any level of training such an approach is practical. In foreman training, rather than preaching about what "good" foremen should do or handing out rules of behavior, little of which is usually seen by the trainee to apply to his specific situation, the foremen can, through role-playing, reproduce their problems including their own behavior, which is frequently the crux of their problem. Data about their behavior drawn from this common experience provide the basis for insight and changed skills. On all levels of training, experience in the training

---

[1] Ronald Lippitt, *Training in Community Relations* (New York: Harper & Bros., 1949).

group can be analyzed to provide understandings and skills in group leadership. Such training, complex as it may be and demanding competent trainers, is rapidly spreading. It is applicable to training situations removed from the job situation and to training situations close to the job.

Reading 3.2

ORGANIZATION-DEVELOPMENT STRATEGY OF TRAINING*

Robert Blake and Jane S. Mouton

The main criterion of a training program is improvement in organization performance. For this purpose the *process training hypothesis* is not adequate. We have replaced it with the *organization-development hypothesis.* This states that to achieve *fundamental* changes in organization performance, it is necessary that the organization's culture —its history and present problems—be the subject of membership-wide study, examination, and planning for execution of change.

The organization-development hypothesis acknowledges the need for aiding individuals in concrete ways to be more effective in their own personal work. Beyond that, it introduces concepts, methods, and skills for changing the organization's culture to promote the conditions of choice under which more productive behavior can occur. Furthermore, the probability that changes in individual behavior will occur is increased to the degree that members study and modify organization culture, such as the values, norms, and so on, that when disregarded, can constitute insurmountable barriers to change.

Several projects have been launched according to the requirements of the organization-development hypothesis. Because of the dramatic improvements in organization performance compared to the limited success following application of educational efforts under the process training hypothesis, significance is to be attached to the differences in strategy of the two approaches. Some of the important distinctions in the

---

* Abridged from Robert R. Blake and Jane S. Mouton, "Theory, Technique and Results from Managerial Grid Organization Development," a paper presented at a seminar on organization change, Graduate School of Business Administration, University of California, Los Angeles, April 5, 1963.

training design, methods and scope of application include (1) use of *The Managerial Grid*[1] as an integrated set of theories about the management of production-people problems, as described in more detail below; (2) replacement of sensitivity training, which used the unstructured T-group, by laboratory learning designs that involve structured interaction performance under time pressure, with results measured through quantitative indices and followed by periods of process review, critique, and evaluation; (3) replacement of the behavioral scientists as trainers by the line management; (4) introduction of a *series* of the follow-up steps for application of what had been learned to concrete problems of work; (5) extension of time perspective for change from the idea of a two-week training experience to a development effort of about five years; (6) reconstituting the organization culture by instituting values, norms, attitudes, involvement, and commitment with the highest possible integration of people into production; and (7) the utilization of action research as the basis for measuring changes achieved and for continuously setting new directions of organization and individual growth and development.

It is with the concepts of change involved in the organization development hypothesis that the remainder of this report deals.

A SIX-PHASE APPROACH TO ORGANIZATION DEVELOPMENT EDUCATION

The general outlines of organization development are simple. However, the details of execution are complex. In a broad way, the approach engages the entire organization membership in studying and perfecting itself as a system of interworking parts integrated around attaining organization purpose. Included are (1) an investigation by each member of his own managerial styles; (2) examination of boss-subordinate relationships; (3) analysis of work team action; (4) exploration of coordination issues of interrelated teams; (5) identifying and defining major organization problem areas such as long-range planning, profitability of operations, union-management relations, promotional policy and incentive awards, new product development, utilities conservation, safety, and a seemingly endless variety of other concrete issues; and (6) planning for and executing agreed-upon solutions that result in changes throughout the organization.

In an organization of substantial size, of as many as 1,000 or more

---

[1] Robert R. Blake, *The Managerial Grid* (Houston, Tex.: Gulf Publishing Co., 1965).

members, these phases may require from three to five years or longer to complete. The length depends on the intensity of the effort, the seriousness of the problems confronting the organization and the amount of development sought.

Self-Administration of Organization Development

The entire effort is administered by the line organization membership itself, rather than by outside behavioral science experts. The behavioral scientist's role is to provide broad consultation on major issues of development, strategy, and tactics of achieving it. The self-administering aspect constitutes a key element. Instead of handing itself over to an outside specialist who teaches or provides step-by-step guidance, the line organization retains full responsibility for executing its own development effort. The participation of the appropriate staff organization is also indirect. It provides the line with consultative and administrative aid. In this way, many sources of "natural" resistance linked to intrusion by experts—outsiders or internal staff—are not encountered. Rather, because the organization's line membership has the responsibility for achieving success through its own efforts, heightened improvement motivation is a highly probable result.

While the phases are not applied in a mechanical step-by-step sequence, but rather are intertwined, the trend of development is in the *direction* to be described.

Part I: Management development within the organization
    Phase 1. Managerial Grid laboratory-seminar education
    Phase 2. Work team development
Part II: Organization development
    Phase 3. Horizontal and vertical intergroup linking
    Phase 4. Identifying organization problem areas and setting improvement goals
    Phase 5. Planning and executing solutions to attain organization improvement goals
    Phase 6. Stabilization

Part I: Management Development within the Organization

Phases 1 and 2 are concerned with aiding individuals and teams to increase their performance capability within the existing framework. The goals of these two phases are concerned with improvement of individual competence and of interpersonal skills of supervision and problem solving.

Phase 1: Managerial Grid Laboratory-Seminar Education. Organization development begins with laboratory learning sessions built into focusing attention of organization members on various approaches to achieving production through people. These are self-taught Managerial Grid laboratory-seminars. The purposes, participants, activities, time applied to the activity and expressed outcomes are briefly summarized in Table 1.

The activities of Phase 1 are designed around two considerations. The first is that intelligent managerial choice of the best manner of achieving production through people is possible where managers understand a *systematic behavioral science framework* and develop a usable common language system through which to exchange managerial points of view. This framework can be employed as the basis for diagnosing organization, intergroup, team, interpersonal, and individual problems and, at each level as appropriate, choosing solutions from among several alternatives, acting out of frustration, on impulse, or being limited to one or two possible actions. The second consideration is that of achieving common understanding of managerial theories by managers at all levels and across the entire organization membership to aid communication control and decision making. Thus, the aim is for organization members to learn the Managerial Grid as a systematic framework. It is presented below in summary form.

The Managerial Grid. The Managerial Grid, Figure 1, identifies several theories of managerial behavior. These theories are based on two key variables. One is concern for production. The other is concern for people. The Managerial Grid shows these two concerns and some of the possible interactions between them. The horizontal axis indicates concern for production. The vertical axis indicates concern for people. Each is expressed as a nine-point scale of concern. The number 1 in each case represents minimal concern. The number 9 represents maximum concern.

The lower left corner of the Grid diagram in Figure 1 shows a 1,1 style. This represents minimal concern for production and minimal concern for people. Moving up the diagram from the 1,1 style to the upper left corner, one finds the 1,9 style. Here there is maximum concern for people but minimal concern for production. In the lower right corner is 9,1. This style shows maximum concern for production and minimal concern for human relationships. In the upper right corner is found the 9,9 style which represents maximum concern for both human relationships and production. In the center of the diagram, a 5,5 style is pictured, and this is "middle of the road" in both areas of

Table 1

PHASE 1: MANAGERIAL GRID LABORATORY-SEMINAR TRAINING

Purpose	Participants	Activities	Time	Expected Outcomes
To replace common sense and intuitive managerial assumptions with a systematic framework (The Managerial Grid)	Total organization—each session contains 12 to 48 members in 6–10 man learning groups composed from a diagonal slice of the total organization membership. That is, each laboratory-seminar contains personnel across departments and levels, but with no actual boss-subordinate working relationships.	Individual study of managerial theory and assessment of own managerial assumptions	80–90 hours	Individual insight into his own and other's managerial approaches
		Standardized problem solving where performance is measured for learning purposes	Individual prestudy of 30 hours	Development of an increased range of alternatives for solving managerial dilemmas
		Team effectiveness critique sessions for assessing and replanning improved strategies of team action	On-site training time of 50–60 hours	Improved team effectiveness skills
		Discussions regarding each individual's managerial style		Development of new standards of open and candid communication surrounding work activities
		Lecturettes on managerial and organization theory		Greater awareness of how traditions, past practices and precedents operate in the regulation of work
		Practice in organization diagnosis		

Figure 1

THE MANAGERIAL GRID

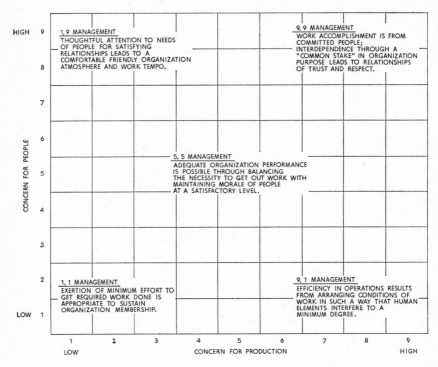

concern. Although these five key managerial orientations are shown, others have been identified. They are described in greater detail elsewhere.[2] The Managerial Grid provides a coherent system and a common language for managers to use in describing their managerial styles in terms of these two interacting key variables.

Phase 2: Work Team Development. Phase 1 helps organization members to develop greater awareness of barriers to and possibilities *for* improving production-people interactions, particularly through greater personal effectiveness. However, general principles and concepts and direct personal learning of the Managerial Grid are unlikely to result in concrete application in daily work *without* additional development phases explicitly designed to insure each application.

The learning activities involved in this phase are summarized in Table 2, which deals with team development on a family work group basis. Through the steps of team development, members evaluate actual difficulties existing among themselves which appear on the surface as

[2] *Ibid.*

Table 2

PHASE 2: WORK TEAM DEVELOPMENT

Purpose	Participants	Activities	Time	Expected Outcomes
To aid work team members to apply directly the learnings of Phase 1 to their team operations	Boss-subordinate work teams—beginning with the top team and continuing throughout the total organization	Team effectiveness activity with performance task and critique to aid members to reconnect with laboratory-seminar way of work	60 hours Individual study of 10 hours; team discussion of 40 hours	Reduction of intergroup blockages that prevent effective communication, control, and problem solving between groups, vertically and horizontally
	Many individuals participate as a boss in one team and a subordinate in another	Discussion of each individual's managerial styles	Career development part of Phase 2 takes place between the boss and each subordinate; time required ranges between 4 and 20 hours	
		Review of job descriptions and job expectations		
		Review of team history, including traditions, past practices and precedents, use of hierarchy, communication, control and decision making, interpersonal conflict, etc.		
		Individual and team goal setting		
		Career development involving boss and each subordinate on a one-to-one basis		

problems of communication, control, and decision making. The significant point here is that the *content* of team development is concerned with examining and eliminating or reducing problems of hierarchy; interpersonal conflict; outworn traditions, precedents, and practices; cohesion; and goal considered from an intrateam point of view.

With completion of Phase 2, the next steps of development are extrapersonal. They relate to broader organizational functioning.

Part II: Organization Development

✓ Within the context of organization development, individual and team learning are only the first two phases, which in themselves are limited in purpose to examining problems, not of the organization as a whole, but from both individual and working team point of view. Education, which is terminated at this point, makes the assumption that insights thus acquired will automatically be utilized, that is, that the organization culture is of little or no significance in governing the action effort that individuals are prepared to apply. This is the process training hypothesis mentioned in the introduction, which experience has shown to be limited in usefulness. Steps beyond, of the kind to be outlined below, give concrete examples of education methods that are applied when the organization-development hypothesis serves as the basis of educational effort.

Additional significant phases are thus needed if conditions are to be achieved under which *total* organization culture is to be integrated toward a higher level of proficiency and sense of individual contribution. Problems posed and subject to resolution in Phases 3, 4, 5, and 6 are in the realm of operations effectiveness. They are problems of the kind that, because they touch on the attitudes, values, and commitments of many (the organization culture), cannot really be solved through the exercise of responsibility by any given individual. These are problems that are subject to solution only through the committed and concrete efforts of several, many, or all. That is, Phases 3 through 6 distinguish *organization development* from *individual management development* or interaction development.

Phase 3: Horizontal and Vertical Intergroup Linking.   Phase 3 is based on the following line of reasoning. Coordination is as necessary between interdependent working *teams* which must mesh their efforts as it is between individuals who are required to pool actions if a job is to be carried out effectively. Yet coordination of effort between organized units can become very unsatisfactory; it can even be broken down to the point where it is nonexistent. Except for solving such intergroup break-downs through mechanisms of formal hierarchy, the standard table of organization makes no explicit arrangements for problem-solving inter-action between groups.

Behavioral science studies picture something of the nature of inter-group dynamics as they bear on industrial life. They show how work groups often either draw invidious distinctions between themselves, which lead to win-lose competitiveness, or withdraw from contact and become insulated against influences from others outside their groups.[3] Under these circumstances, representatives can become so loyal to their group positions that effective problem solving is sacrificed to the desire to win. This in turn can lead to withholding of needed information, reduction of intergroup contacts, or mutual recrimination, attack, and counterattack. Such events as these have been observed repeatedly be-tween organization subunits such as sales and manufacturing, headquar-ters, and field locations or plants, union and management, manufactur-ing and R.&D., purchasing and technical, employee relations, and the line organization.[4]

The significance of educational endeavor in improving the character of intergroup linking is summarized in Table 3. This feature of organi-zation development would be difficult to overemphasize. The procedure is a powerful one as those whose behavior the actual problem affects participate directly in defining its causes and in getting commitment for resolving the difficulties being encountered. When Phase 3 follows and builds on the two preceding phases, the blockages that arise across groups seem more readily solved.

Phase 4: Setting Organizational Improvement Goals. The first three phases above provide necessary background for approaching broader operating problems of organization development.

The idea that organization problems can be solved through the execution of different supervision alone, regardless of its style, is seen here as of limited value. The direction of organization development described in Phases 4 and 5 supplements supervisory approaches with educational methods of problem solving applied to concrete issues of work. Such methods enable individuals to engage in a *study* of problems

---

[3] Robert R. Blake and Jane S. Mouton, *Group Dynamics: Key to Decision Mak-ing* (Houston, Tex.: Gulf Publishing Co., 1961).

[4] Robert R. Blake and Jane S. Mouton, "The Intergroup Dynamics of Win-Lose Conflict and Problem-Solving Collaboration in Union-Management Relations" in M. Sherif (ed.), *Intergroup Relations and Leadership* (New York: John Wiley & Sons, Inc., 1962), pp. 94–140.

Table 3

PHASE 3: HORIZONTAL AND VERTICAL INTERGROUP LINKING

Purpose	Participants	Activities	Time	Expected Outcomes
To achieve better problem solving between groups through a closer integration of units that have working interrelationships	Representatives from the two groups involved: 8–10 per group—significant functional groupings within the organization, either hierarchical or on equal level	Each group develops self-image and image of other group Images exchanged across groups Independently each group seeks to understand why they are seen as they are Discussion leading to resolution of concrete operational problems	Two days for each intergroup sequence, but varies with the severity of the problem	Reduction of intergroup blockages that prevent effective communication, control, and problem solving between groups, vertically and horizontally

Table 4

PHASE 4: SETTING ORGANIZATIONAL IMPROVEMENT GOALS

Purpose	Participants	Activities	Time	Expected Outcomes
To define broadly based, long-term organization goals for performance improvement (*i.e.*, to identify aspects of organization culture for understanding and change)	Total organization in diagonal slices, as well as relevant parts, depending on magnitude and scope of problems	Discussion of aspects of performance that could result in organization improvement From above discussions, broad areas of recurring agreement are identified for intensive, total organization change effort Individual bosses, work teams, and subunits specify aspects of organization-wide problems for which they are responsible and set goals	Depends upon size of managerial force—two weeks to two months; approximately one day per unit	Top team sets direction of performance goals to be achieved Individuals and work teams develop understanding and commitment to general and specific goals to be achieved

of the organization as the subject matter of their own learning and insight. By taking this step, organization members are aided, through using educational *methods* learned and applied in Phases 1 and 2, to comprehend and to solve existing organization problems in a fundamental and more systematic way than they could by employing supervisory practices alone.

Phase 4 gives operational meaning to the concept of *planned* development and identifies the aspects of the organization culture toward which improvement effort is directed. As can be seen in Table 4, the entire membership or, depending on the presumed scope of the problem, that part of the organization membership whose contribution is needed to solve the problem, is involved in identifying problems, defining causes, and setting goals for solution of them.

Phase 5: Implementing Planned Change by Attaining Established Goals. Tactics involved in bringing about organization development in Phase 5, as shown in Table 5, are numerous and varied. They include all of the regular organization arrangements for problem solving and execution of agreed-upon plans, as well as additional approaches of the kind described below.

Continuing intervention in the improvement effort is made as needed by an organization-development specialist who is specifically accountable for auditing, from an achievement point of view, the entire development effort. Also, a new educational strategy is employed in Phase 5. This approach, Task Paragraphs and the Team Effectiveness Design, involves applying learning and methods of enquiry of Phase 1 to solve concrete operational and organization problems. It aids in lifting up the organization's culture for examination and change. Figure 2 lists typical problem areas which have been defined and improved or successfully resolved in Phases 4 and 5 of organization development work.

Phase 6: Stabilization. The final phase is a period of stabilizing the changes brought about in prior phases as depicted in Table 6.

Almost without regard to the effectiveness of the previous phases, the tendency is for the organization as a whole to slip back into patterns and traditional ways of behaving characteristic of the "old" culture. The old ways require less skill and less effort. They afford more comfort, for they are "second nature." A period of time, perhaps a year or longer, is necessary after the completion of the first five phases to identify fade-out trends or throwback tendencies. In addition, corrective action is taken when these fade-out effects are noticed. They are designed to deliberately pull the organization back into its new course. By continuous practice in applying new kinds of performance, members make the

Table 5

PHASE 5: IMPLEMENTING PLANNED CHANGE BY ATTAINING ESTABLISHED GOALS

Purpose	Participants	Activities	Time	Expected Outcomes
To attain goals set in Phase 4	Individuals, work teams, special task forces, total organization, etc.	Regular problem-solving and implementing mechanisms within and between work units	1–3 yrs.	Agreement and commitment among responsible organization members to courses of action; implementation steps determined
		Overriding assignments to specific individuals and groups		Effective realization of goals set in Phase 4
		Study of specific problems using design format from Phase 1 as basis for achieving understanding and problem solving		Specific accomplishments depend on concrete issue facing organization
		Use of organization-development specialist to keep development activities organized, interrelated, and on target		
		Critique of implementation efforts, redefining issues, replanning, etc.		

Figure 2

TYPICAL PROBLEM AREAS WHICH HAVE BEEN DEFINED AND
IMPROVED OR SUCCESSFULLY RESOLVED IN PHASES 3, 4, AND 5
OF ORGANIZATION DEVELOPMENT

Growth and new product development
Long-range planning
Improving corporate reputation and image
Profit sharing
Increasing product outlets
Increasing cost consciousness
Roles readjustment
Burden reduction
Shifting R.&D. values from pure experimental to business-oriented research

Revision of organization structure
Reducing age structure
Revision of promotion policy
Improvement in the organization reward system
Management development
Improved performance appraisal and review
Revision of philosophy of the company organ
Improved union-management relations through contact bargaining, etc.

Integration of headquarter-region; headquarter-field
Reduction of friction between departments such as accounting and technical, employee relations and mechanical, etc.
Relations with government regulatory body
Working with city fathers on property taxation

Improved utilities management
Introduction of running maintenance
Shifting to craft flexibility
Improved warehouse utilization

Defining and gaining understanding of job descriptions
Allocation of space and facilities
Vacation scheduling
Absenteeism
Early quitting
Safety
Pollution control
Waste control
Tool control

Table 6

PHASE 6: STABILIZATION

Purpose	Participants	Activities	Time	Expected Outcomes
To reinforce and make habitual	Total organization	Identify and take corrective action on tendencies to return to or slip into older and less effective patterns of work; special efforts of organization development specialist	One or more years	Build confidence and capability in resisting pressures to revert to old managerial habits. Stabilization of new communication, control and problem-solving approaches to organization efforts.

newer patterns habitual so that confidence in acting according to improved ways of operating also becomes "second nature."

Thus the aim in Phase 6 is not to increase organization effectiveness by setting new goals or directions of change. Rather, the effort is limited to insuring that the changes brought about in the earlier phases actually are able to withstand the pressures toward regression that seem to be present in an operational setting where quick decisions are needed and where crises are a daily occurrence.

As a method of inducing change, organization development has certain limitations in its scope and utility. First, organization development can be no more powerful than the behavioral science concepts on which it rests. Another limitation is the degree of complacency existing in the organization. Complacent people are unprepared to apply the diligence of effort necessary for improvement, and the methods of work involved in organization development are sometimes not of sufficient strength to challenge the motivation of highly complacent people. A third limitation is in the fact that organization development has as yet found most of its application in organizations which themselves have had an extended history and, therefore, strong traditions, precedents, and past practices. A final limitation is with respect to the task of the organization and the character of its membership. Best available evidence suggests that R.&D. organizations may be somewhat less responsive to the change potential of organization development than production and sales organizations. Thus, much more needs to be known before it can be presumed that organization development should be applied without regard for the local circumstances existing within any given organization.

PART II

The Pretraining Phase

Chapter 4

Organizational Collaboration through Clarifying Needs
  Four Degrees and Means of Collaboration
    1. Course Announcement
    2. Meetings with Senior Officers
    3. Homework for the Work Organization
    4. Full Collaboration
  Two Dilemmas of Development
Clarifying Individual Motivation for Training
  Institution and Candidate: Seven Functions
    1. Announcing the Program
    2. Selecting Participants
    3. Guarding against Distracting Preoccupations
    4. Lining Up Expectations More Closely
    5. Requiring Candidates to Do Homework
    6. Increasing Individual Motivation for Training
    7. Involving Participants in Planning the Program
Summary
Exhibits
  4.1. Checklist for Determining Training Needs
  4.2. Cooperative Farm Manager: Some Questions about His Job and Training
  4.3. Five-Step Model for Diagnosing State of Target System
  4.4. Collaboration for Establishing Training Needs between the Institution and the Organization
  4.5. Proposal for Managerial Project
Boxes
  4.1. Motivational Value of Feedback to the Organization
      —H. Baumgartel
  4.2. Individual Motivation for Training—Kamla Chowdhry
  4.3. A Program for Increasing Individual Motivation
      —David McClelland

Organizational Needs and
Individual Motivation

$\int\int\int\int\int\int\int\int\int\int\int\int\int\int\int\int\int\int\int\int\int\int\int\int\int$

"Men wanted. Low wages. Bitter cold. Long months of darkness. Under constant danger. Safe return doubtful. Honour and recognition if successful."

> —*This advertisement in a London newspaper for a polar expedition in 1914 brought 5,000 applications.*

"At any time in history, in order to lose one's identity, one must first have one. . . . Thus, strange as it may seem, it takes a well-established identity to tolerate radical change."

> —ERIK ERIKSON

"A man does not learn anything that he does not love."

> —GERMAN SAYING

THE PRETRAINING stage of training starts in the field, on the job. That is where the needs for new skills arise, where they can be examined in relation to the total change to be achieved, and where detailed training plans can be worked out. These plans then guide the selection of individuals for particular kinds of training. The question of who initiates this sequence is one we need to discuss, but there is no question that this stage calls for very close collaboration between the training institution and the work organization.

How does this close collaboration come about? The first answer to this question must be tangential: usually it does not come about at all. The effectiveness of training is left largely to chance. The institution assumes that it knows the training needs of the participants, presumably out of the experiences of its faculty and its appreciation of currently required developments. It also assumes that the work organization has worked out its training needs and can reasonably expect that sending some staff member(s) to the course will help bring the change about. In its turn the organization assumes that the institution understands the needs of the participants and their organizations and that the course will indeed meet these. In short, the organization assumes that the institution knows *its* business. This roughly is the position with existing organizations. Where training is to precede the launching of new activities and programs for which organizations have still to come into existence or are just in their infancy, the connection between needs and training is even more tenuous.

No production plan would be launched on a factory floor, no product into the market, on the basis of such unproven assumptions. That training can be prepared and offered on this basis generally, not just once but repeatedly, suggests that all involved approach training with a mixture of motives. They prefer to carry on somehow, at low levels of effectiveness if so they be, rather than look at the mixture too closely. The word for this is collusion. Collaboration springs from greater clarity of motivation in the first place.

ORGANIZATIONAL COLLABORATION THROUGH CLARIFYING NEEDS

Demands for training arise most naturally and obviously when organizations expand rapidly, or when altogether new services are to be set up.

For instance, between 1950 and 1965, the State Bank of India increased the number of its branches from 300 to over 1,000. Each branch has an agent to head it, as well as various key personnel. Lower staff can be recruited from outside the Bank, but agents "have to" come from inside the organization. Formerly an accountant could hope to rise to the position of agent in 15 years. Expansion has reduced this period to two years. As accountants rise more rapidly, so others lower down rise to fill the accountants' places.

We will restrict this example to agents. The outline of the training task is quite clear in their case and the Bank both needs and wants training for them. The task is to ensure that 700 members of the staff acquire through systematic training whatever they have not acquired through 2 years' working in the Bank (but might have gained from 15 years' experience).

Similarly clear extrapolations and needs arise from projecting the staff needs of many other organizations. For instance, the decision to cover the whole country with community development Blocks meant, given the original geographical and staffing patterns, that 5,000 Block development officers had to be trained by 1963.

Extrapolations of numerical requirements look simple and concrete. Actually they tell no more about training needs than that they are very large and very urgent. If training is to affect action—and that is the way we use the word here—then training plans have to take into account what improvement or new action is to result from training and the specifications by which these changes can with reasonable assurance be achieved.

This is not the meaning given to training by all people. Motives for training differ. Some organizers are concerned to have certain numbers of staff "in position" by a certain date, even if they can do very little or nothing in those positions. For them, training, *any* training, shows action, and action per se safeguards the new program against accusations of delay. "Real" training, they maintain, can be given later. Others see training as the means by which to make up by numbers what certain services now lack in performance. One person has failed to show results; therefore let there be two. The training plans for some rural extension personnel in India seem to have this orientation, as do the programs of weekend training camps for a half million village leaders. Others again see training as the one massive activity that does not encroach on scarce material resources; or as an activity that defies early challenge. After all, training is an absolute good, surely. Moreover, adequate evaluation of it is difficult. Yet others look to training primarily to tame any new recruits who are eager to change things and thus threaten to make life difficult for their seniors, or to deal with "problem" staff in general. Others, finally, wish only that the name of their organization appear on the list of participants for general publicity, to enhance the standing of the organization.

This paragraph does not by any means exhaust the motives for promoting training. We hope that it lists enough of them to make our main point: that motives for training are not at all simple and are, more likely than not, very mixed. The motives we have listed are reactions to external and personal pressures of various kinds. It is such pressures that people try to allay through training.

Training needs that the institution can try to meet arise from two sources. Once source is the changing nature of jobs and changes required in the internal functioning of the organization. The other source is imbalances and misunderstandings that lower the organization's standards of operation.

The needs for change and therefore training that arise from external sources are usually easier to identify and to dramatize than those that arise from internal discrepancies. A faster machine or a more economical manufacturing process, an important restriction or a new tax, a liberalization of credit for purchasing the kinds of products the organization makes or the launching of a countrywide new extension service—all these obviously demand a response from both the organization and the institution. The organization may adopt the new process, step up its rate of expansion, shift to new lines of products and services. The institution can publicize such external developments and the various possibilities and implications for taking part in them. Institutional participation may be particularly valid if it can foresee significant external developments and needs and forecast their magnitudes and implications. The communication of such facts and estimates may anticipate pressures toward change and serve to initiate training in good time.

The study and communication of needs for change that arise from sources within the organization can occasion similarly useful pressure in advance of the event. Only they are more difficult for the organization to carry out by itself. The difficulty arises partly from people's hesitation to look for such information. On both counts the institution can help. Box 4.1 summarizes the results of using an employee survey to feed back to the organization some facts about itself. The feedback was the beginning of a management development program which focused directly on the problems highlighted by the survey.

The results of this study suggest that the creative use of new information for conferences and meetings at all levels of departmental organization may be one of the best and most dynamic avenues to management development and organizational growth.

The first function of the training institution in the pretraining phase, then, is to highlight the needs for change that arise from both internal and external sources and to allow this knowledge to impinge on the work organization. The institution can do this with just as much clarity and vigor as it takes to galvanize the organization into purposeful action. The last thing the institution ought to do is to soft-pedal the implications of any failure to meet actual and predictable training needs.

Four Degrees and Means of Collaboration

The institution can proceed in a variety of ways. The choice depends on the likely scale of the training program in an organization and on the extent of change an organization may be able to tolerate at any time,

Box 4.1

MOTIVATIONAL VALUE OF FEEDBACK
TO THE ORGANIZATION

H. BAUMGARTEL

An experimental study was carried out in the accounting division of an electric light and power company. Six departments took part. They employed 60 managerial and supervisory personnel and 640 other personnel.

The results of an attitude questionnaire were written up in a brochure. A copy was given to everyone. In the four experimental departments this communication was followed by a program of discussions and meetings. The results were considered and implications for action sorted out. No feedback program was organized for the other departments. The questionnaire was then administered again.

A comparison of the results showed that the experimental departments showed statistically significant positive changes in the majority of items. "To mention only the most important differences . . . non-supervisory employees expressed more interest in their work, felt their work was more important" and had a better image of their supervisors. They also "felt that their group was better at getting the job done, that they were freer to take job problems to their supervisors, that their supervisors better understood their point of view, that their supervisors got along better with each other, and that they understood better how their supervisor saw things."

The results of this experimental study lend support to the idea that an intensive, group discussion procedure for utilizing the results of an employee questionnaire survey can be an effective tool for introducing change in a business organization. It may be that the effectiveness of this method, in comparison to traditional training courses, is that it *deals with the system of human relationships as a whole* (superior and subordinate can change together) and that *it deals with each manager, supervisor, and employee in the context of his own job, his own problems, and his own work relationships.*

We have speculated that the following conditions are essential for such a feedback program to be effective in any organization. There is reason to believe that the same principles apply in the use of sales and production information as well as with data concerning human factors: This information must be about the organization itself—often research findings from other companies do not convince the present management. The information must be quantitative and objective—personal opinions and impressions are often distorted; there must be some external point of reference. The information must have some stimulating quality by being:

—new information—a good cost accounting system provides new data on departmental costs.

—information contrary to common belief—several studies, for example, have shown that older workers produce more than younger workers.

—information about things not ordinarily discussed—how many times do personal feelings about the boss ever get talked out in staff meetings? The information must provide directions for, or alternative ways of achieving, positive changes—just knowing that there is high turnover and low "morale" in department X isn't enough; one needs to know what factors create the problem.

SOURCE: Howard Baumgartel, "Using Employee Questionnaire Results for Improving Organizations," *Kansas Business Review,* Vol. XXII (1959), pp. 2–6.

and also on the institution's own resources to do the work of clarification. Experience clearly favors very close collaboration between institution and organization. From the institution, clarifying the organization's training needs calls for very skillful and hardheaded work. While helping to a maximum, it must leave no room for doubt as to where the responsibility for action or for the implications of inaction or inadequate action firmly rests. This responsibility is the organization's. If the institution can convey this important understanding consistently, through the attitudes of its staff as well as through their approaches and actions, this can save many heartaches later.

Going from the simplest and most distant relationship to the most sophisticated and closest collaboration, we can distinguish four possibilities open to the institution to match its training goals with the needs of the work organizations. The time required usually lengthens as the process becomes more thorough and collaboration closer.

1. *Course Announcement.* As the barest minimum requirement, just a gesture toward collaboration, the institution can publicize its own training goals and the training strategies it prefers and is competent to use. This, at least, puts the decision to apply for training up to "the other," be it an individual or an organization, and is to that extent better than direct "recruitment" of people for training. A second step marks the first real collaboration. This is an institutional requirement that the work organization formally back candidates applying for training. This minimum level of collaboration, the institutional statement of goals and the organizational commitment, can be included in the way the institution announces a training program.

(*i*) *Statement of Institutional Training Goals.* When the institution announces a program in this manner, organizations can promote candidates for the program out of some understanding of what the program is attempting to achieve. A full statement can indicate some of the implications of the program also, and organizations can take these into account in reaching their decision.

Here is an example of such a statement:

> The X Institute was founded in 1957 to develop training, research and consulting services which may help industrial organizations to respond effectively to the many new demands of national independence, modern technologies, and economic policies. Represented on the Governing Council of the Institute are [a list].
>
> The Y program is for executives between 30 and 40 years old who, because they belong to the owning family, have been promoted to top decision-making positions at a young age. It aims in the first place at acquainting them with modern management techniques in the fields of . . . so that they can use better data for their decisions. More than that, it aims at helping them examine the process by which decisions are reached in the company and practice more effective ways of contributing to this process.

After a brief description of the training methods to be used, the announcement adds something to the effect that the institution's consulting wing can consider requests for posttraining services in the organization.

(*ii*) *Requiring Organizational Commitment.* Requiring applications to come with the explicit backing of the work organization ensures that the organization is informed, prepared to grant any necessary leave, and is willing to face at least some implications of training. The commitment is greater if the institution requires the candidate's organization to pay the training fees and perhaps also the candidate's salary during training.

The best course announcements clarify the choice for the organization and the general implications in these ways. They are a definite advance over simple soliciting. But the procedure they initiate is still one-way, take-it-or-leave-it.

2. *Meetings with Senior Officers.* Some institutions make it a practice, before launching a new program, to meet with senior officers of the organizations they intend to serve. The occasions may range from informal discussions with individuals to formal sessions and seminars with officers from several organizations at one time.

The advance in this, from the first to the second degree of collaboration, lies in making the planning of training a two-way process. It also signals clearly the institution's interest in working closely with the organizations whose need it expects to meet. Both can be real eye-openers for an organization's officers. The institution raises for their consideration general developments which either already call for organizational attention or are about to do so. It may present estimates of the likely implications of these developments for organizational changes and training needs. To have discussions on this at high levels and to involve executives and policy makers from several organizations in a meeting underscores the important function training can have in facilitating change and also makes clear that all organizations have training needs, including the best. High-level participation in a formal meeting can also represent a substantial organizational commitment to careful consideration and ensuing action, whereas even a series of informal talks with individuals may leave the extent of organizational commitment in doubt.

Such meetings and seminars hold a temptation into which some training institutions have fallen, with grave effects. Under the guise of consulting with the senior officers and working out together with them the kind of training program to be attempted with their subordinates or colleagues, some institutions have tried quietly to convert the occasion into a training program for senior officers. This temptation is the greater if the training needs look to the training institution both obvious and urgent. Its assessment may or may not be correct. That is not the issue. Either way, the conversion of a meeting from joint exploration of needs to another purpose is not lost on the senior officers. However well meant the attempt, it collects resentment and trust is destroyed just where it is most needed. If the program goes ahead at all, memories of this deception may bedevil attempts at closer collaboration for a long time to come.

> In one new institution, which started as a quasi-staff college for an official extension service, repeated confusion of this kind led to a marked estrangement between the organization and the institution. The resentment became so great that the organization rejected every institutional proposal irrespective of merit, "just to put the institute in its place."

If senior officers are to be trained, then it is this that needs to be discussed and sanctioned. Failures on this score do not at all mean that senior officers have nothing to learn or that they are not prepared to learn after genuine discussions of needs. It means only that they refuse to be belittled, a response which surely commands respect.

3. *Homework for the Work Organization.* As the next step toward closer collaboration the training institution can require detailed information about the changes in the jobs for which the organization wishes to prepare itself through training. If the requirements are general and

call for a series of programs, it can help the organization to work out a comprehensive training plan for some time ahead.

(*i*) *Detailed Analyses of Current and New Job Requirements.* Most job analyses now in use are inadequate even as descriptions of current activities. They specify a series of required qualifications in subject-matter knowledge and technical skill, that is all. To serve as the basis for training designs, job analyses have to go beyond these simple lists and describe how a job has to be actually performed, for example, under what physical conditions and time pressures, and with what access to colleagues, superiors, and additional resources. In short, the job analyses have to be operational. This is so for new jobs no less than for existing jobs. For new jobs, the operational analysis is based on detailed forecasts, that is the only difference. The forward analysis can be revised later in the light of actual experience.

Most useful and economical are analyses focused on the crucial requirements of the job, that is, requirements that make the difference between effective and ineffective performance. On existing jobs, comparing in detail the behavior of an effective and an ineffective performer can pinpoint these crucial requirements. The critical incident technique provides for descriptions both of effective and ineffective behavior on the job, usually in checklist form.

Exhibit 4.1 shows the checklist for determining training needs that the U.S. government uses for the job of administrative officer in the federal service. The next higher officer, who supervises administrative officers is asked to record his observations on this form and to add whatever explanatory notes he feels necessary. His instructions are to:

> Isolate and list each individual duty of position:
> Group related duties into a classified list.
> Establish the nature of responsibility for each duty.
> Estimate frequency, importance, and difficulty on each.
> Evaluate the employee's performance on each.
> Check as training needs any deficiencies which are significant and which can be corrected by training.[1]

An operational job description covers at least four kinds of specifications: knowledge and skill content, relationships involved, time spans, and settings and roles. Exhibit 4.2 shows a list of questions designed to elicit the necessary information for the job of manager of a cooperative farm. This job was new and for an organization yet to be developed.

---

[1] *Assessing and Reporting Training Needs and Progress,* U.S. Civil Service Commission, Personnel Methods Series No. 3, 1956, p. 25.

When technological or other developments call for changes in existing jobs and for possible retraining, it can be very useful to compare what various people expect the incumbent of a job to accomplish. The perceptions of the immediate superior, of colleagues, and of subordi-

Exhibit 4.1

CHECK LIST FOR DETERMINING TRAINING NEEDS

Nature of Responsibility	Duty	Frequency; Importance; Difficulty			Performance†	Check if Training Needed
		F*	I*	D*		
	Personnel Management—Actions					
P S C A	Preparing job specifications	—	—	—	—	—
P S C A	Interviewing applicants	—	—	—	—	—
P S C A	Arranging appointments of personnel	—	—	—	—	—
P S C A	Etc.	—	—	—	—	—
	Fiscal Management—General					
P S C A	Preparing payrolls and vouchers	—	—	—	—	—
P S C A	Issuing travel orders	—	—	—	—	—
P S C A	Awarding contracts	—	—	—	—	—
P S C A	Etc.	—	—	—	—	—
	Office Management—Space					
P S C A	Negotiating space lease or rental	—	—	—	—	—
P S C A	Assigning office space	—	—	—	—	—
P S C A	Planning equipment installation	—	—	—	—	—
P S C A	Etc.	—	—	—	—	—
	Policy					
P S C A	Composing policy statements	—	—	—	—	—
P S C A	Interpreting policies	—	—	—	—	—
P S C A	Etc.	—	—	—	—	—

No. Circle P, S, C, or A: * Use 1, 2, or 3:   † Use +, /, —, or NA:
  P = Perform (by self)   1 = High degree   + = Outstanding
  S = Supervise (immediate)   2 = Average   / = Adequate
  C = Control (through others)   3 = Low   — = Weak
  A = Advise   NA = Not applicable

SOURCE: *Assessing and Reporting Training Needs and Progress,* U.S. Civil Service Commission, Personnel Methods Series No. 3, 1956, p. 25.

nates are commonly at variance, and all may differ again from the way the incumbent himself sees the job. Such discrepancies make for difficulties in the organization. Moreover, an adequate training design can hardly be worked out till the perceptions of those involved are congruent in all important respects. If there are residual differences, they need to be earmarked for later checking against experience. The awareness of residual differences, meanwhile, may enhance motivation for training and action.

Exhibit 4.2

COOPERATIVE FARM MANAGER: SOME QUESTIONS ABOUT HIS JOB AND TRAINING

1. *Technical knowledge.* How much does the *manager himself* have to know about:

   a) Poultry
   Dairy
   Crops
   Soils
   Other farm subjects

   b) His overall functions of:
   Personnel hiring
   Incentive payments
   Job planning and supervision

   c) Finance:
   Budgeting by major items
   Costing by major items to guide production choices
   Accounting

   d) Purchasing supplies

   e) Marketing:
   Finding customers
   Packing and dispatch
   Collecting payments

   f) Equipment repair:
   Pumps
   Electrical
   Vehicles
   Buildings

2. *Relationships.* What are they? With whom? How often? How close? For example:

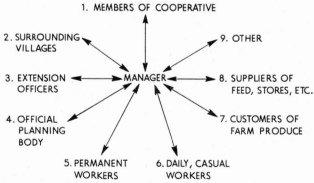

1. MEMBERS OF COOPERATIVE
2. SURROUNDING VILLAGES
3. EXTENSION OFFICERS
4. OFFICIAL PLANNING BODY
5. PERMANENT WORKERS
6. DAILY, CASUAL WORKERS
7. CUSTOMERS OF FARM PRODUCE
8. SUPPLIERS OF FEED, STORES, ETC.
9. OTHER
MANAGER

3. *Time.* To what extent is he responsible for:

   a) Maintenance of buildings and equipment
   Soil—compost, systematic soil improvement
   Livestock—upgrading, etc.

   b) Making farm plan—for example:
   Cropping patterns
   Market and cost estimates
   Investment
   Staff—for example, training

   c) Own career—a life's job? a step to?

Exhibit 4.2 (Continued)

4. *Settings* in which different aspects of the work is done and roles. For example:
    Meets people in groups—villagers, Board?
    Attends meetings away from farm? Leads meetings?
    How many people besides him live on the farm?

(*ii*) *Meshing Organizational Plans for Change with Training Strategies and Methods.*   These new job requirements need to be addressed by the training strategies and methods the institution chooses to use, and these in turn must fit into the organization's plans and ways of working. The latter fit needs to be checked and ensured no less than the first. Exhibit 4.3 sets out a five-step model for checking the readiness of an organization for a specific kind of training strategy and method. Laboratory training in the instance here.

A similar procedure can establish in advance of training what preparations the organization proposes to make for the return of newly trained participants and for using their new competence. If the participant's colleagues are involved in the change, how are they to be prepared? Through what kind of training? How are his superiors to be prepared, and service staff involved in his activities? Through hardheadedly following this line of considerations, the organization may find that it needs a series of different training events for various staff. Out of this core of recognition plus basic information a training plan can then be developed.

> Some organizations collaborating with the National Training Laboratories have worked out a three-step strategy of laboratory training by which key officers develop required skills in human relations, collegiate collaboration, and organization. The first laboratory is for officials from various organizations. The top officials from an organization first participate in this, a "stranger laboratory." The next laboratory is for the next level of key officials from several units of the same organization. This kind is named "cousin laboratory." Finally come "family laboratories" which bring together personnel who normally work together.

4. *Full Collaboration.*   There is a final advanced relationship in which the institution and the organization are in full collaboration, full-fledged, played-in partners in an enterprise of importance to both of them. Questions of initiative and responsibility are then no longer topical; they have been sorted out long since. Close collaboration like this is characterized by general sureness of method and fruitfulness of outcome. As new questions arise, they are considered and dealt with smoothly and efficiently.

Exhibit 4.3

FIVE-STEP MODEL FOR DIAGNOSING STATE OF TARGET SYSTEM

1. Are laboratory training change goals appropriate to target system? If yes, then:

   If not, stop and reconsider appropriateness of laboratory training.

2. Is the cultural state of target system prepared for laboratory training:

   a) Degree and type of value conflict?

   b) Legitimacy of interpersonal phenomena?

   c) Degree, range, intensity, resolution of conflict?

   d) Concepts of control, authority?

   e) Interdependence of target system?

   f) Relationship of trust and confidence between change agent and target system?

   If yes, then:

   If not, stop and examine areas where more preparation is needed or where value conflicts should be reduced.

3. Are key people involved and committed:

   If yes, then:

   If not, stop and examine ways to develop more commitment to program.

4. Are members of the target adequately prepared and oriented to laboratory training?

   If yes, then:

   If not, stop and examine ways to develop more commitment to program.

5. Is voluntarism (regarding participation) insured?

   If not, stop and examine attitudes toward laboratory training: Why people go or do not want to go to laboratories. After diagnosis, attempt to accurately indicate the place of laboratory training in career development.

SOURCE: Edgar Schein and Warren Bennis, *Personal and Organizational Development through Group Methods* (New York: John Wiley & Sons, Inc., 1965), p. 216.

It is useful to distinguish collaboration between the institution and fully operating organizations from collaboration built by an institution into a new organization that it helps to develop.

(*i*) *Collaboration with Fully Operating Organizations.* It is useful to distinguish further between large organizations that need only rare specialized outside help to round off their internal programs and others whose needs are wider and less well defined.

Large organizations generally work out their training needs and plans on their own. They have full-time staff development and training departments for this purpose. These departments also carry out routine training programs within the organization. Large organizations use outside training institutions only for two purposes: specialized training for numbers too small to warrant an internal program; and personal development for middle and senior executives, in which contact with executives from other organizations holds major advantages. Increasingly, too, they draw on outside consultants for help to ensure freshness of view and to subject internal programs to intensive review from time to time.

Medium and small organizations need far more assistance from the institution than this. They may ask for its help for working out adequate job analyses and overall training plans; for designing adequate procedures for selecting and preparing candidates for particular training programs and for receiving them back into the organization after training; and for working out the follow-up services afterwards. Collaboration can range from the provision by the institution of simple devices for use by the organization, for example, survey questionnaires and selection tests, to making training a wholly joint project and allowing it to pervade the whole organization. Joint work on a specific training program can become the starting point and means for getting the organization as a whole ready for widespread and far-reaching development.

The supervisory training project launched in 1964 by ATIRA and four textile mills together is an Indian example of this closest kind of collaboration. It involved intensive studies of the job supervisor, experimental job designs, new recruitment and selection procedures, and reviews of the management structure impinging on the supervisor's job. The mills financed the three-year project. ATIRA provided the research and training staff and undertook to train and retrain all supervisors working in these mills.

(*ii*) *To Establish New Services.*   In rapidly developing countries, training has often to precede the development of a new service and the establishment of an operating organization. But contrary to prevailing practice, this does not mean the absence of collaboration; quite the reverse, in fact. This situation offers the institution an opportunity to work closely with policy makers and headquarters officials from the very start. Later, when the required activities are studied in the field in order to design specific jobs, additional people and organizations can be involved in the new service: consumers, suppliers, local leaders, and others whose interested help will be needed. The last thing that the institution ought to do in helping start a new activity is to be seduced into dreaming up the job and the training needs, as it were, sitting at a desk or at meetings of its own staff.

The Institute of Rural Health and Family Planning at Gandhigram, Madurai District, offers an example of close collaboration in establishing a new service. To prepare itself for training various kinds of family planning workers the Institute first prepared a preliminary set of job functions based on the outline of the National Family Planning Programme. It then placed its own staff members at Block and village levels to perform these job functions. Besides developing this work, they recorded their activities in detail, including time spent, contacts made, problems encountered in relation to the various functions. On the basis of regular analyses of the diaries and of discussions among the staff, the job functions and methods of work were modified. This process continued till the job designs were confirmed in practice. The operational job description then became the basis of a training design for family planning workers. The Blocks in which the job designs had been established became the field in which participants in the training programs could practice the new skills.

The four degrees and means of collaboration between the training institution and the work organization are summarised in Exhibit 4.4.

The primary aim of the training institution in all its dealings with the work organization during the pretraining stage is to ensure that the organization develops realistic training goals and that these goals match reasonably closely the training the institution can plan to offer. The goals become realistic as they take two sets of factors into account. On the one hand are the changing job requirements and the implications the changes will have for the rest of the organization. On the other hand are the time and other training specifications that the institution works out to meet the training needs while keeping within the limits of its own resources. As these mesh, a realistic program gets established.

Two Dilemmas of Development

Two final points: First, the question of who in the organization gets involved in the exploration of training needs and the implications of meeting them can be of very great importance to the effectiveness of training. Logic does not exhaust it. A policy decision by the board of directors to set up training opportunities for young professional staff, for instance, may have sound logic to commend it: the younger staff do not have to break through a crust of outdated experience and they have the longest career ahead of them in which to put the training to use. Yet the decision may harden the senior staff into resisting the change, and it is

Exhibit 4.4

COLLABORATION FOR ESTABLISHING TRAINING NEEDS

	The Institution	*In order to*	*By means of*	*Limits*
1. *(i)*	States training goals	clarify issues for organization's decisions	brochure/course announcement	one-way: no modification through organization's response
(ii)	Requires applications to come through organization; organization to pay fees/salary	increase organization's commitment to training goals	ditto	ditto
2.	Discussions with senior officers	signal interest in collaboration and respect for senior staff	meetings and seminars	relation to job needs indirect and uncertain
3. *(i)*	Requires detailed job analyses	focus organization's attention on operational needs	course announcement	organization's ability and inclinations
(ii)	Requires organization's plans for change	focus organization on complete program of change	ditto	ditto
4. *(i)*	Collaborates with existing organization	ensure matching training goals and motivation for change	extended face-to-face contact	ditto plus institution's resources
(ii)	Collaborates to establish new services	involve related organizations	extended field work	ditto

they who supervise the younger staff. Conflicts such as these are particularly common during periods of rapid development. Rapid development means that senior staff cannot be sure that the knowledge and experience they have acquired over the years is really superior to their younger colleagues'. Their knowledge of technical subjects, for instance, may be outdated and their experience of years ago no longer relevant. Administrative power may be all they have left. Now this last base of theirs is threatened by the policy decision about further training for junior staff. The threat is the greater if the decision was taken without real agreement with the senior staff. We stress "real," because how could they object openly to training the young promising staff? Training for themselves would also be threatening. After all, they are supposed to *know*. It is a real dilemma.

The second point consists in just this: that this and other dilemmas that constantly beset the processes of development do not get resolved by pretending that they do not exist or that they are not important to people caught in them. Recognition may not remove them, but it does ensure at least that the dilemmas can be taken into account in any decision and that the people affected by them know this. Otherwise, on top of the dilemma itself, the affected people feel belittled and brushed aside, even when this was no one's intention.

The multiplication of branches of the State Bank of India may serve to illustrate the inevitable dilemmas and the questions that arise from them. One implication of recruiting 700 agents from within the Bank is that new agents are much younger. On the operative side this runs counter to the popular image of the banker as "guide, philosopher, and friend"—for which a few grey hairs might be more appropriate. Internally, problems are bound to arise from the wide range of ages represented in posts of the same level. Are older colleagues or superiors willing to trust the decisions of an agent with so much less experience than they? Do they provide him easier access to wise counsel to offset his inexperience? Or will the seniors decide instead on controlling their younger colleagues more tightly and take the decisions higher up? If the latter, how can the young man carry authority with his own staff, many also older than he, if he knows that his actions are tightly circumscribed? How much then does the Bank wish to encourage initiative and experimentation at branch level?

Besides facing the dilemmas and implications of development openly in order to smooth the paths of change, the same attitude is necessary in order to arrive at job designs which not only exist on paper but can be carried out in practice. Job designs that allow for prevailing dilemmas then provide the basis for training and the institution's own internal preparation for it. This sequence must be stressed over and over again. There is no other. Training is a service function. If the young bank agent needs to learn to take decisions, training can help him acquire this competence. If, on the other hand, he needs to refer matters to superiors, or can really not be sure of support, then training can help him to stall more gracefully. Which is the proper objective of training is for the organization to decide, and similarly with all dilemmas that face organizations in development. Their resolution cannot be left to the training institution. Lack of clarity on the job is bound to lead to lack of clarity in training. The opposite, that clarity in the job is bound to lead to clear training, is unfortunately not automatically true. Otherwise, the book could stop here. But clarity on the job, in all its implications, is the first prerequisite of sound training.

CLARIFYING INDIVIDUAL MOTIVATION FOR TRAINING

Training needs are in the first place organizational needs. As pressures for change impinge on an organization, from outside or from inside, it responds—through expansion, through adopting new technologies, through developing new functions and reorganizing existing functions, and through a variety of other possible ways. Many of these organizational responses call for training. True, it is people who do all this. But so far we have not concerned ourselves with the question of who in particular, *which* people, need to be trained, how they are to be found and chosen, and how they are to be prepared for training. This section deals with this second dimension, the personal one.

The process is analogous: the training needs that the organization has hammered out in response to various pressures for change become in turn the pressures on individuals to change. To deal effectively with the impending new jobs and situations, individuals find that they need to use new knowledge, understanding, and skills. They may have these already. Or they may need to acquire them, through training.

The individual can respond basically in one of three ways: He can decide to change, if necessary with the help of training. Or he can decide not to change himself but instead change his job, by asking for a transfer within the organization or by going elsewhere. Or, third, he can decide to change neither, and hope that the need for change will pass him by, by chance or by his own active resistance. So much for the theme. Organizational change depends for cost, speed, and smoothness on people deciding to change themselves; that is, to learn, to go for training.

For those people who have been directly engaged in hammering out the training needs, the personal part of the theme will have become vividly alive by the time they have finished that initial task. Somehow—working out training needs may be the most effective and economical way—all affected by the change need to gain this personal awareness. For an individual's motivation toward training is shaped most of all by the meaning he attaches to it. If he is aware that the need for training arises out of the changing job and situation, training will seem reasonable at least. He may see the opportunity for it as recognition by the organization that he has further capabilities to develop. He may feel elated at being chosen—his interpretation—to join the core of people qualified to spearhead new developments. He may see it as a sign that he is on the way to promotion. On the contrary, if he does not see any need for training, for himself or for this particular training, he may see the training opportunity as a veiled criticism of his current performance, as if the organization were telling him, "Improve, or else! here is your last chance!" Or he may see it as an indication that the organization considers him the person easiest "to spare," or wants him out of the way while changes get made in his part of the organization; or as a kind of vacation by way of reward for years of devoted work. Personal motives too come into the picture. An applicant may volunteer mostly in order to have his name associated with a prestigious institution, to have a break, to escape a conflict-ridden situation, or for a variety of other reasons not directly related to a training course.

Motives of unpredictable direction and strength will tend to fade into second place as the changes actually required in the jobs and organizations become clear and demanding. Just as the training institution would be most unwise to do anything to shield the work organization from the full impact of required changes, so the organization would be unwise in turn to shield individual staff members from the personal implications of impending changes. In each case, the limit is only the tolerance of the recipient for such a challenge. With normal, healthy people, that is a limit that is difficult to overstep. The question of how the potential participant in a training course perceives this opportunity strikes us as more important than whether he takes the initiative in requesting the opportunity for himself or whether his organization makes the first move to request him to go.

Institution and Candidate: Seven Functions

The institution has a series of seven functions connected with matching applicants and training requirements and with preparing the accepted candidates for the program.

1. *Announcing the Program.* The initial formal announcement of a training program ought to contain enough information for candidates to apply. Typically the announcement contains a general statement of the needs to which the training addresses itself (for example, export marketing) followed by more detailed training objectives; the categories of people for whom this particular program is meant (for example, age, experience, position); the training and main methods to be used (for example, active participation, field work); the duration, dates, location, and cost of the program; and the admission requirements and procedure. Some institutions introduce the course faculty in the announcement.

2. *Selecting Participants.*   If the organization's training needs are clear and also the minimum qualifications participants should have for a particular program, the motivation of an applicant is the most important unknown that remains. To understand this then becomes the most important and also most difficult purpose of the selection procedure.

Is what the applicant looking for really in line with the needs this program sets out to meet? In part this is a specific question. If he is looking for greater competence in certain mechanical and mathematical skills, it is doubtful whether he ought to go now for a course in management, this even though his organization is sure that managerial skill is what he needs and could use in his future career. At least some steps need to be taken by the organization to line up his expectations with what the course offers. Much more intricate is the mixture of general concerns that the same question commonly hides. In Box 4.2, we summarize a piece of research on a group of 29 middle-level managers who attended a full-time residential program of 15 weeks at the Harvard Business School. About half of them came to the program largely to escape conflicts and to resolve dilemmas involving personal choice. The "conflicted" managers were highly motivated for training and included a high proportion of participants who had themselves requested to go for training and were paying all or a substantial proportion of the cost of training.

Nothing mechanical or absolute is intended—or indeed possible—in suggesting careful procedures to line up what participants look for in the training and what the institution offers. The unforeseen consequences of training are often the most fruitful. What is intended here is to stress the importance of two motivational factors.

The selection procedure—application forms, written tests, interview, individual or group task—can be designed especially to elicit data on these two aspects of a candidate's motivation. In individual interviews, and in observing and listening to candidates working on a joint task, such as discussing a case, it is possible to note the nature and strength of feelings different candidates express and to build a picture of what each seems to be most concerned about. In written tests and applications, it is important to ensure that the questions elicit personal rather than generalized data. The commonly used general question about what the candidate intends to use the training for only yields stereotyped, safe answers. It is more useful to ask the candidate to pinpoint a situation in his recent experience in which he thinks this particular training would have helped him.

Box 4.2

INDIVIDUAL MOTIVATION FOR TRAINING

KAMLA CHOWDHRY

A study of 29 middle-level executives attending a full-time residential program of 15 weeks showed that there were "self-initiated" and "company-initiated" candidates. The break up of these into "conflicted" (experiencing some organizational stress, needing help with critical decisions, e.g. career decision making, or being involved in dilemmas) and "unconflicted" (successful, committed to their progressional roles, and having a sense of achievement) was as follows:

	Self-Initiated	Company-Initiated	Total
Conflicted	12	3	15
Unconflicted	3	11	14
Total	15	14	

Most "company-initiated" executives were "unconflicted" and their attitude to the program was somewhat nonchalant. The "self-initiated" executives, most of whom were "conflicted," were much more involved in terms of their own needs and preoccupations.

The "self-initiated" executives in "conflicted" roles attended the program with twofold purpose: flight from conditions of stress and the need to resolve their dilemmas and conflicts. They seemed to use the development program as a psychosocial moratorium, a place where they could delay their decisions, consider their alternatives, and make their final commitments. On the other hand, the emotional investment for development in the "company-oriented" executives who were in "unconflicted" roles was less. The predominant mood of executives in this group seemed as if they were being rewarded for services rendered rather than a mood of seeking or of learning. This perhaps is more a reflection of the way selection takes place in the company than of the fact that they are "company-initiated." First, it is important that the participants' motivation be strong; and secondly, that it project in directions that have a good chance to be satisfied by the particular training the institution offers.

SOURCE: Kamla Chowdhry, "Executive Needs in Management Development Programs," *Industrial Management Review,* School of Industrial Management, M.I.T., Spring, 1963.

The following series of questions can yield data useful in selecting a candidate for training:

1. Describe a recent situation in which you were involved in which you would have liked to use the training offered in this program. What happened? What did you do? What left you dissatisfied?
2. List the new technical and other skills you would like to have at your command to deal with a similar situation in the future.
3. Would you have been free to use these skills in the situation or were

other changes required also? If other changes were required, list the additional skills you would need to promote them.

3. *Guarding against Distracting Preoccupations.*   Let us assume that the selection procedure has shown a candidate to be suitable for the course. He has the necessary minimum qualifications and experience, and also sufficient motivation to be accepted. The next step is to offer him the opportunity. At this stage, it is necessary to ensure that no foreseeable circumstance will disturb the applicant's training.

Particularly if the program is away from home and family and lasts several months, experience suggests that many an applicant needs to be protected from distracting preoccupations. He needs to be assured, for example, that his family can manage without him for that time and that they have access to any funds and help that they may need. Perhaps his organization can give the little thoughtful care that would free the participant from worry on these scores. In India, family holidays and other traditional events are often more difficult to take care of. The participant's absence from home on these occasions may represent a major break with the past and one that seems, especially to the older generation, out of all proportion to the value of a few days' training.

The training institution had best be quite explicit in advance about the standards it will enforce on these occasions. It is then up to the selected applicant and his organization to decide whether he can join the course on these conditions or whether, even at this advanced stage, he had better postpone his participation for another time.

4. *Lining Up Expectations More Closely.*   Once the selections have been made, and the candidates have agreed, additional information can usefully flow both ways. The institution can send out the list of participants. More important for lining up expectations may be the provision of lists of accessible people who had participated in a similar training program earlier and could answer questions about it, about the institution and the people there, and also about such pedestrian concerns as to what to pack. This sort of preliminary exploration may help to keep the candidate's mind open both with respect to the particular problems he may use the program to deal with and also the kinds of experiences he may anticipate. One of the expectations to be communicated about training is that expectations too may change in the course of it.

Communications from the institution aim to prepare candidates for an experience of real relevance and to assure them of the institution's intention to ensure this. As an example, during the six weeks between the selection of candidates and the beginning of a program in 1965, Siet Institute sent out three batches of information and questions.

The first batch: The brief acceptance letter enclosed three papers: one, on administrative matters, contained details of hotel bookings, the procedure for paying hotel bills and what to bring by way of clothes, bedding, etc., travel plans and arrival time, and the procedure for paying fees. The second outlined the second half of the program. (The first part of the program had been described in the very first letter.) The third paper was a questionnaire designed to help the Institute prepare for it. The questionnaire asked three questions:

(*i*) On which training areas have you chosen to concentrate your attention at the workshop and in your preparation for it?

(*ii*) What kinds of data do you have available about the areas on which you will concentrate? For example, immediate experience and current training data, data from experience elsewhere, reports.

(*iii*) What additional data would you like other participants to bring, if possible?

The second batch 12 days later: The letter contained the list of topics and suggestions already received for the second part of the program and promised a further list a week later. It also included a provisional list of participants.

The third batch, 8 days later: This batch contained the additional list of topics and the confirmed list of participants.

5. *Requiring Candidates to Do Homework.*   To think that the training period can be extended forward by requiring participants to do some systematic preparation before they arrive is pleasant but unrealistic. Experience suggests that it is worth asking only for a little and that little of a limited kind: assembling some data to take along for use during training or deciding on a project proposal on which, after approval by the trainers, the participant can work immediately after he returns from training. Such a request is in line with the practical and personal orientation the institution wants to give the training and with the close connection it has with the participant's work organizaion.

The Indian Institute of Management, Ahmedabad, has used projects successfully in its programs for young executives. Exhibit 4.5 shows the project proposal form which is part of the procedure to be completed for selection. It requires the participant to choose as a project one that he can complete in two months and which has the approval of his organization. The time span is determined by a second training event for the same group. It is scheduled about three months after the end of the main four-week program. For one week, participants then discuss the completed projects with the help of trainers.

To ask for more homework than this seems to run two dangers. First, it is unlikely to get done. If the institution then lets that pass without comment, it raises doubts about the need to do subsequent assignments.

If it does comment, it is likely to sound punitive. Second, if they are heading for full-time training and a long absence, participants will surely be preoccupied with handing over their responsibilities and arranging their personal affairs. Being pressed for time, they are likely to regard a request for homework in advance as indicating that the training institution is out of touch with the realities of the participants' situation, and their expectations would suffer accordingly.

Exhibit 4.5

PROPOSAL FOR MANAGERIAL PROJECT

Name: Designation:

Organization: Contact address:

Telephone No.:   Telegram address:

Title of project:

Background of the project:

Specific issues/problems involved:

Objectives in undertaking project:

Nature and sources of data to be collected:

Approaches to be used in collecting data:

Please check (X) against the following:

    The above project can be completed in two months   ☐

    The above project had been approved by my sponsor   ☐

SOURCE: Indian Institute of Management, Ahmedabad, Program for Young Executives, 1966.

6. *Increasing Individual Motivation for Training.* The institution can take two further interrelated steps to build up the applicant's readiness for training. One is to enhance his motivation beyond the minimum. The other is to involve him in planning the program. Any gain on these scores is likely to be reflected in his quick progress immediately after the program starts. A quick start becomes doubly valuable if it sets the pace and tone for the whole program. These additional steps therefore deserve the institution's careful attention, even though they are less familiar than the rest. They can be organized separately in advance or at the very start of the training program itself.

For enhancing the individual motivation for training, the institution has three kinds of methods at its disposal. The first is part and parcel of the communication the institution makes to the applicant through all its contacts with him. If as a result of these contacts the applicant gathers that the institution's purposes are clear and that it is competent to carry them out, moreover that it shows perceptive concern for the people who will come to the program, he will surely look forward to the experience with increasing interest. He will expect to work hard and to profit from training. Even the most insignificant-looking procedural detail feeds into the process by which the applicant builds up this important advance picture of the institution.

The two other methods aim specifically at increasing the applicant's motivation for training. One consists in collecting data about his present effectiveness on the job and sharing it with him. We have earlier referred to such a feedback procedure for an organization as a whole (Box 4.1, page 81). The personal purpose here is similar and the procedures for it simpler.

> In the case of teachers, for instance, Ned Flanders has found that systematic observations by a colleague of a candidate's behavior in a session and afterwards sharing with him indications of his effectiveness greatly enhanced the candidate's motivation for training. By careful pairing of colleagues and by avoiding evaluative comments, initial hesitations and awkwardness with the procedure were greatly reduced. Only collection and sharing of actual happenings were required. As a result the candidates saw weaknesses and possibilities of improvement that they then decided to explore during training.

The second method to enhance motivation for the training in advance of the program is more elaborate. It consists in organizing a short special program for this very purpose. The courses based on David McClelland's work on achievement motivation and short training laboratories are examples. In Box 4.3 we have summarized McClelland's approach and stated his set of 12 propositions about enhancing people's motivation and the scheme through which he relates them.

In Chapter 5 we will write more about training laboratories as a training method (page 125, *et seq.*). The essence of special courses for enhancing individual motivation for learning is that they lift up for the participant's conscious systematic attention his point of view, feelings, and attitudes, and his relationships with others and with the world around him in which he lives and works. Pondering this picture the participant finds aspects of it that are not to his liking. He looks forward to improving these through the forthcoming training.

7. *Involving Participants in Planning the Program.* The principle behind this step is familiar. The main problem is how to put it to work. The aspect that usually makes for difficulties is the unspoken fear and distrust that the institution may have of the participants: that they will ask for training that it cannot provide and that it will lose control of the

Box 4.3

A PROGRAM FOR INCREASING INDIVIDUAL MOTIVATION

DAVID C. MCCLELLAND

Pilot attempts to develop *n* Achievement have gradually led to the formulation of some theoretical notions of what motive acquisition involves and how it can be effectively promoted in adults. These notions have been summarized in the form of 12 propositions which are subject to research. The propositions are anchored in experiences with pilot courses, in supporting research findings from other studies, and in theory.

PROPOSITION 1.   The more reasons an individual has in advance to believe that he can, will, or should develop a motive, the more educational attempts designed to develop that motive are likely to succeed.

PROPOSITION 2.   The more an individual perceives that developing a motive is consistent with the demands of reality (and reason), the more educational attempts designed to develop that motive are likely to succeed.

PROPOSITION 3.   The more thoroughly an individual develops and clearly conceptualizes the associative network defining the motive, the more likely he is to develop the motive.

PROPOSITION 4.   The more an individual can link the newly developed network to related actions, the more the change in both thought and action is likely to occur and endure.

PROPOSITION 5.   The more an individual can link the newly conceptualized association-action complex (or motive) to events in his everyday life, the more likely the motive complex is to influence his thoughts and actions in situations outside the training experience.

PROPOSITION 6.   The more an individual can perceive and experience the newly conceptualized motive as an improvement in the self-image, the more the motive is likely to influence his future thoughts and actions.

PROPOSITION 7.   The more an individual can perceive and experience the newly conceptualized motive as an improvement on prevailing cultural values, the more the motive is likely to influence his future thoughts and actions.

PROPOSITION 8.   The more an individual commits himself to achieving concrete goals in life related to the newly-formed motive, the more the motive is likely to influence his future thoughts and actions.

PROPOSITION 9.   The more an individual keeps a record of his progress toward achieving goals to which he is committed, the more the newly-formed motive is likely to influence his future thoughts and actions.

PROPOSITION 10.   Changes in motives are more likely to occur in an interpersonal atmosphere in which the individual feels warmly but honestly supported and respected by others as a person capable of guiding and directing his own future behavior.

Box 4.3 (*Continued*)

PROPOSITION 11. Changes in motives are more likely to occur the more the setting dramatizes the importance of self-study and lifts it out of the routine of everyday life.

PROPOSITION 12. Changes in motives are more likely to occur and persist if the new motive is a sign of membership in a new reference group.

VARIABLES CONCEIVED AS ENTERING INTO THE MOTIVE CHANGE PROCESS

A Input or independent variables	B Intervening variables	C Output or dependent variables
1. Goal setting for person (P1, P11)	Arousal of associative network (salience)	Duration and/or extensiveness of changes in:
2. Acquisition of *n* Achievement associative network (P2, P3, P4, P5)	Experiencing and labeling the associative network	1. *n* Achievement associative network
3. Relating new network superordinate networks Reality　　　　(P2) The self　　　　(P6) Cultural values　(P7)	Variety of cues to which network is linked Interfering associations assimilated or bypassed by reproductive interference	2. Related actions: use of feedback, moderate risk taking etc 3. Innovations (job improvements)
4. Personal goal setting (P8) 5. Knowledge of progress (P3, P4, P9)		4. Use of time and money 5. Entrepreneurial success as defined by nature of job held and its rewards
6. Personal warmth and support	Positive effect associated with network	
7. Support of reference group (P11, P12)		

NOTE: P1, P11, etc., refer to the numbered propositions in the text.

SOURCE: David C. McClelland, "Toward a Theory of Motive Acquisition," *American Psychologist,* Vol. XX (1965), pp. 319–33.

process and resources for which it is responsible. So, if there is consultation at all, the institution often restricts it to the participant's organization and to very general questions. If the institution then goes on to consult with individual participants, it often does so to adhere to a principle only and so ends up making an empty gesture that it had far better not make. For if it is not ready to listen, the institution ought not to ask questions. A useful principle is to involve participants in planning the program—or in anything else—only to the extent that the institution is truly willing to take their views into account. Experience assures us that even a small start in this direction will widen the area of willingness in time. It is a more promising starting point than the other extreme: of going the whole way because the principle says so but with fear in one's heart. The fears may then justify themselves.

Involving participants in analyzing their jobs and the requirements of impending changes offers a useful start.

The first two days of Siet Institute's regular three-month courses consist of program consultations on the basis of job analyses and prospects. Much of the work is done in small groups composed of participants from similar organizations. They pinpoint the training needs they share. These groups are then brought together to report to each other and to the faculty. The program also provides for detailed individual study of field reports from earlier courses. The reports indicate the directions and standards of training. From their study of reports, participants can learn what they need especially to study and practice in order to do similar work themselves and recommend these areas for inclusion in the program.

Participants may see these steps initially as gimmicks rather than genuine attempts at joint planning. Experience usually tells them that the institution will not really change the program, whatever the outcome of these sessions, and that the sessions are at best an occasion for courtesy. They may yet be right in this assessment, even where an institution is genuinely interested in making this step work. If it repeatedly runs programs for similar groups, the institution may well get the impression that it already knows the participants' training needs from its own experience. This impression is supported if the participants' training needs sound the same, over and over again. If this is so, it may be well to review the designs of these events. For instance, instead of offering open questions, the institution can present its understanding of the training needs for comment and go on from there. It can also review the task given to the discussion groups and make it more specific and demanding. It is possible too that so early in the program the groups may need more faculty help in order to acknowledge and sort out differences between participants and come up with generally meaningful specifications of needs. Usually the initial doubts last till participants see their views actually reflected in the program.

Another possibility open to the institution is to ask participants to take responsibility for designing specified blocks of time in the program. This can be an alternative or an addition to involving them to a limited degree in planning the whole program.

At the Sloan School of Management, Massachusetts Institute of Technology, experimental groups of students are left to design nine hours' work per week for themselves within broad faculty specifications. They decide on what work to tackle and how, and which faculty members or outsiders to draw into the program. Initial results have been very encouraging. The programs the students have designed are found to be at least as heavy as any that the faculty would have organized, and motivation is very high. The results are in line with industrial experience of letting small work groups fix their own targets.

SUMMARY

In the pretraining phase the three partners in training—the work organization, the participant, and the training institution—build a picture for themselves of the training to come. They do this inevitably; it is well if they do it out of knowledge and understanding. Otherwise they build it out of ignorance, by imagination and emotions. It has been the burden of this chapter to show that it is in the training institution's direct interest, and also within its means, to influence the expectations with which participants come to training. The picture of training with which they come is more realistic and useful if they have had the institution's help in building it. Through systematic efforts more information can be collected, expectations can be reformed, and new stereotypes developed. All this is part of the total process whose next phase is called training.

Underlying this process are questions of motivation, both for the work organization and for individual participants. They are best clarified if the demands of technological and other changes press hard and directly on the organization and the individual. The institution endeavors to make sure that this happens and that out of the impact emerges the motivation for training. If the demands are yet to come, and training has the important function of preparing for change, then the institution can help with forecasting changes and their implications. On no account is its function to shield the organization or the individual from the demands of change. The reverse is true.

The pretraining stage is a stage of forging links. In the first place, it links up the three partners in training. In the second place, it starts the linkage of the three main phases of the training process. Like many other chains, training too is no better than its weakest link. Not only does the preparation for training which the institution does for itself—the subject of the next chapter—depend on this first linkage. The training program too depends on it. The same link has also to bear the weight of the posttraining phase of follow-up services and of generally helping the participant and the organization to integrate the training into normal operations. As in construction, foundations such as these may be hidden from view as the building goes up. But they had better be sound.

Chapter 5

rrrrrrrrrrrrrrrrrrrrrrrrrrrrrr

Training Methods

"To put away one's own original thoughts in order to take up a book is a sin against the Holy Ghost."

—SCHOPENHAUER

"I never teach my pupils. I only attempt to provide the conditions in which they can learn."

—ALBERT EINSTEIN

THE TRAINING needs of the organization and the selected participants impinge on the institution. It now has the task of designing a program that can best meet these needs. Notice that this definition of its task is correct both when the institution takes the initiative in offering a program and when it designs one in response to a particular request. The only difference is that the one design is based on training needs that the institution sees as important, the other on needs seen as important by the organization and then worked out in collaboration with the institution, or at least agreed by it.

When training needs arrive at the institution for action they meet prejudice. This is merely a sharp way of saying that the institution is not a blank space or an empty vessel. Just like other human enterprises, it has views and preferences, characteristic ways of looking at and approaching a task and carrying it out. This distinctiveness is what gives the institution its character; and the organization and participants that look to it for training presumably have some of this in view when they choose it. Particular institutions are noted for their special interests, as the Indian Institute of Management, Calcutta, is noted for operational research and managerial mathematics; or for certain training methods, such as case teaching or in-plant training; or for the strength of certain faculty groups or services.

By the time the institution comes to consider the program it intends to offer, its prejudice—preference, tendency, or point of view may be more acceptable words for the same phenomenon—has already influenced its choice of training strategy, both externally in its relations with the organization and the participants, and internally in the kind of faculty it has assembled and its approach to training design. These initial choices come into play again in choosing training methods and faculty roles. They do so not only because the same prejudices still hold for this next stage but also because the earlier choices of strategy necessarily entail preferences for certain designs, methods, roles, and relationships. These in turn then also call for certain training facilities. For instance, the laboratory strategy of training calls for work in small groups (therefore small rooms). It is best rather isolated from other parts of the institution's work (therefore a block of time rather than occasional sessions sandwiched between others). It calls for highly experienced trainers—otherwise it is better not to attempt it. These trainers have to be the kind of people who do not develop their relationships with participants on traditional authoritarian lines. And so on. Within wider or lesser limits, institutional preference, training strategy, design, methods, and facilities are causally related and support one another. As we examine in this chapter different training methods and their specifications, and how the institution can build them into a training program, it is important to remember this starting point. Possibilities are not all wide open, and that not only for lack of suitable trainers and facilities. The institution will not consider all possibilities logically open to it. It is no use pretending otherwise, for the institution or for others.

We will briefly examine a series of seven different kinds of training methods. They are not the only kinds, but they cover the known range. In this text we will limit description to a minimum and concentrate on the assumptions, dilemmas and choices posed by each method and the specifications it demands in terms of time, faculty, and facilities for its effective use. Fuller descriptions are contained in the readings that follow this chapter, one each for four kinds of methods. We could not find a useful reading for training in the field—which is an interesting fact in itself. And we found none on seminars and lectures that added significantly to what we say in the text.

TWO FAULTY JUXTAPOSITIONS

The sequence we have chosen starts with training in the course of action—on the factory floor, "in the field"—and ends with the generalized lecture in a special place. The choice is not just a matter of convenience or good order. As we study different training methods, we want also to challenge two common formulations about training and go on to substitute others that seem to us more useful. Both are juxtapositions of things that in practice need to be related.

The first is the juxtaposition of training and experience. Learning from experience is often used as a counter to systematic training, as if the two were at opposite ends of some scale, or even glared at one another as foes from two separate arenas. Yet all learning comes from experience; although, as we shall see, the connection is neither direct nor simple. All that effective training can hope to do is to ensure maximum opportunities for relevant experiences to occur and to so organize the opportunities into useful sequences and intensities that the elements of chance and waste in learning are reduced. When technologies and organizations are rapidly changing and expanding, this is a sufficiently formidable task, in extent and complexity, and in value. Far from juxtaposing experience and training, relating them is the valid first formulation, and the major task.

A second favorite gambit in the game of opposites is the juxtaposition of theory and practice. Training is often equated with theory, and practice with experience. "Practical" people decry theory—and training—as useless. A. N. Whitehead, the mathematician and philosopher, on the other hand, saw "nothing so practical as a good theory." At this stage we may suspect that each contestant is busy rating most highly his own kind of interests and competences. One concentrates on specific, individual experiences—and action; the other on attempts to develop useful generalizations from repeated experience—theory. For training, the task is to find ways of relating theory and practice most usefully, to ensure both competence in the individual unique situations which make up life and also the development of useful general guides and ways of thinking: a conceptual framework with which to anticipate the new situations of the future.

EVENTS—REFLECTION—EXPERIENCE

The distinction that seems to us important for trainers to make and to hang onto is between an event, a session in marketing, for instance, and the participant's experience. This distinction embodies two different points of view that the trainer above all has to keep separate. The event is one kind of thing. The participant's experience, from which he learns, is another. The event is external. It is what the faculty can arrange and put into the training timetable. The experience, on the other hand, is personal, internal. It is what a particular participant makes of the event, the meaning he attaches to it, and therefore what he "internalizes." To be quite rigorous, the participant's experience is what he makes of the *time* the event covers. He may daydream instead of tuning into the marketing problem at all, and recall the session later in terms of pleasant memories. The "blue Monday" phenomenon is well known to trainers the world over: many a participant's mind and heart are still on yesterday's holiday pursuits. Or he may be stimulated by just one aspect of the subject, take off from there and work away at it by himself in great excitement, leaving the rest unattended. Or many other things. The point is that the trainer only controls events, and events are at best an indirect avenue to ensuring for participants experiences and learning of predetermined kinds. This tenuous connection between external event and internal experience, between training and learning, accounts for the major problems of evaluating effectiveness in training, or, for that matter, in any communications: The trainer organizes events, but realistic evaluation of those events has to be in terms of the participants' experiences. No easy matter, this. In order to make reasonably sure that participants are "with him," the trainer has to check frequently. This amounts to conveying to the participants something like this: "X is what we had in mind to help you learn. What have you learned in fact? All of X? Some of X? Which? Something else? The opposite—for example, to hate the subject or be frightened of it; to hate us for keeping on with it? Or are you now ready to take the next step?"

One more general thought before we go on to scan some major kinds of training events and examine their uses in a training program. Learning takes time, reflective time. The number of events is no guide to the quantity of learning. Continuous activity, continuous company, may on the contrary militate against learning, may deflect participants from the demanding business of changing their minds and stretching their capacities that we call learning. A training institution, so to speak, is not a circus. It does not exist to entertain, to help people forget their daily preoccupations. On the contrary, it exists to help people understand and to do something with their preoccupations. All that participants may learn from a very "heavy" program is what it feels like to be under heavy pressure for a long time. If this is the learning the faculty intends to foster, fine. There are jobs and positions where pressure abounds, and participants can be helped to experience this. But even that experience, to lead on to something useful, needs reflective time. Otherwise it is only a repeated burden.

Some people reflect best by talking—by putting somebody into a comfortable chair and making him listen to their efforts to discover what they really think. Others do best by sitting still and pondering in apparent idleness, others again by walking alone in the open air. There are people too who state to themselves the problem they are working on and then go about doing all sorts of unrelated things; they trust from experience to a kind of unconscious inner working, may wake up in the middle of the night with the answer ready. Each participant has his own method, or has yet to find it if his environment so far has not led him to this. And at different times, he may find a different method best for reflection. In the last section of the next chapter, we will concern ourselves with the difficult questions of putting a training program together, its sequence, how to think about the training mix. Here it is necessary to stress that the training program needs both to stimulate and also to allow opportunities for participants to think and to internalize events in their various ways. These opportunities too are training events and can be allowed for deliberately. The program needs elbowroom, time for things "to grow on" participants. Experience, learning, is deepening and widening. It cannot be forced. It is more likely to be hindered than helped by too tight a program.

LEARNING ON THE JOB—NINE TRAINING REQUIREMENTS

Learning on the job leaves all these features to chance. There may or may not be time to think; and the help and stimulation of new ideas is limited to whoever happens to work closely together. Just how chancy it is is implied in the terms commonly used to characterize learning on the job: "trial and error," "sink or swim," "learning the hard way," "knocking off rough corners." Yet this is the traditional way of acquiring skill. It runs on unless and until more systematic training takes its place. In developing countries it is still widely favored. An open examination of its continuing appeal may flavor of beating a horse that at least ought in most places to be dead, but this can help us here to delineate more sharply the criterion against which to measure training methods.

There is first a kind of basic reasonableness about learning by trial and error. It covers everything to be learned in that situation, and in whatever way it occurs. Moreover, we all do learn many things by trial and error; walking, for instance. Or to let one's capacities grow over time also makes sense. It is not reasonable to let a 20 year old do a wise man's job. Finally, this is the way father learned his job. So why not the son? It is probably not chance that the familiar expressions we have recalled for this method all have a challenging tone, defiant, as though to keep the sons in their place.

The question is when and where this method of learning is now appropriate. A statement of the assumptions on which it rests will clarify this. There are at least three. The first is that the job and the work situation can be apprehended as a totality; it is a matter of letting one's senses and mind work. The second is that the job will be the same for a long time—like walking—so speed of learning is not a major consideration. The third is that the risks of errors during learning are small, both to the learner and to the organization.

It is immediately clear that these assumptions are no longer generally useful, certainly not for jobs characteristic of our time. Most modern jobs are complex in nature and cannot be grasped or practiced all at once. Moreover, interdependent production organization makes it increasingly difficult to have unscheduled time for reflection or for asking or giving advice and help. Furthermore, the time it takes to acquire a skill is now important. Machinery and organization need to be fully used to be economical. Moreover, technological advances and all the shifts in the environment associated with development—social, economic, political—make the total life of particular skills short. So they have to be learned fast and used soon.

The same speed of change puts a premium on knowing how to learn, again and again. That is something that the subtle processes of growing into a skill over a long time do not raise to consciousness. People who have learned on the job may be alright at what they have been doing, very good in fact; but along comes a new machine or a new condition in the work, and they find themselves unable to do anything other than to offer the standard recipes with increasing determination. They often find themselves, as the saying goes, not with 10 or 20 years of experience but with a half-year's experience repeated 20 or 40 times. And even that half-year's experience may have become out of date. This problem is all around us—in traditional crafts, including farming; including also management, administration, and training itself. Finally, with higher investment and tight schedules the cost of errors on the job has multiplied. So errors too cannot usually be left to chance any longer.

From this analysis we can extract the first four requirements of a systematic training program. It needs to:

1. Provide successive glimpses of the job in such dimensions that the skill required for each can be grasped, practiced separately if necessary, and then put together with other parts when the time is ripe. That is the same as saying that what the program puts forward for the attention of the participant at any time must be real *for him.*

2. Provide time and other resources, such as the trainer's knowledge and experience, in such measure that the participant can convert the training event into an experience for himself.
3. Protect the participant and his organization against personal harm and expensive error arising from lack of knowledge and skill.
4. Make the learning process itself conscious for the participant so that he knows how to set about dealing with new situations as they arise and can go on learning.

In many cases these four requirements, or at least the first three, can be provided on the job. Many organizations now do so. It is in fact a more or less systematic process that most people have in mind when they express themselves in favor of learning on the job. They see the participant as an understudy, apprentice, intern. He is attached to a senior chosen for his sympathy and ability in nurturing new talent. He is given work involving increasingly complex decisions and action in line with his growing skill. Time is scheduled for reviewing the work. Attendance as an observer at departmental and board meetings; consultation to elicit thought, comment, and recommendations; occasional meetings away from work for review and planning—these are all increasingly common in large organizations.

Perhaps the most elaborate provision of opportunities for training on the job is a Junior Board, or its equivalent at departmental levels in industrial organizations. This board is composed of a group of people in line for promotion. It proposes to the senior board fully responsible actions on current and policy issues. It may from time to time and within agreed-upon limits act on behalf of the board. All this is regarded as part of staff development and as quite systematic. The additional burden of time and other resources are regarded as proper investment in staff.

But many organizations do not find this enough. They cannot train enough people in this manner during times of rapid expansion. Also many modern jobs cannot be dismembered into parts for separate practice in the course of day-to-day working. Our list of four basic requirements that a systematic training program must meet has, therefore, to be expanded by five more.

Systematic training must also:

5. Expose participants to ideas and methods beyond those now available within the organization.
6. Provide opportunities for experiment beyond the tolerance of an operating organization and for feedback of results.
7. Give participants the experience of belonging to groups beyond the organization, particularly professional and occupational groups, which can

foster continued exchange of ideas and the development of high standards in the profession.

8. Provide opportunities to step back from day-to-day tasks to think about one's job as a whole, analyze priorities and division of time and how the job fits into the participant's pattern of life.

9. Provide opportunities for very intensive experience through a high degree of consistency and training skill.

Looking at the whole list of nine requirements leaves the impression that from now on learning on the job has most to offer during the later stages of acquiring a skill. These are the stages when new skills have to be put to work under normal working conditions. In terms of our three-partite division of systematic training, this is the post-training phase. It is a phase of crucial importance. It harbors extra difficulties in developing countries where trained but inexperienced staff often work in scattered locations under only distant supervision. Much of their onward training has to be on the job.

Librarians for village libraries in India, for instance, can join for their basic training, but when they get to their jobs they are on their own, each by himself. One training scheme provides detailed "apprenticeship" and supervision for just one difficult aspect of the work: book ordering. During the first year a senior officer does all the ordering. During the next year the librarian does 20 percent of it, during the third 40 percent, and so on. During the first year the new librarian can, therefore, concentrate on getting the rest of the work in hand. As that becomes familiar, he devotes more and more attention to the difficult job of book ordering. More or less systematic schemes on these lines in many fields provide for occasional senior assistance to scattered staff and whole institutions.

At the earlier stages of acquiring new skills, on the other hand, training on the job now has less and less to offer. At that time the participant needs various opportunities that the operating organization cannot offer. He needs less ambiguous roles and tasks than the insider/outsider, training/producing mixtures that learning on the job demands. In short, the participant must definitely be in training, even if he is in the organization's own training center. His task at this phase is to learn. Only later, not while in training, can he apply his skill to production.

1. Training in the Field

Training in the field is the first step back from learning on the job. It can have two kinds of purposes. It can provide the participant with opportunities to test specific ideas and techniques that he wishes to learn in a situation of daily life. It can also, second, offer him opportunities to find out what an organization in fact needs for its development. These two purposes are different. The focus of the first purpose is on the participant's needs to become more proficient in the use of a particular technique. He gets scope to practice it, that is all. In that case, the trainer's task is to ensure that the organization's normal working is not unduly interfered with by the participant's practice. For the second purpose the needs of the organization are the focus. The participant practices diagnostic skills and the building of closer relationships. Talking of the purpose of this training method as "applying" knowledge and skill in the field is only confusing. Whether any particular technique can be usefully "applied" there is quite a different question.

It may in fact be useful to keep field training for these two purposes separate.

Siet Institute has training for both purposes in its regular 12-week course in industrial management, but at different times and in different places. Technique practice, for example, of work sampling or time study, occupies three days in the fourth week and is carried out in a large factory. Practice in diagnosing needs is the starting point of a three-week study of a small factory that begins in the sixth or seventh week. This study leads to recommendations for action which are communicated to responsible executives. Specific techniques may or may not be used in the field study. That depends on the needs of the factory and the participants' ways of clarifying them.

The participant's role in field training is basically that of an interested outsider. He is in a normal work setting but does not belong to it. It would be substantially the same without him: he is supernumerary. Superficially this description might not seem to apply to someone like a management trainee. He is hired in the expectation that he will permanently join the organization, and his training program is an integral part of the operation. But in terms of his experience he, too, is an outsider as he comes newly into a department and, after getting acquainted with its working, leaves it again for another some weeks later. His role and his experience will be significantly different when, a year later, he actually goes to work in one or other of the departments that he visited earlier. The difference comes in the nature and the degree of his involvement and the share he will then carry of responsibility for the department's activities. Training in the field gives a bird's-eye view. It encompasses everything. The perceptive and diligent participant can find out much about any part. But it is all from a distance.

The outsider's role carries several advantages in terms of training. It is easier to be dispassionately analytical in that role. The outsider has no personal stake in what is going on or in the outcome. The role allows great flexibility. The outsider can move about in the organization, follow up cues, take time to reflect and analyze. No one depends on him to be in a particular spot at a certain time or to complete a specified task. He can spend some time in one organization, then move on to another.

From the institution's point of view, training in the field is a very demanding method, calling for extensive and difficult preparation. Four areas for thought and action can be listed: the detailed roles of the participants and of the trainers in the field, choosing the organization for field training, and special preparation of participants.

(*i*) *Clarification of Participant's Role.*   The aim in field training is to combine most promisingly the freedom and other advantages of the outsider with access to sufficient, and sufficiently important, data. This combination, not the kind of work participants do at home, is the main criterion for choosing the field and clarifying the participant's role. Since industrial units associate consultants with useful recommendations for action on real problems, the purposes of training and of the factory's operations may well be combined in the consultant's role. This is the role Siet Institute chooses for participants for the three-week in-plant and in-District training. In other settings, different roles may be appropriate. The intern in a hospital, and the research worker or training fellow in an academic setting are examples.

A number of things follow from the choice of role. Each role implies an agreed-upon bargain between the institution and "the field." If the bargain can be worked out and stated explicitly, so much the better. The consultant role implies that, in exchange for accepting this training opportunity for the participants, the institution commits them to offering something of value to the organization. Whatever the role, it must allow for two different points of view. The trainers specify the training opportunity. The organization has no part in this; it cannot decide what the participants are to learn or how. On the other hand, the organization's view holds for establishing the value of the participants' recommendations. The trainers cannot declare a recommendation, however valid, to be of value if the organization will not accept it. The implicit and differing points of view that are involved need underlining because training in the field is difficult to organize well and the common shortcomings in this kind of training can usually be traced right back to inadequate beginnings.

The following examples illustrate the kind of difficulties that inadequate attention at this stage lead to.

For field *visits* there is really no attempt to strike this bargain. The organization expects nothing of value and is also unlikely to give anything beyond that which good public relations requires. It is doubtful that such visits really give the exposure that are their justification and so warrant the time, trouble, and expense that they cost. At the opposite end are field *placements*. In the United States they are often called internships. Many of these turn out to offer little training to participants, while giving an organization the free use of an eager mind and pair of hands. This is liable to happen, for instance, if the placement is in a social work agency so short of staff that the incoming participant finds himself allocated any pieces of work that "he is able to do." These pieces are usually fairly simple tasks. He may be kept doing them for a long time, no matter what, if anything, he learns after the first day or so.

Or an organization may, halfway through the field training, deny participants access to certain kinds of data important to completing their task. This kind of hesitation sometimes occurs in industrial units over cost data. It amounts to the organization not keeping its side of the bargain. On the opposite side of this, again, are the villages surrounding many training centers that are sometimes talked of as "wasteland." They have received successions of training groups for field work. Each group has established the "needs" and program anew until the villages now need nothing so much as to be left alone. At issue here is not the trainers' or participants' goodwill or intent but what is useful to attempt in a village during field training and what is not.

(*ii*) *Clarification of Trainer's Role.* The role of the trainer in the field calls for clarification both vis-à-vis the participants and also vis-à-vis the organization. These areas are full of dilemmas. How far can a trainer leave participants to their own devices? Leaving them to make up their own minds can be good training. But the consequent errors may deprive the organization of the benefits it was led to expect. Just when does the trainer step in? And how does he step in without belittling the participants' independence and learning? If his own schedule leaves him a choice, how much time should the trainer try to spend with the participant(s)? The more he is present, the more will he be tempted to do something.

A useful rule of thumb for living with these dilemmas may be active training and correction during technique practice but the much more withdrawn role of a resource person during field training focused on diagnosis and relationships. Many trainers find the latter role much easier when they have a task of their own to work on while present in the field. They are there, accessible for consultation, but they need not stand around in between. The role of the trainer in the field vis-à-vis the participant is related also to the role he takes in the rest of the training program.

(*iii*) *Choosing the Organization for Field Training.* The choice of organization and the bargain to be agreed upon with it are largely a function of the chosen roles. One problem at this stage is to avoid settling for either the most advanced or the most backward organizations. Placing participants in a unit that rates among the best would be easiest but would soon leave them discouraged over ever finding a problem to work on and contributing something to the organization's operations. They would feel as if they were commiting a fraud whenever they asked for time from the organization's personnel. What is best in operations may, in short, not be at all the best for training. The worst unit, on the other hand, may have far more, and more difficult, needs than the participants can help with, given their limited time and skills. So they may get very excited but end up frustrated. This is commonly so when the unit suffers from complicated problems of relationships between key people or when field training is organized in too large a unit. The institution may then end up with unfinished business on its hands, which raises a variety of further problems.

Choosing an organization for field training, therefore, involves a series of difficult and time-consuming steps. Many organizations may need to be studied briefly to find the few that suit the training needs of the participants in terms of coverage and complexity and also of the organization's needs and likely response. Exhibit 5.1 reproduces the checklist that trainers at Siet Institute use as a first guide for selecting small factories for in-plant training. The few may be further reduced when the trainers spell out to them the major aspects of the bargain. All this involves much time and care, but the values of good field placements are high enough to warrant this.

(*iv*) *Preparing Participants for Field Training.* Clearly the greater the skill with which participants go into the field, because of tested experience or specific preparation during the earlier stages of the program, the greater the confidence with which the trainers can leave them free to explore and make their way. Working through some of the emotional factors in advance can make participants readier to use the skills they have, and reduce preoccupations over unsettling uncertainties, for example, about collaboration in the group, accommodation and food, and so on. In the Area Development Course at Siet Institute

Exhibit 5.1

CRITERIA FOR SELECTION OF UNIT FOR IN-PLANT STUDY

	Very Good	Good	Fair	Poor
I. MANAGEMENT:				
1.1. *Receptivity of Management:* Receptivity to the type of participants coming to units; Willingness to disclose data; Willingness to come to Siet for receiving report				
1.2. *Quality of Management:* Main problems of the unit: As management sees them; As faculty sees them; Possibility of implementation of recommendations				
1.3. *Language:* Knowledge of English (essential); Knowledge of other languages				
1.4. *Availability of records:*				
1.5. *Possibility of attending Siet training course:*				
1.6. *Local status and influence:*				
II. THE MANUFACTURING PROCESS				
2.1. *Suitability of Plant:* Scale of operations (workers per shift); Scope for application of techniques and diagnostic skills				
2.2. *Type of Product:* (Preference for finished product with adequate challenge for practice of techniques)				
2.3. *Length of Process Cycle:* (Not too long to see results)				

Exhibit 5.1 (Continued)

	Very Good	Good	Fair	Poor
III. LOGISTICS:				
3.1. *Residential accommodation* (Reasonableness of charges)				
3.2. *Distance from accommodation* (Transport arrangements)				
IV. VARIETY(Type of Plant):				
a) Organization				
b) Raw material				
c) End-product type				
d) Type of market				
e) Interesting features				
V. FURTHER OBSERVATIONS (if any):				

SOURCE: Small Industry Extension Training Institute, Hyderabad, India.

participants divide themselves into the required small groups for field study by their own choice and then have a two-day training laboratory to work through anticipated problems of relationships. The trainers can also help participants think concretely about various aspects of the task and design simple aids for use in the field. Exhibit 5.2 shows a seven-step guide for studying village leadership prior to setting up a health committee. This is in use at the Institute of Rural Health and Family Planning, Gandhigram, India.

Happily trainers can count with some certainty on two very favorable forces to emerge as the training in the field gets under way. Most participants feel intensely stimulated by it and respond to the opportunity with unexpected initiative and devotion. If anything, they exaggerate their part in what happens. For its part, the organization usually responds warmly to the participants' earnestness and good sense, and values their thoughtful questions and comments, this even before recommendations get focused and embodied in a formal report. Trainers can, therefore, be of good cheer in organizing training in the field. They can feel assured of its useful purposes and also have the agreeable feeling that they are likely to be moving with the stream, in the direction of everyone's inclinations.

Exhibit 5.3 summarizes the specifications of training in the field.

Exhibit 5.2

GUIDELINES FOR LEADERSHIP STUDY

STEP I

Visit the village.

STEP II

Meet three formal leaders like Panchayat Presidents, Village Munsiff, Karnam, Schoolteacher or Village Level Worker.

STEP III

Introduce yourself in the following way to the formal leaders:

We are coming from the health department. We are interested in the health activities. We have come to your village to find out your health problems and try to help you in solving them. Our idea is to improve the general health conditions of all people.

We usually work along with the leaders in the village because we know that they are interested in public welfare, they know your health problems better and they can carry our ideas to people better and help us in implementing the programme.

Therefore it will be of great help if you as a leader will be kind enough to give us the following information that we require for our work.

Information required:

1. Number of households.
2. Different caste groups in the village and the number of families in each caste or religious group.
3. *a)* Are there any factions in your village?
   b) If so, among whom?
4. Which is the most influential group or community in your village?
5. Please mention the name of the communities which they can influence.
6. Please mention leaders in each of the communities whom you consider are greatly interested in public work and influential.
7. Generally whom do people approach whenever they have a problem?

STEP IV

Prepare a sociogram based on information gathered from questions 1 to 5.

STEP V

Make a list of leaders suggested.

STEP VI

Meet each of them individually and get the names of leaders whom he considers as important and fill up the forms. Introduce yourself as a health worker who has come to help the village to help the people in solving their health problems. Explain to them the purpose of working with leaders and the need for selection of leaders and formation of health committees. Then request him to list out the names of leaders whom he considers as influential and useful and enter their names in the forms supplied and also get the informations specified in the form for each one of the names suggested.

STEP VII

Tabulate all the names gathered, and find out the number of times each one of them has been repeatedly mentioned by the interviewers. Those who have been mentioned most, are the most influential.

Exhibit 5.2 (Continued)

INSTITUTE OF RURAL HEALTH AND FAMILY PLANNING, GANDHIGRAM
LEADERSHIP CHART

Name of Village————————   Sheet No————————

Name	Identification Particulars	Age	Literacy	Caste	Occupation	Group Influences	Source of Leadership

SOURCE: Institute of Rural Health and Family Planning, Gandhigram, Madras State, India.

Exhibit 5.3

TRAINING IN THE FIELD: OUTLINE SPECIFICATIONS

	a) *Specific technique training*	b) *Diagnostic and relationship training*
Participant's role	Outsider: learner	Outsider: helper
Data	Situational	Situational
Trainer's role	Active guide	Resource person, consultant
Time required	Half days or whole days	Regular and frequent, or block of time, eg., 2–3 weeks as a minimum
Trainer requirements:		
Ratio	1 to 12–15	1 to 5
Time for preparation	Little	Very heavy
Follow up	None	Varies widely, can be heavy
Facilities required	Work setting in which technique normally used	1 work setting for 1 to 4 participants, long-term relationship with organization
Special points	None	Long lead time for making arrangements in the field.

2. Simulating Real Life: Role Playing and Business Games

Training in the field is a major venture on all counts, and effective roles for participants take time to establish and to perform. To reduce these costs and to provide practice in a variety of situations and roles, it is possible to design training opportunities which are one more step removed from real life. Instead of taking participants into the field, at the cost of extra time and limited responsibilities and roles, the field can be simulated in the training session itself.

Simulation methods cover situations of varying complexities and roles for the participants. The most elaborate "create" a whole field organization, rotate participants through key roles in it, and have them "deal with" specific situations of a kind they encounter in real life. Management trainees may work at an office desk with ringing telephones and full in-baskets. Each participant has a number of intradepartmental and interdepartmental memos, letters, reports, forecasts, and other data on his desk, such as he might normally receive. They pose a series of problems to handle, perhaps a crisis which the man must correct. He can use the channels of communication normally open to him: telephone, memos, and face-to-face meetings. This simulation method has been called "controlled experience sessions."

Two less elaborate and more common simulation methods of training deal with one half of such "controlled experiences" each. Role playing is one, business games the other. The purpose of role playing is to help participants experience what something "sounds" or "feels like," what the difference is between talking *about* people and talking *with* them, and talking *about* doing something and actually starting action. For this, role playing is very real.

Role playing is a very flexible training method. It may be elaborately preplanned, the actors carefully prepared and specific session time earmarked for the play and the subsequent discussion. Or the trainer can encourage participants to role-play spontaneously during some session. Careful management of time is important for the first version. Otherwise discussion time or repeat plays will get left out. A good rule of thumb may be to allow not less than 10 minutes for the play, twice as much time for discussion as for the play, and time for at least two plays of the same situation. That already adds up to one hour without allowing for an introduction or closure. Informal, spur-of-the-moment role playing requires no specific advance preparation or setting. But it does call for extra time and a high level of training skill. Rather than have participants go on with an unprofitable argument, for instance, the trainer can ask them to assume opposite roles. The results of such a degree of reality in the session may be far-reaching. One is that no time may be left for much else, in this same session! We assume that the trainer is able to handle whatever comes of the confrontation.

Business games pick up the other half of real life. They provide practice in using data about resources and processes that would be

Exhibit 5.4

SIMULATION METHODS: OUTLINE SPECIFICATIONS

	a) "Controlled experience"	b) Role playing	c) Business game
Participant's role	Player	Player/observer	Player/colleague or competitor
Data	Normal working data	Self-generated	Normal working data
Trainer's role	Organizer, conductor of review	Organizer, conductor of review	Organizer, conductor of review
Time required	2 sessions	1 hour 15 mins.	2 sessions
Trainer requirements:			
Ratio	1 to 8	1 to 20	1 to 20
Time for preparation	High, depending on materials	1 to 2 hours	High, depending on materials
Facilities required	Real setting: e.g., desks, working telephones, etc.	Nothing special	One room for each 4 or 5 participants

available to, say, a general manager: production schedules, available finance and facilities for borrowing, staff and market positions, inventories, fixed and variable costs, and others. Participants use these data to reach decisions that have calculable effects on output, costs, sales, etc. These decisions create new situations that call for further decisions; and so on through a number of stages. Several participants or teams of participants can be set to compete with one another. They can receive data on the competitive position at each stage, which they can then include in their considerations of the next decision.

The role of the trainer in simulation sessions lies mostly in organizing and reviewing them. Organization includes preparation of players and of materials, and can be very time-consuming. During the play the trainer is absent or in the background. At most he makes sure through a minimum of action that the play proceeds and also comes to a stop. The trainer usually conducts the review parts of the session, which are of key importance to making these methods valuable.

The major problem in using simulation methods is to ensure that the dramatics do not become so intriguing that the participants get seduced away from the primary purpose: learning something for action. This purpose is different from others for which similar methods can be used. A moment's reflection, in passing, about one of these may recapture the distinction and the point of view that needs safeguarding. Psychodrama and sociodrama are also simulation methods. They are used in therapy to help disturbed people to relive situations that upset them. The play may lead them anywhere. Its importance lies in the process, in the reliving itself. The purpose of simulation methods of training, on the contrary, is to offer opportunities for specified experiences. If they lead anywhere else, the trainers have failed.

Exhibit 5.4 summarizes the specifications of simulation methods of training. A reading at the end of this chapter gives further details about these methods, particularily about role playing.

3. Laboratory Training for Personal and Organizational Development

The purpose of laboratory training is to provide participants with an intensive experience of how they affect each other—and probably other people also—and how a group forms, maintains itself, and deals with relationship problems characteristic also of larger organizations. For intensity of experience and for clarity of data the training group needs to be small: 12 to 15. Some programs specify 8 to 10. The laboratory is shorn of several key aspects of normal working (incidentally also of key aspects of most other kinds of training). For instance, the group has no task other than studying its own working; attention to data outside itself is regarded as misdirected. It has no hierarchical organization other than whatever the group may construct for itself, certainly the trainer will not put himself on top. It depends on immediate and clear feedback beyond any standards normal in everyday living and working. All this makes the experience for the participants very real and intensive. They are *themselves,* not "playing" someone else. They work only on problems that they themselves initiate. The insulation of the setting from ordinary life is emphasized if the sessions take place in a soundproof room. It is then obviously a laboratory.

In terms of Lewin's three-stage model of learning, the unexpected

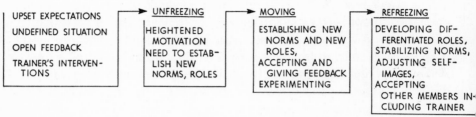

Figure 5.1

CHANGE MODEL OF LABORATORY TRAINING

UPSET EXPECTATIONS	UNFREEZING	MOVING	REFREEZING
UNDEFINED SITUATION	HEIGHTENED MOTIVATION	ESTABLISHING NEW NORMS AND NEW ROLES,	DEVELOPING DIF- FERENTIATED ROLES,
OPEN FEEDBACK	NEED TO ESTAB- LISH NEW NORMS, ROLES	ACCEPTING AND GIVING FEEDBACK	STABILIZING NORMS, ADJUSTING SELF- IMAGES,
TRAINER'S INTERVEN- TIONS		EXPERIMENTING	ACCEPTING OTHER MEMBERS IN- CLUDING TRAINER

behavior of the trainer and the other special conditions of the training laboratory make for rapid unfreezing. Figure 5.1 shows the process of laboratory training according to this model.

A second model for understanding the process of laboratory training hinges on the dissonances created by the trainer's behavior and the needs participants feel to reduce these dissonances. Major dissonances occur in at least four areas:

1. Between the participants' expectations of the trainer and the trainer's behavior in fact. The trainer avoids all attempts to seduce, force, or otherwise get him to conform to initial expectations.
2. Between each participant's concept of himself and his actual behavior and its effects in the laboratory.
3. Between the participant's expectations of the group's reactions to him and how the group in fact reacts.
4. Between the image of himself a participant wishes to impress on others and the image others in fact get.

The trainer's role is to live down right in front of the group the commonly accepted standards of hierarchical relationships and neglect of the effects people have on each other's feelings. His task is to show that these effects need to be, and can be, studied and taken into account, and that feedback can be given that is useful and acceptable. He plugs all avenues, barring one, for escaping from the discomforts of disso-nance. The avenue that remains starts with requiring participants to face both inner and outer realities and then to move away from current habits if these produce undesirable effects.

Shattered expectations and other dissonances make a training labora-tory a disturbing and intensive experience. The same quality probably explains the high rate of retention of what participants learn there. Research findings with the U.S. Bureau of Naval Research put the retention rate at 75 percent, compared with 55 percent of visual material and 35 percent for lecture presentations. But such high intensity has a price. In the first place, laboratories are best full-time. Many participants cannot carry on with other work at normal standards while they are also in a training situation that is as productive of anxiety and anger as a training laboratory usually is during its early stages. That is a major limitation of this training method. Other limitations come up in any attempt to fuse in the same program a training laboratory with other kinds of training. Both to attain and maintain the necessary intensity of experience and to protect other parts from this same intensity, labora-

Exhibit 5.5

LABORATORY TRAINING: OUTLINE SPECIFICATIONS

Participant's role	Himself
Data	Generated by group itself, "here and now" feedback
Trainer's role	Nonauthoritarian, resource person
Time required	15 × 2 hours, preferably in a block
Trainer requirements:	
Ratio	2 to 12–15 or 1 to 8–10
Time—preparation	Very little
Facilities required	Small room: tape recorder (helpful)
Special points	Requires rare training skill; may arouse high levels of anxiety which can affect activities running concurrently.

tory training is best carried on separately or at the very beginning of a diversified program. The high level of motivation for learning that laboratory training usually engenders is likely to carry over to other parts of the program, but that comes later. The severest limitation for this method may yet be the shortage of mature trainers who are also skillful and experienced. Skill and experience are here most clearly not adequate. Or rather, since they are working in the delicate area of participants' perceptions, feelings, and reactions, only people who have a fair insight into their own motivations and a large capacity for accepting others qualify as trainers. Even then training laboratories make heavy demands on the trainer's nervous system and sheer stamina. The learning that a training laboratory promotes, is of course correspondingly exciting and satisfying to the trainer.

Exhibit 5.5 summarizes the specifications of laboratory training. A reading following at the end of this chapter gives further details.

4. Sampling Real Life: Incidents and Cases

We are leaving the realm of action, real or simulated. Participants can no longer talk with the people in the situation they are considering, for those people are not in the session. They cannot influence the situation, for it is over and done with. All they now get is a descriptive record in the form of an incident or a case. Any life such a record is to have for the participants must be put in by themselves. They do this by "seeing themselves" in one or another person in the data, or in several in turn. As a result of this projection they experience the situation vicariously, as if they had been involved.

From this important point of view it may be a disadvantage to have the case on audio-tapes or on films. For the closer the case situation approaches full reality, the more difficult it becomes for participants to identify with the people in the data. They may instead become more conscious of differences in voice, looks, and surroundings and lose the similarities in content and problems between that situation and their own. For learning, not the reality outside but the reality to the participants is the key factor.

One purpose of providing vicarious experience is to multiply, well beyond what they would meet in their day-to-day work, the situations and problems to which participants can be exposed during a course. Another is to present each sample of real life in slow motion, so that it can be studied in detail and participants can learn to get the most out of the data it offers. The communication is that data are limited—and precious.

The third purpose of the case method is to help participants develop the habit of taking more factors into account than they usually do, analyze them carefully, and put them together into an integrated picture to guide understanding and action. These factors include the personal feelings and relationships of the actors in the situation. Because the descriptions of people and situations are taken from real life and resemble people and situations with which participants are familiar, this method also promotes the exploration of one's own attitudes and relationships. Cases provide all available data to participants in advance of the session. Participants are expected to have prepared themselves thoroughly, to be familiar with the facts and with ways of relating them usefully. The incident process developed by Paul Pigors[1] does not as-

---

[1] Paul and Faith Pigors, *The Incident Process—Learning by Doing* (Massachusetts Institute of Technology Series 2, No. 46).

sume this preparation. The incident itself is only a very brief statement of the situation. Additional data are available from the "instructor" of the day, who may be a participant whose situation is for discussion. By questioning, participants can elicit the additional data and explore directions of their choice and on the issues they see in the case. This is a useful thing to practice. To the "instructor," that is, the participant/ instructor, the process provides additional practice in writing up an incident out of available data, making a teaching plan, and leading the discussion/and observing the discussion process.

The trainer's role in the session is to help participants, individually and as a group, to clarify their understanding of the people and situations and to see to what decisions, actions, and implications this can lead them. Further, he builds on the participants' contributions. As he helps generalizations to emerge from the study of the particular situation, he can enrich the conceptual schemes with which participants will approach their work in future. These functions are different from piloting a meeting through an agenda, chairing a debate on an issue, or lecturing on a concept. Trainers develop different personal styles of carrying out these functions. The point here is that they alter the traditional relationship between trainer and participant. This in turn affects other parts of training programs, where this altered relationship does not necessarily develop.

Both shortage of skilled trainers and the acute shortage of adequate teaching materials severely limit the use of these training methods in developing countries. The limitations are interconnected. Experience elsewhere suggests that case research and case teaching are complimentary skills and get developed together. The orientation from which they spring tends to pervade whole courses. Indeed whole institutions are based on their use.

Professor Pigors' courses at the Massachusetts Institute of Technology and the work at the Harvard Business School are cases in point. In India, the Indian Institute of Management in Ahmedabad is developing the case method into its main orientation and method. Its faculty members receive training in the method abroad and have at the time of writing developed over 200 teaching cases in various fields of management, which they use in their two-year degree program as well as in special courses.

In India, apart from very few and partial exceptions, it is only the words "incidents" and "cases" that have become familiar. They are used for a wide variety and quality of materials. Some are not teaching but research cases. They deal with historical themes, or the author's, rather than with the detailed data of a particular situation calling for understanding by someone involved. Others are limited to the point of view of one person; their discussion is, therefore, limited to what this one person saw. Others, again, present the unusual or absurd when the need is for material that can help increase skills that are widely needed for day-to-day operations. Still others are written and used as illustrations of some principle, as if life were an illustration of principles rather than the starting point from which useful principles can be deduced. And much of the material is simply inadequate in coverage and quality so that discussion of it cannot satisfy the purposes for which cases are useful.

The development of material for incidents is no easier and perhaps even less advanced. Though fewer data are given out to the participants in advance, the trainer has to have material quite as full as, or even fuller than, for a case, so that he can answer participants' questions. After the participants become familiar with the method, i.e., after three or four sessions, the trainer can shift the burden of preparing incidents to participants in turn, which also has the advantage of involving participants in discussions of their own experiences. But even if the material is adequate, this still does not guarantee effective incident or case sessions. Few trainers are experienced in using these materials. There is, therefore, a real danger that these methods will fall into disrepute instead of meeting the justifiably high expectations entertained of them. Starting them off with inadequate material, skill, or institutional support, they may boomerang.

The minimum concentration for using the case method is high. For trainers it involves long preparation of their own research and training skills and of materials. For a start, enough incidents and cases need to be available for a self-contained series of sessions, not just for one or two. It takes a series to familiarize the participants with the method. Advance preparation by participants of cases for discussion has to be rigorous and general, otherwise the session tends to become an abstract argument instead of a meticulous consideration of available data, and it will be limited to few participants.

This difficulty in preparation is avoided in the incident process, which starts by questioning only very brief data; in fact, this is the advantage which the process sought to explore. The case series has to be long enough also for the novelty of the trainer's functions and role to wear off, particularly their nonevaluative character. The reality of the data, the demands these methods make on participants to handle their considered points of view in open discussion, and the different role of the trainer, all make the use of incidents and cases thoroughly desirable. But

Exhibit 5.6

SAMPLING REAL LIFE: OUTLINE SPECIFICATIONS

	a) Incident	*b) Case*
Participant's role	Initiator/contributor/leader	Initiator/contributor/leader
Data	Specific life situation elsewhere	Specific life situation elsewhere
Trainer's role	During question time, resource person; then discussion leader	Listener/clarifier/theoretician
Time required for preparation	Session time × 2	Session time × 2
For series of sessions	10 × 1½ hours	10 × 1½ hours
Trainer requirements:		
Ratio	1 to 20–40	1 to 20–?
Time for preparing sessions	10 × 2 hours	10 × 1½ hours
Facilities required	Circular/horseshoe sitting arrangement; large blackboards	Circular/horseshoe sitting arrangement; large blackboards
Special points	High initial cost of material: 1 month's highly skilled work for each incident	High initial cost of material: 1 month's highly skilled work for each case

nothing less than the minimum material and skill will do for starting self-generating programs using this method.

Exhibit 5.6 summarizes the specifications of the incident and case method. A reading at the end of this chapter gives further details.

5. Individualized Training

Tutoring, individual practice of specific skills, and reading and written assignments are traditional methods of individual training. For the many tasks that involve a senior and a junior by themselves, and for others that are for just one person on his own, this method simulates the work situation. In all other cases it means one more step away from reality: colleagues, customers, citizens, and others are now all absent.

The big advantage of individual training is that it puts participants clearly into the position of determining the speed with which training can proceed. The tutor adapts his activities to the participant's rate of learning. With practice and other assignments, the participant's singularity is marked even more sharply. Not only his competence but also his motivation are then on test, both quite exposed.

Social isolation and high cost have until recently limited individual instruction to a supplementary method of training. The development of programmed instruction promises to individualize the simultaneous training of many participants in certain skills. The essence of such a program is that it takes the trainer's place in several important and time-consuming respects. Based on a meticulously detailed analysis of what the participant is to learn, the duplicated program—instead of the individual trainer—confronts the participants with a set of specified steps so designed and ordered as to make it possible that each will progress in the desired direction. Other directions are closed off. The program may be in the form of a teaching machine or a programmed textbook; this is secondary. In the words of Wilbur Schramm, the essential elements are six:

. . . *a*) an ordered sequence of stimulus items, *b*) to each of which a student responds in some specified way, *c*) his response being reinforced by immediate knowledge of results, *d*) so that he moves by small steps, *e*) therefore making few errors and practising mostly correct responses, *f*) from what he knows, by a process of successively closer approximation toward, what he is supposed to learn from the programme.[1a]

> From initial application in school education, programmed instruction has found its way into industrial training. By 1965, industrial companies reported the successful use of programmed instruction in mathematics and statistics, production, maintenance and other managerial activities involving scheduling, basic science and aspects of engineering services, and in increasing number, operator skills. Programs were also developed and tried out in human motivation for supervision, and for imparting knowledge to salesmen and service representatives about a wide variety of new services and products.

One big advantage of programmed instruction over other methods lies in its flexibility, both for the participant and for the trainer, and for the administrator of training programs. Individuals often can work through programs in their own time, as well as at their own speed. They need neither to start nor finish a program together. Experience in industrial settings suggests that the slowest learners take about twice as long as the fastest. When they work on individualized programs, the slow need not feel rushed, nor the fast feel held back by others. This flexibility is most advantageous in training groups which are heterogeneous in terms of specialization, for example, production engineers and

---

[1a] Schramm, Wilbur "Programmed Instruction Today and Tomorrow," in *Four Case Studies of Programmed Instruction*, Fund for the Advancement of Education, 1964.

marketing and financial executives setting out to learn general management. At any time some participants know much more (in their specialized field) than the rest. Programmed instruction can then allow what in schools would be termed remedial teaching: special programs to enable a portion of the course group to catch up with the rest.

A second advantage of programmed instruction is that it provides in private the step-by-step evaluation and feedback that most participants would find unacceptable in front of their peers and trainers.

A third advantage lies in the uniformity of training input that comes from substituting a program for a trainer, or, more likely, for many trainers. When a particular course is taught by more than one trainer, it is almost certain that there will be significant differences in content. It is difficult even for the same trainer to maintain consistency from one course to the next. What he usually has is a general syllabus and a session outline. What he does within this outline is a creative, highly individualized act. Programs, on the other hand, are subjected to empirical testing on sample groups of participants for whom they are intended and finally emerge "high and dry," consistent with objectives and constraints. Research studies show that final examination scores are much more homogeneous in programmed instruction than in other training methods. Few, if any, participants fail.

The problem at this stage of the development of individualized training methods is to sort out what are the exuberances of fashion from what is sound and permanent. It is already clear that many of the original claims for programmed instruction are spurious. There is no indication that adequate individualized instruction requires either fewer trainers or less well-prepared trainers. As for the quality of trainers, the reverse is more likely to be true. This is because participants will be in various stages of the program at the same time and ask questions over a very wide field; also to the extent that the participants feel stimulated by the program they may ask more sophisticated, wide-flung, and deeper questions. Then, appropriate programs are hard to find, and a good one is hard to identify without further testing under controlled conditions. This is a costly and time-consuming process. Moreover, a wide range of programmed materials are required to instruct participants of varying ability. The costs per program vary widely but are certainly high. They are usually economical only when the prospective training population is large and the training objectives stable. Several expensive skills go into making a program. One American company reports paying $1,000 to $1,500 preparation costs per instructional hour.

Some questions of what is actually learned from programmed instruction also remain to be explored. Clever participants seem to develop a knack of short-cutting the program. Others go through the program apparently satisfactorily but are then unable to pass tests or answer questions about what they have been reading or answering in the program. Apparently, the alleged reward from immediate feedback, telling the participant that he has made the right response, is simply inadequate. While feedback and reinforcement in the usual social situation of trainer and participant may be less consistent and reliable, it seems that it is more durable and carries other important values. Com-

Exhibit 5.7

PROGRAMMED INSTRUCTION: OUTLINE SPECIFICATIONS

Participant's role	Individual, wholly in charge
Data	Standardized programmed material
Trainer's role	To answer questions
Time required	Flexible
Trainer requirements:	
Ratio	1 to 20
Time for preparation	Little
Follow up	None
Facilities required	"Programmed" text books, etc.; individual work space
Special points	Preparation of program is quite separate from its use. Its high cost, of the order of one month's highly skilled work per hour's instruction, is economical for training large numbers of participants.

plaints about boredom are the most common complaints participants make about programmed instruction. That they complain about boredom in other training methods too does not help. For in the case of programmed instruction, the complaints raise questions about the very basis on which it rests: higher motivation and truly individualized training. If these objectives were achieved, these complaints would be the first to disappear. But it is difficult to know what this "boredom" really describes. It could describe, for instance, the relentless pressure the participant feels to concentrate on the program, which does not allow him the luxury of "tuning out" that he can have in usual sessions—though hardly in individual tutoring.

A final thought: programmed instruction has a very great indirect advantage. It demands a meticulous specification of training needs and definition of training objectives, and training sequences and methods related most carefully to these objectives. A similar degree of care should, of course, inspire all training efforts, irrespective of method. But it often does not, and here is a method where nothing less will suffice. This reason would be enough to believe that programmed instruction has much to offer India and other developing countries.

Exhibit 5.7 summarizes the specifications of programmed instruction. A reading at the end of this chapter gives further details.

6. Seminars and Syndicates

The purpose of seminars, syndicates, and other general discussion methods is to provide participants with opportunities to exchange ideas and recollections of experiences. Through this exchange they stimulate each other's thinking, broaden their outlook, and also gain experience in the kinds of give and take that commonly occur in meetings of many kinds. This process develops tolerance for the views of others. The methods are most promising if the group consists of people who come from different professional backgrounds and functions but who work in similar organizations and jobs. The contexts and goals are then similar, but the range of ideas and points of view brought to bear on them is wide. The understanding and tolerance that gets developed is appropriate to general rather than functional management and useful for considering issues of broad policy.

> The Administrative Staff College of India, whose work is based on the syndicate method developed at the Administrative Staff College at Henley, U.K., pays major attention to the composition of syndicate groups. Each syndicate has participants from public and private industry and from public administration. In terms of functions, they include engineering and technologies, accounting and finance, personnel and marketing.

Syndicates and seminars differ from the discussion of incidents and cases in that they focus on wide topics and problems, not on a single concrete situation. Nor do they have a carefully specified problem in focus for action. Syndicates and seminars aim generally at widening the participants' horizon and providing opportunities for exercising the mind: reading, preparing material for discussion, and participating in and leading discussions.

The participant's role in these methods is an active one, if he chooses. Studies have shown that in groups of more than eight, some participants tend to be silent, and most groups are larger than eight, at least 10 to 15. Still, the methods depend on participants' speaking. It is common for participants to take turns preparing material for discussion and chairing the sessions. The trainer's role is correspondingly inactive during the sessions; there he is a resource person. He may even sit apart from the group in order to signal that the participants are fully responsible for the proceedings. His active functions are mostly behind the scenes, helping compose the group, thinking of topics and assignments to give the group, and paying attention to participants who seem in difficulties with the method or the group, and perhaps helping them privately.

The purposes of these methods of training also set their limits. They assume that a participant can use at work the general skills that these methods help him to practice. They also assume that the decisions the group reaches at an intellectual level will affect the participant's behavior. These assumptions may or may not be valid. The intended effects are so general that the methods cannot be assessed for effectiveness separately from the effects of the training environment as a whole or from a wide range of background factors.

The most serious possibility is that these methods run counter to some basic needs of developing countries. For instance, where motivation for development is slight or mixed, participants in general discussion may settle for tolerance at the price of new ideas; they may accept verbal agreements at high levels of abstraction at the price of working hard, first, to reconcile difference and widen the areas of real agreement. They may not learn to respect and to live and work with real diversity. The prevalence of "perhaps" and "broadly speaking" in many documents that emerge from these courses confirms one's fears that the group has used verbal subterfuges to avoid exploring the areas of disagreement or even stating the different opinions side by side, unresolved. Yet development depends basically on divergence—dissonance —followed by integration and collaboration, as does training. That these methods are used widely in developing countries and are put forward as major advances is, therefore, disturbing.

The exception to this worrisome possibility is brainstorming. Brainstorming is the very child of novelty: new problems call for "creative" solutions. Nothing is taken for granted, least of all the relevance of past experience. The method deliberately provokes participants to break out of habitual grooves of thinking and come up with fresh approaches to the problem. There is no trainer. The whole atmosphere favors divergence and unorthodoxy. The starkness of this goal goes a long way. Brainstorming frankly favors divergence, and this fact may be sufficient to explain why brainstorming is so little used as yet in developing countries where new solutions ought to carry the highest premium. It is

Exhibit 5.8

GENERAL DISCUSSIONS: OUTLINE SPECIFICATIONS

	a) *Seminar*	b) *Syndicate*	c) *Brainstorming*
Participant's role	Contributor, chairman, presenter of data	Contributor, chairman, *Rapporteur*	Contributor
Data	General topic or problem	General topic or problem	New problem
Trainer's role	Very small, resource	Very small, resource	Stimulator of unusual ideas
Time required	2 hours	2 hours	1 hour
Trainer requirements			
Ratio	1 to 12–15	1 to 10–12	0 to 6–8
Time for preparation	Little	Little	Little
Follow up	Little	Little	1 hour
Facilities required	Circular sitting	Circular sitting	Circular sitting
Special points	Tend to abstraction and verbal agreement		

virtually untried even though its immediate aim is limited to new ideas only, not changes in behavior.

Exhibit 5.8 summarizes the specifications of three methods for broadening the mind.

7. The Lecture

Of the six kinds of training methods discussed so far in successive sections of this chapter, four use as data situations from real life as they occur right in front of the participants in the field or in the training laboratory, or in situations specially set up or reported to them by an observer or trainer, as in simulation techniques, incidents, and cases. The fifth kind of method, individualized instruction, standardizes—that is, abstracts—data from real life for systematic step-by-step learning of certain kinds. It also takes the participant out of the social context of most training events: away from other participants, in tutoring, and in programmed instruction away also from the trainer. The latter method underscores that the participant, in order to learn, must want to learn, and that he will in the final analysis proceed with learning at his own speed. Motivation and speed are thus acknowledged to be at the participant's end of the training process. The sixth set of methods, various kinds of general discussion, reintroduce the social dimension but put the participant to work on general topics and problems, that is, on abstract data.

The seventh training method, the lecture, keeps the data abstract and also cuts out again the social dimension of learning. For purposes of training, which is all we are concerned with here, the assumptions the lecture relies on are numerous. It makes at least five:

1. That participants are motivated to learn. If they are free to choose whether or not to come to the lecture, their coming represents some motivation, although if the lecturer is famous, handsome, or has a melodious voice, the motivation may not be primarily for learning. If attendance is obligatory, as it almost invariably is in training courses, the participants' motivation is an unknown.
2. That the lecturer and participants are on the same wavelength, so that there is a basis for common understanding. It assumes this to be so not only at the beginning of the lecture but also as the lecturer goes along.
3. That the lecturer can hit on a speed of delivery, a set of ideas, etc., which are necessarily the same for everyone with useful results; that he can "feel" when he is engaging the purposeful attention of the majority of participants. He must assume that participants are keeping pace.
4. That the assembly of participants in the same room and atmosphere but with little or no interaction between them produces useful results; i.e., that the social dimension of training can be ignored.
5. That a participant can by himself, with the help of reading and informal contact, build the bridge between the lecture and his work situation, and that intellectual understanding will influence action.

These assumptions are open to doubt, as we have seen in earlier sections. No wonder they make the lecture the most difficult method to use effectively. From this point of view it is remarkable that it is the most common and apparently most durable training method of them all.

As a training method the purpose of the lecture is in fact specific and quite limited. In the continuum of knowledge, understanding, and skill or behavior, the lecture can focus on the second: understanding. When, through reading assignments and experience, participants are fairly familiar with information about a subject, the lecturer can relate the facts to one another and fit them into a memorable scheme, a picture of understanding, a thesis and a theme. This may be more memorable than, say, reading a book, because of the living voice and manner, and "the atmosphere" that will be associated with this picture for the participants. The lecturer can make the facts "come alive," convey enthusiasm and significance.

The effectiveness of the lecture method is, therefore, most closely related to its place among other methods in the same program. The lecture holds its greatest promise when it is a response to questions raised by participants or thrown up in previous discussion, field work, or other experiences. Its duration is an important factor in its effectiveness. Studies show that 20 to 30 minutes may be the maximum time a lecturer can effectively speak continuously and receive attention. A lecturer can break up a longer period by using the blackboard or more elaborate audio-visual methods or by interspersing his lecture with occasional questions to the participants. But these details and devices must not distract us from a kind of awe at this most difficult of training methods to use effectively. The participant's role during the lecture itself is that of individual listener, part of the audience. The trainer is all active; he decides what to talk about, he lectures, he makes what he can and wishes of the reactions of the audience as he goes along.

The main attraction of lecturing as a training method is its deceptive simplicity and the control it is supposed to give to the trainer over what goes on. The coverage and preparation of the lecture can be predetermined. The lectures can be scheduled weeks ahead. Participants can be expected to take notes or be provided with duplicated summaries. Once prepared, a lecture can be repeated on other occasions or even given by a substitute lecturer. Perhaps even more attractive is the predictable course of the session itself. The lecturer can "feel" satisfaction at having given a good lecture. So lecturing holds the position of the established method of training. Other methods have to challenge it in a special way. It is usually not enough to suggest that they be compared to lecturing in terms of the purposes they can serve and their comparative effectiveness and costs.

The simplicity is deceptive most of all, of course, because what the lecturer speaks has nothing directly to do with what the participants learn. This connection, as we have seen, is anything but neat. Some participants will learn nothing of what the lecturer planned. More fearful perhaps is the readiness with which others may accept the lecturer's theme as the last word rather than think it through and choose it, discard it, or vary it for themselves, which would be the way to make it part of their own understanding. The very qualities of a good lecture threaten its value as a training method. The more complete and logically consistant the argument, the more erudite its derivation, and the more appealing its packaging, the more the lecture will tend to be bought as a totality, the final answer, Q.E.D. Many of the satisfactions participants feel with a lecture may be the opposite of those that come with learning: a sense of closure rather than of having to go out and study and think, a sense of being taken care of by knowledgeable elders with whose learning and performance they cannot hope to match their own, a sense of dependence.

The tested results of lecturing, therefore, encourage only its most deliberate use. It has use in that part of the learning process that aims at increasing intellectual understanding. For passing on knowledge it is inefficient. People remember only about one half of the content of a lecture immediately afterwards, no matter how carefully they think they listened. Two months later they will remember about 25 percent or less. Incidentally those who remember most are not the most intelligent.[2] An underlying fact is that people think several times as fast as anyone speaks. Their attention to a lecture has, therefore, a great deal to do with that "spare time."

Some studies have been carried out to throw light on this gap. They are of college students whose interest might be most directly intellectual. Bloom played back tapes of classroom activity to groups of college students and asked them to recall what they were thinking about at the time. He found that students in lecture classes as compared to students in discussion classes reported significantly more thoughts classified as "irrelevant" and "simple comprehension," and significantly fewer thoughts classified as relating to "self," "other persons," and "problem-solving.". . . In a related study, Brinkley asked college students to rate 10 academic activities as to the extent to which they elicited "mental activity." He found great variability among students. He also found that a composite ranking remained much the same for groups of students over a 20-year interval. Group discussion was ranked second and lecture eighth in the composite ranking.[3]

These studies were made in America. During a seminar in India 20 senior officers listened to the erudite head of their own organization speak for an hour. A quick check the very next day revealed that no one was able to recall with certitude more than one out of the five policy points that he had made. Even where there is a tradition of oral communication, therefore, the lecture is a very ineffective method of imparting information.

As a method of changing action, that is, for the objective of training, lecturing is also ineffective. The famous American sets of experiments, one concerned with changing food habits, the other with lessening labor turnover and other disturbances following production changes in a

---

[2] See Dominick A. Barbara, *The Art of Listening* (Springfield, Ill.: Charles C. Thomas, Publisher, 1958).

[3] Quoted in Norman E. Wallen and Robert M. W. Travers, "Analysis and Investigation of Teaching Methods," in N. L. Gage (ed.), *Handbook of Research in Teaching* (Skokie, Ill.: Rand McNally & Co., 1963), p. 482.

garment factory, have been matched in India, with similar results. Only 3 percent of the women in three lecture groups changed their food habits, compared with 32 percent in the discussion groups.[4] Very heavy labor turnover in the factory was almost eliminated through the workers' active participation in production changes.[5]

Developing and deciding to use a new skill calls for a commitment on the part of a participant. This commitment springs from the meaning the changed behavior has for him personally and the degree of

Exhibit 5.9

THE LECTURE: OUTLINE SPECIFICATIONS

Participant's role	Listener, part of audience
Data	General, abstract
Trainer's role	Lecturer
Time required	20–30 minutes. One hour or more if audio-visual and discussions methods used
Trainer requirements:	
Ratio	1 to 00
Time for preparation	Varies
Facilities required	Varies with size of session and subsidiary methods
Special points	Effective for understanding stage of the learning process only.

concensus for the change he can see in the group immediately around him. Lecturing by itself does not address either the individual or the social dimensions of this process. It is proper, then, that "training" through lecturing has been renamed in many places "orientation." That limits its aim to the intellectual and the abstract. But "orientation" is becoming a bad word too. Changes in words do not get at the problem.

The central task is no different in essentials for lecturing or for other training methods. It is to specify the proper time and place for its use in the training process, through careful examination of the aims it can promote and through equally careful evaluation of the results.

Exhibit 5.9 summarizes the specifications of the lecture method.

---

[4] Kurt Lewin, "Studies in Group Decision," in Dorwin Cartwright and Alvin Zander (eds.), *Group Dynamics* (Evanston, Ill.: Row, Peterson & Co., 1956), chap. xxi.

[5] Lester Coch and John R. P. French, Jr., "Overcoming Resistance to Change," in Cartwright and Zander (eds.), *ibid.,* chap. xix.

TRAINING METHODS COMPARED WITH OBJECTIVES, PROCESSES, AND FACILITIES

We have examined in turn seven major kinds of training methods and some major examples of each. There are others. Workshop, symposium, demonstration, and panel-discussion are just some of them. We trust that the reader will have no difficulty sorting these under appropriate major heads. Several are normally used in conjunction with other methods and would appear under several titles. Demonstrations and the increasing range of audio-visual methods are among these.

The choice of training methods for a particular program depends in the first place on a series of three comparisons. These then have to be interrelated for final choice in the same way as a craftsman would assemble a tool kit. The tool kit of training methods does not show in what sequence and how frequently the tools are to be used. To this question, the design of the training program, we will devote the next and final chapter on the pretraining stage.

The three comparisons for choosing training methods for a program are:

1. Methods compared with training objectives.
2. Methods compared with the learning process and its stages.
3. Methods compared with available time, skills, and facilities.

Summary data for these comparisons can be presented in three exhibits.

1. Methods Compared with Objectives

Exhibit 5.10 refers back to the nine training objectives listed on pages 112–14 and evaluates the methods in terms of them.

The ratings are necessarily rough. A skillful, devoted trainer can deflect the tendencies of a particular method. Some contexts are favorable, others unfavorable. But even rough ratings indicate the major tendencies. Where widely varying conditions might make ratings misleading, we have left the space blank. The blank ratings need to be regarded as offering real promise so long as certain conditions are present.

Simulation, laboratory, and case methods are promising on almost all scores. Simulation is down on exposure to new ideas. The laboratory method scores highest: five V. Highs. But its coverage is limited to

Exhibit 5.10

COMPARISON OF TRAINING METHODS AND TRAINING OBJECTIVES

Training Methods

	(1) Field	(2) Simulation	(3) Laboratory	(4) Cases, etc.	(5) Individual	(6) Seminar	(7) Lecture
1. Realistic and manageable part of job	High	V. High	High	High	High	Low	Low
2. Help with internalizing learning	High	High	V. High	High	V. High	Low	V. Low
3. Protection for participant and organization against mistakes	High	V. High	High	V. High	V. High	V. High	V. High
4. Learning to learn	High	High	V. High	High	High	High	V. Low
5. Exposure to new ideas and methods	High	Low	V. High	High	High	High	High
6. Experiments with behavior	High	High	V. High	High	High	Low	Low
7. Membership of new reference groups	Low	High	High	High	Low	High	Low
8. Step back to think about job as a whole	High	V. High		V. High	Low	High	High
9. Very intensive learning	High	High	V. High	High	High	Low	Low

personal and organizational behavior, so thinking about the job as a whole is an uncertain dimension.

Individual training, seminars, and other general discussions cannot meet a number of training objectives and are, therefore, limited to very specific uses. Seminars and lectures do well only on exposure to new ideas and studying one's job in a wider context. The High ratings for protecting the participants and organizations against mistakes indicate that some methods are very distant from the work situation. It was this distance that placed them in sixth and seventh place in our list of methods.

2. Methods Compared with the Learning Process

Exhibit 5.11 rates methods in terms of ten stages of the learning process. Though the stages are listed in sequence here, they overlap in practice. The ratings are again indicative only.

Training in the field and by simulation, laboratory, case, and individual methods score high for the five early stages of the learning process. In its limited field of coverage, the laboratory method is very strong throughout, with the exception of conceptual understanding of a job as a whole. The general discussion and lecture methods do not fare well in this comparison.

3. Methods Compared with Facilities

Exhibit 5.12 summarizes the sectional tables of specifications of different training methods. All items except the first, participant's role, have a direct bearing on the skills and facilities required to use a particular method.

The data in this exhibit is important in that it brings what is desirable in contact with what is possible or impossible for a particular program or institution. The limitations impinge particularly in three ways: inadequate time for preparation and follow up (field, simulation, and case methods), scarcity of suitable materials (cases and individual training), and scarcity of certain training skills (field, simulation, and laboratory and case methods). The time limitation is the easiest to remove. Much of it can be removed by planning further ahead. The rest can be translated into costs. And if costs can be related to the results of training, the additional cost will turn out to be a bargain in almost all cases.

The limitations of training materials are more difficult to remove

Exhibit 5.11

COMPARISON OF TRAINING METHODS AND STAGES IN THE LEARNING PROCESS

	Training Methods						
	(1) Field	(2) Simulation	(3) Laboratory	(4) Case, etc.	(5) Individual	(6) Seminar	(7) Lecture
1. Stimulation by data situation	V. High	V. High	V. High	High	High	Low	Low
2. Interaction and involvement	High	V. High	V. High	High	V. High	High	Low
3. Experience	High	High	V. High	High	High	Low	Low
4. Practice	High	High	V. High	High	V. High	Low	V. Low
5. Feedback	High*	High	V. High	High	V. High	Low	V. Low
6. Repeat practice(s)	Low	V. High	V. High	High	V. High	Low	V. Low
7. Repeat feedback(s)	Low	High	V. High	High	V. High	Low	V. Low
8. Conceptual understanding of job	Low	Low	Low	High	Low	Low	V. Low
9. Conceptual understanding of change process	V. Low	V. Low	High	V. High	V. Low	High	High
10. Creative experimenting	High	High	V. High	High	V. Low	Low	V. Low

* For diagnostic field studies the rating should be low.

because they link into the third limitation, the severe shortage of training skills needed for the use of highly desirable methods. In the case of
diagnostic field training and laboratory training, this shortage is so
severe that these methods have to be left out of the tool kit for all but
the fewest programs, certainly in developing countries, until more trainers become available. But can interested people not learn these skills
"on the job"? Not, we would appeal, when these methods offer participants and organizations least protection of all against mistakes. The
first principle must be to risk no harm.

For most programs in developing countries the methods that sample
real life, incidents and cases, have also to be left out of the kit. Lack of
training skill will do no harm, at least, but the material by itself, even if
it is good, does not make the method effective. And wasting the time of
participants (and their organizations) and bringing the methods into
disrepute ought perhaps not be regarded as harmless after all.

So the shortages generally force developing countries back to using
the training methods which are at best effective for very few objectives
and at few stages in the learning process: general discussion and lecture
methods. Breaking out of this discouraging trend is a two-dimensional
task. One step is to take attention off the general limitations and study
meticulously the methods that can in fact be assembled for a particular
training program. The institution may have a trainer who has such close
relations with a work organization that diagnostic field training would
surely lead to no harm. Another may have a knack for role playing. He
might not be able to describe what he does, or why, but he is effective;
so role playing can be included in the kit. A discussion serves objectives
a lecture cannot serve, even if it is not particularly well led. So that can
be included. It may be possible to include a series of cases or a training
laboratory by borrowing the materials and skilled trainers from another
institution. The point is to augment the tool kit with desirable methods
just as much as possible, each with its clear minimum specifications for
use.

The second step is to use the programs that do offer novel training
methods for enabling more trainers to acquire scarce new skills. Two
ways are possible. Firstly, active trainers can be encouraged and helped
to make the most of their new experiences, through review sessions with
more experienced trainers and through faculty development programs.
Second, the training sessions can be used directly for developing additional trainers. For instance, many kinds of sessions would not be
harmed if additional trainers were invited to sit in and to take part
afterwards in review and planning sessions. Breaking through the pre-

Exhibit 5.12

COMPARISON OF TRAINING METHODS AND OUTLINE SPECIFICATIONS

	Training Methods						
	(1) Field	*(2)* Simulation	*(3)* Laboratory	*(4)* Cases, etc.	*(5)* Individual	*(6)* Seminar	*(7)* Lecture
Participant's role	Outsider	Player-observer	Himself	Initiator, contributor, leader	In charge	Contributor Chairman	Listener
Data	Situation	Partial situation	Here and now	Description of situation elsewhere	Standardized programmed material	General	General
Trainer's role	Active guide, resource person	Organizer–discussion leader	Resource person, consultant	Listener, clarifier, theoretician	Resource person, organizer	V. Little resource	Lecturer
Time required preparation per session	Heavy Heavy	2 hours	15 × 2 hours	10 × 3 hrs. 10 × 1½–2 hours	Varies Varies	Varies 1½–2 hours	20–30 minutes; 1 hour if subsidiary method used
Time requirements Ratio	1:15* or 1:5	1:8–20	2:15	1:20–?	1:20–?	1:12	1:00
Time for preparation	V. Heavy	Heavy	V. Little		V. Little	Little	Varies
Followup	Heavy	Heavy		10 × 1½ hours			
Special points	Long lead time, expensive		Coverage limited to personal and organizational behavior; rare training skill; difficult effects on concurrent programs	High initial cost of materials and long lead time	High initial cost of materials; expensive	Tends to verbal agreement	Tends to dependence
Detailed chart	p. 99	p. 101	p. 103	p. 106	p. 108	p. 110	p. 114

* Technique practice.

vailing shortage of skilled trainers, somehow, must command first priority in developing countries. To some of the ways of doing this we will return in the last part of the book, on the training institution and its development.

Reading 5.1

SIMULATING REALITY: ROLE PLAYING*

Udai Pareek

Role playing is an old method adopted by children to learn new social roles. Children may often be seen acting as parents or other adults. This kind of play activity is a good learning device for children. However, this has been developed into a new technique for use with both children and adults.

Role playing is a method of adopting roles from real life other than those being played by the person concerned and understanding the dynamics of those roles. It is "a method of studying the nature of a certain role by acting out its concrete details in a contrived situation that permits of better and more objective observation." Role playing is a conscious attempt to examine the various roles played in actual life.

Role playing developed as a result of new developments in interpersonal techniques started by Moreno.[1] Later this technique was adapted for its use in various situations in interpersonal relations like education, administration, industry, social work, therapy, etc. Various parallel names have been used for role playing such as leadership training, reality practice, experience practice, spontaneity training, etc. However, the term "role playing" is the most accepted and is more expressive. The technique of role playing can be adopted for various purposes and the nature of the technique would differ for different purposes.

---

* Abridged from Udai Pareek, "Role Playing as a Human Relations Training Technique," *Indian Journal of Social Work,* Vol. XI (1960), pp. 251–59.

[1] In the early twenties of this century Moreno experimented with groups of role players in the theatre of spontaneity in Vienna (see J. Nehnevajsa," Sociometry: decades of growth" in J. L. Moreno (ed.) *Sociometric Reader.* (Glencoe, Ill.: The Free Press, 1960), pp. 707–53. Moreno's major contribution in this regard is available in English in J. L. Moreno, *Who Shall Survive?* (New York: Beacon House, 1953).

While planning role playing, one important factor to be considered is that of establishing rapport with the audience and the role players. The role players should clearly understand the purpose of role playing and should be agreeable to play the roles.

Considerable skill is required in the selection of a situation for a role-play session. The situation should be of challenging nature and should be of concern to those who are participating in role playing; for this purpose a conflict situation may prove better, but it should not involve areas of personal conflict.

Equally important is the technique of role briefing. Those who are to play roles should understand clearly the type of persons they are required to be during the role-play session. It is better to prepare written briefing sheets and distribute them to the persons concerned. In a group role-playing situation, the whole group need be briefed regarding the general situation and group atmosphere. The individuals in the group situation should be briefed separately. Briefing should concern only emotional state and attitudes and should not contain details about the type of things the role player should say during the role-play session.

For good role playing the role players should get involved in the situation. This would depend much on the type of briefing. Involvement is necessary to make the role-play session as near to reality as possible.

The role of the role-play director is of great importance. He should see that role playing is proceeding according to the briefing. During the role-play session he observes the progress of role playing and cuts the role play whenever he feels that it is not proceeding properly and is not fulfilling the purpose for which it is arranged. He can also cut the role play to explain the dynamics behind a particular statement. During the role play he can also interview the role players to show to the observers how the various persons have been feeling.

Sometimes role-play is done by one or more than one expert to demonstrate some principles or practices. In this case the person may be in role for sometime and then may come out of the role to explain the dynamics behind the role being played. It is useful to develop this practice of stepping in and stepping out of the role by role players, to explain to the observers the relevant feeling they would like to report.

The final analysis of role playing is of great importance. After the role-play session is over, it should be thoroughly discussed. For this purpose it is necessary to do some audience briefing in the beginning. The observers may be asked to observe the dynamics of the group engaged in role playing, with the help of an observation sheet or form. Guided observation during the role-play session helps in making the purpose of role play clear. At the end of the role-play session, the role-play director and the observers may interview the various role players to know the dynamics behind the role-play interrelationships. It is sometimes useful to use an *alter ego*—one of the observers who may identify himself with one of the role players to report to the observers the feelings of that player to see the difference between the reportings of the feelings by two persons. After analysis and evaluation of this type the role-play session may be concluded.

SOME ROLE-PLAY PROCEDURES

Role playing is being increasingly used for human relations training. Various forms of role playing are being developed for this purpose. The main requirement in role playing is of assuming roles and playing them out. The following are some of the methods adopted in this connection. The utility of a procedure would depend on the purposes for which role playing is to be arranged, the type of audience, etc.

Simple Role Playing

The usual method adopted may be called simple role playing or what Maier calls "Single Group Role Playing."[1a] In this procedure one role-playing group performs and all others act as observers. The role play can be cut by the role-play director whenever there is a need of explaining the dynamics to the audience. This procedure is quite useful for purposes of demonstration, for developing skills in sensitivity to the feelings of others, for intensive training, and for use with the small groups. In this procedure role play is arranged before the audience, who at the end discuss for the final analysis and evaluation of the role playing. The analysis can be facilitated by the use of an *alter ego* for the major roles in a role play. This arrangement is especially useful to develop skill in sensitivity to the feelings of others by providing the chance to the *alter ego* to view the differences in the perception of feelings by the role player and *alter ego*. There are many advantages in Single Group Role Playing. First, it helps in the training of observation, as all the persons present in the role play contribute to the observation of the session in progress. The various aspects of the role-play session are observed by different persons. Second, it helps in training in the analysis of behavior. Various observers present in the group try to find out the

---

[1a] N. R. F. Maier, A. R. Solem, and A. A. Maier, *Supervisory and Executive Development, a Manual for Role Playing* (New York: John Wiley & Sons, Inc., 1957).

reasons of things said and done and the dynamics behind the behavior of the different roles.

Third, the advantages of feedback are effectively available to the role players, and this helps in developing their insight into the behavior they have been role playing. The feedback is more effective since it comes from various observers. And lastly, there is better training in sensivity to feelings. This is specially so when an *alter ego* is used for the role-play situation.

Multiple Role Playing

When the purpose of role playing is to involve all the persons present in the group, the Multiple Role Playing procedure[2] can be adopted. In this procedure the audience is formed into convenient role-playing groups and the various groups role-play simultaneously. A good procedure to divide the audience into groups is to have two or three persons sitting in the odd rows turn and face two or three others in the even rows, which would make small groups. Written instructions are distributed, and the various small groups start role playing on the same problem. After a specified time the role play is terminated and discussion is begun. It is always useful to have process observers in every smaller group.

The method of Multiple Role Playing has its own advantages. First, every member in the group gets practice in role playing. Second, the solutions arrived at by different groups can be discussed and compared with one another and useful conclusions can be drawn. Third, Multiple Role Playing is good for studying the process of group interaction. When process observers are working with the various groups, their report of the interaction processes are very helpful in developing insight in the participants. Although the same roles are being played by the various groups, the differences due to personality and group factors produce differences in approach.

Audience Role Playing

In this procedure[3] the audience is made sensitive through the use of a specially prepared situation and then is required to react to a change in

---

[2] N. R. F. Maier and L. F. Zerfoss, "MRP: A Technique for Training Large Groups of Supervisors and its Potential Use in Social Research," *Human Relations,* Vol. V (1952), pp. 177–86.

[3] N. R. F. Maier and A. R. Solem, "Audience Role-Playing: A New Method in Human Relations Training," *Human Relations,* Vol. IV (1951), pp. 279–94.

the situation. Some details of a situation are read before the audience so that it is attuned to a particular emotional attitude. Later on new experiences are introduced and the actions of the members of the group are noted through specially prepared forms. The behavioral changes are measured in an artificial situation of attitude change. This kind of role playing is useful in finding out effective ways of changing attitudes.

Skit Completion Method

The procedures of role playing discussed above can be used in a variety of ways. It may sometimes be necessary to gear role-play sessions directly to the conflict problem. For this purpose it may be necessary to cut out preliminary parts of the role play and to introduce the problem direct for the purpose of role playing. To accomplish this, a skit is often presented before the audience, and the audience is required to observe it. When the point of problem conflict is reached, it is left and the role-play session starts. The Skit Completion Method[4] is meant to carry developments to a specific conflict area, which becomes the starting point for role playing.

Dramatized Case Method

A similar procedure is to present a dramatized version on the basis of written dialogues of a situation and then to introduce the role playing at the point where conflict reaches a climax.[5]

Various other changes have been made in the procedures of role play to suit specific purposes. Hendry[6] introduced the idea of complacency shock by debunking his own lecture method and introducing the problem for the role playing. Zander[7] introduced what he called an "Inter-awareness" discussion panel in which the panel discussion procedure was adopted after giving a detailed and specific statement of the problem to the panel and asking the members to assume specific roles during the panel meeting. A clarifier was required to interpret the process and the progress of the discussion to the audience. Other variations have been introduced by different workers in group dynamics and human

---

[4] Maier, Solem, and Maier, *op. cit.*

[5] N. R. F. Maier, "Dramatized Case Material as a Spring Board for Role Playing," *Group Psychotherapy,* Vol. VI (1953), pp. 30–42.

[6] Maier, Solem, and Maier, *op. cit.*

[7] Alwin Zander, "The Interaction-Awareness Discussion Panel," *Journal of Social Psychology,* Vol. XIX (1944), pp. 369–75.

relations training. The idea and basic process of role playing can be tailored to the needs of specific groups.

Reading 5.2

WHAT IS LABORATORY TRAINING?*

Edgar H. Schein and Warren G. Bennis

By giving a bird's-eye view of laboratory training, we hope to highlight and exemplify the differences in assumptions and methods between the laboratory approach and more traditional educational activities. We will use primarily a chronological approach.

Orientation to the Laboratory

Participants in a laboratory, such as the one we will describe, come from various business and industrial organizations. Some have volunteered for the experience while others have been sent by their superiors or at the recommendation of the training department. For most participants, hereafter called "delegates," the total learning experience begins long before the actual laboratory. They have read brochures and articles about laboratory training, have talked with others who have attended, and have been oriented by supervisors or members of the training department staff in the organization in which they work. These contacts build up expectations of what the laboratory will be like, which in turn influence how the delegate approaches and reacts to the actual laboratory activities.

Because of great differences in initial orientation, we find delegates arriving at laboratories with a whole gamut of initial feelings—at one extreme, eager anticipation based on genuine volunteering; at the other, great apprehension and a feeling of having been punished because of "having been sent" without fully understanding why. Most delegates are also puzzled at the outset by the vague and unsatisfactory answers to the question of what the laboratory will be about that they have obtained from acquaintances who have attended laboratories. Some will be

* From Edgar H. Schein and Warren G. Bennis, *Personal and Organizational Change through Group Methods* (New York: John Wiley & Sons, Inc., 1965), pp. 10–27.

frightened; others will respond to this vagueness by being intrigued; all will share a certain amount of uncertainty as they arrive at the conference center.

The great variety of initial feelings and universally felt uncertainty can be directly related to the fact that laboratory training has no cultural counterpart. It is not exactly like school; it is clearly different from psychotherapy; and it shares little with other kinds of training activities. The delegate thus has to form stereotypes on minimum information and is vulnerable to whatever anxieties tend to be aroused by any situation alleged to be interpersonally potent.

Arrival at the "Cultural Island"

Most laboratories are held somewhere away from the pressures of day-to-day.

This newness, the uncertainty, and the apprehension all work toward a situation in which the delegate arrives at his first orientation session busy trying to get acclimatized and to get control of his own feelings of tension and uncertainty.

First Session

The orientation session deals with matters of housekeeping (dining room hours, recreation facilities, how to get laundry done, and so forth), provides an opportunity to introduce the staff of the laboratory, and states in brief form the goals of the laboratory and the kinds of learning activities which hopefully will enable the delegates to achieve these goals.

For example, in a typical introduction, the "dean" of the laboratory or some other staff member points out that the goals of the laboratory are to create opportunities for the delegates to learn about the following kinds of things:

1. Self. The delegates' own behavior in groups and the impact which their behavior has on other members.
2. Others. The behavior of others in a group and the impact which their behavior has on them.
3. Groups. How groups work; what makes them function.
4. Larger systems. How organizations and larger social systems work.
5. The learning process. How to learn from their own experience ("learning how to learn").

These are deceptively simple goals and are in general only vaguely understood when first outlined. The speaker points out that it is easier to explain the method after the delegates have had some experience in the laboratory.

From the delegate's point of view, the initial orientation session may be more meaningful as an emotional introduction to the staff and laboratory than it is in its actual content. Whether or not he is aware of it, the delegate is more likely to be paying attention to how the speaker

Table 1

TYPICAL SCHEDULE FOR THE WEEK

	Sun.	Mon.	Tues.	Wed.	Thurs.	Fri.
9:00–11:00		T-group	T-group	T-group	T-group	T-group
11:00–11:30		Coffee break	Coffee break	Coffee break	Coffee break	Coffee break
11:30–12:30		General session	General session	General session	General session	General session
12:30– 1:30		Lunch	Lunch	Lunch	Lunch	Lunch
1:30– 3:30		T-group	T-group	T-group	T-group	T-group
3:30– 6:00	Opening session	Free time	Free time	Free time	Free time	Free time
6:00– 7:30		Dinner	Dinner	Dinner	Dinner	Dinner
7:30– 9:30	T-group	T-group	Tape listening exercise	Free	Exercise or training film	Free

looks and sounds than to what he says. The kinds of feelings which the speaker arouses in him—tension, anticipation, reassurance, hostility, confusion, or whatever—will make it hard for him to listen attentively and to comprehend. Recognition of this fact has led most laboratory staff to plan introductory sessions which are as short as possible reserving further explanation for sessions which follow the initial meetings of the training group.

The schedule which is given to the delegate will indicate the major training activities of the laboratory:

1. *T-groups.* These are basic learning groups which continue to meet throughout the course of the laboratory. They usually contain 10 to 15 members with one or two staff members or "trainers." T-groups are generally "unstructured," in the sense that the staff provides a minimum of agenda and formal leadership.

2. *Information or theory sessions.* These are general sessions during which a staff member lectures and/or gives a demonstration to impart some concepts or ideas or research findings about an area relevant to the laboratory goals.

3. *Focused exercises.* These are activities which may involve small or large groups. They are usually introduced by a staff member who describes the learning goals and the specific activities, such as role-playing or group observation, which are to be engaged in by the delegates.

4. *Other activities.* Most laboratories involve seminars, two-man interview groups (dyads), informal bull sessions, and other activities which may be introduced during its course. Some of these will be described below in our chronicle. They are usually not included on the delegate's regular schedule because of their informal or optional status.

THE T-GROUP

The T-group is, for most delegates, the major emotional focus of their laboratory experience. Finding out who the other members of their group are, including the staff member, becomes one of the first anchors around which the delegates organize their experience. This anchor takes on additional importance as the delegate discovers the unstructured nature of the T-group.

When the group has settled down, the staff member gives a short introduction, usually lasting less than five minutes, in which he restates some of the learning goals. He points out that the T-group's primary task is to create learning opportunities for its members, and that it has no formal leader, preset agenda, or rules by which it must operate. It is up to the whole group, including the staff member, to decide what to do and how best to learn from its experience.

Whether he emphasizes it in the introduction or later, the trainer makes it clear that it is legitimate and likely to be profitable for the group to try to learn from its own experienced behavior—the "here-and-now" situation—rather than to discuss problems outside the group, from the world they left, the "there-and-then" world. The tape-recorder, which will be running at all times unless the group decides to turn it off, is available as a learning aid to enable the group to recapitulate and study some of its earlier experiences. The tapes are the property of the group and are erased at the end of the laboratory. If the staff member comments on his own role at all, he is likely to state that he does not perceive himself to be the chairman or leader of the group, but rather a person who will help the learning process of the group in whatever way he can.[1]

When the trainer finishes his introduction, the group is suddenly left to its own resources. It is difficult to describe the full emotional impact of the beginning minutes of a T-group because the members are struggling with so many emotional issues at once. They are confronted with a violation of many expectations they have taken for granted in educational settings, most of all that the trainer will define an agenda, some ground rules and some goals which are meaningful for the group. Instead, each member confronts some major problems—"What do we do and what are our goals?" "Who am I to be in this unstructured situation and what kind of role should I play?" "How can I keep sufficient control over the group to prevent it from doing things which will make me too uncomfortable?"

In coping with these problems, different members use different strategies. Some ask further questions of the trainer; some try to get him to be more of a leader or guide; some lapse into an anxious watchful silence; some get angry; and some attempt to organize the group with various tasks like "introducing ourselves." As the members fill the vacuum with their behavior, they begin to generate the raw data from which they will have the opportunity to learn about themselves, their impact on others, others' reactions to them, and how groups work.

How the T-group goes about its business of creating learning opportunities during the first and subsequent sessions is hard to characterize because each group has its own unique history. It has its own particular combination of people; its own particular trainer with his own theory of learning and style of intervention; its unforeseen incidents, dilemmas, and crises. It creates, for each member, a unique set of emotional and intellectual experiences.

T-groups do have in common the kinds of issues or dilemmas which have to be resolved in the process of building a group and learning from this procedure—what to do, how to spend the time, how to distribute power, control and influence, how to develop group standards and a climate which permits maximum learning, how to develop group goals and a sense of group progress, how to keep the group process within

---

[1] We have had to qualify so often this description of what the staff member does because of the huge variation among trainers in how they open the T-group and the kind of role they make for themselves.

bounds. It is the particular solutions to such dilemmas which make each group unique.

A Digression: The Learning Process in the T-Group

What does the delegate begin to learn from the unstructured group experience? In what manner does he first discover for himself the meaning of the laboratory method of learning? For some delegates, learning begins immediately with the opportunity to study their own reactions to this novel experience, and to compare their reactions with those of others. For other delegates, the learning process does not begin until they become involved in some incident in the life of the T-group in which they are confronted with unexpected feelings on the part of others, either in reaction to their own behavior or to the behavior of others. Both kinds of delegates gain an increased awareness of their own feelings and the feelings of others. What is this increased awareness about?

For many delegates, the learning process first focuses around the problem of communication. While most delegates admit at the outset that they are not as good listeners as it might be hoped, rarely do they realize how little listening they or anyone else in the group does during the early sessions. The discovery that they missed many things altogether and that various group members heard the same speaker say entirely different things is shocking and thought provoking. They become more aware of the complexity of the communication process.

For some delegates, the problem of communication is not as salient as the problem of structure and organization in the group. Those who wish to get the group organized often find themselves confronted by others who are comfortable in an unstructured setting and vice versa. An important first learning step for this group is the awareness and acceptance of genuine differences in member needs, goals, and ways of approaching problems.

Another kind of learning which occurs results from a group member getting reactions from others in areas about which he is relatively blind. The person who leaps into the early power vacuum of the group with the sincere motive of getting the group moving may discover that a number of other members perceived him as attempting to dominate and control the group. The silent member may discover that he communicates more of his feelings through his silence than he realizes, and that for many members his behavior is a subtle but powerful way of controlling the group. The person who tries to help by giving reactions to others whenever the impulse moves him may discover that others do not find his "feedback" helpful, either because it is too evaluative, too ill-timed, or too hostile in undertone. The person who hides his own feelings by being constantly analytical about what the group is doing may discover that several members view his behavior as a real barrier to group progress instead of an aid. For all of these delegates, the crucial learning process is increased awareness of their own impact on others which enables them to check the assumptions they have made about themselves.

Some delegates focus their learning effort on the level of group process. They discover that group decisions are tricky things to observe and to manage intelligently. Sometimes a minority pushes the group into action because each of the silent members erroneously assumes that the silence of the others means consent. Sometimes the group votes and then acts on majority rule only to discover that the minority is effectively able to block the action. The group may elect or appoint a chairman only to discover that he is unable to control the vicissitudes of the meeting because the same members who were willing to have him be chairman discover that they are unwilling to have him exercise any kind of control. Sometimes the group sets up an agenda only to discover that the agenda tyrannizes the group and prevents it from doing what it really wants to do. Yet, no one knows how to undo the group decision, particularly if it was hard won in the first place. Increased awareness of how groups function and the consequences of certain kinds of group action are the learning result.

Usually these discoveries result from an emotionally taxing reconstruction of some of the earlier events in the group's life. In the process of making such a reconstruction, members learn how to be better observers of group action, learn what sorts of observation other members have made, and learn what sorts of reaction have been aroused by various incidents in the group's history. Almost in spite of themselves group members become more observant, more analytical, and more cautious in making assumptions about group behavior. They are, in this sense, learning how to learn from their own experience.

Out of increased awareness in all these areas comes the possibility of changed attitudes. The delegate develops new attitudes toward the learning process, toward himself, toward others, and toward groups. Out of such attitude changes will come new behavior and greater competence in dealing with others. The major learning outcomes, therefore, will be increased awareness, changed attitudes, and greater interpersonal competence.

THEORY SESSIONS

It is a basic assumption of laboratory training that experience must precede the introduction of a theoretical concept. Equally important is the assumption that raw experience without some degree of intellectual understanding is insufficient to produce learning which is useful and can be generalized. The delegate must be able to fit his experience into a framework of concepts and ideas which will allow him to relate to situations and persons other than in the laboratory.

In order to optimize learning, delegates attend daily information or theory sessions. The content of these sessions is designed to help them understand the experiences they are having in the T-group by focusing on topics such as the following: what to observe in a group, emotional problems of becoming a member of a new group, decision making and problem solving in groups, the communication process, styles of emotional expression and presentation of self to others.

In designing the content of theory sessions, the staff draws on its general knowledge of what issues the T-groups are likely to be facing at any given time and how these relate to other laboratory and back-home realities. In many instances, however, they will introduce new topics on short notice if it appears that several groups are facing some new issue which was not going to be dealt with. This requires close coordination among staff members and a sharing of what they perceive to be happening in their T-groups from day to day.

During the second week, the emphasis in theory sessions usually shifts somewhat from T-group issues to issues which arise in social systems, organizations, and communities. More attention is given to the occupational role which the delegate plays, to problems of authority and delegation, theories of management and organization, the consequences of collaboration or competition, and the like.

FOCUSED EXERCISES

The purpose of focused exercises is to generate some specific behavior so that a particular area can be studied (e.g., the communication process), or to practice some skill which is important for further learning (e.g., how to observe group action). An example of the former is an experiment highlighting the differences between one- and two-way communication. A delegate is asked to give some complex instructions to a group under two kinds of conditions: one-way communication, defined by the ground rule that the group is not allowed to ask any questions during the instructions, and two-way communication, defined by the ground rule that the group may say anything during the instructions. The one-way and two-way conditions can then be compared in terms of accuracy of communication, length of time taken, feelings of the sender and the receivers, and so forth.

An exercise such as any of these involves practice in several kinds of activities: actually observing others while remaining silent, analyzing observations and reconciling differences between observers, deciding what observations to report back to the group in order to be helpful, and the actual process of giving the feedback in such a way as to maximize learning opportunities.

Toward the end of the first week or beginning of the second week, a more complicated and extensive exercise may be introduced. One frequently used exercise is on intergroup competition. Two or three T-groups are each given instructions to produce some product—a one- or two-page paper on some relevant topic—which is evaluated by a panel of judges consisting of members drawn from the competing groups. In the free time after the work period, one typically sees the groups clustered in separate parts of the conference center reviewing how they worked, expressing confidence in their own product, and generally derogating (though in a joking manner) the other groups. The following morning, the groups meet to look at their own product and that of the other groups.

In line with the general assumption that for maximum learning the experiences which the groups have had must be analyzed and put into a framework, the final portion of the exercise is devoted to an hour or more of systematic recapitulation supported by the results of the questionnaires which had been administered at various points during the total exercise.

In this type of exercise, an attempt is made to simulate the realities of organizations and social systems. The exercise highlights for delegates the positive and negative consequences of intergroup competition, what it feels like to be a winner or a loser, a judge or a group representative. The exercise also begins to refocus the delegate on his back-home situation.

THE SECOND WEEK

The main task of the first week is entry into the laboratory culture. Re-entry into the back-home world is the primary task of the second week. During this week, the increasing attention on back-home problems is manifested in a variety of ways. Sometimes groups are brought together with the task of discussing how they might apply some of their new knowledge to the back-home situation. Or, meetings of groups are held at which members take turns discussing some particular back-home problem they have, while the other members attempt, through interviewing and careful diagnosis, to give help to each other on the problem. The real benefit of this kind of activity is to give the helpers practice in the art of giving help. If the problem presenter gains new insight into his back-home situation, this is a secondary gain. In some laboratory designs, a new set of groups is started with the purpose of giving every member the experience of making a transition from one group to another. The problems of re-entry into the back-home groups can then be assessed in the light of the transitional experience within the laboratory.

OUTCOMES OF THE LABORATORY

As the laboratory draws to a close, a variety of reactions among the delegates is noticed. There are those for whom the opportunity to concentrate on themselves and their own problems has been so meaningful and so realizing that they are genuinely reluctant to see the experience end. They feel that they have become better acquainted with themselves. They may not be sure how this will affect them on the job or at home, but they are sure that the experience has been very worthwhile.

There are others who feel they have had a revelation as to what makes other people and groups work. They have had the opportunity, for the first time perhaps, to study the reactions of others and to observe how a group must struggle with the diversity of its human resources. Sometimes such insights lead to sharply changed attitudes toward groups and group action. Outright hostility toward any form of committee often changes into a more sensitive understanding of groups, and into recognition that groups can only be effective if allowed to mature and work through their initial problems.

There are some delegates for whom the most meaningful experience has been that they have been accepted and liked by the other group members. They go back home with a renewed sense of confidence in themselves. There are others for whom the experience has been primarily disturbing because they may have discovered that they were not as persuasive, clever, or powerful as they had assumed. They will go home with more questions about themselves than they had brought, and many of these questions will remain unanswered for some time after the laboratory.

Still others will see in the laboratory some gimmicks and devices for use in back-home groups, and will attempt to utilize these in spite of entreaties from staff not to take the laboratory method as a model of how to run a work group or a business. For some of these "alumni," the gimmicks will fail; they may then turn against the laboratory method feeling it to be a fraud, without recognizing their own misuse of the method.

Some delegates will cherish the fact that the laboratory provided a two-week period during which they could leave behind their work and family and ruminate about basic issues of life. For them, it offered a retreat and an opportunity to revitalize themselves. Some delegates will find that among their fellow T-group members, roommates, or other contacts, they can now count several close friends with whom they will maintain a relationship in the future. Some of these friendships may be more intimate than any they have in their back-home situation.

Some delegates will suffer intensely during the entire laboratory period because, from their point of view, very little was actually accomplished; they will go home puzzled, confused, and still skeptical.

All delegates, whether they are aware of it or not, go home with greater skills as group observers and diagnosticians, and with greater sensitivity to the complexity of interpersonal relationships. Whether they utilize this increased sensitivity constructively or not depends upon them, but there is little doubt that they have acquired it. All delegates become familiar with a new approach to learning—utilizing their own experience and learning from it. All delegates finally understand why it was so difficult for others to tell them what the laboratory would be about. As they think back over their own experiences, they realize how personal and unique these have been and how difficult it will be to tell others what has transpired.

Reading 5.3

THE CASE METHOD*

Harriet Ronken Lynton and Rolf P. Lynton

The teaching of cases is one of many attempts to get more of real life into classrooms and training programs. Ideally, cases confront the member of the discussion group with situations which faced someone like himself somewhere, sometime. They present a chunk of somebody's real life, but not of the member's own life during training. As pieces of real life[1] they are full of people, not of abstractions, and too complex to be fitted into neat categories, generalizations, and other intellectual equipment. As somebody else's experience, a case can help the member explore his own attitudes and behavior as if by personal analogy, at moments when direct attention to his own experiences would provoke only fear and defence, not learning. Doing it by analogy instead of for himself in the commitments of real life increases his freedom to explore more of the ins and outs of a problem which he might otherwise ignore, and to go beyond his habitual response into an exploration of second and third thoughts instead of settling for the first. This close but not insistently personal quality also allows some concepts to be explored and understood in case sessions which will help in understanding personal experiences.

Degrees of Identification

The place of cases in an educational program, the choice and sequence of cases, and the emphasis the instructor can give in the discussion of them, all revolve around the degree to which members identify themselves with the people in the case. The ideal can be formulated readily enough: The greatest values are gained if a member can identify with one or more persons in the case but not so closely that he himself ceases to be a different person.

For working directly with member's attitudes, there are better ways

---

* Abridged from Introduction, *Asican Cases* (Mysore, India: Aloka Centre for Advanced Study and Training, 1960).

[1] Only names and identifying characteristics have been disguised.

than teaching cases. Cases are not even particularly good projective devices, though they certainly need some of this quality for effective use. Ideally, they serve primarily in helping members conceive that there may be several ways of looking at, thinking about, and acting in an identical situation, to wonder which they might choose if they had themselves been in it, to ask more effective questions of the data life throws up to them, and to go on to learn some generalizations and concepts from this study of field data. Without a limited identification there would be no learning. Without the remaining difference and distance there would be no systematic thought and understanding.

Stating the ideal is one thing; achieving it is another. The line between too much and too little identification is in practice very difficult to draw. Medicine, law, and social work, the disciplines in which teaching of cases has the longest tradition, have sought to limit identification and maintain the focus on the subject matter by abstracting the client into a conglomeration of standard symptoms: these conglomerations of symptoms, not the patient, the accused, or the substandard family, *become* "the cases" and pose "the problem." The person recedes into the background; the problem occupies the attention.

This emphasis looks promising whenever cases are thought of primarily as vehicles for teaching subject matter rather than as analogies through whose examination and diagnosis members can review their own experiences. It is then only one step further for the instructor to conceive of his task as teaching the subject he knows, be it medicine, law, production control, public administration, finance, labor relations, or any of the other fields of personal subjects like human relations, counseling, education itself, which have not escaped this comfortable misconception which finally treats hearing and talking about as synonymous with learning.

One weakness of this approach has attracted more attention than any other: When the student moves from the classroom into actual practice, his orientation puts the locus of change away from the person who is supposed to be most immediately affected. That person then often cooperates, if he does so at all, only clumsily or halfheartedly in carrying out the expert's solution to his problem. Doctors, lawyers, social workers, and teachers may get satisfaction from taking decisions of this kind, but the decisions remain stillborn. At present these specialists are being urged, with increasing impatience, to treat the patient not the disease, the criminal not the crime, the particular poor family on X street not poverty, the learning child and adult not the subject in the abstract. But these urgings may be equally stillborn. For at the personal level, the focus on subject matter by abstracting the people in the case, while surely not for the learner's benefit, still promises much needed immediate comfort and other satisfactions to the doctor, lawyer, social worker, and teacher.

The other kind of cases limit identification and invite attention to their subject matter of human relations in the opposite direction to abstraction: They include a lot of personal details as the person in the case sees them. They therefore lend themselves to learning the complex and manifoldly determined makeup of a "point of view" and "the concept a person has of himself"; to the study and understanding of personal feelings and how they can be seen to affect the behavior of a person; situations of rivalry and social change as they in fact come up to real people in real life, just as illogical and incomplete as it usually is. A member can see himself as *like* Mr. X in the case in many ways, and this may prompt him to reflect about himself. But with so many detailed differences and a different totality he will not see himself *as* Mr. X in disguise. He can learn from Mr. X without becoming him.

Our preference for this kind of case is related not only to the way we believe people learn but also to what we feel is most important for people to learn, at least at this time. The abstraction in the other kinds of cases emphasizes what human affairs have in common, the convergent phenomena, where capacities for development are straining fearfully at every resource, and most basic of all at the people themselves and the communities in which they live. . . . The crying need is for the pioneer, the person who can conceive of diverging from his own and go on, both to take the initiative and then to maintain the new element in his society. But this pioneer must be as much a bridge as an innovator, for, barring the occasional prophet, he can be effective only when he does not break so completely with the traditional society that he no longer has any relationships there.

This social innovator, this pioneer, is caught in his own feelings in the first place. These we work with directly . . . , in study groups and other interpretive sessions as well as in field work. What we expect a member to gain from the cases is a systematic way of thinking about people, including himself, and the assurance that, though the emotional and other demands of change are quite personal to himself, others go through the same kind of throes and are in that sense his kin.

Which Case, and When?

The situations which leaders, administrators, and trainers have to understand and handle are infinitely varied. Moreover, people gain their insights and their understanding of such situations along different routes and at different speeds. Therefore a case which is suitable at some particular stage for one training group may not be suitable for another at the same stage. Ideally, the instructor would have available several cases suitable for the particular stage the training group has reached from which to select the most promising. These cases would be of recent date and present situations of the kind which members of the group might be expected to meet somewhat in the way they come up in the cases.

To guide him in selecting the right case at the right moment, the instructor needs an increasingly intimate understanding of his group, for it is primarily the members that he is teaching and not primarily the case.

The Instructor

Gauging the proper time and way to draw the members' attention now to their own experiences, now to other people's, is the instructor's most difficult task. He cannot escape it if he thinks of himself as someone who helps people to develop themselves, to change their attitudes and their behavior. Both the personal referent and the learning from the experiences of others are valuable. . . . The experiences of other people are most prominent in the case discussions, where the instructor may even discourage references to personal experiences if they threaten to drain off the tensions that belong properly in the study groups and can be better handled directly there.

From minute to minute the instructor is concerned with helping to make the work meaningful to the members. It must be stimulating, personal, disturbing but not so much so that the members freeze. The instructor's task is to help them look instead of state; understand instead of overthink; listen to other people's feelings instead of to the din of their own. What is at stake is learning that is made up of personal growth. So even when he brings in teaching material outside the group's own experience, the instructor still focuses first on the members, not on the cases. What will be most useful now, is the question which persistently occupies his mind.

Reading 5.4

PROGRAMED INSTRUCTION*

H. Oliver Holt

"Teaching machine," "programed textbook," "programed learning" —names which have caught the public fancy (or opposition) in recent years—all describe a new and exciting teaching method. To people concerned with industrial training it is becoming especially important. "Teaching machine" was the term used by Prof. B. F. Skinner when he first introduced the notion in 1954. Later, the term "programed text," which emphasized the importance of the instructional program *per se,* was used. Today the method is variously termed "programed instruction," "programed learning," "automated teaching," etc. I prefer the term "programed self-instruction"; it is more descriptive of the instructive materials and of the way in which they are used.

But whatever term we use, it is subject of great interest and considerable study in the Bell System. This interest stems in large measure from the System's growing need for highly proficient people to keep pace with modern technology. On a System-wide basis, the training job is not only massive in terms of the number of people involved but expensive. For example, in the Operating Companies, some $75 million is spent annually on the loaded salaries of non-management employees undergoing *formal* (i.e. classroom) training. The *total* cost, including *informal* on-the-job training materials and course preparation, classroom space, utilities, equipment and supplies, etc., runs a great deal higher. No wonder then that it is important for us to assess carefully something as promising in terms of greater training efficiency as programed self-instruction.

By now a good bit of evidence is in, and we are able to list several advantages and limitations of the method. But first, here is a brief summary of its characteristics.

Four characteristics are typical:

Small steps—The subject matter is broken down into a large number of small steps organized into an instructional sequence. The student masters these steps one at a time.

* Abridged from H. Oliver Holt, "Programed Self-instruction," *Bell Telephone Magazine,* 1963 (Spring).

Continued responding—As he works through the program the learner responds to each step and in most cases either fills in blanks with missing words or makes a choice among given alternatives.

Immediate knowledge of results—Programed books and teaching machines are designed so that the learner can turn a page, move a slide or turn a knob and know immediately whether the response he has just made is correct.

Self-pacing—Each learner works with his own book or machine and works through the program at his own pace. As a result of this, the teaching environment is quite different from the usual classroom situation.

Most programs are now appearing in programed text or book form. But several are employing audio tape recordings, visual projection and combinations of various media, too. It is unrealistic, therefore, to look upon present materials as representing final developments in the field.

SOME ADVANTAGES

There are several important interacting advantages of programed instruction.

First of all, there are a number of benefits which can result from the self-pacing characteristic and from the fact that learning from self-instruction programs occurs individually rather than by groups. To consider self-pacing first: several factors probably combine to determine each individual's pace. Since most programs are verbal, reading speed is certainly an important factor. Also, the extent to which the learner has prior knowledge of the subject being taught contributes to his speed. Although some studies of programed instruction have reported a correlation between the learners' IQ and the total amount of time spent on the program, these correlations are far from perfect, indicating that other factors are operating. Whatever the causes, individual speeds become apparent in the first few minutes after a group has started a program together. Bell System trainees working on programs have exhibited an interesting consistency in extremes of speed. The slowest learner takes about twice as long as the fastest. This ratio is found in many other similar industrial programs.

How does this speed variation offer advantages over the traditional method of group-paced teaching?

One advantage is the flexibility this allows both the learner and the course administrator. Individuals often can work through programs in their own offices, thus accomplishing two things: they save travel and living expenses which would be necessary if they went away to school; they can work on their program part-time without total disruption of their jobs. In the Bell System these advantages have been demonstrated by hundreds of salesmen who have learned about a new service and a new product by working through self-instruction programs in their own offices.

In addition, some Plant Department schools have found it advantageous to suspend rigid scheduling of their basic electricity courses since the use of programed textbooks has been introduced. Each trainee now stays in school only as long as it takes him to demonstrate his proficiency in the subject matter. He then goes back to his job immediately without waiting for the rest of the group. In addition, since students do not learn together there is no need for them to begin together. Therefore a school may, for example, offer basic electricity from October 1 to May 1 rather than list a series of class starting dates, say two weeks apart. Such an arrangement allows managers more flexibility in assigning men to a school.

Self-pacing and individual learning also constitute major reasons given by trainees for preferring programed self-instruction to more conventional methods. It offers advantages to both slow and fast learners. Slow learners, who may drop farther and farther behind in the conventional class, have the extra time they need to grasp the elements of the subject. Faster students, often bored or even frustrated by the slow pace of typical group instruction, retain their interest by progressing quickly through the material in the course. With the self-instruction method, such people are free to "burn up the course," finishing well ahead of slower fellow students. In brief, self-instruction programs help solve an age-old problem of instruction: allowing for individual differences.

UNIFORM QUALITY

There are several advantages of programed self-instruction which fall under the category of "quality control." First, let us consider what happens under conventional lecture-discussion conditions. Any time that a particular course is taught by more than one instructor it is almost certain that there will be significant differences in content. It is difficult, too, for an instructor to maintain consistency in a course as he teaches successive classes. In fact, it usually is erroneous to assume that a lecture-type course as a stable entity exists. What *does* exist is an instructor's outline. It is the instructor himself who is responsible for translating the outline into detailed teaching sequences and these sequences necessarily are highly individualized interpretations. Thus, there can be no assurance that one is getting a high quality product across several lecture-discussion classes.

The situation is quite different with a properly developed self-instruction program. In the first place, the standard procedure for producing a high quality product is to "cut and try" a program throughout its development. Specifically, this means that it is subjected to empirical trials on sample groups of the trainees for which it is intended. It is tested

Figure 1
PERFORMANCE IN LECTURE DISCUSSION AND PRO-GRAMED INSTRUCTION GROUPS

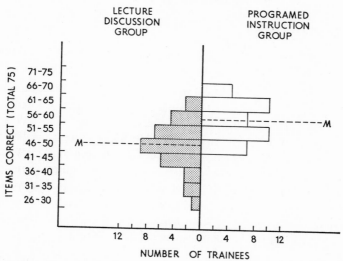

and revised as many times as necessary to make it meet training objectives. The final product, then, not only has been demonstrated to be effective, but remains constant. That is, all students who take a particular programed course take the *same* course. Thus the instructional product can be expected to be much more uniform than the lecture-discussion product even though different groups of trainees work through the program in widely separated locations.

Evidence of one type of quality is offered by several research studies. These studies report a higher homogeneity of final examination scores than is the case with conventional instruction. That is, scores are clustered toward the high end of the scale and there are few if any failing students. (See Fig. 1)

Popular articles about programed study often promise spectacular savings in time. Certainly there are many occasions when a great deal of time is saved, but these do not by any means always occur. A programed course may, in fact, take as much time or more than its conventional counterpart. For example, in an experimental study conducted by the Bell Laboratories, a self-instruction course was written so that its content matched that of a concurrent lecture-demonstration course in basic electricity. Several classes in each method were compared. Although average proficiency of the self-instruction group was significantly higher than that of the lecture-discussion group, the average time taken by the two groups was practically the same. Since the purpose of industrial training is to meet objectives directly relating to job requirements, the emphasis must be on assuring that the objectives are complete, specific and accurate, and that the training meets those objectives efficiently—rather than on time savings.

SOME LIMITATIONS

While programed instruction has substantial advantages, it also has several limitations which must be considered:

An appropriate program is hard to find. There are many programs on the market, but they are primarily academically, not industrially, oriented.

A good program—one that does an efficient teaching job—is difficult to identify. At present it is necessary to rely on try-outs under controlled conditions to assess the quality of programs—a costly and time-consuming process.

Program writing is also time-consuming and often requires the efforts of several people to produce an extensive program. While opinions vary as to exactly what kind of team is required to produce a good program, our opinion is that it takes four kinds of knowledge and skill: program development methods, knowledge of the subject matter, frame writing, and technical and copy editing.

Good programs are expensive. There are various ways of estimating the cost of preparing self-instruction programs, and costs vary widely. Programs prepared under contract generally have cost from $1,000 to $1,500 per instructional hour—or from $40,000 to $60,000 for a one-week (40-hour) program.

A good program which teaches efficiently may be irrelevant to the job being taught. This hazard is not peculiar to programed instruction, but it is sufficiently important to deserve emphasis whenever training is considered. Programed teaching is a *way* of teaching. If our objectives are erroneous, we may do a beautiful job of teaching—the wrong thing.

There are several other conditions which might limit the use of this method. For example: when the subject matter is so unstable that continual expensive revisions would be necessary; when there are so few students that the expense of a program may not be justified; when the self-pacing characteristic cannot be exploited and may, in fact, be detrimental.

Chapter 6

Designing the Program

> "The accent must be on auto-regulation, on active assimilation—the accent must be on the activity of the subject. Failing this there is no possible didactic or pedagogy which significantly transforms the subject."
>
> —JEAN PIAGET

BY NOW THE training institution is clear about the strategies and methods it can employ, given the faculty and the facilities available. The work organization, for its part, is clear about the contribution training can make to the changes to be effected. It has both an overall picture of its training needs and an understanding of the specific training needs of the different kinds and levels of staff involved in the changes. This clarification of training needs has been hard, painstaking, and often slow work. But clear definitions of needs now mean clear training objectives. And clear training objectives in turn make for clear evaluation of the effectiveness of training. So if skimping there had to be, this was not the place for it.

The organization has gone further and shared out the work of meeting the training needs among various training resources available—senior personnel, its own training department, outside training institutions. For any of them, their particular share of training needs have become the training objectives. For instance, the training objective of a branch manager has been defined as grooming at least two department managers for promotion within 12 months. One objective of the training department during the same year is to make 20 cashiers proficient in operating new accounting equipment and another 20 in general sales-work, all prior to installing some new equipment. Meanwhile, the objective of a particular outside training institution is to help to develop 15 departmental managers on the way to promotion from all over the organization; for this they need to gain an understanding of the whole range of general management functions at branch level, and additional skill in staff management without day-to-day supervision. On these objectives, however adequately they are now defined, each agency now brings to bear its resources, and designs a program that holds the greatest promise.

FIVE STEPS IN PROGRAM DESIGN

Five steps are involved in designing the training program. The orderly step-by-step description of them makes them appear mechanical, some kind of mathematical extrapolations. We will lay this stress here on good order and counting but in full knowledge that a high level of creative and tentative work is in fact involved.

1. The first step is to choose a strategy or, usually, a combination of strategies. The strategies in turn favor certain tools in the kit of training methods.

> For instance, the outside institution has been charged with helping 15 departmental managers gain (1) an understanding of general management functions at branch level, and (2) increased skills in independent staff management. The first objective suggests giving weight to activity and organization-development strategies, that is, priority attention to job content and organizational processes. The second objective, to gain skill in independent staff management, suggests combining laboratory and person-development strategies, as they pay the greatest attention to the processes of getting things accomplished on the job and to the conceptual understanding of these processes.
>
> The training methods generally favored by these strategies are simulation and case methods. Field training may be added for working on activity and organization-development strategies, and laboratory methods.

2. The second step is to break the general training objectives into constituent parts. The first rough breakdown is into component knowledge, understanding, and skill.

> The first objective, understanding general management functions, is heaviest on knowledge and understanding and lightest on skill. The second objective, better staff management is heaviest on skill, lighter on understanding; the department managers who come for training already possess or have access to the *knowledge* about staff management that they need.

The initial breakdown of training objectives into knowledge, understanding and skill is not difficult. The more taxing task is to match these components with appropriate training methods, to arrive at estimates of numbers of sessions and other events required, and to clarify for each event the particular part of the objective it is to meet. It is taxing because the component training objectives are only rarely discrete but instead overlap and because it is difficult to estimate how many practices, for instance, may have to be scheduled in order to ensure a given level of proficiency for participants.

The first objective, understanding general management functions, may be attempted by a series of six case sessions. Though all may deal with situations calling for understanding by someone in the position of a branch manager in some organization, four may present problems in different functional areas and two present problems of coordinating different functions. The second objective, of enhancing skills, requires a more elaborate training design. Most appropriate may be a training laboratory, including a series of skill sessions, for example, in interviewing, a series of cases focused on different staff problems as they come up to the branch manager, and perhaps some simulation sessions.

The end product of breaking the general training objectives into constituent parts and matching the components with appropriate training events and methods is a list of events, each with stated purposes and specifications. The data for each event or block should cover eight items: general and specific objectives, content, training method, time, evaluation methods, review time, and person(s) responsible for the event.

Exhibit 6.1 shows a section taken from the curriculum used at the Institute for Rural Health and Family Planning, Gandhigram, for Family Planning Health Assistants who work at the village level. The three-month residential course has a number of such blocks of events. The typed data on each block are given to participants. Additional details, for example, of time for review and reflection, and methods of evaluation, are also provided to both trainers and participants. The value of this method of organizing a curriculum is that training tasks and objectives are specifically linked for every block, a block of sessions as well as a block of field practice.

3. The third step is to use the specifications of different training methods in order to arrive at the total time and facilities required for meeting an objective. This yields the subtotals which can be added together to arrive at a rough grand total of time and facilities required by the program as a whole.

Exhibit 6.2 shows this calculation for the training of 15 departmental managers for these objectives and by the methods indicated earlier. Most striking are the different amounts of time required for attaining different

Exhibit 6.1

SECTION OF CURRICULUM FOR VILLAGE LEVEL FAMILY PLANNING HEALTH ASSISTANTS*

Session Number	Content	Objectives	Job Function	Job Tasks	Teaching Method	Time Required	Faculty Member
Section 4	Village Community and Power Structure	To enable the student to have an understanding of/skill in:					
	1. Definition of "community." Need for the study of community, rural and urban.	1. The word "community" and its meaning.	1. To make a general survey of village including preparation of map, study of social structure and their relationship, etc.	1. Collection of general information.	1. Lecture-demonstration and exercise.	2 hours	Rao
	2. Social institutions—caste—religion—education, etc.	2. Characteristics of a community.		2. Preparation of sociogram of a community.	2. Field visit to study the community structure and social institutions in a village.	½ day	De
	3. What is power structure and leadership? Sources of leadership and types.	3. Social institutions in a village.	2. Identification of leadership in every community.	3. Identification of leadership.	Lecture-discussion.	1 hour	De
	4. Methods of identification of leaders. How is this leadership useful in implementation of Health and Family Planning Programs (source credibility, group acceptance, etc.)? What is a sociogram? How it is useful in finding out interaction between communities?	4. Sources of village leadership. 5. Methods of identification of village leaders.	3. Helping the ANM in selecting female leaders in the village.	4. To help the ANM identify the female leaders. 5. Collection of information on personal attitudes and beliefs of people toward family planning.	Lecture-discussion	2 hours	Rao
	5. Customs, norms, values. Attitudes, beliefs, etc., of the communities and why the Health Assistant (Family Planning) should know these and how to use these.	6. Customs, attitudes, and beliefs of people as related to health.	4. Meeting individually the resistant couples and identifying their barriers.	6. Meeting of the dropouts and resistant couples individually with the leaders; identifying the difficulties and helping them to overcome them.	1. Lecture. 2. Field practical for leadership identification and preparation of sociogram.	2 hours 1 day	Rao De
					1. Lecture-discussion 2. Gathering of information on attitudes and beliefs of people on family planning by survey.	2 hours	Rao De

Exhibit 6.2

TRAINING 15 MANAGERS FOR TWO OBJECTIVES: TIME AND FACILITIES REQUIRED

Objective	Training Method	Time (Hours)				Facilities
		Participants'		Trainer's		
		Prep.	Training	Prep.	Training	
1. Understanding general management functions at branch level	Cases (6)	18	9	9	9	6 cases; discussion room with blackboard, 9 hours
Total	. . .	27		18		
2. Better independent staff management	Laboratory		30	7½	60	Discussion room with tape recorder for 30 hours
	Cases (6)	18	9	9	9	6 cases; discussion room with blackboard for 9 hours
	Simulation sessions (4)	—	6	6	6	Materials; discussion room with blackboard for 6 hours
Total	. . .	63		102½		
Total for whole program		90		120½		12 cases (4 functional, 2 coordinating, 6 staff management; discussion room 54 hours (with tape recorder 30 hours; with blackboard 24 hours)

training objectives. For a series of case sessions to foster understanding of management functions, the total time required is 27 hours for participants and 18 hours for trainers. For improving staff management the corresponding totals are 63 hours and 102½ hours.

4. The fourth step is to decide on the different packages in which this program could be offered and to ask the organization to choose between them.

Package i: Two-week full-time residential program:

This would be ideal because laboratory training requires the isolation and intensity best achieved in a continuous program. The greater the attitudinal component in the increased staff management skill required, the more important the intensity of training experience becomes.

In India the budget for this package would be of this order: (Rs. 7.5 = $1):

```
Residence and facilities for 15 participants ×
17 days × Rs. 25..........................4,500
Two trainers, cases, and overhead...........3,600–4,800
                                            8,100–9,300
```

Any travel for participants and trainers would have to be added. Complete costing would have to add participants' salaries. If they earn Rs. 1,000 per month, the cost of the training program would go up by Rs. 7,500.

Package ii: Two-week full-time but nonresidential program:

This program would be located close to the work and residence of participants. This not only would mean the end of more or less undivided attention on the program but would involve the return of a participant every evening to family and friends whose expectations make changing more difficult for him. Inevitably training by this package will be less intensive. Studies show that this reduction may not affect the result of training that aims at increased knowledge and information but that it does affect training that aims at new attitudes and human relations skills.

The biggest advantage of this package over the first is its greatly reduced cost: Rs. 3,600–4,800. If the trainers come from outside, their travel and residence (2 × 17 × 25 = Rs. 850) would have to be added.

Package iii: Full-time six-day training laboratory followed by 16 sessions of 1½ hours each during or after working hours:

This package, and any others that avoid a full-time program, can only be offered if the trainers reside in the same place in any case or have other work—and payments—that keeps them there. If so, then it may combine to great advantage the features of packages i and ii.

Its budget would look like this:

Residence and facilities for 15 participants × 6
  days 2,250
Two trainers, cases, and overhead 3,600–4,800
_____
  5,850–7,050

If the second part of the program, case and simulation sessions, can be held outside working hours, the total salary cost of the program would be halved. But the program then has to be limited to two sessions a week (plus two long evenings of preparation). This schedule would stretch the program over two months. If this period is too long, it may be worth the extra cost to conduct at least a part of the program, for example, preparation, during work hours, or to double the number of sessions per week in order to finish the whole program in a month.

Package iv: Daily sessions during work or after working hours:

This is the cheapest package and might be a useful design for reaching training objectives that require frequent contact with jobs in their work settings. It is not a promising package for the training objectives we have used as an example here. The cost for trainers, cases, and overhead would be unchanged: Rs. 3,600–4,800. The participants' attention would be divided. There would be a predictable heavy loss of training time as participants change gear every day from operating to training and have to warm up for each session. If the same results are to be achieved as through the other packages, total training time—and the cost of the trainers—would have to be substantially increased.

Other packages are possible, notably full-time weekend programs with part-time programs in between.

The choices of training packages and budgets that the institution can offer the organization are summarized in Exhibit 6.3. For any full-time training the cost of participants' salaries sharply outweighs the cost of trainers and their overhead. As noted above, the fourth package, training outside working hours, is not at all a bargain, as it may seem at first glance.

5. The fifth step in designing a training program is to work detailed training events into training sequences and finally into the shape of the total program package. Both objectives call for special attention here.

OUTLINING PROGRAM SEQUENCES AND THEMES

It is very tempting—and very damaging—to approach the next step in preparing the program primarily as an administrative matter. A description of it on this basis would sound something like this: "There are, let us say, 40 one-and-one-half-hour sessions. If we work a six-hour, four-session training day, our whole program will last 10 days. No faculty member ought to take more than one session a day. Therefore, we will have four different subjects a day." The neatness is tempting. So also is the possibility of avoiding the heavy work which, following on so much detailed work already, certainly has to go into approaching the task as a training matter. The proper approach would once again relate the training objectives, as translated by now into discrete training events, to what we know of the learning process and its various aspects.

Exhibit 6.3

FOUR TRAINING PACKAGES AND
BUDGET ESTIMATES
(In Indian rupees; 1 rupee = approximately 13 cents, U.S.

Package	Participants' Salaries, etc.	Residence	Trainers and Overhead	Total Cost Excluding Travel
1. Two-week full-time residential program 7,500		4,500	3,600–4,800	15,600–16,800
2. Two-week full-time but nonresidential 7,500		. . . .	3,600–4,800	11,100–12,300
3. Six-day full-time residential plus 16 sessions outside working hours (total 8 weeks) 3,750		2,250	3,600–4,800	9,600–10,800
4. Thirty-one sessions outside working hours (16 weeks at 2 sessions per week)		. . . .	3,600–4,800	3,600–4,800

There are a number of relevant considerations. We will concentrate here on five: (1) phasing the program to accord with the learning process, (2) relating the program to prevailing expectations, (3) building the training group, (4) incorporating the grand themes of training for development, and (5) striving for consistency in training.

1. Phasing the Program to Accord with the Learning Process

Kurt Lewin's three-stage formulation of the learning process—unfreezing, moving, and refreezing—is relevant here. We referred to it earlier (Figure 3.1, page 39). It is relevant here both for the grand design of the program and for each of its major parts. It means, in the first place, that the unfreezing, the questioning of established ways of looking at situations and of habits of action, belongs early in the program and early in every constituent part. Before unfreezing, participants do not attach enough importance to the problem to wish for new behavior and, therefore, to learn. The training events that belong early in the program, therefore, are those that offer maximum stimulation and involvement: laboratory, simulation, some kinds of training in the field. Through them participants get sufficiently challenged, churned up, and motivated to have to deal, somehow, with the disturbing discrepancies, dissonances, and inadequacies. The stage of unfreezing is for training what ploughing is for agriculture.

There follows the seeding and planting stage: exploration, new knowledge, experiments with new behavior, trial and error, and all the substantive events to satisfy the need to move, to learn. Cases, individual learning, practicing new techniques in the field, these belong very much in this stage.

Finally comes the stage of fitting new knowledge, understanding, and skill that has proved useful and acceptable in the training situation into personal and organizational patterns of routine day-to-day work and living: the refreezing stage. Churning up at this final stage, raising more dust than can settle, would be inappropriate, irresponsible and perhaps unhelpful. At that time the opposite is required: settling down, consolidating. The appropriate events would stress cases, role playing, individual assignments, and reflection.

At Siet Institute a full-time training laboratory follows immediately the two and a half to three days set aside for opening up the course. This laboratory lasts four to five days. It is followed by two to three weeks of sessions focused on providing new knowledge and practice of area development subjects and techniques. Interviewing is an example of the skills practiced at this stage. The bulk of the program consists of group and individual sessions. A short fieldtrip follows: two days to practice some techniques and to provide a major exercise in collaboration. Review sessions follow, then more work sessions focused on new knowledge. In the sixth week, just before participants leave for the three-week in-District study, there is another laboratory. It is full-time for two days. Its immediate objective is to sort out relationship problems among the participants in the field teams before their big collaborative task.

The District study has a methodology that participants can use when they return to their own places. The subsequent program which occupies the last 3 weeks of the 12-week course, is built around writing and presenting joint reports and clarifying any questions that remain.

2. Relating the Program to Prevailing Expectations

This need comes to the fore most strongly at the very beginning and the very end of the program. At the beginning the expectations that need attention are the ones participants and the trainers have of each other and of the training program itself. To the extent that these expectations can be linked to reality, and uncertainties reduced or removed at this initial stage, participants and trainers, both, can move more freely to the very limits of the program.

An opening speech can be the first step in that process. It can convey to the participants general sanction and approval for the training that they are about to begin. It is a kind of initiation ceremony; to call it a ritual is not to decry it but to describe its primary function. The secondary function of the opening session is to orient the participants firmly away from their usual day-to-day preoccupations, toward the training program. Besides the positive values of this orientation, it can help reduce the guilt that active people often feel about being away from the scene of action and the urge to get back to "doing something." This secondary function of the opening address is commonly confused with a symmetrical function of the final session. That is the proper time to orient participants toward the outside world of work and public concern, away from the training; then, but not at the beginning.

The formal opening session is best followed by a series of events set up so that participants and trainers can talk together, get to know each other, and share expectations of each other and of the program. General discussions, group assignments, individual tasks shared in the group, and time for informal contact can all serve this purpose. We have described an example of this earlier, on p. 104.

The expectations that need to be lined up as the program draws to a close are of a different kind and put the trainers into a different role. They concern the work and home situations, which each participant will be facing, mostly alone, and to which not the trainers but the participant's work organization and family and friends are party. Role playing, incidents and cases, and individual assignments and consultation are appropriate kinds of events for this back-home stage of the program. The roles appropriate for a trainer at that stage are resource person and helper.

At Siet Institute 10 sessions are blocked out for discussions of back-home problems. An individual written assignment earlier in the course has elicited some of these: the problem itself, how it came up, and who were the people involved. Discussion now is mostly in triads. One participant practices helping two others consider the problem one of them has reported. Participants take turns in the different roles, reporting and preparing for action; listening, clarifying, advising, and helping two people have a useful discussion. A case session is inserted from time to time. The case presents a problem faced by someone else. Its discussion serves to remind participants that back-home problems are common and to brush up analytical and diagnostic skills. Additional sessions focus on the helping relationship, both in concept and practice.

3. Building the Training Group

The program needs to reflect also the social dimensions of learning. Studies show that an individual learns, or at least learns better and faster, when he feels the approval of other participants as well as the trainer's and when others openly commit themselves to similar improvement. He needs to be able to check his ideas and his progress as he joins in developing norms of acceptable behavior to meet the needs and in sorting out various functions in the group which facilitate learning.

For participants to know one another and to develop norms and roles in the training group takes time and opportunity. The program needs to allow for these before trainers can hope to have the participants' attention for learning other things. Training laboratories are particularly well suited to speed up and deepen the social processes in learning. In a general program, laboratories are best scheduled right at the beginning, with additional sessions from time to time later in the program when relationships between participants and trainers can be expected to demand attention. If the program has encouraged the training group to become very closely knit, it then needs toward the end to provide opportunities for dismantling the group again in preparation for parting. Otherwise, the last weeks will be increasingly overshadowed by participants' regrets and fears about parting, at the cost of attention to using their training back on the job and to the support that they need and can organize for this.

4. Incorporating the Grand Themes of Training for Development

A fourth consideration concerns the response of the program to the underlying, demanding themes of training needs in developing countries. We have mentioned two in particular: One is the need to introduce divergence and creativity into situations that lean heavily toward convergence and repetition. The second theme is the need to move away from dependent relationships to independence and interdependence.

A training program is a particularly effective means of addressing these needs just because it is, in Matthew Miles's phrase, a *temporary* system. It can provide an environment which meets personal needs, reduces defensiveness, and releases potential for creativity and innovation. It can be precisely fashioned by its designers as a temporary Utopia, with a flexibility that can evoke the best possible contribution from its participants. Hagen's analysis of the innovative personality in developing countries points the direction for particularly salient personal development through training.[1] He describes the high innovator as someone who sees a coherent world about him which he feels will respond dependably to his efforts to change it; who trusts his own

Exhibit 6.4

TRAINING METHODS AND EVENTS FAVORING
DIVERGENCE AND INDEPENDENCE

Training Methods	*Divergence and Newness*	*Independence and Interdependence*
Field training	Medium	High
Simulation	High	High
Laboratory	High	High
Incidents and cases	High	High
Individual instruction	Medium	Medium
General discussion	Low	Low
Lecture	Low	Low

evaluation of his experience; who sees the surrounding world as valuing him if he achieves his goals; who has high needs for autonomy, achievement, order, and for succor to others, and nurture from others. The innovator operates among people with whom the opposite feelings, of powerlessness, failure, meaninglessness, alienation, and interpersonal distance, are extremely common. He has to learn to deal with and live with these feelings and continue to work skillfully.

Well-designed training can provide experiences in all these dimensions. The events and methods can be rated for their resonance to these two basic themes. This has been done in Exhibit 6.4. The simulation, laboratory, and case methods resound to both. Consistent preference for events and methods which are one or two steps in the desirable directions will add significance to the whole training program.

5. Striving for Consistency in Training

Another general consideration concerns the trainers' readiness to think of the program in terms of the total time participants spend in it

[1] Everett E. Hagen, *On the Theory of Social Change* (Homewood, Ill.: Dorsey Press, 1962).

and not only in terms of the time occupied by scheduled training events. The difference between these partial and comprehensive ways of thinking about the program shows up most, of course, in residential training. There the whole day can become meaningful for attaining training objectives. The residential and food arrangements, library procedures, games and other leisure-time programs, the contacts with the administrative wing and staff of the institution, all have training components. All communicate something which participants match and compare with the training they receive in the formal program. There is no neutrality in this. If the communication from these settings is consistent with what the training program is busy developing, it adds and supports. If it is inconsistent, it subtracts and throws doubt.

> At the Aloka International Training Center it was a principle "that arrangements should allow, even demand, a multitude of choices to be made by individual members and small groups of members. . . . [This] principle ran right through the training course. . . . There were spare beds and . . . members chose the cottages in which to live and might also choose to change. House staff, however, was so restricted that the members had to clean their own cottages, lay tables and wash dishes as a matter of routine. They also devoted an average of six hours per week to manual work on the farm. For the manual work there was a reasonable assortment of tools but not enough to provide a complete set for each member. This ensured that the work program they designed had to take account of problems of coordination and many other limitations."[2]

Exhibit 6.5 gives extracts from the document that participants in Siet Institute courses received about their responsibilities outside the formal program.

In question is whether the numerous aspects of the training situation are used to strengthen the program or whether their effects are left to chance, or even unwittingly so arranged that they run counter to the objectives of the program. The question goes beyond formal events to the uncounted opportunities for contact between participants, and between participants with trainers individually, in groups and in a body. All add to the consistency and therefore impact of the training program or detract from it. Even the physical facilities are no exception. They also "speak." Just as a circular horseshoe seating arrangement makes for contact and discussion, so sharing rooms makes a difference—are the rooms allocated to them or chosen by them?—and chairs in long rows or at small tables at mealtime. The great opportunity residential programs have over others is therefore twofold: not only do they cut the

---

[2] R. R. Lynton, *The Tide of Learning. The Aloka Experience* (London: Routledge & Kegan Paul, 1960), p. 28.

Exhibit 6.5

GROUP RESPONSIBILITIES FOR LIVING ARRANGEMENTS

To allow the widest scope for meeting personal preference and also for practice in effective decision making the members will be involved in deciding and organizing many things: within the formal program, the most suitable subjects for discussions; facilities—for recreation and use of games equipment; for leisure time—excursions and other social functions; for the routine of living—questions of accommodation and food.

That effective decisions in these areas will be circumscribed by all sorts of limitations at the Institute is certainly true—indeed a truism; all life, all *effective* decisions, are full of limitations—of facilities, funds, and time of other people and of ourselves. The decisions are effective to the degree that they exhaust the freedom of choice within such limits.

The role of the faculty in this connection will be limited, both informally and at "open air meetings." Faculty members can clarify the limits of the specific situation. For instance, although the members will be asked to give suggestions for subjects for a seminar, these shall be related to the work of the area officers, the objectives of the seminar, and the experiences gathered in the seminar. On the other hand, once the limits are clear, the participants will be free to reach any decision within them, and it will be similarly up to them to change it again in the light of their experience.

Many a question raised by an individual member concerns him only, immediately at least, and the responsible faculty member will settle it directly or ask him to deal with it himself. Questions that concern more participants or the group as a whole will be referred to all, and the group will need to reach decisions on them as a body, taking responsibility for their enforcement and living with their implications.

Faculty Assignments

To facilitate and speed up administration and decision making in which the members are involved, different faculty members have assumed responsibility for the following aspects and should be contacted in these connections:

1. The course program   (Name)
2. Use and care of Institute equipment and facilities, e.g., games   (Name)
3. Social events, e.g., excursions   (Name)
   (The faculty will organize some social events; these will be announced in the weekly timetable)
4. Improvement of buildings and grounds by participants, e.g., through decoration, gardening, etc.   (Name)
5. Accommodation, sanitation, and services in hostel and first aid   (Name)*
6. Food   (Name)*

Organization of This Group

The members can organize themselves for their responsibilities in these connections in any way they choose. They will have charge of any meetings and conduct them and reach decisions on any outstanding questions in any manner they wish. Faculty members will be present only on request, to furnish information about the areas for which they are responsible. Beyond that, if the participants are unable to

* On detailed questions from individual participants, and other matters open to immediate routine action, participants can contact (name), the hostel warden. Only in case of doubt, if differences remain, or if the matter affects several or all participants, will the faculty member get involved, on the invitation of either the group or (name of hostel warden).

Exhibit 6.5 (Continued)

reach effective decisions, they can at any time, as a group, ask for a faculty member to work with them as a consultant in decision making. In that role the faculty member would still leave the group to take any decision within the limits set. His function would be to help the group pinpoint the problems that stand in the way of agreement and the steps required to remove them.

SOURCE: Siet Institute, document for participants, 1963. Abbreviated.

participant off from the impact of the workaday world but they can also focus many events on the training objectives and so achieve a consistency and intensity that is most conducive to learning. This is particularly important and also economical if changes in attitudes and relationships are high among the training objectives.

Nonresidential programs offer fewer opportunities to achieve consistency and intensity. But the principle is the same: It is to use every available possible opportunity, in and out of session, to promote the training objectives.

COMPOSING THE DETAILED SYLLABUS

When program sequences and themes have been established, not once for all but sufficiently to indicate the main emphases and rhythms of the program, the detailed composition of the syllabus can go forward. It is again not an administrative act, not a jigsaw puzzle to be made up of a set number and combination of pieces which can only be put together in one way. Composing the syllabus, too, is a creative task.

We can set out the considerations that need to go into composing the detailed syllabus in four pairs of alternates. "Alternates" is the important word. It is indeed important to alternate, not to discover middle ground. In physical exercises, it is important to stretch and to relax, stretch and relax, alternately. Compromising, settling for a half-stretched, half-relaxed posture, would be no exercise. Similarly, in training it is not the average, the lukewarm, that is important—too many of us spend most of our time in that state already! What is important to embody in the syllabus is the training equivalent of the parental admonition, "When you work, work! When you play, play!"—each with gusto.

1. Alternating Stimulation and Reflection

We have talked earlier of the essential function of reflection in converting external events into personal experiences, that is, into learning. Periods of externally designed and paced training events need to be matched by reflective time, during which participants work out the meaning of the happenings for themselves and digest it.

Alternating may be too deliberate and conscious a word to describe the subtle process that is required. A certain amount of time has to pass for an experience to "sink in." How participants spend that time will vary widely. What is important here is that the program provide the time. To avoid the impression that such periods are idle and waiting to be filled up, it may be best to label these periods "personal study" or, as in one program, "alone time." Whatever the label, reflective time has to be planned, not be left a residual or chancy item at the end of a long day. If this is not done, the days may fill up tight with activity, and participants will return to their jobs possibly feeling that they "have had a ball," but wondering what large parts of the training were all about. This sequence is particularly common in short programs. Irrespective of duration, continuous activity must not become a value per se of a program.

If the program is longer than a few hours or days, participants can be expected to "tune out" of training events from time to time when they need to reflect. They will then be physically present but mentally and emotionally busy with themselves. For such is the wisdom and economy of the human organism that it will insist on satisfying the need for reflection in much the same way as the overtaxed, indispensable executive finds himself laid up with a cold or worse. Such "absence," if unplanned, will throw the program out of gear; and that, moreover, without yielding for sure the benefits that a properly planned and sanctioned period of quiet would give.

We have emphasized the need for reflective time in the syllabus because it is commonly cut out by the pressure to cover "the syllabus." One U.S. governmental agency runs 12-week programs for several thousand participants a year of 11 scheduled hours a day, six and a half days per week. But the opposite error is also made, of offering data for plentiful reflection that have little to do with the training objectives. The ideal syllabus would provide for appropriate new data whenever reflection is about to veer off the training objectives for lack of stimulation and then provide renewed opportunity for reflection.

2. Alternating Personal Involvement and Safe Distance

No involvement means no learning. The starting point is personal experience, that is, events which acquire intense personal meaning. But deep, acute involvement does not favor some important kinds of learning, for example, analysis of data, understanding and generalizing for future action. Therefore, intensive training using personal experiences needs to be matched by sessions which offer analytical and conceptual understanding of this experience. The one is stimulating, personal, disturbing. Members may suddenly freeze inside, stare instead of look, overthink, be preoccupied with the din of their own feelings in their ears. The other is calm: "Now let's look back." The members can shed their preoccupations, look at what happened and understand it, listen to other people's feelings.

The ideal syllabus would move participants in the direction of involvement until they froze and stared, and then immediately backtrack to a study of other people's experiences for clarification and understanding.

3. Alternating Talking about Something and Practicing It

No skill is acquired without practice; and practice throws up new questions and experiences to talk about and study. It is an alternating process, not the one-way process on which many training designs are now based: first theory, all of it, then practice at the end—as if practice were "applied" theory, not theory generalizations from practice.

Where practicing a new skill in full reality is dangerous or too expensive, a simulation method can provide practice. A practice game in sport and a mock flight cabin for the pilot in training are examples. All sorts of training aids can be developed to make practice quite possible, even early in a program. From early practice springs understanding of theory, and also many questions about theory. How very frequent is the phrase from a participant at practice, "Oh, *now* I understand"—and what an accusation it harbors against the trainers! For how much the participant never understood, how much he will not be able to check if practice comes late in the program—answers to these kinds of questions the trainers will never know. Practice provides not only the understanding of theory but the motivation to learn theory.

Continuous practice, on the other hand, will also run dry. It tends to become mechanical, a quality of value in only a few jobs. Some research findings on this are summarized in Box 6.1.

The ideal syllabus would provide practice opportunities until improvement in performance tapered off and threatened to halt short of the training objective; and it would then provide opportunities to think

Box 6.1

CONTINUOUS OR DISTRIBUTED PRACTICE

Bernard M. Bass and James A. Vaughan

Experimental studies have shown, in general, that over a wide range of situations some form of distributed practice will be superior to massed practice. We must be cautious, however, in specific applications of these results. For example, studies involving motor skills have consistently shown a definite superiority for distributed practice, but the findings from verbal learning and other complex learning studies are not so clear-cut. In fact, the results of the latter are exceptionally complicated and depend upon a number of variables such as the response measure, the similarity of the terms used in the material to be learned, and the amount of prior experience the subjects have had on similar tasks. For instance, when the material to be learned is rather brief and not unusually difficult, massed practice has the advantage in that intertrial forgetting is minimized and learning will probably be accomplished before much work decrement has developed. (The primary reason advanced for the superiority of distributed practice in most instances is that rest periods allow for the dissipation of the work inhibition which normally builds up and interferes with learning in long or massed practice sessions.)

With some kinds of very difficult and complex tasks there may be an advantage to a varied attack such as a few massed with more frequent rest intervals followed by briefer practice sessions with more frequent rest intervals. In some situations massing may be more effective than spacing when rest periods are not of the appropriate length and frequency. A number of studies have found that, with the same amount of study time, trainees who moderately massed practice of complex materials outperformed other trainees who distributed their practice in the extreme with long rest periods between each practice session.

Summarizing earlier literature, Bass lists the following as guidelines for establishing efficient training regimen:

1. Generally, greater learning will occur when the rest intervals are shorter early in training and longer late in training. This is preferable to holding the rest interval constant throughout the course of training.

2. The less meaningful the material to be learned, the greater its difficulty and amount, the more will the distributed practice be superior to massed practice. Conversely, if what is to be learned is very simple, short, and meaningful, massing will yield superior performance.

3. The less capable and less experienced the trainee, the more he will benefit from distributed practice. Conversely, the talented, experienced trainee may find moderate massing preferable.

Box 6.1 (*Continued*)

4. Material learning by some form of distributed practice will be retained longer than material learned by massed practice.

(Consider how rapidly you forget the subject matter of a course for which you crammed the night before the final examinations, in comparison to courses in which you studied regularly during the semester.) This principle is of major significance in increasing the effectiveness of study.

SOURCE: Bernard M. Bass and James A. Vaughan, *Psychology of Learning for Managers* (Pittsburgh, Pa.: University of Pittsburgh, 1963), pp. 88–89.

and talk about what still presented problems and so prepare for the next practice.

4. Alternating Individual Events and Group Events

Participants provide stimulation for one another through their different experiences and ideas and through the processes going on in the group. They also provide the individual with opportunities to test and check his ideas and his effectiveness as he sets about changing in certain directions, that is, learning. Studies show that this kind of test and check, followed by early confirmation, are key elements in committing oneself to change.

But studies also show that group solutions to problems are likely to be inferior to the best individual solutions, that in a group setting individual learning tends to be only average in quality and to slow down to a pace that can be kept up by most participants. In short, the pacesetter or the otherwise divergent participant who is so very much needed in developing countries may find his new endeavors stifled in group situations.

The syllabus, therefore, needs to provide both individual and group tasks. The types of objectives that are best attained through group activities include setting goals, planning how to work, diagnosing difficulties, and learning certain essential social skills that permit a participant to test the social consequences of his knowledge. There are other objectives that are best achieved by individual work activities. Examples include writing skills, investigating and organizing specific information relevant to an individual task, and testing ability and knowledge. In individual tasks a participant can take his learning as far as he personally can. Individualized programmed instruction offers possibilities along this line, but only for training with standardized objectives and method. Individual written and practice assignments offer other and often simpler possibilities. Opportunities for individual consulting with a trainer, and individual counseling, provide other settings.

The ideal syllabus would provide a participant with group events for his stimulation, then with individual tasks on which to push himself along as far as he could go; this until he needs another group event which can confirm him sufficiently in his new direction to go on learning.

A syllabus that alternates stimulation and reflection, involvement and distance, study and practice, and individual and group events, seems to get closer to providing the kind of variety that promotes learning than the frequent changes of subject matter that have variety as their main aim. In fact, frequent changes of subject may be both unnecessary and also wasteful. An increasing number of institutions are experimenting with composing the syllabus in subject "blocks" so that participants in any week or month concentrate on two or three subjects only, and those often interrelated. Continuity of subject matter reinforces learning and assures better than the stop-start-stop of the usual syllabus that a meaningful and memorable chunk of a subject will have been learned by the time a block ends. Experience shows that this arrangement economizes time. It is not clear to what extent this economy is due to the arrangement itself or to the painstaking review by trainers which resulted in the arrangement in the first place.

BUILDING-IN FLEXIBILITY

Composing a syllabus along these lines calls for many complicated estimates. What is the minimum block for a subject, and the minimum time for one kind of event before changing to another? Even more subtle are questions about composing one syllabus for individual participants who differ in experiences and needs, and in methods and speeds of learning, and then making this syllabus standard for successive groups. These matters would be difficult to gauge even later, in the middle of the program. The difficulty increases when estimates have to be made prior to starting the program and prior to close contact with participants, and as estimates have to be projected right to the end of a program. At this point the temptation may be to give up.

Lest anyone be tempted to do this and to revert to composing the training syllabus in the classical administrative manner, it is worth underscoring that these same questions confront the task in any case, whatever the approach. The only difference is that we are here trying to

deal with the questions not by summary dismissal or in greater ignorance than necessary but in terms of achieving specific training objectives. For this purpose, the principle on which to proceed without too
much discouragement is not to let the impossible perfect obstruct the
possible good; that is, to use rough magnitudes and reasonable approxi-
mations. After all, a step in the right direction, even one, is progress.
And more insight can come with experience.

The first step is to clarify what of the syllabus really needs to be, and
also can be, decided in advance of the program and what can wait.
Minimum blocks of subjects and sequences of training events for a
subject can usually be planned well ahead on the basis of the subject's
inherent nature and the trainer's experience.

> One course again and again offers a series of six case sessions on organiza-
> tional questions in small enterprises. This block was pretty firmly fixed after
> two trials followed by small adjustments and one substitution. Its timing, too,
> got fixed: one case a day during the week preceding the major in-plant study.
> Another course offers a package on interviewing: a case, then role playing,
> a double session of practice interviews, a review session. This fits into the
> syllabus just before the first District visit which calls for a great deal of
> interviewing. Two more sessions follow the visit to review interviewing in
> practice.

What gets fixed with diligent care can be called the core of the
syllabus. It is important for everybody to arrive at this. Firmness in the
right places leaves both trainers and participants free to explore and
experiment with the remaining parts of the syllabus.

Many other details cannot be fixed and need not be. For instance,
where the most effective sequence and the times of alternating are
difficult to establish in advance, the syllabus can block out the required
total time. The details can then be announced piece by piece as the
participants progress through that particular part of the program.

> The syllabus of one training center is subdivided no further than into half
> days. Many variations can be made within a half day. Another institution,
> which requires for its work expensive equipment that has to be shared
> between several groups, deals with the same question in a directly opposite
> fashion; it subdivides the day arbitrarily into 20-minute blocks. Trainers then
> compose the syllabus with precision but only for a few days ahead at a time.

Some parts of the syllabus can be planned to greater precision than
others. Where major parts join and the program is to shift emphasis, the
important need is to make quite sure that the objectives of the program
so far have in fact been met. A detailed syllabus for the entire course

must be suspect. Concreteness this far ahead is surely deceptive. To avoid dangerous rigidities at these points, one institution had detailed syllabi ready for each major part but for scheduling and issue only when the trainers were sure that participants had mastered what they needed for the next part. When it first developed its courses, this institution did not even go this far but decided the syllabus only week by week on the preceding Saturday afternoon. The main point is to make the syllabus just as detailed as available data allows but not to push it beyond that for the sake of neatness.

What flexibility to allow in the syllabus for variations between participants of one group and then between successive groups coming for the same training must necessarily rest on very rough and arbitrary estimates. Experience over the years provides some guidance as to the normal range of variations. But relying on normal, usually impressionistic, standards can become a deadening habit and reduce the composition of a syllabus to a routine. That it must never be. Systematic evaluation procedures can be put to use here. To attain the training objectives, the detailed syllabus must in the end address the particular individuals and groups in the particular program.

Finally, the syllabus needs to leave room for unforeseen, perhaps unforeseeable, happenings. The deliberate provision in advance of some flexibility for this purpose in the syllabus ought not to occasion surprise. It performs the same functions for training as the limits of tolerance perform in an engineering drawing. In training, as in machining, the aim is not perfection but performance within certain acceptable limits. On the one hand, there will be occasional scrap, also, in training. Some session may simply fail to produce the expected results; or it could not be held because of an administrative breakdown or for some other reason. For new, previously untried programs the allowance for failure has to be extra large. The same applies for training handled by inexperienced trainers. Both conditions loom extra large and are common in developing countries.

Other demands for extra program time may arise from unexpected windfalls. An event in the work organization or the society at large, or a development in the training group, may occasion a shared preoccupation so great that it would be quite unwise to try to proceed with the program as if nothing new had happened. It is often possible instead to direct strong emotions toward a training objective.

A fire in one institution created such an occasion. Of course, the session broke up and participants ran to help put the fire out. Once that was done, the trainer gave an individual written assignment: "What did you see? What cues did you use to decide what to do? How did you chose with whom to work?" This occasion revealed that the one participant who had "learned" fire fighting was in fact spellbound and unable to act. Just this fact provided very useful food for thought.

The need for flexibility arises, therefore, not only from vague estimates of training time and rates of progress. It arises also from unpredicted and unpredictable events which can be used for training or which produce hindrances to learning. These hindrances must be removed before participants can resume progress in the desired direction. Nothing will etch on the participants' minds so sharply the trainers' concern with reaching training objectives as the trainers' responsiveness to such situations.

In a 44-hour training week, a 5 percent tolerance would yield an unscheduled two hours. This may not be too much flexibility to allow in the syllabus for catching up and otherwise adjusting the program.

EVALUATING THE PROGRESS OF TRAINING DURING THE PROGRAM

To alter the syllabus in the light of experiences during the program, trainers need indicators to guide them. They can then decide with fair accuracy when to add a session to a block here, to try a different teaching method there, revise a sequence in some part of the program, provide some extra practice for a few lagging participants, insert an opportunity for reviewing relationships. This amounts to building into the program some procedures for concurrent evaluation of the participants' progress towards specific training objectives. The aim is more skillful navigation now, not a review of the program with an eye for improvement next time. Evaluation for the purpose comes later, second, as also reviewing the relevance of the program's objectives to the needs of the work organization and the job. The latter kinds of program evaluation belong to the posttraining phase and will be considered in Chapter 9. Concurrent evaluation accepts as fixed the training objectives of particular events and blocks in the program and measures how far they are being achieved.

Concurrent evaluation can be carried out in two ways. One is to measure the participants' progress toward the training objectives at specific times during the program. The second is to provide in the syllabus for regular program review sessions.

1. Measuring Progress

Measures for evaluating progress are rooted in the set of objectives laid down for a training event or a block of events in the syllabus. When the event or block is over, the participants are expected to know x, to be able to do y, to have changed their approach and outlook in z direction.

To measure progress towards these objectives requires a series of six steps:

(i) Defining the exact objectives of the procedure and of each part. Usually three objectives and parts are involved:

    a) Assessing the progress of the participants, individually and as a group.

    b) Assessing how stable and lasting this progress is.

    c) Earmarking for later attention what events and methods need reexamination by the trainers to prepare for the next program.

(ii) Defining the behavior of the participant that is to result from the training event or block of sessions. This is the outcome of three steps of which the first was taken when the institution and organization were first in contact over this training:

    a) Defining the detailed changes in behavior on the job that the organization requires.

    b) Translating these changes into closely analogous behavior that can be achieved and measured in the training situation.

    c) Dividing the changes into sequences of smaller changes which can be attempted and measured in a training event or block in the program.

(iii) Developing measurable criteria for the end behavior. Increased speed, accuracy, and quantity of output provide simple criteria for measuring some kinds of changes. For training that aims at qualitative improvement, developing measurable criteria becomes more difficult. Examples of such objectives are greater effectiveness in enlisting local leaders in a cooperative effort, collaborating more closely with colleagues, reaching wiser decisions. For objectives such as these, both the measures and the interpretation of results are complex. The first limit of the measure and the interpretation is the precision with which the criteria have been defined.

(iv) Developing methods for measuring the criteria. Some criteria are far easier to measure than others. The number of pieces machined to certain specifications can be counted. Behavioral and attitudinal criteria call for more complex measurement. Again, the adequacy of the measuring instrument sets the limit to the accuracy of results.

For instance, many programs provide only for a final evaluation in which participants are asked to rate the major parts of the program right back to its beginning. Such an evaluation rates opinions, not behavior, and those opinions are based on recollections reaching far back; they are not current opinions. Moreover, the opinions are no longer individual, having been influenced by the opinions of other participants and by the standards the group has worked out for itself about what to communicate to the trainers. Evaluation procedures also influence the results. Whether the data is to be written or spoken makes a difference, as also whether it is to be presented in the group or individually, signed or unsigned.

The need for measures that are safe from so many pitfalls may suggest that developing them is an enterprise too complex and complicated to be worth attempting. In fact, adequate measures and procedures already exist for most purposes and trainers need only choose which they wish to use and prepare themselves to do so. The measures can look simple and rigorous. Exhibit 6.6 lists and briefly comments on six out of the rapidly increasing body of different kinds of widely available methods of measuring progress during training.

(v) Collecting benchmark data. Against these data the participants' progress can be measured during the program.

(vi) Collecting corresponding data later. This step completes the process of measuring. For the kinds of learning that cannot be considered stable until it is assessed over a period longer than the program provides, this step leads into the posttraining phase.

Exhibit 6.6

SIX METHODS OF MEASURING PARTICIPANTS' PROGRESS

1. *Observation* seems the simplest. Backed by the use of simple tools and cross-checks, it can also be very useful. Only, a general impression is not enough. Whose impression? Based on what data? Observation is, therefore, limited to measuring behavioral criteria and to skillful observers.

2. *Checklists* can ensure that different aspects of training will be observed, and observed with the required frequency. The lists need to be comprehensive and self-explanatory. Exhibit 6.7 shows such a list.

3. *Rating scales* allow measurement of opinions and feelings. Against clear, and wherever possible, operationally defined dimensions of behavior, ratings are obtained on a five-point scale or finer. Exhibit 6.8 shows such a scale.

4. *Content analysis* of written or spoken words can serve well to measure understanding. It reveals recurring themes, emphases, or gaps; also, the degree of sophistication with which participants can relate different parts of a situation.

5. *Analysis of simulation sessions* can indicate the degree of skill with which participants handle situations analogous to those they are expected to handle on the job.

6. *Projective methods* are most useful for measuring underlying attitudes.

The choice of method is one question; the frequency with which progress is to be measured is another. The principle is to measure so frequently that inadequacies and imbalances in the syllabus do not mount beyond the limits of flexibility in the syllabus. The greater the uncertainties, and the shorter the program or the narrower the other limits of adjustment, the more frequent concurrent evaluation has to be.

In short programs, daily evaluation may be appropriate and deserve time and other resources. Exhibits 6.7 and 6.8 show two kinds of

Exhibit 6.7

YOUR IMPRESSIONS TODAY

Your Name_____Date_____

Write your impressions about the day's work. Keep the questions given below in your mind while writing your impressions. Put the date and name on the sheet. The questions are not to be answered—they are only for guidance. You can use another sheet if you want to write more.

1. Did you have some new insights into your behavior?
2. Did you have some new insights into the behavior of others in the group?
3. How did you see the group today? Describe, using some adjectives (e.g., productive, cohesive, fighting, developing, etc.)
4. How did you see the trainer? Describe, using some adjectives (e.g., helpful, confusing, distracting, damaging, etc.)

SOURCE: Siet Institute, Hyderabad, India.

evaluation forms used in short programs for improving human relations.

Using questionnaires need not involve extra work for the trainers. Participants can take turns distributing, collecting, and collating the forms and presenting a brief summary before the next session. In several programs the first 20 minutes every morning have been given to reviewing the results of the previous evening's evaluations, which are then plotted on graphs on display for easy reference.

Whether questionnaires are used or not, it is important to have some procedure that indicates the participants' progress toward the training objectives. The purpose of this is not to test participants, still less to put them on the spot. In fact, these purposes would cut across the primary purpose of the evaluation we are considering here, which is to check areas of uncertainty in the syllabus and to adjust the ongoing program in the light of actual experience. If the trainers do not feel this uncertainty, or if for other reasons they do not intend to take note of the participants' reactions, the case for this kind of concurrent evaluation

Exhibit 6.8

RATING OF DAY'S L-GROUP SESSIONS

Rate the following ten aspects of today's work. For each aspect you need to choose between nine possible ratings.

Of the nine ratings only every other one is stated textually. Words are too imprecise for intermediate categories but you may welcome the extra choice for your evaluation, as we do.

A. How did you feel is the group?
1. Completely uncomfortable and tense.
2.
3. Moderately uncomfortable.
4.
5. Neither comfortable or uncomfortable.
6.
7. Moderately comfortable.
8.
9. Completely comfortable.

B. How was your participation in the group?
1. Very unsatisfying.
2.
3. Moderately satisfying.
4.
5. Neutral.
6.
7. Moderately satisfying.
8.
9. Very satisfying.

C. How much do you think you learned?
1. Learned absolutely nothing.
2.
3. Learned a little.
4.
5. Moderate learning.
6.
7. Learned quite a lot.
8.
9. Learning was at the maximum.

D. Did the conditions in the group help you in learning about the group itself, its members, and how such groups function?
1. Learned nothing about the group and group processes.
2.
3. Learned a little about the group.
4.
5. Learned somewhat about the group.
6.
7. Learned quite a lot about the group.
8.
9. Learned very much about the group.

E. How free were you in the group?
1. Completely closed, hidden.
2.

Exhibit 6.8 (Continued)

3. Moderately closed.
4.
5. About as much closed as open.
6.
7. Moderately free and open.
8.
9. Completely free, open, and expressive.

F. To what extent did you feel part of the group?
   1. Completely withdrawn, rejected, out.
   2.
   3. Moderately withdrawn.
   4.
   5. About as withdrawn as involved.
   6.
   7. Moderately involved.
   8.
   9. Completely involved, accepted, in.

G. The things talked about in the group were:
   1. Completely there and then, outside the group.
   2.
   3. Moderately there and then.
   4.
   5. About as much there and then as here and now.
   6.
   7. Moderately here and now.
   8.
   9. Completely there and now, centred in the group.

H. How many members actively influenced the group approximately?
   1. None.
   2.
   3. A few.
   4.
   5. About half.
   6.
   7. Most.
   8.
   9. All.

I. Do you think the trainers consider today's L-group sessions to be:
   1. Worst possible.
   2.
   3. Moderately poor.
   4.
   5. Neither poor nor good.
   6.
   7. Moderately good.
   8.
   9. Best possible.

J. What do you think of the trainers in today's L-group sessions?
   1. Worst possible.
   2.
   3. Moderately poor.
   4.

Exhibit 6.8 (Continued)

5. Neither poor nor good.
6.
7. Moderately good.
8.
9. Best possible.

SOURCE: A form adapted for use at Siet Institute from the form developed at the National Training Laboratories, U.S.A.

disappears. It is then better not to have it at all. Few things are so galling to the participants and so ruinous for their relations with the trainers as evaluation procedures that turn out to be a sham, an empty gesture.

2. Program Review Sessions

Participants may remember review sessions in school as having to do with spot tests, revision, and teachers trying to go over the same ground again for the benefit of the slow ones. Program reviews, to the contrary, are means for helping trainers adjust the program to the needs of the participants. If they are regularly included, program reviews serve at least four functions:

(i) The very announcement of review sessions as a regular part of the syllabus signals to the participants that the trainers approach the program as a collaborative task. They have no illusion that they are all-knowing even in advance. On the contrary, they expect to learn from the participants' reactions to the program and are both willing and able to adjust the syllabus accordingly.

(ii) The review sessions allow participants to raise questions and make suggestions from their points of view. This is different from evaluation measures which are usually composed and timed by trainers and embody *their* points of view. That the program allows for both sets of points of view supports the design of training as a joint enterprise of several partners.

(iii) Review sessions are more flexible and far-ranging than evaluation measures. Evaluation measures concern an event or a block which embodies clear objectives, rigorous processes of thinking, and measurable signs of progress. Over large parts of the training situation, and some parts even of the program, clarity to such a degree does not obtain. Review sessions allow for tentative thoughts and for thinking aloud over the whole range of the training situation.

(iv) Review sessions can be a good opportunity for trainers to feed back to participants the results of evaluation measures, to check with them the interpretation of evaluation results, and to propose consequential adjustments in the program.

Review sessions and evaluation measures are, therefore, complementary methods of indicating current progress. It would be a mistake to regard them as alternatives.

TRAINING SCHEDULES AND TIMETABLES

The trainers have now taken many steps to prepare a program appropriate to the needs of the participants and their organization. The steps form four sequences:

1. Long ago they *chose an overall training strategy* in the light of the general training objectives and available resources.
2. They then *converted the objectives into a program,* breaking them down, where necessary, into constituent parts and choosing training methods and materials with appropriate specifications for each. The detailed series of steps involved just in this sequence are set out in Figure 6.1.
3. Then, thirdly, the institution correlated the program to the organization's requirements. In doing so, the trainers ensured that the program reflected the different phases of the learning process; allowed time for dealing with expectations, immediate ones of both trainers and participants and also of those arising from the underlying needs of developing societies; and helped the training group to get properly built. The trainers then made the whole program and training situation just as consistent as they could.
4. With the general program in its approved package as a guide, the trainers then *composed the detailed syllabus.* They ensured, in the first place, that all parts of the program were accommodated and tied together effectively. They built in sufficient flexibility to allow for normal variations between groups and also for adjustments to unforeseen events. They provided time and procedures for evaluating and reviewing the participants' progress in the program so that adjustments in the program could be made with accuracy.

Weekly and daily training schedules are the visible outcome of this long series of activities. They are usually worked out by the trainers and announced at the beginning of the program in the form of timetables. Some institutions prefer to involve participants in the process of converting the schedules into exact timetables. Within limits set by the methods specifications and by the trainers, participants are asked to decide on the times for sessions, breaks, and other events in the program. This opportunity arises most readily in residential programs, particularly in institutions that provide housing for trainers right on the grounds.

Figure 6.1

CONVERTING TRAINING OBJECTIVES INTO A PROGRAM

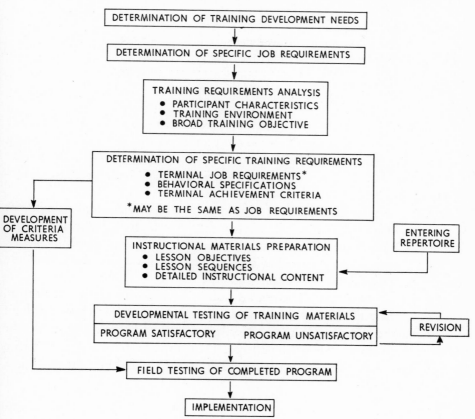

In one residential program for training young community leaders, the weekly schedule early in the course was specified as follows:

	Hours
Manual work (3 × 2 hours)	6
Discussion of manual work and of incidents in living together (3 × 1½)	4½
Case sessions	
Small groups (4 × 1)	4
Whole group (4 × 1½)	6
Review and discussion of program	2½
Village demonstration	2½
Field visit	6
Case preparation (estimated 4 × 1½)	6
Individual written assignment	2
Evening discussions (2 × 2)	4
Total	43½

The three days that had both manual work and case sessions were to have the following events:

	Hours
Manual work	2
Discussion of manual work, etc.	1½
Case session	
Small group	1
Whole groups	1½
Total	6

Participants were then asked to work these events into a timetable. A weekly review and planning session provided the occasion for revising the timetable. Substantial variations occured from course to course, and often within the course, as the participants experienced successive versions and explored new ones.

The engineering concept of tolerances and of working to limits has basic importance in training. It can help reduce the wild, erratic swings of opinions about training and shift concerns from all or nothing, attack or defence, endlessly detailed syllabus or no syllabus at all, to the middle range of action and improvement.

Not all programs and not all training groups are equally successful, and often the causes for the variations are not clear despite valiant efforts to disentangle them. Nor, even if they become clear, can the course of events always be altered. That is the human condition. Trainers need to do the best they can. That is all. But nothing less will do.

Reading 6.1

JOB SPECIFICATIONS AS A BASIS FOR TRAINING DESIGN*

Betty Mathews and K. Pisharoti

In developing countries, such as India for example, the National Family Planning Program requires thousands of workers to be trained to carry out new functions and new ways of working with community groups. In spite of the importance of these needs in many countries and

---

* Abridged from Betty Mathews and K. Pisharoti, *Job Description as a Basis for Training Design* (Action Research Monograph no. 2 [Gandhigram, India: Institute of Rural Health and Family Planning, 1966]).

although considerable time, effort and money are invested in training, the result has not always been as successful as it might be. It is useful therefore, to examine the building blocks that underly the job training process.

Specifying the Training Needs

The trainer is faced with four questions not only to be answered but answered in precise order: What is it that the trainee must learn? In what order should it be learned? How will I know when he has learned it? What teaching methods and materials are best suited to provide learning experiences most effective for the trainee to learn it? . . .

The relation between employee performance and program goals often is difficult to define, and it is not always possible for administrators to specify exactly what terminal behavior is desired. When such questions arise, there are unfortunately no magic answers. One useful solution has been for the training institution and the program organization to work cooperatively in field testing jobs as a means of identifying the specific tasks and terminal behaviors required to meet program objectives. For example, the Institute of Rural Health and Family Planning, Gandhigram, working with the Central Directorate of Family Planning, assigned several of its own staff members to perform the roles outlined for family planning workers at the Block and Village levels. A critical analysis of activities performed in relation to program achievement led to a set of job specifications on which to base job training. Below is a sample of two job functions taken from the 18 functions specified for the Family Planning Health Assistant responsible for organizing family planning programs among a rural population of 20,000.

Task-Behavioral Analysis

Once the job functions are clearly stated and the tasks required to fulfil each function specified, the purpose of the training is clear. The tasks describe the behaviors that will be expected of the trainee on the job—what he must learn to do. To further break down these behaviors the trainer addresses himself to the question: In order for the trainee to do this task, what knowledge and what skills must he learn? For each task the knowledge and skills are specified as in Figure 2, which illustrates the analysis of three of the tasks under job Function A for the Health Assistant.

Figure 1

EXAMPLE OF TWO FUNCTIONS TAKEN FROM JOB
SPECIFICATION OF HEALTH ASSISTANT,
FAMILY PLANNING

Job Functions	*Specific Tasks*
A. Make a general survey of each village chosen for initiating the Family Planning Program including a village map, study of social structure and group relationships.	1. Visit the village to meet concerned leaders and explain the activities he wishes to carry out in the village.
	2. Collect information from leaders and officials re number of households, location of caste groups, relations between castes, vital statistics for village for the previous year.
	3. Prepare outline map of village showing important landmarks, streets numbers of houses, caste groupings and their relationships, *panchayat* leaders' houses, other leaders.
B. Identify health and family planning leaders in the program village.	1. Select every tenth house and interview the male spouse using a standard interview schedule.
	2. Help the Auxiliary Nurse Midwife to select another sample of every tenth house to interview a female spouse with the same schedule.
	3. Interview each person named by respondents as a leader for health and family planning to ascertain his willingness to serve on a family planning committee.
	4. Conduct a group meeting of those accepting the leader role to fix a time and place for a one-day training camp.

Organizing the Data for Learning Purposes

From the job description for any one worker there may be as many as two or three hundred separate tasks specified and five to ten times as many specifications of the knowledge and skills to be taught. From these specifications the trainer knows what the trainee must be taught. He wants to organize these data into a pattern that will be most meaningfully related to the learning process. To do this he needs to analyze again the job functions and tasks to determine whether the tasks are performed in a sequential chain, that is, are all the tasks for Function A to be performed before the tasks for Function B can be per-

Figure 2

JOB FUNCTION A—KNOWLEDGE AND
SKILL SPECIFICATIONS

Tasks	*Knowledge*	*Skills*
1. Visit the village to meet the concerned leaders and explain the activities he wishes to carry out.	The specific activities that are to be explained, how they are to be carried out.	How to explain his role and the activities in a way that enlists the interests and cooperation of the leaders.
	Methods for finding out who are the concerned village leaders.	How to approach village leaders and what to say.
2. Collect information from leaders and officials and records { About number of households, caste groups, and group relations.	Method of preparing interview plan. Types of relationships between caste groups and their indicators. What officials to contact.	How to interview individuals or groups for general information. How to elicit indicators of caste relationships.
{ About vital statistics for previous year.	What vital events are needed.	How to work with a village registrar, how to read, and how to record, needed data.
3. Prepare outline map of village showing streets, numbers of houses, caste groupings, caste relationships, locations of *panchayat* leaders and other leaders.	Why a map is needed, and how it can be used as a tool in getting job done.	How to tour a village to draw outline map and mark relevant data.

formed? In the illustration of the Health Assistant job, the tasks do form a sequential chain of events to be repeated by the worker for each new program village. With such a chaining pattern built into the job itself, the trainer need only order the knowledge and skills for each task. For example, before the health assistant is taught how to explain his activities to leaders, he must know what activities he is to carry out.

As jobs become more complex, however, less chaining of tasks occurs. For example, the tasks of a shop foreman, who supervises a number of workers, serves as technical expert and as liaison with upper management, will have much less chaining than the tasks performed by a lathe operator. When the tasks defined for a particular job have only minimal chaining, the trainer, in order to transpose the data into teaching-learning experiences more effectively, may need to impose an order on them. For this purpose the knowledge and skills themselves can serve as a basis for organizing the data into subject blocks. That is, all the tasks, knowledge, and skills that relate to community education and working with community groups are grouped together in one block and ordered in terms of what is to be taught first, second, etc., within the block. For example, before a student learns how to draw and use a sociogram of a community he must have learned about the concept of community, power structure, leadership patterns, channels of communication, social norms, and how to identify and study these community dynamics. Likewise, tasks, knowledge, and skills concerned with the supervisory process are grouped into a subject block; tasks, knowledge, and skills about family planning, such as anatomy and physiology of reproduction and methods of contraception, are grouped and so on. Care must be taken to maintain the identity between each task and the knowledge and skills related to that task.

Grouping the tasks, knowledge, and skills by subject areas, however, does create a new set of problems for the trainer. First of all, the total job, although it may lend itself to subject groupings, is to be performed by the graduated trainee as an integrated whole. Ultimately, he will be required to use technical skills and knowledge, supervisory skills and knowledge, problem diagnosis and problem-solving skills together in a single event. Although to teach specific knowledge and skills may require this temporary separation of functions, the training design needs to specify how these separately taught areas are to be reintegrated. Some ways of doing this include (*a*) close teamwork and coordination by trainers teaching different areas so that students are guided to relate these different subject areas to the same practical problems day by day; (*b*) case problem analysis involving the multiple dimensions found on the job, and (*c*) field practice in the real job situation followed by review sessions.

Framing the Objectives

To address himself to the question of how to know when the trainee has learned, the trainer needs to think in terms of the required terminal behaviors to be expected from the trainees. To be useful an objective must specify what the learner is doing when he demonstrates that he has learned, that is, the terminal behavior that is to be observed and measured. Also, the objective must specify the minimum level of performance that is acceptable evidence of learning. For example, *To know or to understand the local language as used by villagers* does not specify an observable behavior, nor does it specify an acceptable level of performance. Whether the trainee *knows* or understands cannot be directly observed. What the trainer really means is that he plans to sample some observable behavior from which he can infer *knowing or understanding.* That is, he wants the trainee to list, to write, recite, identify, compare, contrast, differentiate, apply, interview, solve, collect, etc.— behaviors that are observable and measurable in terms of some standard. Next, the objective must state the standard by which the behavior is to be judged. If the trainee is to identify words and phrases commonly used by villagers, perhaps we need to specify the conditions under which he is to identify and how many words so identified will be considered an acceptable level of performance. Such an objective might read as follows:

> *Given a list of 100 words and phrases, to identify 50 out of a possible 70 that are commonly used by villagers.*

Such specifications of the expected outcomes of teaching and learning are not as difficult as it might seem at first because the job-task for which the knowledge and skills are to be learned has already been specified and serves as a focus for the learning objectives. For example, the objectives for Task 1 in Figure 2 might look something like this:

> *To be able to write a description of all the activities for making a village survey (that appear on the study-discussion list) in the order in which they are to be performed.*

The terminal behavior is specified as *to write a description of all the activities for making a village survey,* is a specification of the content area; the words *all,* and *in the order in which they are to be performed* is a statement of the minimum level of acceptable performance and, finally, the conditions under which the performance is to be carried out are indicated by the identification of a particular *study-discussion list.* This objective, then, may be said to meet the criteria for framing an objective, but is it adequate to fulfil the requirements of Task 1? Further examination of the task, the knowledge, and skills required suggests that at least two additional objectives are needed:

> *To be able to describe orally these activities that are to be carried out in a village in a classroom setting simulating the village situation (role playing) so that the listeners feel that they want to cooperate.*

> *To be able to describe orally these activities to village leaders in the field and actually gain evidence of their support and cooperation for carrying out the activities in their village.*

These three objectives lead the trainee step by step in the learning process so that by the time he carries out the third objective, he has demonstrated his ability to perform that task successfully in terms of a performance standard.

The Training Design

Once all the objectives have been framed, the trainer has before him a training design that specifies the subject matter to be taught, the behaviors expected of the trainee in relation to that subject matter, the conditions under which the trainee is to perform, and the level of performance required of him. The final step of identifying the kinds of learning experiences to be developed for the classroom and for field practice has become much easier than usual, partly because the very process of framing an objective has resulted in identifying the kinds of learning experiences required to fulfil that objective.

From the statements of learner-objectives, the trainer is able to plan for series of learning experiences that are designed to develop the trainee's mastery of each objective. From his past experience the trainer is able to make a fairly accurate judgment of the time each experience will require. Once this has been done for each objective stated, a training course design has emerged that is rationally tailored to the job specifications of the Health Assistant.

To complete the training design one further operation is usually required. The trainer may find, as he reviews all of the learning experiences for a chaining job, that some rearrangement of their order is required to adapt them to local conditions. For example, rather than sending the student for field practice in relation to each task, he may want to group a number of tasks together for field practice to prevent fragmenting the field program itself. In the example given in Figure 3, for instance, when the trainee carries out the third objective under actual job conditions, perhaps he should be able also to begin carrying out the survey activities and involve the village leaders in this process. If so, then the trainer would schedule all the classroom experiences first, to be followed by a block of time for all the field practice experiences related to a series of tasks. Whatever the rearrangement, it will depend directly upon the action program operations carried out by the training institution and the variety of field laboratories it has developed or is able to develop in cooperation with the organization requesting job training.

For job specifications with minimal chaining, it will be recalled that the tasks, knowledge, and skills were grouped into subject blocks. At this stage of design then, objectives and learning experiences would have been organized under each subject block and ordered in terms of what is to be taught first, second, etc. This is often called a vertical sequence. But suppose, for example, that the job for which the trainee is

Figure 3

TRAINING DESIGN FOR FUNCTION A, TASK 1;
FOR HEALTH ASSISTANT

Function A: Make a general survey of each village chosen for initiating the Family Planning Program including a village map, study of social structure, and group relationships.

   Task 1: Visit the village to meet the concerned leaders and explain the activities he wishes to carry out.

   Knowledge: a) The specific activities that are to be explained.
   b) How they are to be carried out.
   c) Methods for finding concerned leaders.

   Skills: *a)* How to approach village leaders, how to explain his role and activities in a way that enlists interest and cooperation of leaders.

Subject	Objective	Teaching-Learning Experiences	Time
Explaining program activities to village leaders.	1. To be able to write a description of all the activities for making a village survey that appear on a study-discussion list in the order in which they are to be performed.	1. Guided discussion of activities on study discussion list.	2 hours
		2. Field observation of village survey.	½ day
		3. Seminar on field observation.	2 hours
		4. Written exercise.	1 hour
		5. Review of written exercise.	½ hour
	2. To be able to describe orally the activities to be carried out in a village in a classroom situation simulating the village situation so that listeners feel they want to cooperate.	6. Skill practice for describing activities to village leaders.	
		Role play: Divide into five groups—four given leader roles.	2–3 hours (Extra staff needed.)
		a) H.A.—approaches and describes activities five minutes.	
		b) Critique by leaders; list points on chalk board —15 minutes.	
		Repeat process for each member, taking critique into account.	
	3. To be able to orally describe activities to village leaders in the field and gain evidence of their support for carrying out the activities in their village.	7. Field practice Students go to assigned villages with field instructors to contact leaders.	1 day.

being prepared requires him to conduct a village community survey that involves study of community sanitation, family planning, health knowledge, and attitudes of the people and the social interaction of the community as well as survey technique. If each area of knowledge and skills involved were organized under different subject blocks and taught as distinct and separate events, the trainee would be left to discover and to build connecting bridges between subjects, which he might or might not be able to do. In any event the relationships between subject blocks as they effect an integrated job performance is too important to leave to chance. The trainer, therefore, has the task of ordering the learning events to a calendar of time in such a way that the trainee has the opportunities to learn the knowledge and skills from each subject block that are relevant to a given task before he is required to demonstrate his mastery of that task.

With the learning experience organized in a timetable that makes the best use of the training institution's resources, the trainer has before him a training design that answers the four questions: What is it that the trainee must learn? In what order should it be learned? How will I know when he has learned it? What teaching methods and materials are best suited to provide learning experiences most effective for the trainee to learn it?

This may seem, at first, to be a rather difficult and complex process for answering these questions. It *is* difficult! Training is difficult and demands the highest quality of skill and effort from trainers if it is to be freed from the elements of chance and waste. And training is costly! In fact, cost accounting analysis will reveal that in most training institutions in India 600 to 800 rupees are required to support *one hour* of training. Training is successful only to the extent that trainees are provided opportunities for learning that are relevant to the tasks they are expected to perform on the job. To plan for less is to plan for waste!

Reading 6.2

THE INSTRUCTIONAL PROCESS*

Stephen M. Corey

Inasmuch as this paper is intended to bring to bear on teaching and the teaching process a scientific and disciplined rather than a literary

---

* Abbreviated from a manuscript first prepared as a working paper for a project aided by the American Council on Education and devoted to an examination of correspondence study. Subsequently, and in substantially modified form, the manuscript appeared as Chapter I in the 1967 yearbook of the National Society for the Study of Education, *Programmed Instruction*.

point of view, I want at the outset to suggest this operational definition of instruction: Instruction is the deliberate manipulation of the environment of an individual in order to get him to emit or engage in specified behavior in response to specified situations.

The first implication of this definition is in the word "deliberate." Instruction is neither whimsical nor accidental. Instruction is a planned activity. The quality of the planning may leave much to be desired in that the consequences of the instructional plan may not materialize. It is my view, nevertheless, that by being *deliberate,* instruction requires some plan, some strategy, some design. Not all activity that might be referred to as teaching is deliberate in this sense. Some teaching involves providing the learner with a very lush environment (a long bibliography?). What he chooses to learn is up to him.

The second cluster of implications is in the phrase "manipulation of the environment." These manipulations may and actually do become extremely various. The learner may be talked to, requested to read, requested to listen, asked to do things with apparatus, to move objects, to look at pictures, or to go someplace to observe things and events. All of these represent planned or deliberate manipulations of the learner's environment in our sense. The assumption is, of course, that these environmental manipulations are attended to, or better, responded to, by the learner. The lecture must be heard, the pictures seen, the directions followed, and so on. Taking such responding for granted rather than attempting to determine its actuality is a common cause of unsuccessful instruction. The instructor may manipulate what he *thinks* is the learner's environment. He may speak and gesture and demonstrate and give directions, but unless the learner responds there is no telling whether or not it is *his* environment, in contrast with *an* environment, that has been manipulated.

The third implication, and one that may not be at all obvious, is the separation this definition of instruction suggests between curriculum planning and the process of instruction. Curriculum planning is the process whereby the ultimate behaviors to be taught are established. Instruction is the process whereby the learning of these behaviors is facilitated. Curriculum planning is replete with value judgments of a philosophical type. It is this curricular planning that results in decisions that various populations at various times should be taught to appreciate certain kinds of literature, to master accounting skills, to spell conventionally, to understand national history, and so on. The process of instruction starts with these "givens," preferably stated as behaviors rather than as vague aspirations, and develops programs that are designed to achieve them. This means several things to me. First, it suggests that instruction is empirical in that its effects must be determined and these effects used to improve the process that generated them. Second, like any distinction between ends and means, separating *curriculum planning* as the process of determining educational ends or objectives from *instruction* as the process of achieving these objectives or ends cannot be carried to extreme lengths. Ends and means are in general too interdependent to warrant more than a separation of convenience for conceptualizing. It probably should be noted here that differentiating between curriculum planning and instruction, with almost exclusive attention to the latter, leaves the bases for curricular decisions unattended to. These decisions are, of course, of great importance in the development of any course of study or program of courses.

The final implication of this definition of instruction is that the consequences of instruction must be known, must be observable, for the process to continue and to become more effective. The planning of instruction is based upon the prediction, often unformulated, that certain types of manipulations of the learner's environment will have certain effects upon him as manifested by his behavior. These "hypotheses" can only be confirmed by observing whether the anticipated consequences of the instruction actually result from it. This means to me that whatever is intended to result from an instructional plan must be observable to those who planned and/or implemented the instruction. If the consequences of instruction are not observable, it is impossible to establish any "cause and effect" relationship between instruction and learning. In order that these consequences of instruction be observable, they must be described as behaviors or the products of behaviors— something that is written, recorded, constructed, etc. No instructor has access to the mind of the learner. The only consequence of his instruction he can observe is what the learner does.

Given the above definition of instruction and its implications I now turn to a consideration of the several activities that seem to me to constitute instruction. The contention is that any instance of instruction involves making a choice among alternative activities in respect to each of a sequence of identifiable operations. The quality of these decisions determines the efficiency of instruction. While instructional efficiency is not often made the explicit focus of attention in any type of institutionalized instruction, some efficiency considerations seem to me always to be implied. Admittedly these considerations are more often implicit than explicit, but I can remember no instances of a deliberate choice on the part of instructors to employ the less efficient of alternative instructional procedures each of which is judged to be generally effective in reaching stipulated objectives. Time seems always to be a factor in instruction as it is in life. If the same things can be accomplished in less rather than more time, the former is chosen. This assumes, of course, that efficiency data of some appreciable degree of reliability and validity are at hand. Such is often, or even usually, not the case in instruction. Strong opinions are held regarding the consequences of this or that instructional procedure, but the bases for the opinions are rarely verifiable.

My reason for commenting below and at such length on the several aspects of instruction is the belief that an analytical approach to the process may provide a useful conceptual framework for describing and evaluating specific instances or specific programs of instruction irrespective of their purposes or auspices. It is quite likely that the extent of my analysis would try the patience of the practioner whose work assignments so far as the planning of instruction is concerned have been based upon traditional and common sense notions of what is involved.

Seven Tasks

Developing or planning instruction requires that the instructor, or as may more often be the case, the several persons responsible for the instruction, accomplish a number of separate tasks. While these tasks generally come in a roughly predictable sequence, there are many interactions. This point is elaborated later. I want now, however, to describe the several things that anyone responsible for instruction must do.

(*a*) *He must describe (i) the behaviors intended to be the ultimate outcomes or objectives of the instruction as well as (ii) the situations or stimuli to which these behaviors are considered to be appropriate responses.* The ultimate behaviors or ultimate instructional objectives are, as I have said, the result of decisions made by curriculum planners in contrast with instructional planners. The behaviors described as the intended outcomes of instruction might be verbal or nonverbal or a combination. I am thinking of nonverbal or sensorimotor behavior as that which operates directly on the environment in some fashion. An illustration of a *symbolic* instructional objective for a very limited instance of instruction might be: "Says 'Christopher Columbus' in response to the oral question (auditory stimulus): 'What person subsidized by Spain is generally believed to have discovered America?' " An illustration of a nonsymbolic or sensorimotor instructional objective might be: "Adjusts the lathe to a tolerance of .008 inch when directed to do so by his supervisor."

Several points may need emphasis here in connection with any description of the terminal behaviors that define the purpose of an instance of instruction. First, it is not sufficient, although it is certainly necessary, for the persons planning and/or implementing the instruction to be the only ones who are clear and explicit regarding its intended outcomes. It is important, too, for the learners to be clear and explicit in their understanding of the behavior the instruction is planned to get under their control. Few instances of academic instruction designed to result in modification of verbal behavior pay much attention to acquainting the learner with the ultimate behaviors the instruction is designed to result in.

A second implication of the "terminal behavior description" aspect of instruction is that the situations to which these behaviors are judged to be appropriate responses *must also be specified*. For a pupil to behave by saying "Christopher Columbus," for example, in response to the stimulus "Whom do Americans often call the *Father* of their country" would not be acceptable.

The third point needing emphasis in regard to stating instructional objectives as behavior is that there must be some indication of the minimum quality of this behavior that will be accepted as evidence of successful instruction. This designation of quality, or standard of acceptability, would be included, of course, if the description of the instructional objective were sufficiently complete. Usually, however, it is not. For example, this statement of an objective for instruction in shorthand is not adequate in this respect:

> Translates oral speech into shorthand symbols and subsequently reconstructs the speech by translating the symbols orally.

This statement is better:

> Translates 30 minutes of nontechnical speech delivered from manuscript at an average rate of 100 words per minute into shorthand symbols and subsequently reconstructs the speech without error so that it conforms to the original MS.

Finally, these instructional objectives must be so stated and described as to make it possible to get evidence of their existence (see item [c] below). In other words, whatever it is that the instruction is intended to accomplish must be observable.

(*b*) *He must identify and describe the characteristics of the population to be instructed.* For efficient instruction these characteristics often need to be stated in considerable detail and may involve a range of conditions and behaviors. A specified chronological age might be one condition for admission to a particular instructional situation. An illustration of a more academic behavior that might be stipulated for the population to be instructed is: "Has mastered the multiplication tables through 15." What I am referring to here is the need to make clear the assumptions an instructor makes about what the persons to be instructed must already know that is relevant to the instructional objectives or what physical conditions they must meet. These "entering" behaviors or characteristics must be present before the individual "enters" the instructional system or instance of instruction being planned. These "entering" behaviors or conditions represent those components or aspects of the terminal behaviors (terminal objectives) that have resulted from a disciplined behavioral analysis of these objectives *but will not be taught.*

One important aspect of the establishment and description of the behaviors and conditions that should obtain in respect to the population to be instructed *before* instruction as such starts has to do with the learners *readiness* to do what the instructional plan demands of him. These demands—that he put forth effort to attend, to read, to listen, to respond, to manipulate objects, and so on—as they are assumed in any program of instruction are often incompatible with the learners' actual readiness or willingness to engage in such activities. When this appears to be the case, those who have planned the instruction generally blame the learner for his limitations. They rarely view their own instructional plans as being at fault.

Describing the requisite conditions and characteristics of the population for which the instruction has been designed, is, of course, closely related to the formulation of terminal objectives or behaviors. The latter must be considered in relation to the population that will acquire them.

(*c*) *He must construct a terminal test for determining whether or not the terminal behavior representing the instructional objectives can be engaged in at the specified level of quality and in response to the appropriate situations or stimuli.* The responses to the *terminal test* are the evidence that the person instructed has under his control the behaviors the instruction was designed to teach. The construction of a *good* terminal test is usually a major task. First and of extreme importance, it must be valid in the sense that the behavior required to cope with the test successfully is the same behavior the instruction was designed to teach. If instruction has been designed, for example, to teach the correct spelling of words a learner *chooses* in order to express his own ideas in an essay, and the terminal tests consists of spelling words dictated by the teacher, the test may not be valid. The reason is that the test was not constructed so as to determine the existence of the behaviors the instruction was designed to teach.

A second requirement of a good terminal test is that the number of responses and situation sampled by the test must be sufficient. To illustrate this requirement consider a test to determine whether or not the following terminal behavior has been brought under the control of the learner by instruction:

> Responds with the correct answer to problems involving the determination of cube root.

The terminal test question this behavioral objective raises has to do with providing a sufficiently extensive *sample* of cube root problems to enable the learner to cope with all of the exigencies such problems present.

In developing a program of instruction, it is helpful to work on the "terminal behaviors" and the "terminal test" at the same time. The need to devise a method of getting evidence that the behavior presumably taught will actually be emitted in response to given situations often reduces the tendency to state terminals vaguely or to have unrealistic expectations in regard to them. As a matter of fact, one way to define instructional objectives *operationally* is to describe the testing situations to which a learner must respond appropriately if the objectives have been achieved.

(*d*) *He must analyze the "terminal objectives" or the "terminal behaviors" of the instruction into their elements or components.* This is often a complicated and demanding task and one to which relatively little explicit attention is paid in many instances of instructional planning. This is noticeably the case in connection with instruction designed to result in the verbal behavior identified with *knowledge.* Principles are taught with inadequate attention to teaching the concepts upon which the principles are based. Concepts are taught with inadequate attention to the basic discriminations the concepts require.

The careful analysis of an instructional objective that has been stated in behavioral terms may result in a long list of component behaviors. Various ones of these components will be assumed to be known before instruction and will be designated as entering or prerequisite behaviors. The remaining behaviors may either (*a*) be taught in the instructional program or (*b*) controlled through effective directions (manualized).

The behavioral analysis of instructional objectives has as its eventual purpose the identification of the instructional units.

(*e*) *He must construct* tests *or other procedures to determine whether or not the prerequisite behaviors and/or conditions (readiness, normal eyesight, etc.) obtain in respect to the population to be instructed.* This screening is done so that only the learners for whom the instruction is designed will be expected to undergo it. Generally, and for reasons of efficiency, an instructional program should be planned and developed for a relatively specific and homogeneous population of learners. When characteristics of the population to be instructed, such as its general educational level and its command of the subject matter considered prerequisite, are stipulated *and enforced,* this substantially reduces population heterogeniety. Given current teaching and promotion practices, however, it is *very* hazardous to *assume* background knowledge if the assumption is based on the fact that the persons for whom the instruction is intended have completed and "passed" certain grade levels or even certain specific courses. There are many data to support this caution. Failure of instruction to do what it was designed to do often results because the entering characteristics and behaviors that were assumed were not in fact present. The construction of screening tests to determine the existence of prerequisites involves the same validity and sampling problems that were noted under (*c*) above in relation to the terminal test.

(*f*) *He must develop an effective sequence for teaching the behaviors which resulted from an analysis of objectives and were put in the category "to be learned."* The sequencing of instructional units so as to result in the most efficient establishment of behavior control, verbal or otherwise, has been subject to little careful study. There are many bases for establishing sequence—chronology, as in history; from simple to more complex, as in spelling; from easy to more difficult, from the specific to the general, from the general to the specific, according to the wish of the learner; and so on and on. Choices among sequencing possibilities are usually made without much supporting data.

(*g*) *He must create environments that will elicit and reward the behaviors represented by the instructional objectives.* Creating these environments represents the central task of instruction and is accomplished by the use of instructional stimuli of great variety. In the broadest sense, and within the general context of instruction, *instructional stimuli* are those stimuli that are consciously used in the instructional process to describe, elicit, and reinforce the behaviors to be learned. When these instructional "stimuli" exist in some "stored" form, as is the case with books, models, simulations, charts, maps, films, or tapes, they are *instructional materials.* Advocating the use of a "variety of instructional materials" is a generalized recognition of the fact that some instructional stimuli are more likely to elicit specific desirable behaviors than are other instructional stimuli. Appropriate responses to situations involving automobile driving are more apt to be elicited by actual steering wheels than by symbolic stimuli (words) referring to steering wheels.

(*h*) *He must arrange for an appropriate practice and reinforcement schedule so that the desired behaviors once under the learner's control will continue to be elicited by the appropriate stimuli for as long as is deemed desirable.* This aspect of instruction has received little direct attention. Arranging for "review" is common, but when the desired terminal behavior once appears to be under the learner's control, and by this is meant that he can respond appropriately when he is requested to do so, the ravages of forgetting are either completely overlooked or it is assumed that they will be dealt with in other than an instructional context. One of the expensive and pervasive sources of waste in institutionalized education results from the almost complete lack of attention to *postinstructional reinforcement.* The learner is discharged from the instructional situation as soon as there is evidence that the terminal behavior has just been learned. Little is done to increase the likelihood that the learner's control of his responses will continue.

Flexibility for Adjustment

While there is some operational logic to the sequence of the activities described above that seem to be necessary for instruction as I am conceiving of it, the sequence is not to be viewed as rigid and there is considerable interaction among the various aspects of the total task. Work on the terminal test, for example, often forces a reformulation of the objectives. Similarly, identifying "prerequisite behaviors" often requires a reconsideration of other aspects of the instructional plan.

As I have said, aspects of instruction (*e*) through (*h*) above are always subject to modification *in light of their consequences.* This conception of instruction as an empirical process that is constantly made more effective by having its consequences taken into account is inherent in the concept of instruction that has been developed. It is perfectly clear, however, that in the vast majority of instances of instruction no precise or comprehensive evidence of consequences is sought and the failure to do so is interestingly rationalized. The rationalization most commonly used whenever even a slight *bit* of evidence seems to question instructional procedures that are familiar to and valued by the instructors is that the ones being instructed are not living up to their obligations.

The consequences of instruction can be observed in at least two different ways. First, as the various instructional situations are being developed, they can be tested by having two or three learners respond to them in order to determine whether or not they are effective. Second, when the instructional plan is completed, it can be field tested with the populations and under the circumstances with which it was designed to deal. Needless to say, neither procedure is used with any frequency as instructional plans and programs are developed by most institutions providing instruction.

Required Competences

The various tasks that have been described as constituting instruction can be accomplished with varying degrees of care, discipline, and objectivity. The point I would like to stress, however, is that to the degree the planning and implementation of the instruction represents careful, systematic, and objective action and evaluation, the purpose of the instruction is more apt to be achieved. In order for there to be discipline and objectivity, it seems to me that instructional planning and the implementation of instructional plans require the following kinds of competencies:

1. A specialist in the behaviors that constitute the objectives of the instruction. This means someone who knows a great deal about *whatever behavior* the instruction is designed to result in.
2. A behavioral analyst. This analysis of the gross behavioral objectives is undertaken to identify the singular components and elements of instruction and to establish a tentative sequencing of these behaviors. This aspect of instruction is widely neglected.
3. An "instructional environment" or medium specialist who is able to make good decisions about the kind of stimuli (oral, written, pictorial, three dimensional, etc.) that promise to be most effective given the task to be achieved by the instructional program.
4. A perceptive interviewer who will arrange for procuring an interview-type reaction to the instruction by a few subjects of the type who will benefit from it *as the instruction is being developed.*
5. An expert in the experimental (field) testing of instances or programs of instruction.

Needless to say, these kinds of competence exist in all degrees of quality and several of them may be represented in the qualifications of a single person.

Summary

The conception and analysis of the instructional process that has been elaborated at some length in the preceding pages suggests that the basic instructional unit or module consists of stimuli that:

a) Describe or otherwise make clear to the learner the behavior he is to acquire control over.

b) Describe or otherwise make clear the situation to which this behavior is an appropriate response.

c) Attempt to elicit this behavior as a response to the appropriate situation.

d) Reinforce or reward the behavior as soon as possible after it is emitted.

Speaking generally, and being aware of the risks such generalizing entails, it seems clear to me that the great majority of instances of institutionalized instruction bear down heavily and *almost exclusively* on the first aspect of instruction as listed above. By this is meant that the instruction emphasizes to the effective exclusion of almost everything else, the description of, or statement of, the ideas, concepts, principles, definitions, and so on that the learner is subsequently expected to emit as verbal behavior. Much less attention is directed to making clear the situations for which these verbal behaviors are judged to be appropriate responses, to trying continuously to elicit these behaviors or give practice in their emission, or to reinforcing the correct behaviors as soon as possible after they are emitted.

PART III

The Training Phase

Chapter 7

Developing the Group
and the Climate

╭╭╭╭╭╭╭╭╭╭╭╭╭╭╭╭╭╭╭╭╭╭╭╭╭╭╭╭╭╭╭╭╭╭

"No single thing is so important to every man as to have for neighbours intelligent, companionable persons."

—BELLAMY

"A teacher will not be successful in instituting a plan . . . for achieving a given learning objective unless the social dimensions of the group are in harmony with it."

—G. JENSEN

THE PARTICIPANTS have assembled. They have at hand the general description of the program and the detailed timetable, at least for the opening days. For better or for worse, the main preparatory stage is closed. The might-have-been's no longer matter, whether the choice of participants, the composition of the training group, or the program design. These are now all fixed. The trainers' task is to do the best possible job within the limits that now in fact exist for the program. As for the rest, well, that is an opportunity for learning—for future programs.

From the moment the participants arrive, a process starts that seems to have little to do with subject matter: a social process. Participants explore who else is in the program and what they are like. This question of theirs concerns other participants and also, very much, the trainers. Participants have explored these questions already in their imaginations and with participants of earlier programs that they have met. On the basis of hypothetical answers, they have built up their expectations. Now they watch for cues to check, elaborate, change, confirm. Early interactions have these questions as background. Social questions, these and others, often demand so much attention that they crowd out other

227

aspects of the program, such as the content of opening lectures or of early discussions. It is just as well, therefore, if trainers do not expect too much recall of the content of these initial events. It is better to set the events up in a manner that promotes this essential social process.

In short, a new community is being born: a training group. It has a very special importance in residential programs, with their built-in closeness of living, as well as learning, together. But a group forms in any training program. With the possible exception of very spasmodic training sessions, the nature and direction of this group will affect the outcome of the training program in a major way. It is the trainer's task, perhaps the basic statement of it, to influence the social process in such a manner that the group will focus on the training objectives, and develop norms, relationships and a climate that all promote learning.

The idea that there is such a task still strikes many trainers as very strange. For some, the formation of a training group is not something desirable and potentially valuable but an inescapable evil. They see it as a nuisance, as something they are not able to stop but wish they could. For others, the phenomenon only arises because of administrative convenience and economic necessity. They would much prefer a tutorial relationship. Only it cannot be had; a pity. If they can admit at all that a "good" training group has value, it still does not amount to much. At any rate, they see the social process as quite unpredictable and not open to deliberate influence. It is just something with which they are blessed or cursed lightly, something they must live with either way, like fair weather or foul.

In that last they are right: like the weather, groups are with us, like it or not. Trainers with a positive orientation toward participants see groups as serving a variety of functions: a retreat from everyday work and living, a setting in which to try out new ideas and be stimulated by others, an association allowing experimenting during training, and continuing contact. To this general orientation only few trainers bring the skill necessary to actually handling participants in groups.

The sharply contradictory attitudes are reflected in prevailing approaches to handling participants in a group. Some trainers seem to aim at keeping participants as separate as they can, with as few interactions among them as possible. Interactions beyond a minimum are classified as indiscipline. The opposite approach, equally individualistic and for a time advocated as vigorously as the first, is to let every participant have his own way. The idea is that he knows how to maximize his own growth. Either way, when a participant's performance falls greatly below what the trainer expects of him, the trainer's characteristic response is to exhort him to do better. If that produces no result, he then discounts his own expectation of the participant. If, on the other hand, a participant excels, the trainer may hold him up for emulation. Both kinds of acts assume that the difficulty or the "success" lie primarily with the individual participant.

Yet in their heart of hearts—we will return to the location of that knowledge in the next chapter—most trainers know better; as, of course, do the participants. Experience throws up questions that are inescapable. For instance, how are they to explain that trainer X gets cooperation and learning in a group that trainer Y is so discouraged about? How is it that trainer X gets effective results with pretty much any group, and trainer Y with distressingly few or none?

The forces at work, complex though they are, can indeed be understood and influenced. The development of a training group is basically no different from the development of groups elsewhere, at work and in the neighborhood. It passes through similar phases, thrives on lots of contact, throws up its own leaders, diversifies the roles of various participants, has characteristic ways of working and of dealing with strangers without and strangers within. In a network of factors the trainer's behavior is undoubtedly the most important. The trainer is not omnipotent—as some like to think. He is not impotent—as others fear—or prefer. He simply exercises the most important single influence. His task is to use this influence effectively for training.

THE SOCIAL PROCESS: THREE ASPECTS

Participants coalesce into an effective group as they share common objectives and develop common tasks, develop common ways—norms—of attaining them and of generally dealing with the world, and build increasingly realistic relationships with each other. To be effective for training, the trainer's objectives, standards, and relationships must become part of this social system. Otherwise, the group develops apart from him or in opposition.

We will examine the development of tasks, norms, and relationships separately, although in real life they overlap and interwine.

1. Establishing Common Tasks

In the course of joint preparatory work, and certainly in its announcement of the program, the institution will have stated the training objectives in broad terms. Hopefully the participants arrive regarding these objectives as worth the effort and time they will spend in the program. If they themselves have chosen to come, this is indeed likely, and the size of the fee they or their organization have paid is some indication of the importance they attach to this training. But often the first possible gap is right there. His organization, or his father, may have put the participant forward for the program. There is then no knowing what effort and time the participant will want to invest.

The most critical stage for establishing shared goals is right at the beginning of the course. Even great diligence during the pretraining stage does not seem to do away with differences between the announced objectives of a program and the purposes that participants hope to achieve by coming to it. Discrepancies on this score are least surprising in cross-cultural programs. The extracurricular attractions of an international program are great, and applicants are especially inclined to put their qualifications into the most favorable light; and, from the other end, the institution has extra difficulty checking on marginal applicants at long distance. Similar difficulties beset local programs, too, only in a lower key. A participant may arrive, for instance, fully expecting a technical rather than a managerial course, or at any rate so preoccupied with technical questions that he cannot focus attention on managerial ones. When the discrepancy is very wide, it may be better for all concerned if the institution asks the participant to drop out of the program right at the start or suggests he try it for a limited period.

The more common situation is that participants project their own preoccupations into the general statement of objectives. Everyone sees there what he wants to see. One sees the opportunity in a junior executive course to learn about cost accounting, which is his work area; another to learn in the same course how to set about diagnosing general management problems; another to learn to lead discussions, or to get some new product ideas, or to write reports; yet another to meet interesting people. All these are apparently reflected in the same broad statement of objectives. They may well be. There can be no certainty about what the program will in fact cover until the trainer has provided opportunities for setting detailed objectives or refused it. Some individual desires can be included, others will have to be left out. The procedures used for this at Siet Institute were mentioned earlier in Chapter 4. The institution's concern with useful objectives can hardly be communicated more clearly than by accommodating in the program those items and priorities which participants have helped to work out through careful examination.

Other critical stages in establishing common tasks develop from time to time during the program. One begins whenever participants working toward what appear to be positive and clear goals find themselves confronted with severe and unexpected difficulties. Insufficient time may be such a difficulty, the need for information that turns out to be inaccessible, or a procedure that does not yield the expected results. When that happens, either the task needs to be changed or steps must be found to deal with the difficulty. If neither is done, frustration will result, along with despondency and other undesirable side effects. Each occasion provides the trainer with the opportunity to show that he is committed to realistic tasks and not to some mechanical notion of training, like covering the syllabus.

2. Developing Norms or Standards of Behavior

Just as participants and trainers bring various, unstated personal objectives to the program which need to be sorted out and brought together into common objectives and goals, they also bring with them implicit standards of behavior. If they come from various backgrounds and parts of the country, they find that the standards they have taken for granted in their lives are not in fact part of everyone's. The questioning and adjustment that follows this realization can be unsettling and difficult, but also valuable.

To these differences trainers add the standards of behavior that they regard as appropriate for the program. Some of these standards are institutionwide, others vary between trainers themselves. Many may be greatly at variance with standards that participants recall from school or college days which they assumed would apply again in the training situation. Examples of school and college standards that get resurrected are that the trainer will lecture and participants will only speak when asked by him; that participants will take notes and be tested on their recollection of these notes; that assignments are individual and competitive, on no account to be shared; and that participants will have to "get together" outside rather than in the program, away from the trainer, not with him. Instead, they may find a situation in which the trainer seems to welcome questions at any time in the session, expects the participants to carry on the discussion for long stretches without him, and encourages personal and social developments in his sessions.

If the institution has clear standards on certain issues, it may have stated them in the advance literature to participants and their organizations.

> For example, the Administrative Staff College of India states in an advance circular that participants will not be admitted after the starting date, that they will not be released till the end except for quite grave unforseeable reasons,

and that no holidays will be observed other than Republic Day and Independence Day. Other norms are implied in the statement of training methods. For instance, participants will be expected to prepare material for discussion, to participate at their own initiative, and to take turns chairing the syndicate. The corresponding standards for the training staff will be to observe and listen, and to speak rarely.

Additional standards get communicated when participants arrive, through written rules or unwritten conventions. Examples are that participants wear suits, that they stand up when a speaker comes into a session, and that all training staff are present at all general sessions.

The standards that can be stated in advance are usually simple and are soon associated widely with the institution. Even then, dilemmas still arise when it comes to enforcing a rule: to stop short of enforcement would render the whole system of norms untrustworthy and unsettle the training process; to enforce it would offend someone, perhaps an important organization.

The rule of not admitting a participant late for a program is an example. Sending back a latecomer is embarrassing and can entail lasting anger on the part of his organization. In one case the anger became the greater when two foreign participants who arrived late did get accepted on the grounds that the rule simply could not be enforced in their case. The national organization stopped sending participants it turned out, for a row of six programs.

Most standards are too subtle to set and to share in advance. They grow. Some concern the amount of work that participants and trainers will put into the program, in sessions and by way of preparation, and what quality and time limits are acceptable.

Advance statements on standards such as this do not help much to establish these standards. For instance, admonitions during the opening session "to work hard" are usually heard as just noise, and a very patronizing noise at that. It is more useful for a trainer to describe what he regards as acceptable. He might say, for instance, that a particular assignment ought to cover two or three sheets and that he will collect it first thing Friday morning. He may go on to set the standard that assignments be used in a scheduled session and returned to the authors with comments at a specified early time. The trainer may open this schedule to discussion. He may even turn over to the group the problem of dealing with any laggards.

These are examples of standards that the trainer communicates. He is, in fact, very influential as a model. This is so in any culture. He and his colleagues have organized the program. Participants expect them to know what standards are appropriate for it. They truly depend on the trainers to show them. So they look to the trainer as a guide to their own styles of action. This is different from dependence that is inappropriate and hinders development.

If the trainer encourages and helps the group set standards for itself, these are often stricter than any he would have set and tried to enforce. High work standards would, of course, show that the group is motivated toward the training objectives and that they see the trainer and the program as making a valuable contribution. Other standards delimit what participants will and will not talk about with the trainer present and how they keep in line those who behave in unacceptable ways. The reading from Charles Orth's book on the first-year section at the Harvard Business School (Reading 7.2, p. 258) describes several groups as they develop their standards.

Often it is not a statement by the trainer but his getting down to work which sets "the tone." His behavior is not only a pointer to the quantity of work he expects but also to his direction, emphasis, and manner. If the trainer attaches importance to participants' developing their initiative and collaborating closely with others, he can show interest in that kind of behavior whenever it occurs. And he can set the example by collaborating with participants. Many standards emerge in this informal way over time: listening carefully to others before speaking, giving opinions freely, answering questions thoughtfully; treating questions as genuine expressions of doubts to clear, not as challenges to be resisted. Indeed, it is often unwise to state standards explicitly before they have really become clear in practice or to state them too sharply or generally.

In the opening session of one program the principal stated that the trainers would make it a point "always" to be helpful, that this indeed was their main standard of behavior. But helpfulness is open to many interpretations, and occasions developed during the course when participants accused trainers of having misled them. They did not see the trainers' behavior as helpful on some occasions and whipped them with the opening statement.

Trial and error is a normal part of the process of setting standards. Participants, and trainers too, test out what behavior is acceptable and what is beyond the limits of tolerance. This testing out can be a trying process, but this price is small compared to the importance of the process. Training partly consists of, and partly depends on, enhancing generally accepted standards—of commitment, quality of work, ways of behaving with others. The trials show, above all, that this essential process is in fact under way.

3. Building Realistic Relationships

Common objectives and standards are worked out in the course of personal contacts and interactions. It is open to the trainer to limit interactions or to multiply them. He can so behave as to limit contact and interactions during the program and thereby slow down the development of the group and pretty much exclude himself from it. This happens if he does most of the talking and takes the decisions, and if he treats participants as uniform and separate individuals. Or he can so behave that interactions are numerous, joint tasks and standards are established quickly, and he himself is a member of the group with particular functions and responsibilities. He does the second if he throws the program open to discussion and to collaborative work and decision making and if he himself is readily accessible to the participants.

To maximize interaction, the size and physical arrangement of the group become of great importance. The trainer cannot interact readily with a crowd of participants sitting in rows facing him—the normal lecture arrangement. Horseshoe and circular arrangements are better but limit the size of the group to about 20. Twenty is still too large if all participants are to be actively involved. Groups as small as eight characteristically have one member who speaks less than 5 percent of the time; the number of silent members goes up as the size of the group increases. If the groups are larger than eight, for other reasons, a trainer who is eager to foster interactions has many opportunities to subdivide it: into buzz-groups of three or four, for instance, for which participants need only shift in their seats; or into small work or decision groups in different corners of the room or out somewhere in the field.

The trainer can also speed the development of the group if he encourages participants to sort out their different roles in the group openly and also to experiment with unfamiliar roles. For the silent to speak or the normally passive to take initiative are common examples of such explorations. They are time-consuming but can produce most worthwhile and far-reaching learning for everybody present. The talkative can try to listen and the leader to accept another's leadership. Role exploration and differentiation are subtly linked to specific situations and tasks. In time, their complexity and sophistication can indicate the level of maturity a group has attained. In a group that has developed far, X may lead in case discussion, Y in fieldwork, W in the group's social life, Z when it comes to helping a participant who has difficulty in taking an active part in the group's activities; O may characteristically become active to oppose the trainer and to express the group's resentment at some unreasonable pressure. When O does this, P may encourage others to join in. And V may finally smooth it all over and state what is to be learned.

By the same process, the trainer's own role is clarified. This is a most important matter since it directly affects the participants' motivation, freedom, and resources to explore and learn. Only one trainer role is simple: the steady authoritarian one. In this role a trainer can surely cripple the most significant motivations and learnings. As this simplicity disappears, with the trainer's decision to share authority and to encourage the development of the training group, his own role becomes the great unknown in the group. Many other role explorations have to wait on this clarification.

> The sequences of stages in a training laboratory illustrate most sharply the difficulties and possibilities that follow a trainer's refusal to be a traditional authority figure. At first participants see the trainer's attempt as a gimmick, a test. They try to force him back into the familiar authoritarian role. If he resists this, they find among themselves substitute leaders to reestablish the familiar structure. Several participants usually compete for this role. This competition leads to anger and to renewed appeals to the trainer to stop "the game"—and the pains of development. Only when his determination is clear and the various explanations for his obstinacy wear thin does the group turn to discover resources within itself. Participants then begin to notice the varied roles that they and the trainer can realistically perform.
>
> Similar but less dramatic and open sequences take place as the trainer takes the role of consultant in the field: "Why don't you guide us more?"; of the discussion leader in a case session: "What is *the* answer?" (i.e., *your* answer); of the resource person: "Why don't you just tell us?" As he resists these attempts to push him back, the struggling is followed by a kind of liberation that enables the group to take leaps forward.

The roles the trainer performs are not stage roles any more than the roles the participants work out. In fact, the notion—hope?—that they *are* staged and that the trainer is "only playing" is among the last strongholds before liberation.

> One of us recalls vividly even now the demeanor of a tradition-laden foreign participant as he came up after a session to ask a personal question. "Professor," he ventured, "is trial and error your method of teaching?"
>
> TRAINER: "You are very uncomfortable with what has been going on. (*Pause.*) If you thought I had planned this chaos you would be able to accept it."
>
> PARTICIPANT: "Yes."

TRAINER: "Maybe you are not quite sure just now whether I, your professor, know what I am doing?"

He looked as if his heart had missed a beat, turned and literally bolted the room. For two days he did not speak in a session. After that he participated more than ever before, and became more freely personal and involved.

Carl Rogers has summarized a lifetime's experience as a trainer in a few pithy sentences on just this point. They are stated in Box 7.1. We will return to a fuller examination of them in the next chapter.

To help participants see that he is genuine, that he really means it, the trainer may have to go through many trials and survive many traps expressly set to test him out. He will be watched not only in the session but outside, in his contacts with his colleagues, staff, and family. His

Box 7.1

TRAINER–PARTICIPANT RELATIONSHIP

CARL ROGERS

If I can create a relationship characterized on my part:

by a genuineness and transparency, in which I am my real feeling;
by a warm acceptance of and prizing of the other person as a separate individual;
by a sensitive ability to see his world and himself as he sees them;

Then the other individual in the relationship:

will experience and understand aspects of himself which previously he has repressed;
will find himself becoming better integrated, more able to function effectively;
will become more similar to the person he would like to be;
will be more self-directing and self-confident;
will become more of a person, more unique and more self-expressive;
will be more understanding, more acceptant of others;
will be able to cope with the problems of life more adequately and more comfortably.

I believe that this statement holds whether I am speaking of my relationship with a client, with a group of students or staff members, with my family or children. It seems to me that we have here a general hypothesis which offers exciting possibilities for the development of creative, adaptive, autonomous persons.

SOURCE: Carl Rogers, *On Becoming a Person* (Boston: Cambridge: Houghton Mifflin Co., 1961), pp. 37–38.

role crystalizes out of the picture participants form and share of him, the total picture.

That the development of common tasks, norms, and relationships constitutes a process with a more or less set sequence underscores the importance of so constructing the program that it promotes early, plentiful, significant contacts between trainers and participants. Informal and personal occasions can help them greatly to get to know each other. As this process of close acquaintance gets underway, the other developments take place. The trainer need not hold back because he is not a perfect copybook trainer. Who is? On the contrary, a trainer's inconsistencies and errors, particularly if they can be openly discussed, have the advantage of making him more human to participants: fallible, doing his best, also engaged, like them, in the process of learning.

INDICATORS OF GROUP DEVELOPMENT

The development of common tasks, group standards, relationships, and roles are all aspects of the same social process. We have here separated them out only for clearer understanding. The pity is that the trainer faces this whole complex process, indeed its trickiest stages, right at the beginning of the program. That is the time when he knows the participants least, both individually and as a group.

Yet the early stages are most important because they prejudice what follows. The progression, in either direction, toward closeness or distance, shared or unilateral decision, becomes increasingly difficult to reverse. Very few training programs go on long enough to allow the trainer the one hundred days of honeymoon of an incoming political government. His sensitivity and tools need to be fine enough to pick up with minimal delay even tiny indicators of the social process and to join them into a general running picture of the group's development. This perception of the group guides the trainer's actions.

The data unroll before his very eyes and ears if he can only be attentive to them. He sees facial expressions, ways of sitting, who sits by whom. He can hear not only words but feelings conveyed by words. Before long, patterns emerge: of participants who speak frequently and others who are silent, some who are listened to, others who seem to rub everyone the wrong way. Individual preferences also emerge.

> For instance, participant Rao seems most of all concerned with winning, with coming out on top. In a simulation game set up to practice understanding the decision-making process, he seems instead to concentrate on figuring out how to win, and proceeds to do so. Having won, his interest seems to flag.

Singh, on the other hand, focuses on how the people set about the task. The results of this particular game seem to interest him less than what he can learn that might be of use to him in decision-making situations in the future. Teja seems to be very impatient with the game but does not say this. Maybe he holds back from fear of what an expression of these feelings might bring. The three are learning different things. At least Teja may need the trainer's early attention.

The trainer's own interventions evoke answers, or silence, or argument. There are masses of data for the trainer to attend to, as well as he is able. He can see that a direction or evaluation from him will shift the participants' attention away from the group and the task to the trainer's wishes. Evaluations, particularly unexplained evaluations, tend to make participants close ranks. They cover up for each other and seem to be pitting their wits against the trainer rather than working with him. Presenting the group with a problem has quite different results. The problem may consist of a description of what participants or someone else set out to achieve, how they set about the task, and the extent to which their performance fell short of the goals. Attention then focuses on the consequences and on finding ways that may be better next time.

In terms of content, the discussion may often lack logical direction. In fact, it may seem quite chaotic, with successive contributions having no apparent connection, and awkward silences or outbursts occurring in odd places. Through all this the trainer can watch for indications that the group is in fact passing through successive stages of the developmental process. Sometimes the indications are clear, at others quite obscure. But each stage does have characteristic indications for the trainer to note. Blaming others for shortcomings is characteristic of an early stage. Blaming oneself comes next. A third stage is characterized by growing disregard for blame fixing altogether and a growing attention to learning how errors occurred and how they might be avoided in future. By this stage the group is already pretty far along with working out its initial relationships. But often the trainer's role is still unresolved even then. He remains present in the inhuman guise of the single, best way in which to do the job, and the group is preoccupied with discovering *his* secret. As the group grapples with this, the aura surrounding the trainer dissolves. In its place emerges the value of acceptable and contingent alternative actions which the trainer can help explore. Operating procedures then become viewed as the-best-working-hypotheses-to-date rather than as rigid rules. When this degree of adaptability in the group shows up, participants have attained considerable acquaintance with and closeness to each other and the trainer. As the saying goes in football, they are played in. They know what they can expect of each other.

The trainer can multiply the data by involving participants in making such observations and establishing their meaning. This has several additional advantages over his making the observations quietly for himself. He thereby signals his preference for freshness and openness in confronting all kinds of data. He provides realistic objectives: observation, listening, understanding the progress of a meeting, and seeing the effects that people have upon one another. He can ask participants to take turns observing the group's development and reserve 10 to 15 minutes at the end of the session for the observers to report what they have seen and heard. Very simple classifications and forms can assist this exercise. After some practice with these, the trainer can proceed to simple sociometric and role studies. A few questions can bring the relationship pattern out into the open: For instance, "To whom in this group do you go for help with work? Or with a personal problem? To whom do you look to take initiative in a work assignment? To ask questions in sessions? To organize a social event?" What participants learn most from such studies is not so much the data—those they are usually familiar with in a general way—but that data like these can be shared openly and discussed. The same data can then serve as a kind of benchmark against which to note progress.

In these ways, the trainer can learn much that is new to him and important. Often he will review his impression and change his behavior. For instance, a bright participant to whom he pays a lot of attention emerges from the data as rather isolated from the others. The trainer's special attention may isolate him yet further when the opposite is required. Or a participant with slovenly work habits turns out to be very influential in the group. The trainer then needs to consider how to ensure adequate standards of work in the light of this fact. A third participant, who is having difficulty with the work, does not figure in anyone's choices. Is he having difficulty because of his isolation there or does his isolation have something to do with his difficulty with keeping pace? Either way, singling him out for individual comment would only increase his isolation and so, perhaps, the difficulty.

In role studies it is important to collect information specifically related to the training tasks. It is important to know which participants are most interested in X subject or are the hardest workers. When those who are seen as working hardest and most effectively are at the same time the lowest in social influence, the trainer can anticipate major struggles in the group. If they at least enjoy the respect of other participants, and if the social leaders are also reasonably effective at work, both the training objectives and the social processes are well in hand.

DIRECT AND INDIRECT INFLUENCE: THREE SITUATIONS

If we look now at the trainer for detailed indications of effective and ineffective behavior, there seems to be a useful distinction to draw between the kinds of behavior that influence participants directly and those that influence them indirectly. This is the difference, for instance, between telling the participants exactly what to do and describing to

Exhibit 7.1

COMPARISON OF KINDS OF STATEMENTS BY TRAINER
WHICH HAVE DIRECT AND INDIRECT INFLUENCE

Statements of direct influence are those in which the trainer:	Statements of indirect influence are those in which the trainer:
a) Expresses or lectures about ideas or knowledge.	*a)* Accepts, clarifies, and supports the ideas and feelings of participants.
b) Gives directions or orders.	*b)* Praises and encourages.
c) Criticizes or deprecates participants' behavior with intent to change it.	*c)* Asks questions to stimulate participation in decision making.
d) Justifies his own position or authority.	*d)* Asks questions to orient participants to the task or to the topic of discussion.

them a task to be accomplished. When a trainer says, "Please stop talking and listen to me," things happen along several important dimensions: he takes responsibility for a task yet to be specified, sets a standard of behavior, centralizes authority in himself, and restricts interaction between participants. On the other hand, when he says, "There is just one day left before your plan for fieldwork is due," he points toward the task and his standards but hardly interferes with the relationships and roles already operating in the group. Direct influence narrowly limits the acceptable range of participants' activities on the task, setting standards and developing relationships, all three. Indirect influence expands the range of possible activities, on all three. In short, by direct influence the trainer inhibits the development of the group. By indirect influence he fosters it.

These are generalizations from a major series of studies at the University of Minnesota. The kinds of statements that characterize direct and indirect influence are set out in Exhibit 7.1.

Not that there is a single pattern of influence that a trainer should strive continually to maintain—even if he could. There are situations in which indirect influence is less appropriate than direct influence. More-over, the identical act of a trainer may appear highly directive in one situation but indirect in another. What studies show is that a below-average proportion of direct to indirect influence over an extended period of time will establish more desirable participant attitudes and superior patterns for work. Participants working with more directive trainers, on the contrary, tend to (*a*) imitate the trainer and use more direct influence in their own interaction, even in the absence of the trainer, (*b*) have less positive attitudes toward the trainer, the group, and the learning tasks; (*c*) demonstrate less spontaneity and initiative and make fewer voluntary social contributions; (*d*) be more easily distracted from the task and respond with greater compliance to, as well as rejection of, the trainer's direct influence. Independent studies using different research techniques in a laboratory situation show similar results, adding that these participants report doing less assigned work and less extra work.

Ned A. Flanders relates these generalizations about direct and indi-rect influence by the trainer to three situations common in training: when the task is not clear, when it is clear and attractive, and when it is clear but unattractive. Box 7.2 states the four hypotheses he has formu-lated. They are of particular interest to us here because every one is concerned explicitly with the effects of the trainer's behavior on one of the two basic themes of development, the importance of reducing tendencies toward inappropriate dependence. Indirectly the hypotheses also address the second theme, the need to encourage innovation and divergence. Divergence is conditioned by independence and interde-pendence. Of the three situations the first, lack of clarity of the task, is of the very nature of the development process. It occurs again and again as a society gropes for the directions and steps for its singularly appropriate development.

1. The Trainer's Behavior when the Task Is Not Clear to Participants

Even in a well-prepared program the training task is not clear on two kinds of occasions, as we have seen: right at the beginning of the program, when expectations remain to be sorted out and common tasks established; and again from time to time later, when the task goes out of focus because it looks too taxing or because for some reason it cannot at

Box 7.2

TRAINER'S BEHAVIOR AND PARTICIPANTS' DEPENDENCE—
FOUR HYPOTHESES

NED A. FLANDERS

We will arbitrarily assume a particular structure of goal orientation and deal with situations in which, first, goals are ambiguous; second, goals are clear and attractive; and third, they are clear and unattractive. We will further assume that just two conditions can exist for each social structure: the structure of authority is either centered in the teacher or distributed rather evenly among students, and social access is either free or restricted.

Hypothesis One: When goals are ambiguous, direct influence by the teacher increases dependence by centralizing the authority structure and/ or restricting social access.

Hypothesis Two: When goals are ambiguous, indirect influence by the teacher increases independence by decentralizing the authority structure and/or freeing social access.

Hypothesis Three: When goals are clear and attractive, direct influence will tend to increase dependence and indirect influence will tend to decrease dependence, but only to the extent that the student cannot see the relationships between the teacher's comments and the clear goal.

Hypothesis Four: When goals are clear and unattractive, direct teacher influence is necessary to sustain work by restricting social process and centralizing authority, through a system of rewards and punishments, producing high dependency.

SOURCE: *The Dynamics of Instructional Groups* (59th Year Book of the National Society for the Study of Education [Chicago: University of Chicago Press, 1960]), Part II, pp. 206–11.

this time be achieved. In these situations participants are likely to develop great dependence on the trainer.

A trainer can find many reasons to justify his inclinations toward exercising direct influence at these times. The participants want it; they obviously do not know what to do or how to proceed. The temptation then is to remind them of the task or give them "a little guidance." Other trainers may succumb to the same temptation, but out of the conviction that the participants do not like these tasks and will have to be forced anyway, or that they are incompetent, lazy, and contrary people. Without going further, the direct approach of simply giving the assignment or "telling what to do" looks very appropriate.

Irrespective of his motivation, a trainer may at times get into the following sequence: (1) he decides that participants are confused; (2)

he guesses at the cause of their confusion; (3) then, acting on this diagnosis, he proceeds to give information, direction, and perhaps criticism. He expects that this will help the participants get on with the work. The result, in fact, is that he strengthens their habit of looking to him for indications of whether they are doing well or badly, expect him continually to tell them what to do, next time, too, and the time after, and develop little imagination or initiative to seek their own solutions to a problem. In all three aspects the reaction of participants to this sequence would be directly contrary to some increasingly common and important training objectives: skill in situations of increasing complexity; independent operation; and initiative, imagination, and flexibility.

Studies have shown that trainers inclined to direct action give twice as many directions as indirect trainers and on an average criticize eight times as often. Many trainers seem to think that plentiful criticism is the best way to make participants "tough." Studies do not support them. Indirect trainers are far tougher when they put participants in the position of facing the consequences of their own ideas, opinions, and decisions. They show that, far from helping, criticism and threat of criticism interfere with many kinds of learning. They evoke childhood fears of change, lead to preoccupations with immediate and simple steps at the cost of even perceiving the complex tasks of reality. What many participants learn from frequent criticism is either to worry or not to care. Any pressures from the trainer to show results, too, need to be timed very carefully if they are not to vitiate learning in areas particularly important to development.

To exercise indirect influence at times when the task is not clear, the trainer can ask participants to choose among alternatives. If these need to be clarified first, he can participate in that process. This is a demanding task and he can expect many attempts, some subtle and angry, to give this job back to him. Holding out against these pressures from participants can be time-consuming and hard on the nervous system, and nothing tangible may be achieved for a while. And all this calls for a high degree of flexibility in the program, which puts pressures also on other trainers and administrators.

Then comes the breakthrough. The participants face the task of choosing, perhaps of clarifying the task and establishing roles. They practice diagnosing the problems, setting up alternatives and choosing among them. Irrespective of the particular outcome, these skills occupy an important place in the objectives of many programs.

In short, the trainer has to make up his mind at a particular moment whether participants now need greater or less freedom in order to go on learning. A predominantly indirect approach will increase his freedom to choose while a more direct approach is likely to restrict it. It is important to stress that the distinction we are making here is not between active (= direct) and passive (= indirect). Indirect influence may come from quite active behavior. Active guidance by the trainer may well be essential when the task is not clear and when the deterioration of activities indicates a need for help. The point is that the trainer needs to be active in the direction of helping participants understand their difficulties and deal with them and in seeing that this understanding does not come from reiterating the task. Nor does it come if the trainer by himself guesses at the difficulties and proceeds on this understanding. Even if his understanding were correct, the participants would still not understand. Certainly if the trainer proceeds by direct action, then he increases the participants' dependence.

2. The Trainer's Behavior when the Task Is Clear and Attractive

This is the situation that every trainer tries to set up and maintain. The participants work away and see themselves advancing toward the objectives. No problem arises so long as the trainer's behavior is perceived by the participants as helping them with the task. He may influence directly through giving information, directions, and criticisms, or indirectly by asking questions or expanding a participant's idea. The trainer has the opportunity to help broaden the participants' perspective of a problem, challenge their understanding, help them evaluate their procedures, and get the most out of this particular task. When the task is clear and attractive, the effects of direct and indirect influence are quite different from the effects in the earlier situation when the task is in question.

An area of doubt arises in this favorable situation only when the trainer's influence, direct or indirect, seems to the participants not logical or relevant to the task. Much then depends on the participants' general assessment of the trainer and their relationship with him. They may see his incongrous behavior as simply an error to be ignored. They may wonder about it, wait and watch, and so give the trainer some extra attention. They may see it as a kind of trick, something to test them. In short, when the meaning of the trainer's behavior is not clear to the participants, the effects on them are similar to the effects of the trainer's behavior when the task is not clear, i.e., the first situation. Direct influence then will increase dependence and indirect influence decrease dependence.

3. The Trainer's Behavior when the Task Is Clear but Unattractive

Most trainers see this as a standard situation for direct action. The trainer in that situation uses his authority "to see the task through." The tools for this are rewards and punishments. The rewards can take several forms. He can break the unattractive task into pieces and intersperse them from time to time with other tasks that are attractive, rest periods, or jokes. This is a kind of sugar coating; the task remains bitter. Moreover, though the trainer may be accomplished in using these tools, he cannot avoid increasing the participants' dependence by using them. Even if he manages to jolly the majority of participants along somehow, there usually remain the few who resent the task, resent him for imposing it, and resent him even for his attempts to lighten it. By tuning into the underlying anger, these participants often acquire influence powerful enough to spoil the task and the learning from it.

A safer and more effective approach is to share with the participants the task of finding out what is wrong—the indirect approach. This requires asking questions, encouraging participants to express their opinions, exploring with them the implications of doing the task in various ways and of not doing it at all, and relating feelings expressed by participants to learning tasks. Trainers who have the skills necessary to manage such procedures can help participants to reassess their own goals and to make new plans for reaching goals. This procedure strengthens the participants' commitment.

Trainers who fear to subject tasks to such a review because the whole situation would become unmanageable or the tasks formulated by the participants would bear no relationship to the objectives of the program, either grossly underestimate their influence on the participants' activities or are themselves unsure about the value of the task. Experiments with leaving participants even wide open choices of program content and methods are entirely reassuring on this point and in line with the results of similar freedom in other settings. The same indirect approach holds good in dealing with individual participants who experience difficulties. By asking questions, clarifying opinions and feelings, and reaching the participant's own assessment of his difficulties, the trainer and participant together can examine different courses of action.

Taking account of the likely demands and consequences of each, they can then settle on the action that looks best.

We have looked at three common situations that arise in the course of establishing common training tasks. Establishing tasks is itself only one of the three dimensions into which, for clarity's sake, we have chosen to divide the social process of developing the training group. The trainers' behavior affects all parts of the process similarly. When the trainer relies on direct influence through making decisions himself, imposing discipline, and regulating other critical aspects of the task, he thereby also restricts interaction among the participants, centralizes authority, and fosters standards of submissive and rebellious behavior. When, to the contrary, he uses indirect influence in any of the three, he thereby develops shared responsibility for the task and at the same time increases interactions, distributes authority, and fosters independent and collaborative standards of behavior.

The characteristic effects of the prevalence of either kind of behavior on the part of the trainer can readily be seen even in a single session and even by an outsider. The prevalence of direct influence shows in dominance by the trainer or by one or more participants favored by the trainer; dependence on certain participants who lead the class; silence among large segments of the group during discussions; fixed and limited roles among group members; disruption and breakdown if the trainer is absent. Expressions of semireverence toward the trainer and his abilities, combined quite possibly with expressions of resentment against the institution, can be expected outside the trainer's presence. The prevalence of indirect influence by the trainer, on the other hand, would have a different set of indicators. It shows in a number of ways: spontaneous interaction among participants; possibly some difficulty in identifying the trainer or the participant leaders; low predictability as to who will take what role and high predictability that a particular role *will* be taken at a particular time; high commitment to decisions made by the group; strong feelings of responsibility for group action; and a feeling of ease and comfort whether the trainer is present or absent. Outside the sessions much of the discussion may still be concerned with the training tasks.

THE TRAINING CLIMATE

Out of the detailed training situations and interactions grows a general training climate, an atmosphere, a tone. This general pervasive phenomenon has much to do with the rate of progress towards the objectives of the program and the satisfaction trainers and participants feel in the process. The same climate may pervade the whole institution and all aspects of the program; to this important dimension we shall return in the last part of the book. Whatever the institutional climate, each trainer is responsible for creating, so far as he is able, a favorable training climate for his own part of the program. This, in fact, is his continuous contribution to the climate of the institution as a whole.

Climate, atmosphere, tone—whatever the word, the phenomenon it labels is pervasive. Also, it tends to perpetuate itself, carrying the quality of the relationship forward, whatever it is. One trainer sets a task. The group accepts it eagerly, perhaps as a challenge, and does extra work. Another trainer sets the same task. The group refuses it, quotes the timetable against him, and appeals to the principal. One trainer makes a mistake. He may end up being liked the better for it: he is human and accessible. Another trainer makes the same mistake. He is ostracized for it. If the climate is favorable, nothing seems to go wrong in the program. If the climate is unfavorable, it becomes almost impossible to do anything right in it. Trainer and participants approach new situations with expectations which then fulfill themselves, either way, and so confirm and strengthen similar expectations for the next session. Unless the grossest interference interrupts the cycle, fair or vicious, it goes on and on, self-fulfilling and self-reinforcing.

In earlier sections of this chapter, we talked of the trainer's actions, one by one or in series—his behavior. The training climate has more to do with feelings that underly behavior. The participants' feelings influence their understanding of the trainer's behavior and the meanings they attach to his actions. They find expression in many "languages"—behavior, words, omissions. The feelings themselves, though, tend to be persistent, being deeply rooted in experiences outside and preceding training. To mark this shift of levels we will stop talking of the trainer's behavior and continue the discussion in terms of the feelings: the feelings he expresses, the feelings that he evokes in the participants, the climate that comes about through this interplay, and the feelings that are carried forward to the next situation.

A favorable climate develops when the trainer moves close to the participants as a person, cares about their needs and difficulties, accepts them as valued people, and is eager to share the tasks of constructing and running the best possible program. The participants respond to this with friendly feelings, feel free to express themselves openly and to explore new directions, and accept difficulties and errors as unintended. These shared feelings of freedom, closeness, and enthusiasm character-

Figure 7.1

THE FAVORABLE TRAINING CLIMATE—
ROOTS AND EFFECTS

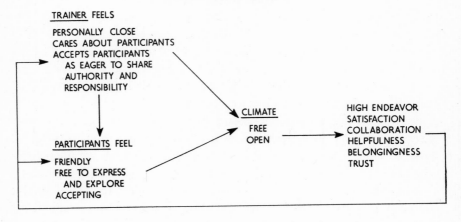

ize the climate favorable to learning and lead readily to high endeavor and satisfaction, eagerness to collaborate, sensitive and perceptive giving of help, and greater openness and feelings of belonging together. It is these feelings that then are carried forward.

This scheme can be summarized in a flow diagram, as in Figure 7.1.

With each round this climate affects all involved more deeply and becomes more firmly embedded in satisfying experiences and expectations. At best the trainer and the participants engage in a truly joint enquiry in which all persist in trying to find solutions to problems and carry through joint tasks. They see learning as the common quest. To this each contributes what he can. Learning to learn from others and collaborating with others are both necessary and fostered in the climate.

The climate unfavorable to learning is similarly summarized in Figure 7.2.

It is easy to see how the unfavorable climate interferes with training while the favorable climate facilitates it. An unfavorable climate is full of interferences. Both trainer and participants wonder anxiously what each is going to do next to the other. Participants deflect attention from the task so that they can "keep their own ends up," avoid attack from others, and defend their self-image. It is a self-defeating pattern, very different from the other. There, in the freedom of the favorable climate, the trainer stimulates without dominating, participates and encourages sharing without losing control, responds to the needs of individual participants but in the context of the small society of the training group, and allows the time and accepts the angry feelings that come and go as

Figure 7.2

THE UNFAVORABLE TRAINING CLIMATE— ROOTS AND EFFECTS

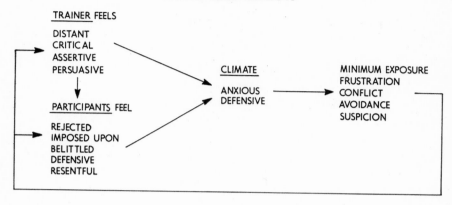

participants veer towards self-motivated and self-disciplined activities. In this process all grow, trainer as well as participants.

Reading 7.1

THE TRAINING GROUP AS A SOCIAL SYSTEM*

Jacob W. Getzels and Herbert A. Thelen

The class may be conceived as a social system with characteristic institutions, roles, and expectations for behavior. The class as a social system is related to the school as a social system, which in turn is related to the community as a social system, and so on. Ideally, the goal behaviors of one social system are "geared in" to the goal behaviors of the other related social systems. Within the class itself, goal behavior is achieved through the integration of institutions, the definition of roles, and the setting of expectations for the performance of relevant tasks. In performing the role behaviors expected of him, the teacher "teaches"; in performing the role behaviors expected of *him,* the pupil "learns."

But roles are, of course, occupied by real individuals, and no two individuals are alike. Each individual stamps the particular role he

---

* Abridged from Jacob W. Getzels and Herbert A. Thelen, "The Classroom Group as a Unique Social System," in Nelson B. Henry (ed.) *The Dynamics of Instructional Groups* (Chicago: University of Chicago Press, 1960), pp. 53–82.

occupies with the unique style of his own characteristic pattern of expressive behavior. Just as we were able to analyze the institutional dimension into the component elements of role and expectation, so we may, in a parallel manner, analyze the individual dimension into the component elements of personality and need-disposition.

To understand the behavior and interaction of specific role incumbents in an institution, we must know both the role expectations and need-dispositions. Indeed, needs and expectations may both be thought of as *motives for behavior,* the one deriving from personalistic sets and propensities, the other from institutional obligations and requirements.

Figure 1

NOMOTHETIC DIMENSION

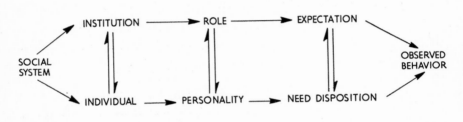

IDIOGRAPHIC DIMENSION

We may represent the general model pictorially as shown in Figure 1.

The nomothetic axis is shown at the top of the diagram and consists of institution, role, and expectation, each term being the analytic unit for the term preceding it. Thus, the social system is defined by its institutions, each institution by its constituent roles, each role by the expectations attaching to it. Similarly, the idiographic axis is shown at the lower portion of the diagram and consists of individual, personality, and need-disposition, each term again serving as the analytic unit for the term preceding it.

A given act is conceived as deriving simultaneously from both the nomothetic and idiographic dimensions. That is to say, social behavior results as the individual attempts to cope with an environment composed of patterns of expectations for his behavior in ways consistent with his own independent pattern of needs.

Behavior in the classroom group remains a function of both role and personality, although in different degree. When role is maximized, behavior still retains some personal aspect because no role is ever so closely defined as to eliminate all individual latitude. When personality is maximized, group behavior still cannot be free of some role prescription. Indeed, the individual who divorces himself from such prescription is said to be autistic, and he ceases to communicate with the group.

The major problem of social or group behavior involves exactly this issue of the dynamics of the interaction between the externally defined role expectations and the internally defined personality-dispositions. To put the problem concretely we may ask: How is it, for example, that some complementary role incumbants understand and agree at once on their mutual privileges and roles or with each other?

The essential relevant concept we should like to propose here is *selective interpersonal perception.*

When we say two role incumbents (such as a teacher and a pupil or a teacher and several pupils in the classroom group) understand each other, we mean that their perceptions and private organization of the prescribed complementary expectations are congruent; when we say they misunderstand each other, we mean that their perceptions and private organization of the prescribed complementary expectations are incongruent. We should like to mention however briefly, two other relevant dimensions.

There is first the *biological* dimension, for just as we may also think of the individual in personalistic terms, we may also think of him in constitutional terms. The individual's personality is embedded, so to speak, in a biological organism with certain constitutional potentialities and abilities. The need-dispositions of the personality are surely related in some way to these constitutional conditions, probably as mediating between constitutional and nomothetic factors. In this sense, we must bear in mind that underlying the psychological dimension is a biological dimension, although the one is not reducible to the other.

Secondly, there is the *anthropological* dimension. Just as we may think of institutions in sociological terms, we may also think of them in cultural terms, for the institution is embedded in a culture with certain mores and values. The expectations of the roles must in some way be related to the ethos or cultural values. The pupil cannot be expected to learn Latin in a culture where knowledge of Latin has little value, nor can he be expected to identify with teachers in a culture where teachers have little value. In this sense, we must bear in mind that interacting with the sociological dimension there is an anthropological dimension, although again that one is not immediately reducible to the other.

If we may put all the dimensions together into a single, and we are afraid rather unwieldy, pictorial representation, the relationships would look something like that shown in Figure 2.

Figure 2

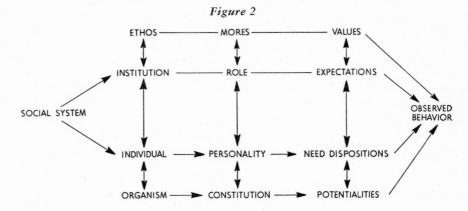

We should like to apply the model to issues dealing with the *nature and sources of conflict* and with the *nature of teacher choices in changing classroom behavior.*

APPLICATIONS OF THE MODEL I: CLASSROOM CONFLICT

We may identify for present purposes four major types of conflict, although these do not necessarily exhaust the list:

1. Conflict between Role Expectations and Culture Values

Consider the potential conflict of the so-called gifted or creative child or *teacher* in the classroom. If the potentially creative person is to be productive and inventive, the cultural values must encourage, or at least be receptive to, personal independence and autonomy. If these people are to express their exceptional talents, they must be able to maintain firm commitments to their own standards and to their own beliefs. But recent studies suggest that our values are coming to prize conformity more than autonomy, moral relativism more than commitment. We are not here arguing the validity of the substantive data—we are illustrating one potential source of conflict in the classroom, i.e., the incongruity between values and expectations.

2. Conflict between Role Expectations and Personality Dispositions

The child is in the classic conflict situation and he must choose whether he will fulfill individual needs or institutional requirements. If he chooses the latter, he is liable to unsatisfactory *personal integration* in the classroom; he is frustrated and dissatisfied. If he chooses the former, he is liable to unsatisfactory *role adjustment* in the classroom; he is ineffective and inefficient as a pupil. In practice, there are usually compromises and accommodations, but the point we want to make here is that the nature of the classroom group activity is quite different when the expectations and the dispositions are incongruent than when they are congruent.

3. Role Conflict

There is a whole range of conflicts that occur when a role incumbent is required to conform simultaneously to a number of expectations which are mutually exclusive, contradictory or inconsistent so that adjustment to one set of requirements makes adjustment to other set of requirements impossible or at least difficult. Role conflicts may arise in several ways.

(*a*) Disagreement occurs within the referent group defining the role. For example, the principal of the school may be expected, by some teachers, to visit them regularly to give constructive help and, by others, to trust them as professional personnel not in need of such supervision. Or the pupil may be expected by some teachers within the school to conceive of learning as essentially the rote remembrance of information provided by the teacher, and by other teachers as essentially the solution of problems meaningful to the pupil himself.

(*b*) Disagreement occurs among several referent groups, each having a right to define expectations for the same role. The university faculty member may be expected by his department head to emphasize research and publication. It is clear that the time given to implementing the one set can be seen as taking away time from implementing the other, and to this extent, they *do* conflict.

(*c*) Contradiction may exist in the expectations of two or more roles which an individual is occupying at the same time. It is here that we have all those problems arising from the fact that pupils and teachers are members of numerous different groups in addition to the classroom group.

4. Personality Conflict

Just as role conflict is a situational given, personality conflict is an individual given and is independent of any particular institutional setting. No matter what the situation, the role is, in a sense, detached from its institutional context and function and is used by him to work out personal and private needs and dispositions, however inappropriate these may be to the goals of the social system as a whole.

APPLICATION OF THE MODEL II: CLASSROOM LEADERSHIP IN CHANGING BEHAVIOR

We wish, finally, to apply the terms and categories of our model of the classroom group as a social system to the problem of changing behavior in the teaching-learning situation. In the terms of our model, changing behavior may involve, at one extreme, the *socialization of personality*. At the other extreme, changing behavior may involve the *personalization of roles*. In attempting to achieve change, i.e., learning in the classroom, the teacher as the formal group leader always works within these extremes, emphasizing the one, the other, or attempting to reach an appropriate balance between the two. The way the possibilities between socialization of personality and personalization of roles is handled in the classroom determines the kind of group that is achieved and the kind of learning that results.

In this context, we may identify three types of group leadership or, more specifically, three teaching styles:

1. The Nomothetic Style

This orientation emphasizes the nomothetic or normative dimension of behavior and, accordingly, places stress on the requirements of the institution, the role, and the expectation rather than on the requirements of the individual, the personality, and the need-disposition. Education is defined as the handing down of what is known to those who do not yet know. It is assumed that, given the institutional purpose, appropriate procedures can be discovered through which the role is taken, despite any personal dispositions of the learner to the contrary, so that he will incorporate the expectations. It then follows that if roles are clearly defined and everyone is held equally responsible for doing what he is supposed to do, the required outcomes will naturally ensue regardless of who the particular role incumbent might be, provided only that he has the necessary technical competence.

2. The Idiographic Style

The orientation emphasizes the requirements of the individual, the personality, and the need-disposition rather than on the requirements of the institution, the role, and the expectation. Education is defined as helping the person know what he wants to know, as it were. This means that the most expeditious route to the ultimate goal is seen as residing in the people involved rather than in the nature of the institutional structure. The basic assumption is that the greatest accomplishment will occur, not from enforcing adherence to rigorously defined roles, but from making it possible for each person to seek what is most relevant and meaningful to him. This point of view is obviously related to particular individuals who fill the roles at a particular time, and expectations must be kept vague and informal. Normative prescriptions of the sort included in typical role expectations are seen as unnecessarily restrictive and as a hindrance rather than a guide to productive behavior. The teacher frowns upon a priori class "lesson plans" and is not embarrassed to ask the individual pupil, if we may exaggerate the typical case somewhat, "Well, what would you like to do today?"

In short, the emphasis is on what we have called the personalization of roles rather than on the socialization of personality. In many ways, neither the nomothetic nor the idiographic definitions of the teaching-learning situation make any demands on the classroom group as a group. The fact that the roles and personalities exist in the classroom within the group context is more or less irrelevant.

3. The Transactional Style

This orientation is intermediate to the other two and is, therefore, less amenable to "pure" or even clear-cut definition. It is not just a compromise. Instead, the aim throughout is to acquire a thorough awareness of the limits and resources of both individual and institution within which the teaching-learning process may occur and to make an intelligent application of the two as a particular problem may demand. Institutional roles are developed independently of the role incumbents, but they are adapted to the personalities of the actual individual incumbents. Expectations are defined as sharply as they can be but not so sharply that they prohibit appropriate behavior in terms of need-dispositions. Role conflicts, personality conflicts, and role-personality conflicts are recognized and handled. The standard of behavior is both individual integration and institutional adjustment. In short, both the socialization of personality and the personalization of roles is taken into account, and the processes in the classroom may be seen as a dynamic transaction between roles and personalities.

In this mode the actual balance of emphasis on the performance changes as a function of interaction within the classroom group. Account is taken of the common or deviant perceptions of existential objects and roles, and of explicit or implicit agreements on how to deal with conflicts and deviant perceptions. In this sense, the group *qua* group is of crucial significance. It mediates between the institutional requirements and the individual dispositions. On the one hand, it can support the institution by imposing, if necessary, certain normative role expectations on the group members; on the other hand, it can support the individual in expressing, if necessary, certain idiosyncratic personality-dispositions. In working out this balance between the institution and the individual, the group develops a "culture" or, perhaps better here, a *climate,* which may be analyzed into the constituent *intentions* of the group; in effect, the group climate represents another general dimension of the classroom as a social system:

Social System $\longrightarrow$ Group $\longrightarrow$ Climate $\longrightarrow$ Intentions $\longrightarrow$ Group Behavior

The stability and concomitant flexibility of the group in moving between the nomothetic and idiographic extremes depends on the *belongingness* that the individuals feel within the group. The development of this belongingness is accompanied by increased security for all the members of the group. The greater the belongingness, the greater the ease of significant communication between the teacher and the pupils and among the pupils themselves and the greater the shared pride in the achievement of both institutional *and* individual goals. What was an "accidental" and compulsory group becomes a planful and voluntary group. The rigidity of the *platoon* or the *instability* of the *crowd* is changed into the resourcefulness and flexibility of the *team.* They "know" what to expect, what to give, what to take. They find emotional support for their risk taking, and the consequent increased individual security encourages "open" transactions between personality and role. The boundaries between the private world and the public world become permeable, and the overlap in the perception of a given situation within the classroom is enlarged. There is, at once, both greater autonomy and heteronomy for the individual. The depth of the person's involvement in the classroom is increased, and, in this sense, learning becomes more meaningful.

Within this framework, this then might be conceived as the ideal-type model of the classroom as a social system: (*a*) Each individual *identifies* with the goals of the system so that they become part of his own needs. (*b*) Each individual believes that the expectations held for him are *rational* if the goals are to be achieved. (*c*) He feels that he *belongs* to a group with similar emotional identifications and rational beliefs.

By way of summarizing the characteristics of the several dimensions presented, we offer in Figure 3 the final pictorial example selected from the categories of goal behavior.

In this final picture we have located the classroom as a social system. From this point of view, the most impressive characteristic of the classroom group, despite the apparent uniqueness, is that it can be studied systematically like *any* other group, be it a board of directors, a neighborhood club, or working team. The fundamental dimensions and concepts remain the same, and in studying any given group within a unified model, we both gain from and contribute to the study of all groups. The dimensions and concepts we have used are derived from

Figure 3

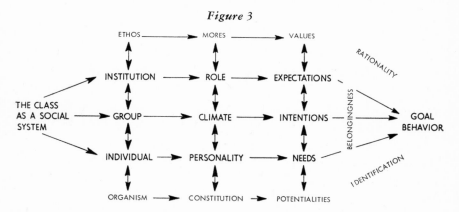

the social sciences, and we believe that is one implication of our effort. Insofar as there is going to be a "science" of education, it will be related to concepts, findings, and propositions from the whole range of disciplines called social science. It will be an integrative structure of ideas about the ways in which cultural, institutional, group, individual, and organismic factors interact and, in the process of interacting, change and bring about change.

The appropriate application of science to a particular situation is an art. Educational science is translated into educative outcomes through making choices, and this calls for the exercise of judgment. We see the learning group as an emergent reality developing out of the transactions between role and personality in the classroom. The nature of the group is determined ultimately by the way the teacher responds to the specific behavior of the students. But the judgment of the teacher on how to respond depends not merely on his ability to perceive the behavior to which he is responding as an immediate act but to look behind the act and to comprehend the behavior as a transaction within the social system as a whole. For it is within this sort of comprehension that not only the particular group but the particular individual within the group can be most readily understood. And it is through this understanding that the teacher can wisely judge how to respond.

One fundamental concern of teacher and student alike, then, is surely the nature of the group they are establishing. If they are working at cross-purposes, the likelihood of educational achievement is slim, for the chief preoccupation of the individuals will be the problem of dealing with a situation in which they cannot perceive order and consistency—at least not *their* order and consistency. Yet, if the classroom is to be genuinely challenging—and it must be this to be educative—dislocation in goals, expectations, potentialities, needs and intentions is bound to arise, for the relationships among the various factors in the social system are continually undergoing change, and are, if we may put it this way, always transacting with one another.

It appears to us then that these considerations tell us something about the image of the classroom group that is needed. This is a Utopian ideal. It is not the image of a social system in equilibrium. It is rather the image of a system in motion or, if you will, in dynamic disequilibrium. It is the image of a group continually facing emergent complexity and conflict (if not confusion) and dealing with these realities, not in terms of sentiment but in terms of what the complexity and conflict suggest about the modifications that have to be made in the goals, expectations, needs, and selective perceptions of the teachers and learners. It is through this experience of recognizing and dealing with complexity, conflict, and change in the classroom situation that we can educate children to take their places as creative and autonomous participants in the other social systems that constitute the larger social order.

Reading 7.2

TWO TRAINING GROUPS COMPARED*

Charles D. Orth, 3rd

[This is an adaptation, based on extracts, from a book containing a description and analysis of how training groups actually develop their

---

* Adapted from Charles D. Orth, 3rd, *Social Structure and Learning Climate. The First Year at the Harvard Business School* (Cambridge, Mass.: Graduate School of Business Administration, Harvard University, 1963).

distinctive "personalities" and how these affect academic performance. The author concentrates attention on two "sections," A and E. They are matched in composition, like other sections, but develop in very different directions and end up showing very different academic results. The author calls the pattern of Section A an "Internal Cohesive Pattern" and contrasts it with the "External Adaptive Pattern" of Section E. Section A developed close relationships among participants but mainly around social events. It may be worth underlining that these very different patterns emerged in the same School the same year and that "even an acute observer would have difficulty in seeing much apparent difference between one section and another" in terms of age, professional and geographical distribution, and test scores upon entering the School.]

Section A

To the members of Section A, the most important element in their experience as a section during the first year was the development of close relationships with each other and consequent avoidance of competitiveness, particularly in the classroom. Their basic orientation was social, and their pride in themselves as a section was based on their successful parties, their winning teams, and their ability to elect their members to important posts in the Student Association and campus clubs.

The leaders of Section A were the socially and politically adept members rather than those students who demonstrated ability to master the challenge of the academic program. The social system which evolved was a very cohesive one, with a strong "in group" at its core and with well-defined and highly restrictive norms governing the behavior of members. Section A was known among its members and on the campus as "the friendly section." The aptness of this title should be evident from the preceding account of their activities and attitudes. Their primary (although not overt) concern almost from the beginning of their history as a section was to limit the competitive academic atmosphere which they believed would evolve if matters were allowed to proceed as appeared likely after such events as the excellent recitations delivered by Ivan and Paul and the aggressive classroom behavior of some of their sectionmates.

The gradually emerging leadership of Mike and the other single students who were taking an active interest in athletics and parties served to point the way toward an alternate competitive route aimed outside the section. The success of the football team and the feelings of solidarity which resulted from this widely participated-in activity dem-

onstrated that a sense of accomplishment could come from other directions than the classroom. The election of Ray—a social leader—as
section representative, displacing Paul—a work leader—was an event
that clearly reflected the emerging social atmosphere of the section.

The in-group was well defined by this time. The cohesiveness, well-
defined leadership, and influence of this group gave section members
the impression that the section was well organized and able to accomplish almost anything as a group if they set their minds to it. In the
meanwhile they were struggling along in the classroom and believed
their problems there were of the same magnitude as those experienced
by the entire first-year class.

The evidence that this was not so provided by midterm grades and
the resulting warning letters was a real shock to Section A. They reacted
by looking to their leaders for direction, and their leaders did the best
they could. They brought the gripes and concerns of the section to the
attention of the faculty and, to the best of their ability, organized review
sessions for the students in trouble. As before, however, their major
concern was not so much to enhance the learning process or to reach
toward academic excellence, but rather to ensure that their sectionmates
would pass. Their greatest worry on the academic side was not how
many men would achieve Baker Scholar rank, but rather how few the
section would lose.

Their final achievement—that of engineering the election of section
members to a number of important campus positions—was one more
indication of how the need for "success" can be channeled away from
the academic and toward other areas of the first-year experience.

In many ways, the achievements of Section A were highly functional
for members of the section in relieving them of the stress of academic
pressure. In any case the social orientation, the channeling of competitive energies toward nonacademic pursuits, and the strong push to
organize participation in such activities were all symptomatic of the
internal-cohesive pattern of adaptation to the pressures and conflicts of
the first-year program.

While it was clear to the researchers that this pattern was the dominant one in Section A, it was also apparent that not all of the students
went along with it. There were some, such as Roger, the aggressive,
competitive student who was punished by his sectionmates for this
behavior, who tried to behave quite differently. Besides Roger, there
were other deviants who were "bucking the system." Two of these men,
Jonah and Vernon, were to finish the year with the highest grades in the
section. During the year they talked in class often and made no effort to

disguise their academic ambitions. For their efforts, these men were rewarded by the faculty in terms of grades but severely punished by their sectionmates, who rejected them socially and exerted considerable pressure on them to conform to the level of academic performance considered tenable by the majority. In addition to the obvious deviants, a sizable minority, mostly married students, addressed themselves rather seriously to the academic task throughout the year. While these men participated in athletic and social events to some extent and conformed to the sanctions governing classroom behavior, it seemed clear to the researchers that this group, under different circumstances, would have reacted differently and perhaps more functionally in terms of learning potential to the academic and social pressures of the first year.

One example may serve to illustrate the kind of standard of behavior that got established in the section, and how. A section member is talking.

> One type of classroom behavior that is not acceptable is drawing on outside experience. This is perceived as breaking the group norm. That is, you shouldn't pull in knowledge you have learned in undergraduate school. Intellectual material is frowned upon. It seems that you don't go beyond the small world of the case; that is getting yourself too involved. The class seems to have the feeling, "What is this guy trying to do?" It is unfair competition.

The men who tried to "score" by using their previously acquired knowledge were "punished" by their sectionmates—in A they were hissed, for instance, or remarks were made outside of class which were phrased to let the student concerned know that he was overstepping the limits of sanctioned behavior. Again Seward said:

> I think Moses tried at the beginning of the year to bring out sociological references in Ad Prac. This wasn't accepted. He was laughed at, which was much more serious than getting hissed.

These norms which restricted academic behavior had a predictable effect on both individual and group achievement in Section A. No real stars emerged in this section, although there were a number of men whose predicted grade averages were as high as those of the men who emerged as stars in Section E. Furthermore, the quality of classroom discussion was clearly lower than it might have been—so much so that the students themselves were aware of the difference. By the time they had experienced some second-year case discussions, some of them were able to spot some of the reasons for the lack of quality that characterised their first-year experience. For instance, Ray told us in the fall of 1960:

It seemed to me that our general level of class discussion was not outstanding. There weren't many men who were willing to really speak out. There were a couple but they weren't the ones the class was looking for. I don't think that the class knew who they wanted to do it, but the men who tried to do it weren't looked upon with great favor by the class!

Section E

Whereas the members of Section A turned their attention inward and concentrated on their relationships with each other, Section E, as a section, appeared to concentrate their attention outside of their own social system and devoted most of their effort to coping rather directly with the pressures of the academic program. The section was essentially task or work oriented as contrasted with the social orientation of Section A.

The cohesiveness and pervasive friendliness which were so characteristic of Section A never developed in Section E. On the contrary, as we will note shortly, the section was very explicit about its desire to maintain the right of individuality for its members. While there were, from time to time, dominant subgroups in the section, their influence tended to be disruptive rather than integrative.

A sociometric questionnaire administered toward the middle of the academic year established what may be called the "Serious Group," which was not apparent as a separate entity as a result of the previous questionnaire. The group was composed of the academic elite of the section, the men who were among the most influential and most respected task and social leaders of the section and the two formal section representatives. The group, therefore, embraced both the formal and almost all the informal leaders of the section. This group, as leaders, came closest to realizing the academic and social norms which the group values most and on which, as a result of the scheme of interaction, the group focuses; that is, they received more choices from outside their group than any other single or married subgroup.

Socially the largest group of the section did not develop nearly to the same extent as Section A. One student said:

> They (the "Senior Group") got together on an exclusive basis. When they gave parties, they were at a private apartment, or something like that. Attendance was really by invitation only, and only a handful from the section ever got invited. By taking their social leadership away from the section, I think the rest of the section never developed socially.

The dominant pattern of activity in Section E was one emphasizing the individual and fighting any attempts from any source to organize activities, constrain academic output, or emphasize the values which many students felt inhibited their right to be different.

At the same time, the section as a section worked to *adapt* their behavior to the requirements of the School and in so doing listened seriously to what their professors told them. Their focus was *external,* they were situationally rather than socially oriented, and they were anything but cohesive as a social organization.

From this comparison one can question some of the assumptions and goals the faculty regard as appropriate. One assumption is that participants come to the program eager to learn new things and will therefore be eager to explore and experiment. Instead we find that the possibility for experimentation in a laboratory sense, where judgment was suspended temporarily in an effort to explore and learn more about the problem at hand, was seldom a real possibility for the first-year student in the case method classroom. He was engrossed in attempts to perform to his and his fellow's satisfaction and, therefore, was unable to contemplate the consequence of tests that might not succeed or experiments that might not work.

The classroom environment had more of the flavor of the arena than of the laboratory. Each student who recited was trying to "score"; to convince the instructor and his classmates that he was on top of the work and knew what he was talking about. Since few students were sure, particularly at the beginning of the academic year, what criteria were relevant, some experimentation was necessary. This took place, however, not in the classroom but in preclass study groups.

We are now convinced that the major lesson *many* students learn during their first year at the School is how to get along in the social milieu of the section while maintaining a level of academic performance sufficient to ensure their passage from the first to the second year. This level of performance is set by the norms of their section and is often considerably below the potential of many students. The majority of the students become, in effect, "on-line producers." Much as they may like to believe that they are independent individuals and much as they may regard the "organization man" with distaste, they would dislike even more to take the punishment they see being administered to deviants in the section or to endure the loneliness of the social isolates. They avoid these fates by conforming to the norms.

In case any doubts remain as to the effectiveness of these social pressures, it may be added here that fully 70% of the Section A members were "on-line" producers compared to 54% of Section E, and that of the students who received little or no social support, more than three times as many underperformed as overperformed. Now, are these students denied social support because they perform poorly or do they perform poorly because they are denied support? An answer to this hen-and-egg question is attempted by studying the isolates and by seeing what happened when the student body was reorganized for their second year. As for the first, Section A had 11 isolates three months after the year started. One became the highest overproducer in the section. Predictions were made for nine more, five single and four married men. Of the five single men, all underperformed in final grades, including the man who had had the highest test score in the entrance test; three were failed out of the School. Of the four married isolates, three overperformed. They were older, kept away from the section and spent their time with their families. The fourth was younger and tried to get social support. He failed. Predicted to rank in the second quartile within his section, he ended up in the eighth.

The differences in performance between the two sections show up most clearly at the very top level. Only one student in Section A managed a grade average more than 3.0 points higher than that predicted for him as against the 11 men in E who overperformed to this extent. These 11 men were all stars; in fact 4 of them became Baker Scholars on the basis of their first-year performance. It is interesting to note, in this connection, that of the 13 men elected Baker Scholars at the end of the first year, Section E had far more than its share, while not a single man from Section A was elected. It is even more interesting to note that, at the end of the first term of the second year, when the men went to class as individuals and were divorced from their sections, four Section A men became Baker Scholars (as did three more men from Section E). While not conclusive, this evidence indicates that there were men with high potential in Section A who found it difficult to perform at the level they might have reached in a different social environment.

The implications of the data appear clear. While we would not for a moment claim that social support or the lack of it was the *primary* influence on academic performance of first-year students, it does seem as though the strong correlations we have noted are telling us that the standing of a student in the social organization of his section was an extremely *important* influence on academic performance. This was true of all students, but especially of the single men who were living and working at the school and were therefore unable to compensate for lack of support from their colleagues by depending on the emotional strength of their familiar relationships. The research was not designed to test the degree to which marital relationships were perceived by the students as offering support, but we would guess that a further inquiry which was so designed would reveal a considerable correlation between married students who underperformed and those who felt their wives were not giving them the emotional and intellectual support they would like.

Reading 7.3

SOME PRACTICAL QUESTIONS ABOUT TRAINING GROUPS*

Dorothy Stock and Herbert Thelen

Our research observations and theories, tested in our own practical experiences during the period of the research, offer tentative suggestions with respect to a number of practical problems.

Problem 1: *How important is the composition of the group, and, assuming that one can select members for certain group jobs, what factors should be considered?*

Our research indicates that for purposes as searching and demanding as human relations training, the composition of the group can make the difference between success and failure.

Presumably for purposes requiring involvement of less of the "whole person," composition would be less critical. It is our belief that the composition of the group determines how far the group can go in training, and that the leadership determines how fast it will go and the extent to which it will realize its potentials for development.

Three factors seem to be the most important: (1) the extent of communality in the group with respect to expectation to work and expectation of degree of intimacy desired; (2) the extent to which there are persons who can openly express attitudes for and against fight, dependency, pairing, and, possibly, flight; and (3) the extent to which

---

* Abridged from Dorothy Stock and Herbert A. Thelen, *Emotional Dynamics and Group Culture* (Washington, D.C.: National Training Laboratories, 1958), pp. 255–61.

the leader's own problems of accepting and dealing with anxiety are different from the group's.

Considering groups in general, we would add a fourth factor: the extent to which the member have and can give the information and skills required for working on the task problems.

Problem 2: *How large should the group be?*

This depends on the purpose during each activity. In general, if the group is to plan and carry out action, it needs a lot of affective and cognitive communication and plenty of opportunity for individuals to talk and test their feelings and ideas against those of others. In general, from 3 to 25 probably represents the minimum and maximum. The more vaguely defined the task, the smaller the group needs to be.

In general, we would advocate the smallest group that contains within it all the resources listed above, with least duplication of roles.

In practice, group size is relatively unimportant for the reason that it is no trick to divide a large group into smaller groups when the various kinds of problem realities demand it. Thus, in the case of a classroom, we would advocate substantially smaller subgroups, from one-person groups up. For organizing one's past experience and bringing it to bear upon a problem one feels is important, subgroups of one person each seem reasonable. For drilling on spelling, vocabulary, memorization, and the like, groups of two seem right, with one person reciting and the other checking or quizzing. For groups to work out projects, groups of five or six seem the largest, because it is too difficult for all to stimulate one another and share views if a group gets larger. For planning an experiment under teacher supervision, a group of 12 to 18 gives enough persons so that there will be a sufficiently large variety of suggestions and hypotheses from among which to select. And so on.

Problem 3: *What is required for maximum creativity in the group?*

In general, our experiences with training groups bear out the notion that creativity is the result of prevention of inhibition and threat on the one hand, and of stimulation, motivation, and clarification on the other.

The group must be motivated: it must want to solve the problem, and this means that it probably needs to have firsthand experiences that put the members under tension. Then there must be the opportunity to discharge the tension by grappling directly with the problem, rather than, for example, by fighting the leader, scapegoating a member, or shifting responsibility to something outside the group. To grapple directly with the problem requires alternation of solitude, during which one collects his thoughts and hopes for insight, with stimulation and sharing, during which ideas get kicked around, elaborated, and defended—this is the process of finding new meanings that would not occur to one by oneself. To engage in this latter process with others requires conditions such that one not only can take the risk of sticking his neck out but will, in fact, be rewarded for so doing. Risk taking seems to be easiest when the group is not too deadly serious, because a serious group is too conscious of time-wasting: It is too intent on the goal to be able to back up and approach it by the kind of circling maneuvers through which new ideational territory can be discovered. The group must also be under pressure, so that there will be expectations of performance and reward for performance, but it should probably arrange the pressures for itself through consideration of deadlines for each step; and these deadlines should be easily modifiable through orderly processes of examination of progress, difficulties, and energy and time resources. We note that these conditions for creativity are also the conditions for getting work done, and we propose that constant talk about whether the group is creative may simply add to its anxiety without increasing creativity over and above the amount that goes with effective working.

Problem 4: *Does a group need a designated leader? If so, under what conditions?*

Our studies of group growth are suggestive. In general, a group does not need a leader if all the members are thoroughly familiar with all aspects of the problem to be solved and want to solve it. Under these conditions they can listen to one another and understand one another and have the will to do so. We have never seen a group like this at its first meeting, but we have seen groups approach this condition over time.

When a problem is so large that each person has hold only of a limited part of it, there must be some provision for coordinating contributions into a single group effort. When a group is heterogeneous with respect to values, it can make use of a "referee," as, for example, the chairman under parliamentary rules (who must lay down the gavel when he participates to take sides). When a group contains persons whose personality predispositions are dominated by one emotionality (for example, dependency), a liaison person is needed who has some tendencies in several directions. (Such a person has enough need for dependency himself that he can respond to it, but he also has tendencies of other sorts so that he can interpret the persons to one another.)

From time to time the group needs a different sort of central person, and a perceptive designated leader can do a great deal to help activate the person needed most at particular times. Thus, we see the designated leader as primarily a methodologist, concerned to see that the group has the help it needs from the members who can best give it. And the actual leadership itself is distributed, not by chance nor on an equal participation basis, but in terms of who can best give the group the guidance and help it needs for maximum productivity.

Problem 5: *Is there any best leadership style? What in general can be said about all leadership situations?*

We have seen good training jobs being done by persons of widely different "styles." We do not have any evidence that would support a definition of leadership at the level of an approved pattern of specific behaviors. We have also seen leaders behave quite inconsistently at different times, especially with respect to degree of directiveness.

Although the arrangements for the personnel of leadership have to be worked out fresh for every group, every purpose, and every situation, still we believe that there are some basic functions that leadership embodies—regardless of how it is provided:

First: Purveyor of institutional realities within which the group operates. Within an institution, groups are set up for particular purposes, and they are expected to move toward attainment of these purposes. Often there are further authoritative expectations of the manner or method by which this movement is to occur. Since these limits are given arbitrarily by someone else, the members of the group cannot reasonably be expected to discover the limits through deliberation, and they might just as well be told.

For completely "free" interest groups, this function is unimportant, because the group has within itself the resources to test the feasibility of boundaries to its scope of action.

Second: Interpreter of the group to the "outside world."

Third: Continual diagnosis and clarification of purposes the group seems to be striving for. This is sometimes assigned to an observer, but in our opinion most nonparticipants build up too much frustration at not being allowed to participate to be able to handle this function with the required objectivity.

What is needed here is not a censor, policeman, or guardian of morals and manners. The need is for diagnosis of purpose so that the inactive members will know how to get into the act, and the active members can use their intelligence to achieve their purposes more directly.

Fourth: Leadership continually defines the demands the group must meet whenever the demands change, or are forgotten or knowledge of them is being repressed. This is the other side of point three.

Fifth: Leadership is continually concerned to maintain a close balance between emotionality and work in the group.

Sixth: Leadership always talks to the group, not to particular individuals. It is assumed that the group must cope with its problems once it sees what they are, and that it will cope with these best on a voluntary basis.

Problem 6: *Is member satisfaction a sign that all is going well?*
Should participation in a group be pleasant and easy?

The answer to this one is yes and no. When everyone agrees that "it was a swell meeting," this might be due to a number of causes: complacency, relief at having survived, progress toward group goals, enjoyment without pain of thought, and so on. A good meeting is one in which members listen to, and respond to, one another's ideas, where there is progress toward explicit goals or toward cleaning up whatever conditions stand in the way of goal progress, where members try hard to contribute needed behaviors, and there is production and reduction of tension.

In general, a small steering committee, which has rehearsed the problems the group will run into, can help a great deal to break big problems into smaller problems into still smaller problems and to clarify process without at the same time stultifying freedom of thought.

In general, a hard-working group has hard work. It assumes responsibility for its recommendations and actions and tries to understand the subtleties of its own psychosocial existence.

Reading 7.4

GROUP DEVELOPMENT IN A CASE SESSION*
Harriet Ronken Lynton and R. P. Lynton

Case (X) is very flexible in use and can therefore be fitted into various places in a course. Taken early it lends itself to systematic practice in paying attention to detail and in putting together uniformities as a second step to understanding the person. Later in the course it lends

---

* From *Asican Cases* (Aloka, Yelwal, Mysore, India, 1960), pp. 27–28.

itself to interpretations at a deeper and more embracing level for which the instructor may want to use the term "self-concept." As a personal life story it offers much scope for projection. Early in a course members ⌐ likely to fight shy of using this—it is "too personal"—and may ⌐ ' into paying very close attention to the details in the case, perhaps *ad nauseam.* Later they may readily see in the case someone in their own group and talk directly about him.

One or the other of two openings seems to occur again and again. Often a hitherto silent member uses the case to make his debut into case discussions. Usually he does so by listing facts in the case as they are stated, such as where the writer was born and went to school, and what his activities are now. Such an opening statement may be long and may range over the whole case without adding anything to it. The importance of it lies in the member's making it. Beyond letting him finish, the instructor may acknowledge his effort and encourage the member's continued participation in several ways. This kind of listening lends itself to repetition on the blackboard; of this more below. The instructor can also comment on the wide range of this opening statement, classify the material into two or three sections, and ask the member to expand on what he has said about one of them if he wishes before the others go on from there.

The other familiar opening is an argument over whether the writer is "successful" or not. Those who see him as successful can point to his "hard work" and his "ambition," to such facts as his numerous high examination results, his rapid promotion and wide responsibilities for over one hundred employees. Early in the course protagonists of this view may have no open opponents because members then generally assume that a case is a success story, a kind of demonstration of how they ought to develop; and if they cannot readily see the success in it they will be silent rather than say so. Later in the course there will be open opposition. The same facts can be interpreted quite differently. These members will regard the frequency and elaboration of examination results in the writer's life as an indication of his dissatisfaction and his anxiety to prove himself over and over again, to seek security in a pile of diplomas. Similarly they may look at the number of people the writer says he directly supervises and conclude that, since "direct" supervision of over one hundred employees is either impossible or meaningless, the statement points to the writer's need to build up his importance in the eyes of others.

In any case the contributions probably lend themselves to a threefold classification: facts and happenings mentioned by the writer, their meaning to him, and their meaning to the speakers in the group. This is a useful distinction for the members to practice and can easily be done on the board. Though the meaning to the speaker is not important for an understanding of the writer, it is yet important to leave this category on the board. For one thing, many contributions will belong to it. More importantly, the members' views matter. By keeping them as a separate classification the instructor accepts them as that, important but different from the other kinds of data.

If the first category, that of happenings, presents any problems, they arise out of abundance. There is no need or value for the instructor to "go after" more and more facts. He may in fact interfere with any straight listing by asking the speaker what the meaning of a happening is that he offers for inclusion, particularly its meaning to the writer. The flow of facts will die down as members notice how repetitive they are. Again and again there is the same kind of fact, such as the writer ending "just below top grade" in examinations and job and his explanation of his falling short in terms of circumstances beyond his control: the achievement of political independence of his country, defective vision, shortage of engineering colleges. In this category belongs anything taken from the case itself, the explanations the writer gives no less than the events for which he gives them. The explanations are at best the writer's understanding of the events, which is not the same as the meaning of the event. They also contain what he wishes the reader to see. Even leaving aside meanings of which the writer may not be aware, there are instances in the case of the writer's wishes rather than his understanding presented as explanations.

The grouping of the facts becomes clear only as members begin to understand the meaning to the writer of the happenings he reports, the second category on the board. But members may have real difficulty going beyond what the writer says. It carries the threatening possibility that the instructor and also the other members of the group could similarly go beyond what the speaker himself says and writes. Some members may be silent, therefore, while others may proceed by guessing. What will hold this part of the discussion together is that most members do in fact have an overall view of the writer, for which the instructor will keep on referring them back to the data in the case, to check, refine and particularise. Presumably the grandiose jumps into overall explanations may become useful tentative steps towards greater understanding.

The members' own experiences can be brought in directly to help in this process. Almost certainly there will be someone in the group who has, like the writer, changed schools often as a child, or lived away from home. The instructor may ask them to describe what this meant to them. Inevitably it entails frequent starting and finishing of relationships with teachers and other school children and allows little opportunity to form deep, lasting friendships. Someone may remember this time as a difficult one, another as fun. Referring back to the case someone may notice that the writer does not mention this aspect of the experience except for his having learned the skill "of working with others." It is a short step to go on to notice that the only relationships the writer mentions in the whole case are working relationships and those in terms of functions, not of people. A three-word sentence deals with his married life. There is no mention of a friendship. Perhaps there is none. Perhaps it means that he does not get close to other people. Are there some other data in the case which may throw light on this? If the discussion continues in the area of the writer's relationships the rest of the period may well be spent on it. Otherwise we will want to return to it.

Once a start has been made, the instructor can usefully work to and fro between the categories of meaning and happenings, helping members group the happenings in the case, wherever reported, around the meanings. The writer seems to be concerned with being first. Data besides the way he talks about his examination results fit into this: e.g., his mention of coming from a high-caste family and of his father being in government service, his going to a 'leading' concern for work, his working with an international group of consultants. But usually he does not quite become first. He does not call that being second, but being "just below top". His urge to keep on taking examinations and the exhaustive listing of them part by part has probably a good deal to do with this need to be on top. Members may wonder what this eagerness does to the writer's social life, for the top position is a difficult one from which to make friends. Presumably someone may notice that gardening and reading, the hobbies the writer mentions, are individual activities. When he mentions his ability and his need to work with other people he does not seem to mean a close personal association but a superior—subordinate relationship. He may wish to associate more with others but he does not.

Since so much of a person's development and present life depends on his relationships, the instructor may wish to focus on them, in this and other cases.

The discussion may not get this far. To help members check their understanding and see the reality and importance of it, the instructor may want to allow some minutes at the end to raise some action questions. For instance, would the members ask the writer of the case to work with them in their organizations? What position would they have in mind for him? Can they anticipate some problems that he would be likely to meet there and could they help him with them?

Another possible end to the discussion is for the instructor to refer the members back to the case and to wonder with them, in the light of their understanding now, how early in the case they could have got some inkling at least of this understanding through careful, skilful reading.

Chapter 8

/ /

The Personal Needs of the Trainer

The Trainer's "Realness" under Pressure: Three Dilemmas

1. Participants' Expectations versus Trainer's Intentions

2. Individual versus Group Needs

3. Consistency versus Flexibility

Different Training Styles

Exhibits

8.1 Categories and Components of a Training Style

8.2. Seven Clusters of Training Styles

Figure

8.1. Two Sample Profiles of Training Styles

Reading

8.1. The Trainer as Change Agent—Edgar H. Schein and Warren G. Bennis

The Trainer

/ /

". . . . the shaman heals through the use of personal power, using craft, charm and cunning; the magician heals through his knowledge of archaic and complex rules, and his ability to follow ritual precisely; the priest claims no personal power, but achieves his healing capacity as an agent or vessel of an omnipotent authority; the mystic healer relies on insight, vision and wisdom, through which he cures the sick soul; the naturalist (the present-day physician) is impersonal, empirical, task-oriented."

—JOSEPH ADELSON

LEARNING takes place within the individual as a result of a confluence of diverse, intertwining, and occasionally opposing influences. It shows not in test performance—that need only show that the participant has memorized an approved response—but in action. It lasts. And it stimulates and supports further learning. The function of the trainer is to entice this mysterious process to develop within the participants, each one of them if possible.

To this task the trainer brings in the first place an adequate standard of competence in his field of training, be it health or accounting, or training methodologies themselves. He needs to be thoroughly familiar with the subject matter of this field. There is no substitute for this, not even, studies show, individualized programmed instruction. If this condition does not exist, the trainer is a nonstarter so far as we are concerned. He had better become a participant in some program first and allow us to address ourselves here to the trainers in that program. It is time to recognize that ever increasing knowledge of a subject in no substitute for adequate training skill; but neither is training skill a substitute for familiarity with the subject. On this minimum requirement we will not spend time here but regard it as home base. We will

275

consider later how the trainer can keep his subject matter knowledge and familiarity alive and up to date, as he must.

This condition satisfied, we turn to the trainer's actual behavior during training. We find that we have to consider several levels. How a trainer behaves effectively in different kinds of training situations is open to observation, thoughtful listening, and understanding. This is one part of what participants do—pretty well all they do, perhaps, at the very beginning of a program. So we hear the trainer making sure, by the comments he makes in field training and the way he makes them, that participants become aware of problem areas but he avoids depending on ready-made answers which would cut short their enquiry. In role playing he leaves all action to the participants, while he ensures adequate time for preparation and playing and stimulates an insightful discussion afterwards. In case discussions he again lets the participants carry the ball; he himself elicits contributions, states underlying assumptions, helps participants think them through, and draws contributions together into memorable conceptual wholes. In laboratory training he addresses directly the underlying relationships and personal issues which interfere with the group's progress.

Whatever the label of the event or the training method with which he starts, we see the trainer again as he changes his behavior in whatever direction promises most learning. As a lecture or an individual task begins to drag, he says, "Alright, we have sat long enough. Let's go out and have a look" (field visit, demonstration). Or, "You have been listening just to me (lecture). Let's hear some others" (discussion). Or: "That is your experience (discussion). Now consider another person's" (incident, case). Or: "You keep on talking in the third person, *about* people. How about a little practice now talking *with* someone, about something that concerns you" (role play, skill practice). Or: "We have done enough of this for now. Here is a reading (writing) assignment for tomorrow." He is the craftsman at work. Intent on the utility and elegance of the result, he varies his pace to achieve it. In his art, he hits on the learners' best pace.

Circumspect timing of inputs of new data and of different kinds of activities and concerns is one of the trainer's most delicate tasks. The whole process has proper seasons. Some times are ripe for disturbing and questioning—ploughing, others for seeding and fostering growth. This farming language is far better for describing the trainer's orientation and activities than talk about "making" or "requiring" people to learn. Notice the similies in Thelen's description of teaching: "the art of the sophisticated teacher manifests itself in the ability to capitalize on the wide range of natural tendencies that exist in the class: to work with them rather than suppress them and to teach . . . behaviors through which (these) tendencies can be expressed."[1] It is no coincidence that medical analogies also come easily, for the word "doctor" is itself derived from the Latin *docere,* to teach. Or managing, which comes from "training by exercise." Craftsman, farmer, doctor, manager—an effective trainer is apparently a brother to all of these.

We have seen, further, that no description so far—not training event, nor method, nor the trainer's actions—yet tells us much about the trainer's effectiveness. What matters is not the event or the act but the meaning that participants see in it. And this meaning has a lot to do with the social process through which the particular training group develops its distinctive character and reaction. A recent book on teacher effectiveness draws the distinction between these two levels very strongly:

> Literally thousands of studies have been conducted on teacher excellence since the beginning of the twentieth century. Investigators have looked at teacher training, traits, behaviors, attitudes, values, abilities, sex, weight, voice, quality and many other characteristics. Teacher effects have been judged by investigators themselves, by pupils, by administrators and parents, by master teachers, by practice teachers, and by themselves. The apparent results of teaching have been studied, including pupil learning, adjustment, classroom performance, sociometric status, attitudes, liking for school, and later achievement. And yet, with all this research activity, results have been modest and often contradictory. Few, if any facts are now deemed established about teacher effectiveness, and many former findings have been repudiated. It is not an exaggeration to say that we do not today know how to select, train for, encourage, or evaluate teacher effectiveness. And many education researchers have abandoned the field of competence research as a simpleminded approach to a vastly more complex topic: the study of classroom interaction.[2]

Finally, we have seen that the nature, quality, and effectiveness of the interaction we call training depends primarily on the feelings that the trainer communicates to the participants through his behavior. From this next deeper level springs the training "climate," a pervasive phenomenon that tends to self-fulfilling and self-reinforcing continuity. With this further step we leave the layers of knowledge, understanding, and skill, even of social skill. That this would be necessary is itself

---

[1] Herbert A. Thelen, Some Classroom Quiddities for People-Oriented Teachers," *Journal of Applied Behavioral Science,* Vol. I (July–September, 1965).

[2] Bruce J. Biddle and William J. Elena (eds.), *Contemporary Research in Teacher Effectiveness* (New York: Holt, Rinehart & Winston, Inc., 1964).

nothing new. We have always known, in our heart of hearts, that neither great erudition nor social skill was enough to make an effective trainer, that his "personality" finally mattered, too. And it may matter a great deal. To put it most simply, for a trainer to express the kinds of feeling that evoke an effective training "climate," he first has to have them.

THE PERSONAL NEEDS OF THE TRAINER

The kinds of feeling that matter for a favorable climate include an absorbing interest and feeling of excitement in his subject and his work of training; eagerness to share the task and help participants grow into taking more responsibility for it; acceptance of the participants as people with differing needs and personalities, and responsiveness to them; and trust in himself and in others. With increasing skill, as it comes with experience and practice, the trainer can communicate these feelings of his more effectively. But all the skill in the world is no substitute for the feelings themselves. If the trainer's interests and concerns lie in other directions, in research, for instance, or in promotion or power, his training skill is dead. Devoid of personal roots, any training skill will be experienced by the participants as manipulative, calling for submission or opposition, and increasing their dependence. At issue is the development of personal understanding and trust between the trainer and the participants; and this is a matter primarily of feelings.

In an atmosphere of trust even an outrageous piece of behavior may "carry" the participants. If it is a real gaff, it may even have the bonus of increasing their acceptance of the trainer as a fallible person who is putting himself out to do his very best but does not always succeed. One of the authors once found himself after the close of a training course in personal conversation with some participants whose travel plans had left them at the institution for an extra day. In the informal atmosphere he found it comfortable to inquire, "Why did you give the Trainer X such a hard time?" After listening to their complaints he added, "But when I made similar mistakes you helped me." "Oh," came the rejoinder, "that's different. You like us." If, on the other hand, the trainer fails to "come through" as a trustworthy person, even the most proper, correct behavior on his part will only confirm to the participants that he is a cold fish; and not a cold fish only but a dangerous one, just because he is so competent and so inscrutable. In a recent survey of 1,000 college students in America aimed at eliciting what characteristics in their instructors they found most helpful, even a steady temper rated insignificantly low. Top score went to enthusiasm.

The trainer's choice of events and methods in his work tells in the end more about the person he is than about his intellectual assessment of the effectiveness of some events and methods compared to others. He settles on those that "suit" him and that he is most likely to be "good" at. Trainers who rely on lecturing are often those who feel a need to talk, who like order and neatness, both in their sessions and generally, who are afraid that they might lose control or show up unfavorably under testing questions. Lecturing satisfies these needs. If a lecturer's table is provided, perhaps on a raised platform, this is not merely a convenience but also a welcome symbol of superiority: that is where he, the knowledgeable man, stands, to whom all eyes are directed, who starts and finishes the session, allows or refuses questions, dispenses approval and disapproval. This kind of lecturer may not welcome the extra distance of this arrangement at first, since it segregates him from the participants. But he is party to choosing a process that by its very nature increases social distance. Like the moat around an encampment, lecturing will indeed protect him from disturbing challenges. He is safe. If an institution has many trainers with these needs, good lecturing is likely to be the main avenue to promotion and all the advantages linked with promotion. In that institution a young lecturer may well feel confirmed in using a method that is so well attuned to his personal needs and his surroundings. This skill he then develops in use, and the others atrophy and become less attractive.

Probably on no other dimension do training methods differ more, and more importantly, than on the control *the trainer* feels he needs over the participants. To this need is bent the traditional deference to the scholar, the wise man, the priestly teacher. Any trainer who sets himself up as the authority figure in control of a training event assumes that this deference is due to him.

> One recent study describes a trainer who was preoccupied with "talking, whispering and horseplay" among participants. He tolerated such behavior up to the point where it became a challenge to his authority and then took some action to suppress it. What is important to note is the point at which the trainer stepped in. It was not the point where the talking, etc., interfered with learning but the point where it became a challenge to his "status."

The next step of this kind of trainer is to insist that control is, *sine qua non,* a necessary condition for effective training. Many trainers stand by this assertion in such vigorous terms that the underlying personal needs are quite plain. When a trainer who has got used to gratifying his personal needs through maintaining a central, controlling, dominating, distant role, he can all too easily seek and find evidence to back his stand. If, as a matter of fact, participants do not take responsibility for improving the training situation, the trainer concludes that he therefore has no alternative to hanging on to control, "whatever theory may say." And these trainers then choose colleagues and successors to fit this same debilitating pattern: a vicious circle.

The relationship between personal needs and choice of training method and behavior is not necessarily simple and direct. It can be inverse. The same need to control may push a trainer to advocate collaborative and permissive methods. He may do so to avoid acknowledging to himself and to others his own need to control. So he hides it behind "permissive methods" and looks to friendly human relationships for confirmation. Anxiety and lack of spontaneity are the mark of this trainer. His heart is not in participation. He does not engage himself but stands aside. If the relationships become friendly at all under these conditions, they are usually superficial and dependent. Moreover, they are achieved at the expense of the task. This trainer indulges participants in his need, not theirs.

The close link between the trainer's personal needs, his behavior, and the methods he uses need not surprise us. It is part of what makes much of the world go round. Industry, for instance, is full of managers who shape whole organizations so that they express and reflect their personal needs. We all experience satisfaction from such congruence and seek it in many ways, for instance, by our choice of occupation. The same congruence, after all, but in appropriate directions, brings out the enthusiasm, care, and concern that we look for in an effective trainer. Truth and perversion are reverse sides of the same coin, in this as in other matters.

What this realization ought to evoke is an adequate examination, at this personal level, of persons being selected as trainers. How does the applicant regard himself and where does he look for his satisfactions? As a scholar, primarily concerned with advancing his subject? As an administrator or organizer who looks for efficiency, perhaps power? As a public servant "able to do anything"? As someone who learns on and on, with the help of others?

We do not know how far the personality factors relevant to effective training are fixed by the time a person becomes a trainer. We do know that for many trainers in India now, training has not been their first or even their second choice. For many, it has been the only road open to earning a "respectable" living, or an activity seen as a step toward some other career. We also know that a developing society may quietly favor an ineffective pattern of training as a way of protecting itself against major change. It looks for trainers who confirm the image it has of itself rather than for trainers who rock the boat. This cultural protection then exaggerates the inherent bias that training everywhere has toward starting off on the wrong foot. Participants feel most dependent on the trainer right at the beginning of any training. The trainer in turn just then looks to the new group for reassurance and confirmation. The prevailing tendency, therefore, is to start the relationship off to a pattern of high dependence. This pattern is particularly difficult to modify afterwards. To this built-in bias in training the world over, developing countries add their pervasive protective bais—all on the same unpromising side.

To expect people who did not choose to be trainers and who value society's traditional deference to the teacher's status and functions to do more than lecture and possibly chair a general discussion, would be inappropriate and also unfair. Their hearts cannot be in striving for more significant training. It would be wrong, and possibly harmful both to them and to the participants, if these trainers ventured into using more personal training methods.

So far as they are concerned, we have only one more thought to express. We doubt whether the cost of their inadequate or erratic motivation for effective training is at all comprehended, by themselves or by others. It is very great, in economic, not to include human and developmental, terms. If people in charge of training schemes continue to recruit these unsuitable people and saddle them with high expectations, it can only be because at that level too the same self-perpetuating defensive process is at work that we have already described. After all, by definition development depends on people behaving in new ways. Trainers of these people have to be themselves in the forefront and to demonstrate the essential novelty. We conclude that the development process would be better served if the training effort were limited to a scale that can be effectively staffed. We know trainers here and there, in India too, who do have the personal qualities required; and there are surely many more who have the makings of effective trainers but need to develop themselves further: to nourish their inner strength and to develop more skill in communicating their attitudes effectively. It is to them that further professional training and these pages need to be addressed.

THE TRAINER'S "REALNESS" UNDER PRESSURE: THREE DILEMMAS

Any basic flaws the trainer has will show under pressure, when he reacts spontaneously, "out of his guts," from the depth of the person he is. Pressures in the training setting arise from many sources and directions. Pressures of time, for instance, and sheer quantity of work are most common. We will focus on the last minutes of a session.

> Time is running out and the trainer has another two or three major points to make. But participants are busily following up an earlier thought. The discussion is lively. It is drawing in some who have not spoken earlier, and now speak haltingly and rather slowly, and not very directly to the point, perhaps. Where does the trainer's attention go then? To "rounding off" the subject, no matter at what interruption of learning in the group? To letting them go on doing what they like? Or to refocusing the group on the main training objectives?—for instance, by stating the choices now open to the group in terms of the little time left. It is a spot judgment, and with the best will in the world, subject to many errors. But the very manner in which the trainer proceeds, in whatever direction, tells about his feelings and about him as a person. In such a situation, one trainer reasserts himself quite roughly, as if the discussion had not taken place or had been an undesirable interlude. Another does nothing, because he has lost sight of the objectives of the session or fears the group's displeasure if he reminds them. A third way is to remind them, but gently. He acknowledges that the current discussion may be more important and that the "rounding off" might yet be done by using the break or making some extra time elsewhere.

In observing the trainer's reaction, a useful summary question may be: Where is his attention mostly? On the subject "to cover," the relationships among the participants, bringing one or two "slow" ones along, their relationships with him, his relationships to colleagues and principal? If the trainer experiences the pressures in this quite common situation as a challenge to his authority, he will look for ways of dealing with them in quite different directions from a trainer who sees them as arising out of the participants' endeavor to learn and out of his own human limitations.

It may be useful to list, with a brief comment for each, three dilemmas built into most training situations which bring pressures on the trainer.

1. Participants' Expectations versus Trainer's Intentions

Participants carry a burden of history, in the form of expectations, as they first meet the trainer. They have some picture of "him" long before they in fact know the particular trainer. And their getting to know him is bedeviled by interpreting his current behavior in the light of the participants' memories of other trainers. Whether these interpretations are rosy or black, they are certainly limiting and, from his point of view, chancy. The new trainer is classified in advance, cast for a part he cannot know and one which may differ for various participants.

An informal opening through which the trainer intends to communicate friendliness and closeness may strike some participants as a sign of incompetence, others as lack of authority, yet others as a challenge and promising fun, and others as fearfully vague and threatening disaster. Participants whose expectations are violated by this initial informality will react suspiciously: "What does this mean?" "Can I trust him?" Or, at a different level, "Can I trust myself with him?"

Trainers need only to reflect on their experience of simply asking a new group, "Are there any questions?" His intention may be to test how well he has been understood. But no questions may come. Or the few questions that do come give him no answer to his question, really. He has learned from experience that some (unknown) participants hesitate to ask for fear of appearing stupid or unprepared before him and others; others (unknown) do the same, to avoid the charge later of "playing up" to the trainer; others again to avoid the risk of ridicule. For all of these, silence is simpler and safer. Those who do ask questions, for their parts and also unknown, may be concerned mostly with assuming leadership in the group or with showing the trainer that they are "good students" who were paying attention.

A similarly wide range of reactions may greet a suggestion that the trainer threw in to stimulate thought and make an idea concrete. Many participants immediately conclude that this is not so much a suggestion to examine as a hint, something to be implemented or opposed.

The pressures out of this discrepancy between participants' expectations and the trainer's intention can become so great that trainers can be heard to sigh that their groups seem "determined to misunderstand and misconstrue" their every action. When this happens, what does the trainer do? Express anger to the participants? Ignore the pressure and "battle on"? Or look for ways to get closer to participants to understand the block and to give participants a better chance to understand him? Two conditions make the pressures that arise from this dilemma extra difficult to bear or to live down. One obtains when participants did not choose to come for training, indeed might have preferred not to come. Not only does this cloud their expectations, but their dislikes are then so general and free-floating that the trainer may be able to do little to offset them. The other obtains when one trainer behaves very differently from other trainers working in the same program or elsewhere in the same institution. The signals to the participants are then confusing and arouse their suspicion. Participants may come to feel treated as toys to be played with, or perhaps experimented upon and manipulated.

2. Individual versus Group Needs

Participants differ in interests, methods of work, speed of learning and interpretation of the trainer's behavior. But except for minor modifications, the trainer's one action has to be the same for all. To whom does the trainer then pay most attention and address his endeavors? The talkers or the nontalkers, the quick or the slow, the agreeable or the attackers? It is all too easy for him to get mesmerized by the obvious, often clamorous, needs at one extreme or another. Many trainers find it indeed difficult to forego the clamor and challenge in order to deal with the less stimulating but often more numerous assortment of participants in the middle. It is well for him to acknowledge the satisfactions he finds in working with the bright and the agreeable and the dislike he feels for those who tax his patience or get his goat. The extremes challenge the trainer as a person and bring his own needs—to be liked, to succeed, to defend himself—into sharpest focus. But the main needs in terms of learning are likely to lie elsewhere.

3. Consistency versus Flexibility

The widely varying and changing needs of individual participants call for flexible behavior on the part of the trainer. Like any skilled craftsman he seeks to respond appropriately to the immediate situation, taking into account as best he can its multiple moving facets. Participants, on the other hand, look to the trainer for consistent behavior, preferably faultless behavior. They know how to deal with him then and what to expect. They can make of the trainer the all-knowing god (or devil) who can be kept at a safe distance. The trainer's flexibility and humanity then can be disquieting to the participants, denying them the certainty and security that they feel they need and to which they feel entitled. Accusations of favoritism, incompetence, and manipulation to retain power often follow.

Trainers know all these dilemmas from experience. They also know, or can find out, how they can reduce the pressures. They can work towards bringing conflicting expectations out in the open and make common plans; face the participants with a pair of suggestions to choose from instead of just one; work in small groups to take care of individual variations in learning; deal with some individual needs of participants outside the session; state and restate the orientation and objectives of the program; encourage clarification of doubts about the trainer's behavior—and so on, down the list of all the desirable behavior we have described in various parts of the book.

The difficulty lies not in knowing but in doing and in acting quickly when the occasion arises; and then again not in doing, in the first place, but in feeling like doing—in the trainer's disposition. If his disposition is not in line with effective training, then he adds a fourth dilemma which really *is* unmanageable: trainer's needs versus participants' needs. We suspect that it is this basic dilemma and the pressures that arise from it that so many trainers seek to deal with by authoritarian, distant, and impersonal behavior and by choosing training events and tools in the reverse order of effectiveness: abstract when something situational is needed, distant instead of personal, individual instead of social, a focus on outward behavior instead of on feelings.

Training in developing countries is beset by these same dilemmas magnified. Trainers there have to be exceptionally strong and able people if they are to be effective at levels of training that make a difference in development. The experiences and expectations that participants bring are, by definition, sharply at variance with effective training for the future: They place the trainer firmly into the position of authority and participants into positions of dependence. These expectations resist major modification, partly because dependency needs are deep-seated in the participants' personalities and also because they continue to govern so many important relationships. Participants are used to the satisfactions of dependent relationships at work and in their families. In those settings they are in authority and have others dependent on them, or can look forward with assurance to a time when this will be their position. Any rebellious feelings that they have experienced against people in authority, and perhaps even expressed in action, have not taken them far along the road of personal and social development. They are commonly what psychologists call "counterdependent"; the focus of attention for their feelings is still the trainer vested with authority.

Effective training in such a situation calls for opportunities to experience pressure from many sources and make individual decisions under these conditions, opportunities of living with intense personal and social demands. Lecturing and general discussions do not have much to offer in these directions; they promote conformity or intellectual debate without testing disagreements in action. Training, on the contrary, must provide opportunities in which participants can practice differing from others and collaborating with others across these differences. To be effective in these directions, trainers need in the first place to have these very qualities and must be able to demonstrate them. They must feel this personal freedom and interdependence themselves so that they can express these feelings in the ways they behave with participants and in the kinds of training events they organize.

The trainer expresses this freedom at the personal level through what Carl Rogers calls his "realness," and the interdependence by his responding to others in ways we have described in the last chapter as "indirect training." Rogers writes:

> Learning will be facilitated if the teacher is congruent. This involves the teacher's being the person that he is, and being openly aware of the attitudes he holds. It means that he feels acceptant toward his own real feelings. Thus he becomes a real person in the relationship with his students. He can be enthusiastic about subjects he likes, and bored by topics he does not like. He can be angry, but he can also be sensitive or sympathetic. Because he accepts his feelings as *his* feelings, he has no need to impose them on his students, or to insist that they feel the same way. He is a person, not a faceless embodiment of a curricular requirement, or a sterile pipe through which knowledge is passed from one generation to the next.[3]

The basic importance of the trainer's realness is confirmed by an increasing body of studies based on elaborate recordings of discussions and statistical correlations between predicted and actual ratings. Denial by the trainer of his own feelings is accompanied by lower effectiveness.[4]

Helping a trainer learn to accept his own feelings more fully and so become more real can be attempted through programs of laboratory training and various kinds of counseling. Collaboration can also be practiced systematically. Ned Flanders specifies three objectives for such training for the trainers: first, practice in accepting, clarifying and using the ideas of participants in planning the work and diagnosing difficulties; second, increasing the trainer's recognition of acts that restrict

---

[3] Carl Rogers, *On Becoming a Person* (Boston: Houghton Mifflin Co., 1961), p. 287.

[4] John Withall and W. W. Lewis, "Social Interaction in the Classroom", in N. L. Gage, (ed.), *Handbook of Research on Teaching* (Chicago: Rand McNally & Co., 1963), pp. 683–714.

participant reactions and those that expand them; and third, developing the trainer's understanding of theories of instruction that he can use to control his own behavior as he guides communication in practice.[5]

To keep on developing himself and resisting the dominant pressures toward familiar authoritarian and directive patterns, the trainer needs above all regular reliable information about his own behavior and its effects on participants. A sympathetic colleague can be an excellent source for this information. If colleagues pair up and take turns providing this information to one another, any threat implied by such checking can be greatly reduced. Not evaluation but information about interactions is required. The question is not what should have happened but what in fact did happen. Self-improvement tends to follow this sharing.

Training trainers for greater effectiveness, then, means changing the authoritarian image which tradition has taught the trainer to have of his role into something closer to the image of a resource person who is able to help participants in the process of their learning. The new image is usually not one that the trainer has experienced. Nor has he received such help or given it, at least with much awareness. In the absence of this personal experience, the new image is likely to have little real meaning for trainers. Even apart from feelings he might have about helping others in ways that he in his day had to do without, there is also the difficulty that the new approach to training has no model. The trainer can point neither at himself nor at some immediately visible figure as example. Finally, the ideal he works toward with the participants' potential is remote: a developing society, something largely intangible and difficult to describe.

The new approach demands from the trainer great acumen, sensitivity and adaptability, and continuous application. The only reward it promises is the personal satisfaction that comes from greater effectiveness. In the institution and program in which he works, the rewards of status and reputation will almost certainly continue to run in the traditional direction of subject knowledge, research and publications, and this for a long time to come. Status and reputation for more effective training may yet be far ahead.

DIFFERENT TRAINING STYLES

Out of his "realness" and striving for interdependence each trainer develops a personal style of his own. He grows to prefer certain kinds of training events and methods and is also most effective using these. The

[5] Flanders, Ned A. "Teacher Influence: Pupil Attitudes and Achievement" (mimeographed; Minneapolis: University of Minnesota, 1961).

events and methods are structures that he fills with his personality. Different methods and different styles are effective because they are congruent, "natural," to the trainer; they express the particular person he is.

One study has delineated seven styles among a group of adult teachers that were all assessed as effective.[6] Teaching style is defined as "a pattern composed of classroom behaviors of a teacher which are consistent over time and which distinguish him from other teachers." The categories used and the seven styles delineated in the study are set out in

Figure 8.1

TWO SAMPLE PROFILES OF TRAINING STYLES

Dimensions	*Profile A*	*Profile B*
1. What does he think is important?	Teaching subject matter or content	Developing participants or process
2. How does he relate to the group?	Impersonal or lacks empathy	Personal or full of empathy
3. How does he communicate?	Talks or teacher-active	Elicits or participant-active
4. What method does he prefer?	Cognitive	Experiential
5. How does he react to change?	Rigid	Flexible
6. How far does he control the group?	Controls completely	Allows full freedom

Exhibits 8.1 and 8.2. Discussion with these teachers brought up four important questions that determine a teacher's style:

1. Which element of the learning situation does the teacher think most important: the student, the subject matter, or the world of the student?
2. What pattern of interaction does the teacher tend to encourage: student-student, teacher-student, or teacher-subject matter?
3. What is the "gratification focus" of the teacher, or, where does the teacher get most of his kicks: relationship with the student, interest in the subject matter, or the act of teaching?
4. What role does the teacher tend to primarily assume: director, star actor, or stage manager?

In constructing a profile of training styles, the trainer's behavior is the all-important focus, not his intent or his feelings. Figure 8.1 shows two basically different styles delineated along six simple dimensions.

From several studies, two general points stand out. The first is the wide variety of training goals and styles through which trainers can

---

[6] Daniel Solomon and Harry L. Miller, *Exploration in Teaching Styles* (Chicago: Center for the Study of Liberal Education for Adults, 1961).

Exhibit 8.1

CATEGORIES AND COMPONENTS OF A TEACHING STYLE

Perceptual-Cognitive

Goals (the type of change which the teacher attempts to produce in the student):

1. Increase student's fund of facts.
2. Give student ability to use certain practical methods and techniques.
3. Give student ability to relate subject to social and/or practical problems.
4. Give student ability to use method of analysis, of thinking.
5. Produce feeling of intellectual discovery and/or intellectual self-awareness.
6. Get student excited and involved in subject.
7. Change basic attitudes or values of students.
8. Produce greater self-awareness, emotional discovery.

Direction of Interest (that aspect of the class to which the teacher directs his major emphasis):

1. Students.
2. Subject matter.
3. The act of teaching.

Class Orientation (the teacher's perception of the class with respect to "needs"):

1. Individualistic.
2. Pluralistic.
3. Unitary.

Behavioral

Control (the degree and type of direction produced by the teacher in the class situation):

1. High dominant.
2. High dominant (responsive).
3. Medium dominant (responsive).
4. Low dominant (responsive).

Emotional Qualities (the manner in which methods are used by the teacher):

1. Protecting (reassuring).
2. Relaxed (accepting).
3. Threatening.
4. Nonaccepting.
5. Enthusiastic.
6. Disinterested.
7. Insecure (uncomfortable).
8. Sensitive.

Methods (Specific behaviors of the teacher in the class situation):

A. Methods of stimulating students.
B. Methods of allaying anxiety.
C. Methods of presenting subject matter.

SOURCE: Adapted from Daniel Solomon and Harry L. Miller, *Exploration in Teaching Styles* (Chicago: Center for the Study of Liberal Education for Adults, 1961).

Exhibit 8.2

SEVEN CLUSTERS OF TEACHING STYLES

	Cluster 1 Businesslike, Objective, Impersonal	Cluster 2 Emphasis on Communication	Cluster 3 Personal Approach	Cluster 4 Self-Involvement	Cluster 5 Sensitivity toward Students	Cluster 6 Protective Behavior	Cluster 7 Stimulating the Student
Goals				To provide greater self-awareness, emotional discovery		To give student ability to relate subject to problems	To get student excited and involved in subject
Direction of interest	Subject matter			The art of teaching	Students		
Class orientation	Unitary						
Control components		Low dominant (responsive)					
Sequence	Fluctuating: medium and high dominant (responsive)	Fluctuating: low, medium, and high dominant (responsive)					
Emotional quality	Relaxed (accepting)		Relaxed (accepting)				
Methods of stimulating students	Presents materials without expressing opinions	Encourages class discussion of students' work	Gives student chance to practice particular method of discipline.	Presents material and expresses opinion	Is sensitive to the need for continuation	Actively supports group process from interference	"Playing the ham"
			Poses problems and asks questions regarding individual experience	Uses small groups		Encourages agreement among students	

Exhibit 8.2 (Continued)

	Cluster 1 Businesslike, Objective, Impersonal	Cluster 2 Emphasis on Communication	Cluster 3 Personal Approach	Cluster 4 Self-Involvement	Cluster 5 Sensitivity toward Students	Cluster 6 Protective Behavior	Cluster 7 Stimulating the Student
Of allaying anxiety		Opportunity to communicate with instructor				Acceptance of expansion of students' contribution	Use of humor
Of presenting subject matter					Use of analogy		

SOURCE: Adapted from Daniel Solomon and Harry L. Miller, *Exploration in Teaching Styles* (Chicago: Center for the Study of Liberal Education for Adults, 1961).

promote learning. Some trainers state their primary goal in terms of developing self-awareness; others aim at relating the subject to practical problems; others again at increasing the participants' urge to study. The trainers' primary direction of interest varies accordingly toward: the participants, the subject, the process of training. In action, some trainers express their opinions, others do not. Some address the participants as a group, others address mostly individuals. Some exercise much control, others little. Through it all, participants may or may not learn what is intended.

But the uniformities are also striking. In the study comparing seven training styles, the word "responsive" accompanies every mention of control or control sequences. All trainers are "relaxed, accepting" even the "businesslike" trainers. The "businesslike" trainers are just like the others in presenting their subject without expressing their own opinions. In another study, trainers differed in the frequency with which they interacted with the students, but when they did interact they all did so in an indirect manner. All the trainers, whatever their style, were very flexible and were able to vary their roles and methods to suit the changing needs. Such flexibility comes from feeling at home in the style and the situation. Altogether, effective trainers range far wider in style and behave far more flexibly than ineffective trainers.

Different styles, methods, and events can be accommodated in the same training program. They are not confusing to the participants. They make the program more stimulating. More importantly, the variety itself communicates, first, that different kinds of behavior can be equally effective in a situation so long as the behavior is genuine; and, second, that participants have the very personal task of developing styles of behavior personal to themselves, styles which truly express the person they each are. What does confuse the participants and can seriously disrupt a training program is a mixture of genuine and "fake" trainers. This leaves the participants wondering in which direction to look and to proceed. Placed among the conflicting pressures of developing countries, they are very apt then to conclude that they are being manipulated, teased rather than trained, and this experience is almost sure to freeze them in their traditional rigid patterns. When that happens training is a waste, or worse. A consistently "real" training environment, on the other hand, is supportive. Participants can feel sure of a genuine response, can see the effects of their new behavior. They can develop their personal styles, which just like the trainers' will surely be more varied and more flexible than the styles they come with. That is the direction of effective training for development.

Reading 8.1

THE TRAINER AS CHANGE AGENT*

Edgar H. Schein and Warren G. Bennis

The idea of change agentry, as we are using the term here, is very new. Because of its novelty, its fundamental outline is still emerging. Thus the role of the change agent is protean, changing, difficult to grasp, and practically impossible to generalize. There are a number of things we would like to call attention to about the role of the change agent. The change agent's role is: professional, marginal, ambiguous, insecure, risky.

1. Professional

The change agent is a professional. He counts heavily on a body of valid knowledge in order to realize his aims, under guidance of certain ethical principles, and with the client's interest, not his own, in mind. This last point should be emphasized; the change agent must defer his own personal gratification in his dealings with the target system, his client. Particularly in dealing with something as important as a large and complex organization—where the change agent's actions may affect thousands of individuals—he must continually check his own needs, motives, and wishes against the reality of the client's needs.[1]

2. Marginal

The change agent is marginal. He does not have formal membership in the target system or with a band of colleagues working close by. Typically he works alone, and his marginality can work to his advantage and to his discomfort. On the positive side, the marginality can

---

* Abridged from Edgar H. Schein and Warren G. Bennis, *Personal and Organizational Change through Group Methods* (New York: John Wiley & Sons, Inc., 1965), pp. 216–19.

[1] The change agent must be made painfully aware of some of the unconscious gratifications of his role, too, so that these can be brought under control. We have in mind such fantasies as high-powered manipulation, an uncontrollable quest for power and omnipotence.

enhance his detachment and perception; it can also create insecurity and an absence of mechanisms (like colleagues) for reality testing. In any case, both the target system and the change agent have to come to terms with the idea of marginality.[2]

3. Ambiguous

The role of the change agent is ambiguous. Essentially this means that the basic concept of the change agent is not widely understood and evokes a wide range of meaning. If one responds to the question, "What do you do?" with the answer, "I am a psychologist," it does not evoke the same bewilderment as the response, "I am a change agent." (In fact, the responder might be well advised not to answer in that vein.) The ambiguity of the role betrays its lack of legitimacy as well as credibility. It also involves certain risks such as drawing suspicion and hostility because of its ambiguity. On the other side, it can be helpful in providing the necessary latitude and breadth which more precisely defined roles do not allow.

4. Insecure

The role of the change agent is insecure. This stems from a variety of causes: the precarious employment basis of the change agent (the fact that he may be the most expendable person under certain conditions); the lack of guidelines and adequate knowledge to guide many of his actions; the profound resistances which develop in attempting to change an organization. All of these factors tend to make the role insecure.

5. Risky

Related to the insecure elements in the change agent's role is the risky quality inherent in it, the risk not only to the target system but to the agent's professional status. As we shall see in the next section, the complexity of organizational change and some of its unanticipated consequences can lead to totally undesirable outcomes.

---

[2] In a recent case which we heard about, a change agent reported to work for his first day on the job, and the plant manager requested him to do some work which seemed to be inappropriate for a change agent. It was work that one of the managers should have been doing. The change agent refused to carry out functions which properly belonged to management. In this case the manager could not come to terms with the marginal role of the change agent.

Change Agent's Competence

The competence of the change agent must encompass a wide range of knowledge including: (1) conceptual diagnostic knowledge cutting across the entire sector of the behavioral sciences; (2) theories and methods of organizational change; (3) knowledge of sources of help; and (4) orientation to the ethical and evaluative functions of the change agent's role.

In addition to this intellectual grasp, the change agent must also possess (5) operational and relational skills: of listening, observing, identifying, and reporting, of ability to form relationships and trust, of a high degree of behavioral flexibility. The change agent must be able (6) to use himself, to be in constant communication with himself, and to recognize and come to terms with (as much as is humanly possible) his own motivations. Particularly in the diagnostic stages of the work, the change agent must observe how the target system deals with him. Quite often, as we mentioned earlier, the interface between the change agent and the target system is crucial for understanding and reaching a conclusion with respect to the state and readiness of the target system. In short, the change agent should be sensitive and mature.

Finally, the change agent should (7) act congruently (authentically), in accordance with the values (meta-goals) he is attempting to superimpose upon the target system's value system. The change agent must not impose democratic or humanistic values in an authoritarian or inhuman manner. If the change agent is concerned with creating more authenticity, and collaboration, he must behave in ways that are in accord with these values. We say this not only for the obvious ethical reasons but for deeper reasons as well. The fact of the matter is that so much of the change agent's influence grows out of his relationship with the target system and the extent to which he is emulated as a role model, that any significant discrepancies between the change agent's actions and his stated values cannot help but create resistance.

These are the requirements for the effective achievement of the change agent's role. We would not expect to find many such supermen among us, but we would expect this job description to be used as an aim.

PART IV

Posttraining Phase

Chapter 9

Redressing Four Common Imbalances in Training Programs
1. Input Overload
2. Unrealistic Goals
3. Alienation
4. Linkage failure

Supporting Innovation at Work
Continued Personal and Organizational Contact
Supplementary Services

Evaluating Training
1. Evaluating the Training Program
2. Evaluating the Training Objectives
3. Evaluating the Participants

Exhibits
9.1. Four Main Questions for Evaluating Training
9.2. Letter and Rating Forms for Evaluating a Human Relations Program

Boxes
9.1. The Transfer of Learning: Six Models for Man in Transition—Kenneth D. Benne
9.2. Training Objectives versus Organizational Disposition—Edwin A. Fleishman, Edwin F. Harris, Harold E. Burtt

Figure
9.1. Four Common Imbalances in Training: Effects during the Posttraining Phase

Support and Evaluation

"If the Atlantic could have been crossed as easily as it can be today, most of the Pilgrim Fathers would probably have returned."

—MATTHEW MILES

THE PROGRAM has run its course. The participants are leaving, on their way back to their jobs. They will now "show what they have learned." If the program was full-time and residential, going back to work is a major event. If it was long and located far away, perhaps abroad, everything conspires to magnify the changeover. But in a very real sense every training program, even one just around the corner and part-time, took the participants "abroad." If it did not it failed, right from the beginning. To the extent it did, there is now a distance to bridge, a transfer to manage.

Kenneth Benne labels participants according to the six different ways in which they return "from abroad" and characteristically set about the problems of transferring what they have learned to their work situation. There is the easy convert, the tourist, the expatriate, the missionary, the mystic, and the learner-critic. His classification is set out in Box 9.1. The learner critic is the most promising model.

Participants can be assumed to have come to the program with well-ingrained tendencies to behave predominantly according to one or other of such models. The program sought to affect these tendencies, to strengthen the effective ones and to modify the others. So when participants go back to work in their organizations, not only they but also the program is under test. If some programs fail through not taking participants "abroad," many more fail, or substantially fail, through not equipping them adequately for the return. Or, more accurately, shortcomings

299

Box 9.1

THE TRANSFER OF LEARNING: SIX MODELS FOR
MAN IN TRANSITION

Kenneth D. Benne

The entry into the Laboratory culture and the reentry into the back-home culture present similar problems to the person. He brought certain established behavior, attitudes, ideas, loyalties with him that were relevant to his memberships in back-home groups. These have been challenged in the training culture, have confronted him with *personal emergencies.* As the emergencies have been resolved here, behavior, attitudes, ideas, etc., of the person have undergone certain modifications. Therefore, he is returning as a somewhat different person and is therefore faced with a reentry problem. The incongruence between the two cultures has to be reduced by the person.

There are certain models of man in transition which give us a picture of how the problem may be solved.

1. *The easy convert:* He has been passive in the Laboratory culture, taking it in with no struggle or fight. When he goes back home he will quickly put on the old shell, and no one will see any difference with him. He will continue to behave in the groove with no change.

If, however, we take the view that the two cultures are different and that the person has had involvement in each, then conflict is inevitable. The conflict may be resolved in several ways:

2. *The tourist model:* He has been a visitor, inspecting what goes on in the training and returns home with a kit of techniques and papers but no real change inside.

3. *The expatriate model:* He left home and deeply involved himself in the Laboratory culture. He may feel unhappy when he goes back home because "things don't happen there the way they happened at Bethel."

Neither the tourist nor the expatriate models forecast change in the person in the enduring back home situation. Three models admit the possibility of transfer of learnings to back home. These are:

4. *The missionary model:* He came to change and may be overeager to spread changes to others back home.

5. *The self-mystic model:* He changed but cannot explain what happened to him. "It was a terrific experience." He may communicate and transfer learnings after more time has passed and he sorts things out.

6. *The learner-critic model:* He has taken a tough-minded, reality-testing attitude toward the Laboratory culture. He has continuously compared and contrasted the two cultures, accepting differences and

Box 9.1 (*Continued*)

resolving conflicts in his overlapping membership roles here and back home. He is the best bet for transfer of learnings.

Some suggestions for enhancing the learner-critic function (which to some extent is available already to all of us):

THE LEARNER-CRITIC MODEL

1. Stay marginal or in transition as far as possible so both cultures are available and valued.
2. Accept the greater potency of back home because of its demand and enduring satisfaction.
3. Be critical of back home and a deeper student of that culture—risking negative reaction of colleagues and work through resistances.
4. Accept the potency of a new culture—Bethel—as a reference group against which you can rehearse the application of ideas and behaviors back home.
5. Meet the honestly expressed needs for change back home by making your learnings available to others for them to test as you tested them when learning at Bethel.
6. Accept yourself as a person with more autonomy and spontaneous competence as you contact puzzling human phenomena, diagnose them, act to change them and be ready to receive feedback.

SOURCE: Theory session of National Training Laboratory for School Executives, July–August, 1961, Washington, D.C.

during the earlier pretraining or training phases show up now, at the posttraining phase.

REDRESSING FOUR COMMON IMBALANCES IN TRAINING PROGRAMS

Matthew Miles attributes difficulties in the posttraining phase to the failure to redress four imbalances in many training programs. He calls these input overload, unrealistic goals, alienation, and linkage failure.[1]

1. Input Overload

The program stimulated the participants so much that they came to the end of it too excited for their own good, or for the good of their

[1] Matthew B. Miles, "On Temporary Systems," in Matthew B. Miles (ed.), *Innovation in Education* (New York: Teachers College, Columbia University, 1964), pp. 437–90.

organization. This overload may have come about through several kinds of errors on the part of the trainers. The trainers may have attempted to cram too much into the program. This is very common. Or they may have scheduled a major group task so late that participants could not "decompress" again before the end of the program. Programs that build up a late assignment into a dominant indicator of the program's overall success or failure often suffer from this weakness. So that participants show up at their best, trainers deliberately tend to hold the assignment until the last possible moment—a report of fieldwork, for instance. They then go on to mistake the level of excitement at the end for a true measure of the success of training.

Either of two things follows input overload. The participants may feel exhausted and overextended, and so aware of what they have *not* learned, even now, that they get back to work deflated and discouraged. Or they go back to work at the same frenzied pitch with which they ended the course; their assessments of work situations then lack balance, and they strain at the nerves of their colleagues with unending chatter about the training program.

2. Unrealistic Goals

The second imbalance may have occurred when setting goals of training. In their initial enthusiasm, participants, severally and jointly, set themselves goals that are excessively high. And though these unrealistic goals were unattainable all along, the trainers failed to dislodge them from the participants' minds.

The freer the training, the more prone is it to develop this imbalance. In the freedom to explore and learn the limitations in the work situations, a kind of hothouse atmosphere ensues in which realistic goal setting is difficult. The trainers may have exaggerated this tendency by not controlling competitive goal setting; perhaps they even welcomed it. In the process, their attention was diverted from the realities of the work situation. The characteristic list of requests from participants at the end of almost every program indicate at once the eagerness and the anxiety they feel about implementing the goals they have set for themselves. A standard request asks for training their superiors, "so that they understand us." Another is for some kind of continuing association of participants as a separate body of trained people. A third is for continuing live contact with the trainers and the institution.

If unrealistic goals are still in view at the end of the program, one of two things happen. Looking back, some partipants may sense the lack of realism in the goals, feel they are returning to work unclear about what they can usefully attempt to do, and so entertain doubts about the practical value of the training program as a whole. Others, who take the unrealistic goals to work, are bound to fail and to become disenchanted then.

3. Alienation

As participants have drawn closer to each other during the training program, they have also separated themselves from colleagues who stayed behind at work. The separation is widened (except in remedial training) by the new things participants have learned. The gap is particularly noticeable if it occurs in the realm of attitudes and values: to the extent that they have become more egalitarian, open, and trustful among themselves, for instance. Others have become "different," less enlightened. This is alienation. Any alienation left unresolved at the end of the program interferes with even the most realistic plans participants have to communicate their learning to others. Often it heads them into general resentment and isolation at work. This unintended and unexpected result can be most painful and disillusioning.

Compared to their necessarily improvised, untried, and tentative attempts to change things, existing methods of working, sanctioned and supported, then look wonderfully solid and invite continuation. Why try to change them when only anger results? Sooner or later, the initial impetus of training wanes, and the participant doubts the utility or wisdom of continuing to wander in the wilderness of novelty and pioneering. Response from all around urges him to forget his training just as soon as possible. The crudest example of alienation is the plight of many participants in long overseas programs who felt like fish out of water when they returned to their home country, and so left it again. Some cling to an indefinite idea of trying to return again later, but the second try usually looks more difficult even than the first.

4. Linkage Failure

The very detachment which made the training program clear, fascinating, and productive may have blinded the participants to what they will be up against when they return to ordinary life. There the simplicity of the training situation is replaced by role conflicts, work pressures, and vested interests. If important sections of the work organization did not approve of the training in the first place, or if participants went on their own to programs of which the organization did not know or might not approve, then the problems of effectively linking training and work are bound to be acute. Even without these additional complications, there is a built-in linkage problem. In the first place, the very existence of the training program, after all, implied some inadequacy on the part of the organization: A need for change, an inadequacy of routine mechanisms, called for the exploration of ideas and behavior beyond the organization's normal tolerance. If training has succeeded, these challenges invade the organization itself, through the returning participant: a Trojan horse of unknown contents and implications present right in the midst of everybody.

Changes derived from the training program, therefore, their appropriateness and quality, do not determine the prospects of successful innovation by themselves. The organization's preparedness also matters greatly; and, if preparedness is there, the adequacy with which participants have been helped to anticipate the strategic problems they will encounter at work, and been enabled to cope with them, matters a great deal.

> The following extract from a letter well catches the frustration of a participant who has just returned to work and encounters unpreparedness and also his own lack of skill: "The last four to five months are enough to make me fed up with the things here. What a difference! During the training both Roy and I were working like mad people. Work and work and work, and what a joy! And here—as soon as I reached I got the first sad taste of inaction. As if I have sinned in going for training in the first place. . . . I have none to blame except myself—for interpersonal incompetence. We take sessions on temporary systems, we talk about 'linkage failure'. We talk about back home job re-orientation. That's it. Cognitively we all are experts. But when it comes to experiencing and action, we are no better than lay men."

Each of these four common imbalances has its roots way back in the program or in the pretraining phase of training. They figured in the training strategy and in the overall relationships between the participants, the institution, and the work organization. Figure 9.1 shows the effects of the four imbalances in the training programs on the participants and their organization.

For future programs a training institution can iron out such imbalances of approach and methods. For instance, it can take steps to increase the organization's awareness, and that of the participants, of the difficulties they have to face at the end of the training program. It can adjust the program to a volume and rhythm that leave participants in good shape to deal with the difficulties of transfer. It can make struc-

Figure 9.1

FOUR COMMON IMBALANCES IN TRAINING: EFFECTS DURING THE POSTTRAINING PHASE

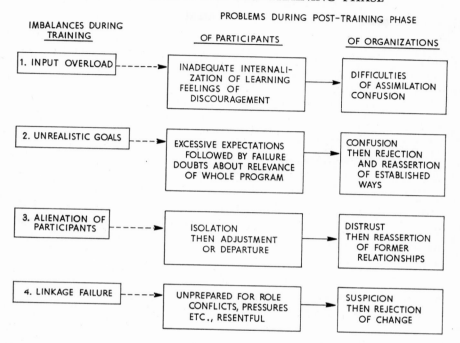

IMBALANCES DURING TRAINING	PROBLEMS DURING POST-TRAINING PHASE	
	OF PARTICIPANTS	OF ORGANIZATIONS
1. INPUT OVERLOAD	INADEQUATE INTERNALIZATION OF LEARNING FEELINGS OF DISCOURAGEMENT	DIFFICULTIES OF ASSIMILATION CONFUSION
2. UNREALISTIC GOALS	EXCESSIVE EXPECTATIONS FOLLOWED BY FAILURE DOUBTS ABOUT RELEVANCE OF WHOLE PROGRAM	CONFUSION THEN REJECTION AND REASSERTION OF ESTABLISHED WAYS
3. ALIENATION OF PARTICIPANTS	ISOLATION THEN ADJUSTMENT OR DEPARTURE	DISTRUST THEN REASSERTION OF FORMER RELATIONSHIPS
4. LINKAGE FAILURE	UNPREPARED FOR ROLE CONFLICTS, PRESSURES ETC., RESENTFUL	SUSPICION THEN REJECTION OF CHANGE

tural changes in its program to avoid disabling alienation; for instance, by breaking one long continuous program into a series of shorter separate programs, or by putting stress on training quickly an adequate minimum concentration of participants. Such steps represent the institution's own learning from experience. Systematic evaluation of current programs can help it learn, as we will see further in the last part of this chapter. Right here we are concerned with the program that has just finished and the participants' return to work. If the imbalances are in the picture at this time and participants are beset by difficulties as they return to their organizations, the institution is unlikely to be able to affect the main issue. For better or worse, the participants are substantially on their own. Only if the imbalances are not too great is the institution in a position to carry out posttraining functions.

SUPPORTING INNOVATION AT WORK

The problems, great or little, that the returning participants face as they attempt to work on their jobs with new skills and attitudes are intrinsically difficult: the same problems, basically that face attempts at innovation anywhere. Dealing with these problems involves a chain of three-step sequences: first, stimulating and ensuring sufficient interest on the part of colleagues; second, helping colleagues evaluate the proposed change as an idea, and, third, trying the change out in practice. However good the program has been at the institution and however able the participant, the training will be effective only to the extent that he and his colleagues at work in fact proceed with such sequences. The organization may ask the institution to help with this process. That is ideal. In any case, the institution is so concerned in the successful use of its training that it goes ahead and provides support and services, at least directly to the participants.

Back at work, every participant is a key figure in the process of change. It is he who is to get others interested, to stimulate them to assess the new ideas, to try them out, and to go on to develop ideas of their own. With his return to work, his immediate colleagues and others to be affected by changes therefore become the learners and the participant himself the *quasi*-trainer. Has the training program prepared him for this? Perhaps it has, through involving him in planning and running various parts of the program, and through exercises stimulating his role of change agent back in his organization. Does his place in the organization offer him a fair chance of working as a change agent? A negative answer to this question should have excluded him from the program in the first place. It means that he may not even get a hearing when he returns. If he is well enough placed, the change agent's role is still formidable. He lacks experience of it. That he returns to an organization to which he has belonged all along, an insider, holds some advantages but also adds some complications to the task of introducing changes. Certain it is that the participant as he returns to his work needs access to all the experience, wisdom, and help that the institution can offer him. These are rightfully his by virtue of the agreed purposes for which he has been trained: to effect change on the job in his organization.

If the organization has carried out its particular responsibilities in the process, much work will already have been done to arouse interest among the participant's colleagues in the impending changes and to evaluate their likely implications. This is the continuation of work started during the pretraining phase. The dispatch of the participant for training was then a token of the organization's commitment to change. While he was away in training, the implications of changes were further examined in the organization, and preparations were made for his return. If all is well, the organization has looked forward to the moment of his return time and is thoroughly ready to go ahead.

At worst the organization's interest in the change has disappeared, perhaps for good. Maybe further examination revealed the prospective change as less desirable, or the idea was overtaken by unfavorable events. This can happen even with the best will in the world, particularly when general conditions alter as precipitously and unpredictably as they often do, not least in developing countries. Failure of organizational interest in change is one of the wastages that must be expected even in good training. The usual situation lies between these extremes. The institution has had some contact with the organization while the training program was going on. It is aware, in a general way, of the organization's receptivity for change and of the kinds of problems that are likely to face the participant upon his return. It will have included in the program some preparation for him. So he arrives back at work with the institution's realistic encouragement and some access to its resources.

What he commonly finds is that his colleague's interest in his training and the changes it is to bring has gone underground: It was stifled during his absence by more immediate preoccupations. His return, in the first place, is a reminder. Dormant interest is rekindled and refocused now that he is back. The time has come to try any change in practice.

The institution's help at this stage can range widely in content and assume manifold forms. Most important is continued contact with the participant and his organization. This is important in itself, and also as a basis for other services.

Continued Personal and Organizational Contact

We can distinguish three degrees of closeness and continuity in the continuing contacts between the training institution and the participants' organization. The closest amounts to doing some joint work right on the job in which the participant, his colleagues, and the institution can be involved. In this way, the introduction of the change becomes a joint collaborative effort and one backed by some extra professional resources. The linkage is complete and maximum resources are available at the point of most difficult action.

An example of such collaboration occasionally occurs in the intensive plant counseling of the Central Small Industries Organization of the Government of India. The scheme of intensive counseling is itself an outgrowth of Siet Institute's field training. The counseling team at work consists of one or two Siet Associates working together with colleagues to make up the necessary assortment of disciplines. Siet Institute undertakes to attach one of its trainers to such a team for up to a week. He works along with the team in much the same relationship as he worked with the participants during their in-plant study in the training program. He is a consultant and resource person. At other times extension officers of the CSIO collaborate with Siet trainers on a demonstration or training program. The Associates take the lead. The trainer joins them for planning, evaluation and sometimes for part of the program itself.

The second best contact, running far behind the ideal, is direct contact with the participant from a distance. The institution can encourage participants to get in touch whenever they meet with difficulties that they think a trainer might help remove. During the training program the trainers may have avoided personal counseling because of the inordinate time it might take and because it would conflict with some kinds of training events. Postprogram requests for counseling do not hold these risks. They tend to come from few participants and can be encouraged safely.

A high proportion of requests are for further information on matters mentioned during training which become real and urgent only after the participants return to work. Requests we have ourselves received refer to teaching cases we used during the program which then turned out to be directly relevant to the participants' situation or arose from readings which participants had taken back with them. Others, the most desirable but also the ones most difficult to meet, have asked for contact in person over problems on the job.

In one kind of situation, counseling can be of direct help. This arises when the participant, facing a heavy sudden increase of pressure on the job, knows what to do and uses his enhanced skill but unexpectedly finds it inadequate. He then has the unsettling experience of having done everything correctly but ending up with the wrong result. The trainer may then give reassurance by helping the participant see that his specific steps were not at fault at all, but rather his assessment of the situation as a whole. Expectations of the scale and speed at which colleagues will get involved in changes are most often at fault; unaided, the participant may slip into undue despondency.

Another step back from giving concrete help on the job is exemplified by offering general refresher courses. These may be located in the organization or a town, or back at the institution. The Administrative Staff College of India recalls the participants of a particular course for a week's program two years or so later. Other institutions organize events for participants of several programs who work in the same organization or locality. It is important to safeguard the working purpose of such events against the very natural tendency to emphasize the pleasures of reunion with old friends and acquaintances. Provision in the programs for plenty of informal contact between participants ouside working sessions can help in this.

Posttraining contact between the institution and participants and their organizations is readily agreed to be the kingpin of adequate follow-up services but is in fact rarely attempted in a systematic manner. It is one of those crucial areas in training in which good intention is often left to stand in for action. If personal contact occurs from time to time, it does so as a chance by-product of some other program of the institution. Meetings with associates tend to be short and mostly social. They are pleasant enough while they last but not meaningful as support to participants on the job. Or, instead of a trainer involving himself in a job problem of a participant and his organization, he uses willing participants to organize or administer a local program of the institution. Examples of sound sustained contact are in fact very hard to come by. We see in this wide discrepancy between professed intent and action a further weakness of training strategies which limit their vistas to the beginning and the end of the formal training programs and barely have peripheral vision for who comes to the programs or what they accomplish afterwards. Helping participants and their organizations to implement changes following training is too important and far-reaching a matter to be left so unplanned and so unattained.

Supplementary Services

Regular follow-up services of most institutions are limited to the issue of periodic news sheets and encouragement to new and old associations of participants. Without roots in continuing contact with participants and their organizations, these services soon atrophy. By themselves they are too slight and may be double-edged.

News sheets, even those eagerly proposed by participants at the end of the program and organized as collaborative ventures between participants and institution, have almost nothing in them that originated with the participants. They are carried on with increasing grimness by the institution. Associations of participants are shortlived if they have no realistic base in the organizations or the locality. Where they continue, they do so because one or two people strain to keep them alive, often for mixed reasons. If participants value the association for its exclusiveness, they perpetuate the damaging separation of those who have been trained, perhaps even trained in a particular program, from those who have not. Before long, the association becomes predominantly a social organization and so avoids the difficulties—along with the possible advantages—of associating with colleagues in order to evaluate progress toward work goals, and to give and receive professional support.

As part of a systematic set of follow-up services, the same means of news sheets and associations can have real value. News sheets can include descriptions of participants' work activities, problems encountered, and experience gained. Some institutions have expanded the news sheet into full-scale journals that appear regularly and contain, besides the usual personal and institutional news, long sections of professional matter and new information.

> The National Training Laboratories, for instance, provide all participants in the Management Work Conferences with a one year's free subscription to its journal, *Applied Behavioral Science*. These participants and their organizations are free to continue this subscription after that period if they wish.

Similarly there are associations of participants that serve as effective contact points with the institution and become a local clearinghouse for participants' experiences and for professional contact and consultation.

For the training institution, developing posttraining contacts and supplementary services is part of its primary task. This point must be stressed, for clarity and for economy in the use of institutional resources. These contacts and services are required for achieving the original task effectively and efficiently. That is in question, not courtesy or good fellowship. The same criterion sets the limit to what is required. Posttraining services need to be developed and sustained sufficiently for the task, no more, no less. To make this judgment calls for sound criteria and procedures for evaluating the training process and its results.

EVALUATING TRAINING

If, as we maintain, training aims at definite changes on the job in an organization, then two criticisms of prevailing evaluation attempts must follow. In the first place, the usual rough and ready "measures" of training simply do not suffice for our purpose. One, the "number trained" tells nothing at all, even about the participants' learning. They may have learned, in large numbers, very little or next to nothing. They may even have learned the opposite of what was intended, for instance, that training is a hateful experience and a waste of time, or a time of rest, or an avenue to high status. If this is so, the training experience has done damage, and the participants may have carried away with them a jaundiced anticipation of future training opportunities for themselves and others and of the reputation of the training institution and its courses. These feelings they will, we can be sure, spread among their friends and colleagues. These possibilities are all generally accepted; e.g., the "number trained" is used mostly to justify faculty strengths and training budgets, not to measure the effectiveness of training.

Measures of the participants' learning at the end of the program provide a much more promising criterion of the effectiveness of training—but at the risk of a different kind of confusion. These measures look specific and often quantifiable. They satisfy the urge to concreteness that helps trainers cover any uncertainty they feel about the effectiveness of their activities. Was it worthwhile? Did we do our job well? Sure! Rao is now able to handle the machine, Latiff can now do a cost study, Sarwar can now speak before a large group. Their before-and-after tests show it. Ergo, they have learned something. But even these tests cannot show what really matters. Even if these were things that Rao, Latiff, and Sarwar needed to learn, the tests cannot show whether they can use the new knowledge and skill on their jobs, and make them truly part of themselves through continuous practice. This requires acceptance of Rao's, Latiff's, and Sarwar's new behavior by the people with whom they work, particularly their immediate superiors and colleagues. Measures of what they know and what they can do simply do not take us far enough for our purpose.

For completeness' sake, a third common criterion needs to be mentioned and peremptorily thrown out: that participants praised the course and were tearful at parting. They commonly are so moved. But it is a whole mixture of feelings they are expressing. It is impossible to unscramble even the genuine impressions they may have at that moment of the effectiveness of training, let alone any indications of the effectiveness of training on the job.

The second thought that follows from our understanding of the aims of training is that evaluation and ensuring consequent action is not the institution's task alone. The effectiveness of training is determined by all three partners in it: the participant, the institution, and the work organization. Just as the strength of the whole chain is determined by its weakest link, so the least contribution from any one partner becomes the maximum possible overall level of effectiveness. By no means every weakness or failure in training is therefore one that can be attributed to the institution or assessed or removed by improvements in its program. Perhaps a participant was simply not up to it, though his organization insisted that he was the man to introduce the change. Or the organization may itself be too weak to use well-trained participants. These are just two of many possibilities.

We will concern ourselves here only with questions that most directly call for evaluation and action by the training institution. They boil down to two sets. One is, what can the institution learn about the effectiveness of that central phase in the change process in which its responsibility is largest, namely the training program? The second is, how can the institution best help the other two partners evaluate their parts and improve them, so that the training process as a whole becomes more effective? An example of the second would be inadequacies in the participants, which may be remedied by renewed attention by the organization to selection procedures and preparation of candidates for training. Both sets of questions can be explored adequately only if the institution collaborates closely with participants and their organizations.

Exhibit 9.1 sets out the four main questions in terms of purpose: what to evaluate, when to evaluate, how to evaluate, and who is to do the evaluating.

1. Evaluating the Training Program

For evaluating the program the basic question is, simply, to what extent did the program achieve what it set out to achieve. It is, overall, the same question that trainers ask of every session, block, and part of the program. That is, the program started with a set of objectives: that, when it is over, the participant should know X, be able to do Y to Z standard, have developed an outlook A. Now that it is over, to what extent has the program in fact succeeded in these terms, and how far does the participant actually behave differently at work? Evaluation at the very end of the program tells about the new knowledge, understanding, and skill that the participant has gained during training. The same kind of data at various stages of the posttraining phase shows how stable these gains are and to what extent they have survived transfer to the work situation. By way of an example, Exhibit 9.2 shows the letter and rating forms used to evaluate a human relations program for trainers two months after its completion.

A comparison of repeated ratings can yield four different results:

1. If the ratings steadily fall within the satisfactory range of performance and show improvement when repeated, this means that the program was sound; that both the participant and his organization were ready to use the training; and that the participant had learned enough during training to keep on improving his performance through practice on the job.

FOUR MAIN QUESTIONS FOR EVALUATING TRAINING

Purpose	What?	When?	How?	Who Evaluates?
Training to help the organization change	Training objectives	Once every three years or so		Institution and organization
I. Evaluating the training program				
a) To improve the effectiveness of the program as a whole	Contents and methods, including timing and sequences of training inputs	At end of program and again at regular intervals after training	Generally available tools chosen in terms of training objectives of program	Institution with the help of participants and their organizations.
b) To increase effectiveness of different inputs and sequences of the training program	Content and methods	Before and after inputs to be evaluated	Specially designed tools, assignments, etc.	Participants and trainers
c) To give the participants effective feedback to help them improve	Participants' attitudes and behavior	Regularly during training	Tests, assignments, questionnaires	Trainers and participants
d) To improve the trainers' contribution	Trainer behavior and its effects	Regularly	Content analysis	Trainer with the help of colleagues and participants
II. Evaluating the training objectives	Participants' behavior on the job	Regularly for set period after training	Interaction analysis; output, etc.; observation of participant and colleagues	Institution and participants with help of organization

Exhibit 9.2

LETTER AND RATING FORMS FOR EVALUATING A HUMAN RELATIONS PROGRAM

DEAR X,

It is just two months since the program ended, enough time, perhaps, to get some idea of its effects on our relationships at work and at home. Such an evaluation is not only a matter of good housekeeping. It can also help establish similar programmes of various kinds as a regular activity.

The enclosed forms may make this evaluation fairly simple. There are three:

A. Your rating of yourself to indicate the changes you have noticed.
B. Ratings of you by colleagues along the same lines as A.
C. Some general questions.

The general results will of course be communicated back to you and some may find a place in the general report. I would like to get the report out this month, so can I expect your answer before _____.

RATING FORM A

How do you perceive yourself, your skills, your relationships, etc., before and after the program? Put on the ladders *b* for *before* (where you thought you were) and *a* for *after;* 1 is the lowest, and 10 the highest. Your responses will show whether you moved up or down.

1. Satisfaction with your role as a trainer.	2. Effectiveness in your role as a trainer.	3. Skill in working with others.
10_____	10_____	10_____
9_____	9_____	9_____
8_____	8_____	8_____
7_____	7_____	7_____
6_____	6_____	6_____
5_____	5_____	5_____
4_____	4_____	4_____
3_____	3_____	3_____
2_____	2_____	2_____
1_____	1_____	1_____

4. Relationship with your colleagues who did not go to the program.	5. Relationship with those who went to the program.	6. Understanding of colleagues.
10_____	10_____	10_____
9_____	9_____	9_____
8_____	8_____	8_____
7_____	7_____	7_____
6_____	6_____	6_____
5_____	5_____	5_____
4_____	4_____	4_____
3_____	3_____	3_____
2_____	2_____	2_____
1_____	1_____	1_____

Exhibit 9.2 (Continued)

7. Behavior with participants.	8. Understanding of self.	9. Behavior with family and friends.
10_____	10_____	10_____
9_____	9_____	9_____
8_____	8_____	8_____
7_____	7_____	7_____
6_____	6_____	6_____
5_____	5_____	5_____
4_____	4_____	4_____
3_____	3_____	3_____
2_____	2_____	2_____
1_____	1_____	1_____

The B form was similar to A, edited for use about a colleague. The C form left space on one foolscap sheet for answers to three questions.

1. Have you noticed changes in any other dimension than those assessed in Parts A and B that you wish to mention? Which?
2. Give one concrete incident to show a difference in behaviour that you attribute to the training program.
3. To what do you attribute the change? Give three main factors in order of importance.

SOURCE: Siet Institute, Hyderabad, India.

2. If the ratings tend to decline with repetition, this means that the participant and his organization found the training less useful than they had expected or that the participant did not have enough training during the program or enough support on the job to carry on successfully.
3. If the results show a sharp drop at first and then rise, this shows that the transfer from training to action was unexpectedly difficult, but that the participant and the organization have overcome the difficulties and are making headway.
4. If the results show a sharp drop and stay down, this means that the organization and/or the participant were not prepared to make the change on the job or that the training objectives turned out to be unrealistic.

These results are clearly important to the institution as a guide to further action. In most cases, detailed study will be required before strategic difficulties can be located and their strengths assessed. For instance, (2) and (3) suggest linkage problems in the transition from the training and work situations. More adequate support for participants on the job may obviate these in future programs. But their removal may also call for more time and rigorous work on back-home problems in the training program itself. (4) and possibly also (2) suggest renewed work on the original training objectives.

2. Evaluating the Training Objectives

If the objectives were inadequately formulated in the first place, even a "good" training program had really no chance to be effective. Faulty job analyses sometimes lead to this result. Or participants are shifted from job to job so frequently that no one job analysis or training can be relevant to their future work. This is the position of government officers who are regarded as interchangeable. They may be sent for specialized training in one field only to find themselves posted upon return to work in another. This is an instance of training failures that occur whenever training objectives are not rooted in definite plans for changes on the job or when the change process as a whole falters through inadequate organizational commitment and support.

The study summarized in Box 9.2 describes a situation in a large American company where a wide discrepancy between training objectives and organizational readiness for related changes led to some surprising evaluation results. In the first place, when the evaluation instruments used at the end of the training program were used again sometime later, after participants had been back at work, they showed diametrically opposite results. End-of-program evaluation is clearly not an adequate final evaluation of training program. Second, wherever the ratings remained steady, the participants' new learning was supported by their superiors. Third, a review of training needs revealed wide differences between production and service departments. The same training was therefore not effective in both.

This program suffered from incompatible training objectives, a weakness common to many programs. Behind this weakness lies confusion between lists of wishes and realistic company policy. In this instance, speedy technological change, freedom from conflict, and immediate efficiency were all among the objectives. But no detailed thought had been given to the question of how they might be combined. A deliberate policy is required for this, which can then guide the establishment and revision of training objectives.

Where overall policy is realistic and clear, regular and frequent evaluations followed by marginal adjustments can keep training objectives in tune with shifting needs. This assumes a close relationship between the training institution and the work organization.

The burden of drastic changes is extra heavy for developing countries: changing tasks, changing situations, and changing divisions of functions. Training needs there are especially difficult to define and then

Box 9.2

TRAINING OBJECTIVES VERSUS ORGANIZATIONAL
DISPOSITION

E. A. FLEISHMAN, E. F. HARRIS, AND H. E. BURTT

An evaluation study of a supervisory training program in a large American company shows clearly how a major discrepancy can arise between the objectives of program and the training needs and possibilities on the job. The objectives of the program were in the general area of improving human relations among the workers and between workers and management. Specific objectives included reducing conflict and promoting greater job satisfaction. By these routes greater efficiency was to be achieved. Foremen were to be the change agents for these improvements. The program was to train them for this function.

Preliminary studies established two clusters of supervisory behavior which could serve to evaluate the training in terms of its objectives. One cluster included kinds of behavior that could be classified as "considerate": attention to workers as people, listening to personal problems, helping and the like. The other consisted of behavior that stressed formal relations, written rules, and keeping to production schedules. The authors formulated these objectives into two operational criteria. One they called "consideration"; the opposite they called "initiating structure." Factorially sound and highly reliable instruments were developed for measuring leadership attitudes and behavior in terms of consideration and initiating structure.

From these instruments, applied before and after residential training, clearly favorable training results were established. The foremen showed significant decreases in initiating structure and corresponding increases in considerate attitudes. But when the same instruments were used again later, after the foremen had returned to work, they revealed the opposite result: trained foremen tended to be lower in consideration and higher in initiating structure than did the untrained foremen. A check with workers under these foremen confirmed these results. Clearly the effects of this human relations program were not stable.

The general interpretation of these results was that the program succeeded in making the foremen more considerate but that it at the same time separated them sharply from the workers. The foremen themselves became more aware of belonging to the management. Singled out for special training in a program that was obviously expensive, they concluded that they had definitely crossed over to the other side. Certainly the workers saw this as the main meaning of the supervisory training program. The result was that the more considerate attitudes that showed up in the immediate posttraining questionnaire were offset by the foremen's tendency back at work to assume more determined leadership roles. The

Box 9.2 *(Continued)*

discrepancy between these two evaluations at the end of the program and later on the job illustrates well the danger of relying only on the first when the acid test of effective training is the second.

The authors then correlated the "contradictory" results with the "climate" set up by the foremen's superiors. The correlation was direct: trained foremen who continued to show more "considerate" attitudes on the job were those whose superiors were "considerate." The others dropped the considerate attitudes they had gained in the training program in order to conform with superiors who were strong in initiating structure. The implication of this for a more effective training strategy would be to provide training for the foremen's superiors and perhaps for *their* superiors also.

The authors also took a second look at the training needs of different jobs in order to establish whether more considerate attitudes in fact produced greater efficiency. This reexamination led to a useful distinction. In production divisions where meeting time schedules and production targets produced great stress, foremen with the highest proficiency ratings showed more initiation of structure. In the service divisions, on the other hand, where these stresses were not so prominent, the higher proficiency ratings went with more consideration. This finding suggested differentiating between training objectives for foremen in production and service departments and changing the criteria for selecting participants.

The results have wider implications. They call for formulation separately of long-range and short-range objectives of training. The relative importance of work satisfaction, freedom from conflict, speedy technological change, and immediate efficiency need to be decided in the work organization. "Perhaps immediate efficiency," the authors conclude, "may not be so important as a long-time balance between efficiency and morale."

Source: Edwin A. Fleishman, Edwin F. Harris, and Harold E. Burtt, *Leadership and Supervision in Industry* (Columbus, Ohio: The Ohio State University, 1955).

to keep up to date and embodied in organizational policies. In that situation, well-designed and operated evaluation procedures are particularly important, to help bridge the gaps that surely occur between needs and policies and between training objectives and training needs.

For bridging a gap of any sort, something has first to exist on the other side. We have seen training institutions struggling to evolve sufficiently clear training objectives out of inadequately defined needs. Either of two results has invariably followed from thus putting the cart before the horse. In some cases the key relationship between the institution and the organization has deteriorated. It is as if the institution were caught in quicksand, and its later struggles to put the relationship and the training objectives on a sound footing only made the situation worse. Every move led to accusations that the institution was improperly usurping functions and overstepping its responsibilities. If the institution replied that it could not mark time while the organization caught up with neglected responsibilities, successful in-fighting rather than effective training quickly became the dominant objective for action.

In other cases the training institution has taken an early hint and withdrawn from any attempt to evaluate its training objectives as a whole. It has limited its evaluation to meeting the training objectives within the confines of the formal program, without pursuing the question of efficacy to the participants' job and organization. The result of this very understandable reaction has been uncertainty and low morale among the trainers. At no point could they be sure that their devoted and diligent efforts had any value in practice.

In short, evaluation of training objectives is the responsibility of the work organization in the first place. The institution can contribute procedural expertise and consistent and sustained interest. Collaboration between the organization and the institution ensures rapid use of evaluation results, in selection and preparation of participants, in program designs, and in preparing the organization for change.

3. Evaluating the Participants

With training objectives formulated clearly in terms of changes to be effected at work, the work organization is in the best position also to evaluate the effects of training on individual participants. The question remains, what is such evaluation for? The organization may use it for the same legitimate purposes that the institution used it for during the training program: to provide participants and trainers with information about progress toward various training objectives and about any difficulties that require attention on the way. This involves feeding the evaluation results in the first place back to the participants, and proceeding to any subsequent action with their agreement. An increasing number of organizations have set up individual evaluation procedures for these purposes and in this manner, merit rating schemes, for instance. For these purposes the institution can help the organization develop regular and rigorous procedures for collecting data from the participants and from their superiors, colleagues, and subordinates. It can also help in analyzing the results.

If, on the other hand, evaluation is to be used for other purposes, or is to be confidential, that is, confidential from participants, the institution had better stay away from it—even where prevailing traditions require the opposite, perhaps especially there. Nothing so inhibits participants from developing a free and close relationship with trainers as the idea that the institution will be in touch about them with their organization. Instead of exploring new methods, they will hold themselves back and shrink from taking the risks of learning, and they will be preoccupied with pleasing the trainers; all this is to ensure as far as possible a good report. Ethics apart, this price is excessive. Such limits and preoccupations are wholly inimical to every phase of the training process. Even so, private communication between the training institution and the work organization about individual participants is still common, directly in line with the general tradition of confidential reports. Instead, the institution should announce publicly that it will not provide confidential information about participants to the organizations.

There remains the help that the organization can rightly expect from the institution to decide the most suitable placement of participants after training and the specific support participants may need to carry through the planned changes on the job. This is reasonable enough. Particularly if the training has been residential and long, the trainers may have got to know a participant so well that their comments and advice can be of direct help in settling such questions.

Some institutions have formulated two principles with which to handle requests for information about participants from the organization. The first is to get involved only in those cases in which it can contribute information and clarification that others cannot give. This principle eliminates many requests that could be answered far better by the participant himself or his colleagues in the organization. The other principle is to inform the organization that the institution will deal with the questions in collaboration with the participant himself. Any information and suggestion will then be known to the participant and already have his agreement by the time it reaches the organization. Some organizations have welcomed this procedure, others have dropped the request.

Evaluation of participants is also a basis for reviewing the criteria by which participants are selected for training programs. Many times study reveals that a particular program is of greater profit to participants with substantial working experience or with some minimum standards of competence in a basic subject, such as mathematics. Other programs may be made suitable for those with less. As in the study described earlier in this chapter, detailed evaluation of participants may also reveal repetitive patterns of difficulties which point to a more precise delineation of the population for certain kinds of training—for example, production foreman or service foreman, instead of both mixed. Finally, this evaluation can guide decisions about supporting programs for participants and their colleagues anywhere in the organization.

PART V

The Institution and the Future

Chapter 10

‎ィィィィィィィィィィィィィィィィィィィィィィィィィィィィ

The Training Institution and the Future

///

"Education remains the only major profession without the guts to look at itself."

—FRANCIS KAPPEL

IN THEORY the contribution of the training institution to the training process is clear. It is threefold. The first contribution is to the participants. Staffed by competent, flexible trainers and administrators under a responsive principal, the institution provides participants with a program and an environment that consistently promotes learning relevant to more effective behavior at work. It is a live model of organizational standards such as the participants hope will shape their work at home. It is a setting that keeps on motivating them to learn more and to improve their performance, that offers stimulating challenges they can handle, that provides the opportunities to discover effective responses and then reinforces them. So much for what the institution is to the participants.

For the trainers, second, the institution is to provide steady support: the collaboration of colleagues, where necessary; supporting services of many kinds, easy of access; a climate that is both stimulating and satisfying. These are all immediate and day-to-day. For the longer term, the institution provides trainers with opportunities for further professional growth, through a satisfying range and variation of roles in which they can gain experience, through contact with colleagues in other institutions, and through special faculty development programs from time to time. For the society in which it works, finally, the institution is an agent for development. It permeates the social fabric with its own qualities of inquiry, active response, and evaluation of effectiveness, above all with its enthusiastic and skillful engagement in society and its tasks.

If this theoretical picture were even broadly descriptive of training institutions in practice, there would be little need for this book. As it is, the theory provides a framework into which we can order for consideration the main dilemmas encountered in practice, along with some estimates of the main directions, the minimum support, and the working methods which would help training institutions develop more adequately. Patchy though this account will be, we propose to proceed with it. We have no wish to add to theory when action seems held back for other reasons.

We will start by stating the prevailing standards sharply. Most of the data we use is from our immediate personal experiences and those of colleagues whom we have consulted. That nothing more general and organized is possible underscores the secrecy with which trainers and principals of training institutions surround themselves. Studies of trainers in action are very few; and the few are mostly by outside researchers, not reflective studies carried out by trainers themselves for their own improvement in the first place. Data on the actual operations of training institutions are fewer still. There are almost no descriptions of how training programs are decided upon, planned, and carried out in fact; how trainers operate as the "teams" we talk about; how a training institution rejuvenates itself. Given the size of the training effort, its cost, and the promise effective training holds for development, it is surprising that training goes on year after year, and even expands, with so little self-evaluation and deliberate improvement.

The only explanation we can offer is that trainers and training institutions are caught in the same vicious circle that circumscribes and enmeshes society at large: change is threatening; it is wiser to leave the cocoon undisturbed; God knows what the explorer would find if he untangled it! But unravel it we must. Certain it is that if we trainers are unwilling, severally and jointly, to learn from our experiences, we ought not to expect participants to learn from theirs.

Where training needs are as great and skilled trainers as few as they are in developing countries, the individual trainer's part in the vicious circle usually consists, first of all, in an excessive work load of training activities. Steady loads of 15 sessions a week are quite common. Then, as soon as one batch of participants is "through," the next batch arrives—a relentless flow. In many institutions, courses are separated by less than a week. Prevailing pressures urge ever larger numbers per session and more courses per year. They leave little room for improving the quality of training in terms of greater effectiveness on the job. Research, even a minimum of professional reading, often go by the board. Inevitably it is not long before the trainers are out of date and their wellsprings of creativity run dry. In that situation any proposals to evaluate the work in terms of effectiveness becomes a further burden and a threat. This is one dilemma.

The same dilemma stands in the way of closer contact among trainers as colleagues and consequently of any joint attempts to develop the institution further. Colleagues tend to work as individuals, carve up the training pie into separate, though logically related, wedges. Each trainer pleads shortage of time when someone suggests going beyond this mechanical sharing. They do not expect collaboration to lighten their burdens but only to lead to open displays of weaknesses and rivalry. The very occasional meetings of trainers usually confirm these anticipations. Many trainers use the lack of professional contact with colleagues also to symbolize an implicit contract. Its explicit version would be, "So long as I do not question your work, I expect you not to question mine." When pressed, trainers may even defend this separateness as academic freedom. The result is that trainers work as teams in only a few institutions, and consistency of approach to training programs is by and large a matter of good fortune.

New institutions have recently come up which embody attempts of consumers and well-wishers to help the field of training out of such dilemmas. They have been set up as autonomous bodies separate from universities and all ongoing programs. This is to guarantee the greatest chances of avoiding the contagion of harmful traditions. The hope has been bought at a price: the price of separateness, of lessened contact with existing institutions, and of possible rivalries with them. Within the institutions the trainers' work loads each week have been reduced, in some cases to six or eight training sessions for nine months of the year, and trainers are encouraged to engage in research and consulting.

It is too early to see the eventual outcome of these attempts to step out of the past. Meanwhile the difficulties that these new institutions are experiencing show just how broad-based and pervasive prevailing traditions really are. The reduction in work loads has not by itself led to greatly improved programs or a corresponding upsurge in other activities. Collaboration between trainers, institute-wide agreement on training approaches and evaluation of effectiveness, support for experimentation and adaptation, these still tend to be marginal. The general trend is still away from training for increased job effectiveness toward academically oriented programs, away from sensitive, flexible training toward routinized take-it-or-leave-it teaching, away from stress on the participants' self-motivation and independence. This assessment is sharp. We wish it were wrong.

Only by very deliberate and sustained efforts, apparently, can institutions push beyond these standards. Even generally agreed policy and the provision of mechanisms for collaboration seem insufficient. For instance, faculty meetings are certainly necessary for integrating the work of different trainers and for adequate forward planning. But they serve these purposes only where there is deep understanding of the training process and determination to make it maximally effective. How to spread this understanding and determination is the question. In their absence the same kinds of meetings tend to lose their professional direction and degenerate into excessively complicated and time-consuming mechanisms for reaching administrative decisions. The time then goes into such matters as library procedures and course dates rather than into considering course designs and trainer roles. And where administrative concerns predominate, the principal is functionally in charge and trainers often compete for his attention.

Besides the establishment of some new institutions and their attempts to develop high standards in crucial segments of the training process, three general developments are taking place which may also hold real promise.

The first is a mounting dissatisfaction among the consumers of training. The growing opposition to the community development program in India and its very large training apparatus is just one major example of this. It is important that this divine dissatisfaction of the consumer not be dissipated through lack of focus or simple destructiveness. Second, while the reduction in trainers' work loads has not removed institutional reluctances to change, it has freed some resources to work on innovation. Many institutions now have the resources for significant development. Third, our own experiences and the indications we have from elsewhere suggest that unraveling the cocoon will reveal hidden strengths and talents ready, or nearly ready, for initiating this development.

Trainers can therefore proceed to institutional learning with good cheer; with the same trust and confidence, in fact, with which they recommend learning to participants and their organizations.

A CONSISTENT TRAINING ENVIRONMENT FOR PARTICIPANTS

We have had earlier occasions to stress the importance of making all parts of the training activities and environment contribute toward the training objectives. This is so, even for individualized programmed instruction which could be assumed to be most immune from institutional influences. That method, too, seems to flower only in favorable climates. "Truly individualized instruction," concludes Thelen, "can be achieved only by a really major change in the context of teaching and learning. [It] can't go forward with business as usual."[1] Otherwise, he adds elsewhere, "procedures change with each new fad, but the attitudes—the spirit—that animate schooling keep change from reaching any vital organ. . . . The new vocabulary merely promotes hypocrisy —the hypocrisy of schoolmen masquerading as educators."[2]

Participants are entitled to expect consistency in at least four facets of the training environment.

1. Between a Trainer's Statements and His Behavior

This is the most obvious consistency: A trainer's behavior must be reasonably in line with what he teaches; otherwise all his teaching is thrown in doubt. Since behavior has deep personal roots, the point for early action may be to avoid statements about what trainers will or will not do that they are unlikely to live up to. This includes statements about how consistent they expect to be.

> Phrases like "always ready to help," "never" angry, "patient at all times," and the like invite trouble. The same consideration reinforces our view that it is risky and possibly harmful to ask a trainer to use a training method that he does not find congenial. He may test new methods in the safe environment of colleagues. With participants his genuineness is of greater importance than his novelty. Genuineness avoids the recurrence of the classic lecture (behavior) about the value of frank and full discussion (statement); of the exhortation (statement) to participants to take their own decisions and act on them while the trainer in fact insists on his preferences (behavior); or of repeated assurances (statement) that nothing matters so much to the trainer as that they get all the help they need, immediately followed by his cutting short a discussion (behavior) in order to leave for home.

Participants depend on reasonable consistency between the trainer's statements and behavior not only in the program but also wherever else he is visible. They watch for it in the ways he behaves with colleagues and staff and with his family. The higher the standards he recommends during the program, the more exposed the trainer is to the risks of disappointing and confusing the participants.

[1] Herbert A. Thelen, "Some Classroom Quiddities for People-Oriented Teachers", *Journal of Applied Behavioral Science,* Vol. I, No. 3 (1965).

[2] *Four Case Studies of Programmed Instruction* (New York: Fund for the Advancement of Education, 1964).

Trainers in residence with the participants or out in the field with them full-time find themselves in many unplanned situations and unguarded moments in which to maintain consistency. They need to be selected with an eye to their capacity for this. Laboratory trainers who take participants farthest into experiencing personal stress and expressing angry feelings need to be able to maintain consistency under the consequent pressures. Many decide to limit their contacts with participants outside the laboratory for fear of not being able to maintain their orientation in all situations. Even then their reputation and behavior during chance encounters need to be in line with their behavior "during training."

2. Between Different Trainers in the Same Program

The program as a whole needs to display consistency of orientation and priorities. So long as trainers share this, they need not behave alike. In fact, being persons of different makeup they will express the underlying unity in many different ways. One comes through best in case sessions, another in field training, yet another in lectures. The trainers have different styles, and the more these suit their different personalities the better. What they need to share and express consistently are genuineness and openness, and pervasive concern for the training task and for improved performance. Not unison but harmony is the outcome of this consistency.

Achieving this consistency in a training program is the outcome of sustained endeavor. It cannot be achieved once for all, but is something to work away at. Trainers need to be teamed up for a program with this consistency in view. Besides encompassing the required knowledge and skills, they need to feel basically compatible and ready to be drawn into close professional and personal relationships. This is important because inconsistencies among trainers may cancel out required learning and may before long so confuse participants that they shut themselves off altogether from conflicting influences.

The danger of inconsistencies between trainers is built into attempts to run training laboratories and other process-oriented training alongside knowledge-oriented sessions. Participants may end up learning from neither the one nor the other. This can be avoided by concentrating the different orientations—and trainers—at separate stages of the program or by having separate programs for each.

When all possible allowances have been made in the design of the program, the institution still faces the dilemma of how to promote at the same time each trainer's individual style and creativity—which immediately make for good training—and the consistent, integrated experiences required by the participants. Much as a trainer may want to experiment, and much as the institution may encourage him, participants will be suspicious of radical differences in the behavior of different trainers. Suspicion is particularly likely to meet the innovating trainer, that is, one who goes counter to the expectations of participants. He is constrained within the limits of tolerance of the participants and also of the institution. He simply is not a wholly free agent, for he is also an extension and carrier of the prevailing institutional standards. Given a sensitive principal and an institutional climate that favors high standards, this dilemma can be addressed by varying the trainer's roles and functions from time to time and by a number of other specific steps to which we will return in greater detail shortly.

3. Between Training Objectives and the Physical Environment

Not only the trainers by their behavior, but the inanimate physical surroundings and administrative procedures of the institution, too, convey to the participants signals that are in tune or at variance with the training objectives, and so help or hinder training.

For instance, democratic values and participatory methods call for a new layout of session rooms. The traditional layout of a podium and table for the trainer, on the one hand, and participants' chairs in parallel rows, on the other, signal in advance that the trainer will speak rather than listen, that he will be personally distant from the participants, and that the training method will not include much discussion among participants. Chairs in a circle, with the trainer sitting side by side with participants, make a communication consistent with the new values.

Luxury may be as inconsistent with the training objectives as cramped facilities. If programs for shop-floor trade-union leaders are held in an expensive seaside hotel, participants (and their constituents) may conclude that the primary object is to buy them over to the side of management. The centralized residential training program for foremen mentioned in Chapter 9 (page 317), harbored this kind of inconsistency.

Propriety is the relevant criterion; that is, consistency with training objectives. Since any training is intended to promote high standards of performance, every item in the training environment needs to perform well. Documents need to be well laid out and well typed, physical facilities need to be neat and clean, and above all, appropriate for their functions. It may be possible for trainers and administrators to go so far as to allocate office space and facilities, such as secretarial services, transport or air conditioning, not in terms of hierarchical status in the institution but in accordance with job requirements. In countries where air-conditioning equipment is not widely available, it is not unusual to find it limited to the offices of foreign "experts" and often of the institution's principal. Functionally, it would be far better to air-condition some of the classrooms. Where office accommodation is tight, as it often is in fast expanding training institutions, the situation could be eased by allotting the scarce air conditioning to the typing pool or to the duplicating room. By doing this the trainers will effectively under-score in practice the functional emphasis on organizational relationships and on decision-making processes that they talk about in the training program.

4. Between Training Objectives and Institutional Administration

If efficiency, personal concern, flexibility, and speed of decision and action are among the values to be promoted through the training program, then the administration of the training institution needs to exemplify these same values in practice. This, again, will avoid damaging confusion and delays and also underscore the relevance of these values and demonstrate their efficacy to the participants.

The need for consistency on this score is greatest at points where participants and the administrative staff of the institution come into direct working contact. This usually happens when travel and finances are to be arranged, training documents are to be issued, and, in full-time programs, when living arrangements and food are to be provided. In residential programs, training and administration intertwine so often and closely that they often cannot be separated. Administrative contacts with participants can have training components so large that they can affect the progress of a program in a major way.

> The classical example is food. Food often becomes the subject for complaint at stages in the program when participants feel unsettled and deprived of their habitual landmarks and supports. They feel uncared for, wish they were back home with their families and in surroundings they know. The unfreezing stage of the training process is characterized by pervasive feelings of this kind. Complaints about food are often their major expression. To handle complaints about food as a mere administrative matter would then miss their central meaning.

In their manifold contacts with participants, the institution's administrative staff has a quasi-training function. Beyond this, participants notice the administrative standards and the general climate of the institution around them and draw conclusions that affect their learning. This makes it very important for trainers and administrative staff members to associate closely together in developing the institution's orientation and in designing living arrangements and "administrative" procedures that are consistent with the training objectives.

Some institutions hold regular meetings of trainers and administrative staff to make the overall approach consistent. They may go on deliberately to reduce to a minimum the working contact between participants and administrative staff. They detail trainers to be the liaison persons for all administrative matters. In this way, they hope to ensure that any training components in administration receive due attention and at the same time that the administrative staff can get on with its work, protected against pressures displaced from the training program. Some institutions turn over to the participants large portions of the administration of "their" program. At Aloka for instance, when participants complained about the food, they were informed of the budget for food purchases and of other limits set for catering, and were then encouraged to take over the planning, purchasing, or preparation of the food.

Some of these steps may be too time-consuming in short programs. But the principle holds: to bring administrative concerns in line with training concerns. Participants can effectively take responsibility for library and documentation procedures, game equipment, and many other administrative items. The ensuing activity, besides providing direct practice in accounting, storekeeping, and other useful managerial competence, may have the additional benefit of developing the attitudes and skills of collaboration and leadership.

In residential programs, above all, the institution has both the wonderful opportunity and the taxing task of achieving consistency throughout the participants' stay, in session and out of session. The unscheduled time deserves special attention there, for it accounts for at least half of the participants' working hours. With one day off each week, the proportion of off time may in fact be close to two thirds. There is no doubt that conflicting influences during this time can offset a large part of what is achieved "during training." Alternatively, if off-time influences are in line with the training, they can powerfully reinforce the progress of the program.

The major limitations and wastages of part-time and nonresidential training in fact arise from inconsistent, perhaps conflicting, influences on the participant from various sides: the training program, work, family, social contacts. In training he may be treated as a responsible, trustworthy person, when at work he must limit himself to carrying out instructions. His family and friends may resent the time he spends on the program, and so belittle the program's importance. It is such inconsistencies rather than the mixture of work and training activities that constitute the problem in off-time, part-time, and even full-time but nonresidential training. Two steps forward followed by one step back may be good progress for the pilgrim participant in these programs.

To sum up: The training institution has the function of lining up just as closely as possible all the various influences on the participants. Some part of this is achieved through contact with the participants' organizations. In the program the institution tries to offset the ill effects of other inconsistencies outside its control and its influence. For instance, it can prepare the participants to expect some inconsistencies and encourage their discussion. Many more detailed points could be made. In the end, of all possibilities open to appropriate action the most important is to ensure that the institution itself has one orientation and one voice for the participants.

THE INSTITUTIONAL "CLIMATE" FOR THE TRAINERS

Because of specialization and economies of scale the private tutor and "guru" have been replaced by the training institution. Not only has the institution to do that tutor's job, it also needs, we have learned, an image, some distinguishing characteristics, what some call an organizational personality. More precisely, to do the job of training well, the institution has to become personal and engaging. An institution is never finished with striving to develop such an orientation and character and to speak with one voice to participants and the society around. The image must forever be achieved afresh, and renewed. For one thing, its very function requires the institution to have one foot in the future, and to that extent to be ahead of the present and at variance with it. Twice before in this book we noted and commended such a split stance: first, in Chapter 6, when we considered the conditions during the program that favor effective training, particularly the close relationship between trainer and participants; and again, in the last chapter, when we visualized the participants' return to their work after training and their attempts to initiate some innovation in their organizations. In every case, and this third is no exception, standing with one foot in the present and the other in the future calls both for individual initiative and also for collaboration with others. Both attempts flower and yield their fruit only if a climate of support pervades the institution.

The institutional structures for a supportive climate have been summarized by Herbert A. Thelen. His nine specifications range over emotional as well as technical support from collegiate groups, the provision of additional resources, links with the community and faculty-wide workshops. The list is reproduced in full in Box 10.1.

In the training session the climate depends in the first place on the trainer. In the work situation it depends in the first place on the participants' superior. Just so in the training institution it depends in the first place on the principal. This is most unreservedly so in developing countries where tradition favors hierarchical authority and where train-

Box 10.1

INSTITUTIONAL STRUCTURES FOR A
SUPPORTIVE CLIMATE*

HERBERT A. THELEN

Specification 1: Improvement of teaching calls for improved performance of teachers in the classroom.

Specification 2: Only the teacher can change the performance of the teacher.

Specification 3: To do this, he requires the emotional support and technical help of a small, friendly group of colleagues.

Specification 4: Resources will be needed and should be available to the small training groups.

Specification 5: The total faculty group, with the help of a steering committee, provides the members for the groups, creates expectancy for performance, and assimilates the results of the training groups' experience.

Specification 6: To do this, the total faculty must itself be a group with shared purposes and outside demands or expectancies to be met.

Specification 7: The "outside" must be composed, for this purpose, of responsible citizens representing the community as a whole, or defined groups such as parents, merchants, civic leaders, etc.

Specification 8: Teachers must maintain interactive contact with the outside, so as to get necessary feedback for the faculty as a whole.

Specification 9: As the program rolls along, the faculty must be able to identify its shared needs for further training and make use of faculty-wide workshops and other devices to meet these needs.

All the above specifications and the suggested plan itself (with slight changes in wording) can be seen to apply to in-service training in hospitals, engineering firms, libraries, and other institutions.

SOURCE: Herbert A. Thelen, *Dynamics of Groups at Work* (Chicago: University of Chicago Press, 1954), pp. 91–92.

ing institutions are still new and have as yet no deep-rooted traditions of collegiate responsibility.

Even in other countries the principal has a very important and often dominant effect on the institutional climate. His direct influence seems to be greater even than that of the head of some other types of organizations. Though many industrial and commercial organizations, for instance, reflect the personalities of their heads, they are also shaped very directly by the impact of technical and commercial requirements. The external demands on training institutions are more diffused and indirect, and the principal's influence is correspondingly more insistent. We may wonder in passing about the satisfactions that this unquestioned importance may give to principals of training institutions. The prevailing reluctance to evaluate the effectiveness of training on the job may well draw support from that high quarter. Wherever it comes out in terms of results, effective evaluation would mean sharing authority, at least with the facts of the situation and the demands that they make.

There are other reasons, too, why a principal in a training institution is accorded extraordinary importance. The difficulties inherent in evaluating the work of a trainer leave his reputation—and often advancement—at the mercy of the principal's opinion; there is usually no other overriding criterion. This gives the principal extra power in the eyes of the trainers. And this in turn reinforces the characteristic personality trait we have earlier noted about trainers: that, as a group, they tend to be just as dependent on signs of approval from the principal as they themselves want participants in the session to be dependent on signs from themselves. This interlocking pattern of dependence—principal-trainer-participant—is most difficult to break, even under the most favorable circumstances. Where it has the support of the culture beyond the training institution, very few principals open themselves to anyone's attempts to do so. Yet they can hardly be expected to initiate them.

In the following sections we will distinguish between institutions that offer an unfavorable, a tolerable, and a favorable climate for their trainers. We will talk of the principal as the person primarily responsible for the climate and trace his influence through the trainers on the outcome of the training effort.

1. An Unfavorable Climate

In this case, the principal is against changing the traditional pattern. The institution, then, instead of playing a significant part in development, strengthens the status quo. We do not know how many institutions in India belong to this unfavorable category, but the proportion is bound to be very high. In the American school system this kind of principal and the next, who tolerate change but do not initiate it, are estimated to account for four out of five principals.

Reinforcing the general drag toward the status quo are two specific factors. One is the grave shortage of principals in the face of the training explosion in developing countries. As a result many institutions run for long periods without a principal or with successive principals occupying the position only temporarily, expressly so; or, finally, with principals whose interests and experience do not lie in training but in, say, administration. Logically, this weakness at the top could leave trainers as a group freer to shape the institution according to their needs. In fact, it leads to uncertainty so severe that any attempts by trainers to move ahead are divisive and raise prevailing anxiety yet further.

The second factor to reinforce the status quo operates strongly in institutions that are part of a work organization—the training department in an industrial company, for instance, or in a government department. In developing countries, governments are particularly active in establishing departmental staff colleges and training centers of many kinds. We noted the scale of some of them in the introduction. Many other formally autonomous institutions are so dependent on official finance and other support that their freedom to innovate is restricted within narrow limits. The problem posed by this structural arrangement can be delineated sharply: training in that situation represents a secondary function. The top management on which it utterly depends for support, often for its very inception and continued existence, has its attention on the primary service or profit-making tasks of the organization. In that setting any training activities that appear to interfere with the performance of "the work" are likely to be restricted within narrow limits or even suppressed.

Whatever the origins for the unfavorable climate that results for trainers, institutions that have it are characterized by a series of disabling features which also explain the absence of development.

Just about all the energy of trainers and administrators goes into current operations and maintenance.

The principal insists that he cannot get additional financing and staff for the diagnosis, planning, and innovation that institutional development calls for.

The principal says that the bodies to which he reports will not approve innovation; that he is powerless to act.

Departments and sections in the institution stand apart in suspicion and tend to ever greater distance from one another.

Evaluation, if any, is not in terms of total effectiveness of training on the job—that would mix up the contributions of different departments and sections—but in terms of parts only, and those parts are confined to the training program. Evaluation proceeds by loops within each department. It is self-confirming and stabilizing, not innovative. Development in one department tends to be "written off" by another. It may be ignored as insignificant or it may be belittled as no better than what has been done long since elsewhere in the institution without any fanfare. Or it may lead to real interdepartmental troubles. It may give the participants opportunities to play off some trainers against others, aggravate existing rivalries between trainers and departments, and provoke additional interference from the principal and higher bodies. The innovating department is then seen as "causing" difficulties, and attempts are made to correct this by attacking or eliminating the offending part of the institution.

Such "correction" does not lead to lasting improvement.

Lest this list seem too discouraging in its relentless direction and complexity and its lack of promise for action, this may be the place to recall that institutional developments in other fields face the same difficulties. Moreover, and more importantly, this moribund trend can be reversed by a principal who wants to act, and acts with skill.

As to the first, the scientific approach to any field involves important social problems. Medicine provides a well-known example. Many 19th-century physicians bitterly resisted such scientific innovations as Semmelweiss' statistically supported plea to surgeons to wash their hands and save childbearing women from death. Other innovations, based on inadequate research, created medical "fads" and contentious schools which resisted rational correction. As medical science developed more adequate research methods and knowledge, it still required a heroic effort to reform the institutions of medical training and the standards of admission to medical practice. These changes were introduced only by calling upon strong professional organization, strict government controls on admission, outside support from enormously wealthy foundations, and a public willingness to pay for competent medical care. Despite this progress, there remain to this day serious problems in the organization of medical research and the transmission of scientific knowledge to medical students and practicing physicians, to say nothing of medical economics. Out of these problems has grown a new field of study, medical sociology.

A principal who is determined to change the institutional climate will, as the saying goes, find a way. As a first step he will probably separate out what is fantasy from what is reality. Some of the disabling features in the list may give way even at this point. For instance, though financing and staff may be required for a change, he is almost certain to find enough of both available in the institution to make a start. To cast the principal as the victim of the budget is misleading. He is limited by the budget to be sure, and change might well be easier if there were more money and more trainers. But the principal also *shapes* the budget and has much to do with the disposal of the energies of available trainers and of other resources. Nor is he powerless before his governing bodies. American studies show that these structural relationships do not determine the rate of innovation. Farmers or physicians, who are quite independent of work organizations, change no faster than managers or principals. In any case, no principal we have yet met really maintains that he is at the mercy of his governing body. More likely he quietly secures the support of the members of that body, severally and jointly, for what he himself wishes to do.

But who is this principal who is likely to set about improving the institutional climate and how does he get appointed? Matthew Miles has analyzed a series of studies of these questions and formulated a set of generalizations.[3] The set includes the following pointers:

> The major impetus for change in institutions comes from outside. In the case of departmental training institutions, training departments, and staff colleges, "outside" means the other parts of the organization. The "consumers" of training, participants and their organizations, demand greater effectiveness of training on the job. Such outside pressures can be blunted by inadequate evaluation and by inadequacies in linking the effectiveness of a trainer's work with his advancement in salary and status.
>
> The degree and duration of change are directly proportional to the intensity of the outside pressure for change. So, "consumers," don't stop pressing! But if the initial response is slow and is then followed by an excessive response, these are the signals that the institution is becoming too dependent on outsiders for effectiveness, perhaps for survival.
>
> Improvement is more likely to be started by a principal selected from outside the institution than by one promoted from the inside.
>
> The change will proceed from the top down.
>
> The rate of change will slow down after the initial burst. This is as it should be. For as the new principal takes hold, the institution develops a more effective climate for trainers.

2. A Tolerant Climate

A more promising situation exists where the principal, though he does not take the initiative, tolerates some change. He is willing to step

---

[3] Matthew B. Miles (ed.), *Innovation in Education* (New York: Teachers College, Columbia University, 1964), pp. 431–35.

out of the prevailing system, at least for a try, perhaps to go along with trainers eager for change. Administrators who have been put into the position of principal often belong to this category; also others who do not personally depend on the traditional system but have no experience of any other, and the many who have no urge to take the initiative in a new direction.

In a climate tolerant of change the initiative lies with a few trainers bent on innovation. Their success depends on accurate estimates in the first place about the principal's range of tolerance for change. The tolerances in question cover the particular direction of change and also the amount of disturbance created by it in the institution as a whole. The latter is particularly difficult for innovating trainers to assess. It involves close contact with many colleagues just when they may prefer to keep their anxieties and resentments to themselves. Silence is a safer way to protest when the principal is condoning and perhaps even supporting the change and does not seem to be put off by anxieties. At best, introducing change under these conditions is risky. And if the estimates are out, or an unforeseen event overtakes them, the attempt may fail.

The safest step to attempt is what Kenneth Rice calls "a protected experiment."[4] The trainers secure agreement for going ahead with a limited change and for letting it run for a while without interference or interim judgment. If the change affects a marginal area and can be isolated from the rest of the institution or program, this agreement is easier to secure. The difficult problems of integrating the change, if it turns out to be successful, with the rest of the institution are postponed until later. While the experiment is on, close contact between the innovating trainers and their colleagues is perhaps the most important preparation for dealing with the problems of integration.

> The lid blew off an unstable situation like this in one institution around the continuation of laboratory training as part of the regular residential training programs. With the departure of the principal who had supported this and other institutional developments, anxieties and resentment which had accumulated around all sorts of issues burst into the open and focused on laboratory training. The innovating trainers were accused of having forced changes down their colleagues' throats by using the principal director as a ramrod. They were seen as hungry for power, to be stopped and punished at last. When they suggested that the effects of laboratory training be evaluated

---

[4] A. K. Rice, *Learning for Leadership* (London: Tavistock Publications, Ltd., 1965), pp. 184–85.

on the job, this only threatened to restore them "to power." Unlike the outgoing principal, the new principal came from a closely related organization. He dealt with this turbulence by isolating "the offenders." As he happened to be sensitive to any insinuation that he might be used by trainers, these or others, he made it a point to remain distant from all trainers.

Effective use of a tolerant climate for innovation is easier if the principal can be convinced that the change will benefit the institution as a whole and the work it carries out. Verbal persuasion, even facts and figures, may not be of much help for this. Such conviction comes from personal experience followed by insight and informed understanding. This may be the main objective and promise of advanced training programs for principals. They offer opportunities for sharing experiences with principals of related institutions in the same country or new experiences in the different conditions of a foreign country. And many such programs enhance the principal's status and sureness, particularly when he returns from training abroad.

3. A Favorable Climate

Finally, there is the principal who is eager for change and both willing and able to take the initiative to develop the institution in significant directions. He certainly has a large and continuing task, and one that is potentially very effective and personally satisfying.

This principal's contacts, like those of an effective trainer, are characterized by openness and genuineness. As far as he is concerned, any question can come up for discussion. Tasks and ways of carrying them out are the dominant points of reference. He encourages explorations for more effective and economical methods of work, whatever the unfamiliar directions in which they may lead. In this sense he favors a functional atmosphere, plays down differences of age and status. But he is genuinely personal. To him people matter. He openly expresses his feelings, feelings of dissatisfaction and anxiety as well as pleasure and excitement. By doing so he frees the trainers to express their feelings to him and to each other. That is the climate, and these are the ways in which it permeates the whole institution.

This favourable climate gets reflected in at least five areas of specific action by the principal.

i) Sharing Routine Responsibilities, Including Discipline. The principal increases the trainers' responsibilities. He refuses to take certain decisions himself or even to check on, let alone interfere with, decisions reached by the trainers in the areas delegated to them.

Problems of discipline among participants may offer an early opportunity for this. One principal informed the trainers soon after his arrival that he considered them well able to handle most disciplinary problems and that, therefore, he would prefer not to deal with these. That sufficed to bring the number of referrals down sharply. It stayed down. Even in major cases, calling for action by the principal, he can insist on a specific recommendation for action from the concerned trainers and usually follow it.

The need for flexible behavior by the trainers and the delegation to them by the principal of maximum responsibility and power is particularly strong in residential training institutions. With administrative and training concerns intertwining, this delegation needs to include some administrative decisions. With this freedom and support, the trainer in turn is in the position to share freedom and responsibility with the participants. As part of his interest in avoiding disfunctional formality, this principal also encourages direct professional contacts between trainers and their colleagues in other institutions.

ii) Gearing the Internal Organization to Function Efficiently. Most institutions have, below the principal, functional departments. Each department is headed by a senior man: economics, sanitation, accounting, management, research. Like professors in the academic world, these department heads ensure the continuity and development of their specialities in terms of personnel and program. There are signs that this organization no longer suffices in academic institutions. Interdisciplinary programs and centers are sprouting up with increasing speed. It has even less chance to suffice in training institutions which are directly concerned with improving participants' continuing and undifferentiated behavior on the job.

Designating some trainers as course and project directors—leaders or coordinators are other titles common for this position—suggests a useful direction to pursue. Trainers team up for a particular task, with one of them in charge. The team as a whole is responsible for all aspects of the work. Full-time and part-time trainers may be included just as required. The program director himself heads "his" course. He may at the same time be also a member of one or more other teams working on other programs. The functional emphasis is clearest when the principal himself is a member of the institution's pool of trainers from which he is drawn along with others into programs and projects. Trainers then work in various combinations that are collaboratively assorted according to the needs of the work, on the one hand, and to their individual interests, competence, and personal and professional development, on the other.

The arrangement is smoothest where the program director is designated well in advance. If he is appointed by the time the preceding similar program starts, he has a direct interest and opportunity to study the on-going program with an eye to instituting improvements in "his" program, to be out in the field studying the problems there, to make contacts to secure applications, and to compose "his" training group. To ensure adequate evaluation, reflection—and also rest—after "his" program is over, a trainer ought not to be director for several programs in quick succession.

The program or project form of organization ensures widely shared responsibility. It scatters points of initiative throughout the institution. It is very flexible, a doubly important consideration when demands on the institution are changing rapidly and can be expected to continue to do so.

Some institutions, in India too, have gone further and are experimenting with having trainers take turns at being head of a department—only experienced trainers, of course. The welcome result is the rapid development of trainers able to head long-term developments. In this way experienced new principals are developed for the country's growing and increasingly numerous institutions.

iii) Diversifying the Trainer's Functions. A third large area for concern and action by a principal eager to develop the institution is the organization of the work of the individual trainer. If, like a mechanic, a trainer thinks he is so routinized that he can do the job "in his sleep," he has long ceased to be the kind of trainer who communicates the values of inquiry, inventiveness, enthusiasm, and high standards through his activities. Quite likely his training sessions will be outdated as well, in content and certainly in the examples he uses. In short, training alone is not a good full-time job. It must not become a routine. The same applies to research and service activities that emphasize the applied and practical, as they must in a training institution. Each trainer needs to keep two facets of his competence fully alive in himself. One is his firsthand experience of using research results and providing services under operating conditions, for example, of plant management or area development. The other is his continued growth in his professional field. He must be in the mainstream of his field through professional contacts, reading, reflective practice, and participation in occasional special programs for this purpose.

Cutting the training load may be the first step toward these. But it does not guarantee them. Nor does the work load have to be invariably cut. Trainers may not need relief from work so much as changing activities and roles. The academic world has used sabbatical years for this purpose: a year off after five or six years of teaching. For trainers the changes need to be rung more frequently, probably in a major way every year. They need time for major research in the field and the kind of responsible action that is the hallmark of good consulting with operating organizations. Some institutions in the field of scientific research have found ways of offering their research workers occasional temporary assignments for managing an industrial unit. It is difficult to imagine a better way than this to help a trainer regain his feel for the real work situation of the participants in all their complexity and conflicting demands, and their pressures for action within given limitations.

The principal's task in this connection would not be well described in terms of having trainers do different things in some more or less mechanical sequence. The principal's task is rather to set up opportunities for each trainer over the years to develop and express in action his inclinations and competences. It includes making sure that no trainer rates his capacities too low, including his capacities for change.

The provision of some of these opportunities has structural and financial implications. This is so with instituting regular sabbatical leaves. The provision of other opportunities will call only for indirect action. For instance, the principal may draw a department head's attention to some desirable or undesirable limitations in the activities of a particular trainer.

> For instance, trainers who prefer group methods sometimes find themselves virtually participants in terms of their role and their complete preoccupation with the ongoing program. Some other tasks, usually the long-term ones, may then suffer; it is the responsibility of their colleagues to draw their attention to this.
>
> At the Aloka International Training Centre, junior faculty members had to live with another kind of conflict. By age and experience as well as by residing in the same buildings with course participants (though in separate rooms), they were closer to the participants than other trainers. This was part of the training design. The young trainers who performed this function were often torn between the confidences participants shared with them and the contribution they could make to improving the program by sharing the confidences in turn with other trainers. To safeguard their closeness to the participants, the principal saw to it that these trainers took no part in the most emotionally demanding training sessions. He also planned to have two trainers in this position in every program so that they could at least share with one another the stresses of their conflicting roles.

Any trainer's formal role set should ideally embody the following six major functions:

a) Training participants, using at least two major types of training methods regularly.

b) Directing a program or project.

c) Research, enough to feel fully abreast and acknowledged in his professional field.

d) Self-development through participation in systematic programs for this purpose. We will return to this in the next section of this chapter.

e) Consulting with the kinds of work organizations from which participants come for training. This is important partly for "keeping one's hand in" and sustaining the severely practical bias in training. Beyond this, consulting provides the trainer with a valid check on his continuing competence. When an organization asks—and pays for—his services, the trainer has a measure of his standing with some influential people outside the institution. So consulting can increase the trainer's work satisfaction and self-respect, as well as his income.

f) Managing an operating unit or project. The values of this are readily seen, but it is difficult to arrange outside the institution. Much of the value can be secured by putting the trainer in charge of some administrative or developmental tasks right in the institution itself. A residential institution can readily offer a wide range of opportunities for management by trainers. It is a society in miniature. It needs, for instance, routine purchases, budget and inventory control, materials management, building maintenance, perhaps new construction; certainly organization and staff management, and forward planning. It also has to relate itself to other organizations in the locality, market its services, and deal with public relations. The size of the unit to be managed matters less for the purpose under discussion here than the fullness of the trainer's responsibility for its efficient functioning.

Some institutions go further. At least one sends a trainer to manage an industrial unit while the regular manager comes for training. Principals of some other institutions encourage trainers to start and run enterprises of their own, a rural clinic, for instance, or a commercial establishment, such as a restaurant.

Some of the examples come very close to suggesting the employment of part-time trainers. This would put the mixture of roles on a regular basis. Or managers and other kinds of practitioners could be engaged as full-time trainers for limited periods, say, two or three years. Part-time employment can work well as long as the training function does not, for reasons of declining interest or external pressures, become the least favored activity. While an industrial consultant, for instance, can usually control his time so that he can regularly function as a trainer if he wishes, an industrial manager usually cannot. Full-time employment of practitioners as trainers for limited periods has other severe problems and is, in fact, worth attempting in only very rare circumstances.

The main problem in all these attractive shortcuts is that practitioners usually lack training skill in serious measure. They have little understanding of how people learn. Developing them into trainers is not simply a matter of helping them acquire some new training techniques. They may have good working knowledge of their subject without the ability to generalize it. They are unlikely to be familiar with developments of concepts since they finished their own formal education. By attitude and personality, too, the practitioner may not have the makings of a good trainer. He may not be satisfied with the indefinite, hard-to-measure, and longer-term results a trainer works by. He may not be at ease questioning the practitioners' habitual perceptions and normal ways of working, which is part of the trainer's function. Even if he wishes to do so, developing appropriate attitudes and skills may demand more time and skilled effort than he can repay the institution, short of adopting training as his main career.

For all these reasons experience suggests that the continuing base had best be the institution and that the trainer's functions need to diversify beyond its boundaries, not vice versa. This diversification may well include provision for trainers going on leave of absence for a year or two for operational assignments.

The principal's task goes beyond general encouragement to trainers to diversify their functions periodically. The principal needs to ensure that time and opportunities are available for this on a regular and accepted basis. Unless he does this rigorously, he will almost surely find that the immediate demands of training programs push out the other functions completely or do not allow adequate concentration and intensity of experience. For these reasons it is doubtful that a principal should encourage any trainer to shoulder more than two of these functions at any one time. It is better that he engage himself in the different functions in turn.

iv) Improving the Professional Competence of Trainers. Trainers can enhance their professional competence through many day-to-day activities. They can join and learn from each other's sessions, collaborate on joint projects, read, and so on. The principal can, in addition, facilitate professional contact outside the institution and encourage special programs for the further development of trainers. He can encourage trainers to be members of professional societies and to contribute to meetings and journals. Studies of innovation show that widespread professional contacts characterize innovative institutions in many fields: education, agriculture, industry, medicine. Trainers in these institutions are more cosmopolitan and also more widely read than trainers in other institutions.

The principal can give his particular attention and interest to trainers who wish to try out new ideas and new methods. He can help them

Figure 10.1

COMPARISON OF LEARNING PERIODS OF COMPARABLE GROUPS OF PARTICIPANTS

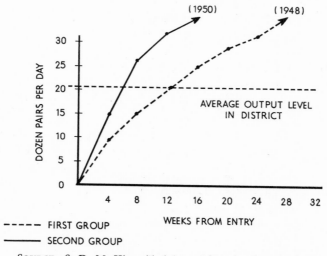

SOURCE: S. D. M. King, *Training within the Organization* (London: Tavistock Publications, Ltd., 1964), p. 241.

secure necessary outside assistance, for example, supervised practice of a new skill until the trainer can use it independently. Substantial improvements can result from a combination of methods. Figure 10.1, for instance, shows the performance of successive groups of participants learning an operating skill from the same trainer. The early groups hit average output levels after 12 weeks of training and full output after 28 weeks. Later groups reached the average in six weeks and full output in 14 weeks. The groups were similar in composition. Though many influences affect training results, the trainer's greater skill undoubtedly accounted for a very large portion of the improvement.

At Siet Institute newly recruited trainers start by taking one of the regular courses as full participants. They thereby gain inside familiarity with the kinds of people who come for training and also with their reactions to the training program. When the course is over, the new trainers have notebooks full of ideas about what they would like to do differently in their turn— questions about course design, timing, specific sessions, training methods.

For developing a specialized skill for limited application, several Indian institutions collaborated in an interinstitutional faculty program in 1965–66. Trainers from six institutions first joined a 16-day training laboratory and training skills session. After some sorting out, 12 trainers then proceeded through a four-stage internship program for laboratory trainers, practicing at various institutions from time to time in the course of the year. At the end of the program a two-week laboratory was planned at which trainers would also organize themselves for the collaboration needed for this kind of work in different institutions.

Special programs for trainers have an importance beyond that of sharing new information and experiences. They signal that the institution and its principal are interested in seeing the trainers develop further and in ensuring the highest possible quality of work. Where trainers are as few and as inexperienced as they mostly are in developing countries, such programs are especially important. We are not thinking of programs abroad, which, at best, can cover a small fraction of what is needed, but of regular programs, some within different institutions and others organized by several institutions in collaboration. All are parts of systematic plans to upgrade the quality of training through raising the motivation and competence of trainers.

But the shortage of trainers and the prevailing low standards of training make it extra difficult to introduce such programs as a regular and permanent feature of the life of an institution. The heavy pressures for quantity even at the cost of quality and the requirements for unfamiliar kinds and degrees of collaboration lead to this dilemma. This makes the principal's task the heavier and the more important.

v) *Developing Institution-wide Responsibility for Plans and Programs.* The principal's most difficult task may be to combine the encouragement of individual, team, and departmental initiative and responsibility with developing responsibility for plans and programs by the institution as a whole. Emphasizing individual initiative and flexibility at the cost of institutional responsibility would blur the total orientation and effectiveness. It almost certainly would also lead to damaging internal rivalries. If the principal, instead, emphasized institutional responsibility at the cost of widespread initiative and responsibility, he would equally lower effectiveness in operation and stifle morale. Happily the two directions, contrary though they sound, in fact spring from the same source. The same favorable climate that encourages the freedom to explore and to take responsibility also engenders a readiness to get close to other people and work jointly on tasks that require collaboration and joint responsibility. The problem lies in balancing the two sides.

Three tasks, in the main, require institution-wide collaboration and joint responsibility:

a) Periodic redefinition of the institution's objectives and of the range of organizations it seeks to serve. This involves agreeing on priorities.

b) Planning the main lines of training, research, and service activities, and the facilities required for them.

c) Defining the criteria for selecting new trainers, and setting standards of work.

We can use the introduction of a new program to illustrate institution-wide responsibility and the processes by which the principal can foster it. The principal would take no action by himself on a program that has no place in plans already agreed upon. It would come up for discussion and agreement among the trainers meeting as a body. Irrespective of its point of origin, with an individual trainer, a department, or the principal himself, it can be accepted only if it is sufficiently central to the main objectives and methods agreed upon for the period in question. If so, agreement on it encompasses the requisite priority for time and other resources. If it is not central, it may yet be accommodated in the standing provision that departmental budgets have for additional exploratory work. If this also is not possible, it may still go ahead under the institution's auspices, provided only that it meets accepted standards of work and is designated as an individual, departmental or, for that matter, an outside contributor's responsibility.

The main point is that the principal, far from regarding the making of plans as his special responsibility by virtue of his position, involves the trainers in all stages of the process. He thereby secures access to the whole range of their ideas and understanding. At the same time he also secures the sharing of views and drawing closer that occurs in the process of working for agreement on joint plans. The end result, the agreed upon plans and programs, then carry more weight on several scores. And their execution commands the trainers' energies more readily because responsibility and satisfactions are shared.

By way of summary, Exhibit 10.1 juxtaposes some major facets of institutional climates that favor or detract from development. The point of view is the principal's.

Exhibit 10.1

INSTITUTIONAL CLIMATES FOR THE TRAINERS: THE PRINCIPAL'S POINT OF VIEW

The Principal's	Favorable Climate	Unfavorable Climate
Self-image	Influential innovator, needs others' support	Powerless, overworked, self-sacrificing. Disciplinarian, toward himself and others.
Image of trainers	Capable of self-motivated work of high standard and of collaboration in joint activity and responsibility. Will enjoy development.	Need continuous prompting and guidance. Disinterested, in conflict with colleagues.
Areas of attention	Diagnosis of current activities, long-term plans. Developing sound relationships within the institution, and between the institution and its clients and the locality.	Current operations; rules, checks on individual performance.
Behavior	Listens, encourages expressions of feelings and views on all aspects. Encourages innovation. Joins in making joint plans which commit trainers to heavy work.	Works separately, makes plans by himself. Works through impersonal logical rules and orders. Keeps trainers and departments separate.

THE LANGUAGES OF RESISTANCE

To promote a favorable climate for development the principal assumes functional roles and divests himself of authority and power sanctioned by tradition. As he does so he meets the same kinds of initial difficulties that the trainers run into when they move in a similar direction with participants. The usual first reaction of the trainers is defensive, full of distrust and suspicion. They feel manipulated rather than freed. They see the principal's endeavors to draw them closer as a more clever and hence more frightening manner of exercising arbitrary power. What is genuine is seen as technique.

The first murmurings may well come around the greatly increased number of meetings required to establish the new climate and to reach general agreements on broad outlines of development. "Alright," trainers say to one another, "so he wants us to meet. It is all a waste of time. We will carry on afterwards as we always have, you will see." Or: "He is asking us to speak only to test us out, to see who is with him." Listening to trainers discuss institutional questions among themselves one might conclude that this principal is an obstacle, not a help. He is not doing "his" job; "he is the one who needs training".

As the principal persists in the new direction, the apparently inevitable period of incredulity may start: "It is a gimmick, it can't be true." The trainers continue to experience the change as an imposition and resent the extra burden the principal seems to put on them; that is, basically, the burden of reaching agreement among themselves and of living with the consequences of joint decisions.

Then they test him out: "Let's see if he really means what he says. I bet he doesn't." This is perhaps the first recognition of the possibility that he might mean it after all, contrary to all expectations. This testing out can take many forms. For instance, when the principal delegates to course coordinators both more functions and also the corresponding authority to take action, his behavior is open to several unfavorable interpretations. Trainers can regard it as an attempt to stay out of trouble, or to save himself work, or as confirmation that he is not in the least interested in participants, that he is "just an administrator." If they see the transfer of responsibility in any of these ways, they do not assume the new functions with any enthusiasm. At best they proceed with a wary eye, glancing back over their shoulder. This period is characterized by strong ambivalent feelings, difficult to dislodge. A very important set of experiences and expectations is in question. As trainers, like other people, wish their early expectations to be proved correct, this twilight stage can last a long time. The point to underscore is that right through this period, it is the principal who has to carry the burden of change. Most difficult of all may be the emotional burden of remaining friendly and outgoing, open and patient with the trainers even while his endeavors seem so little appreciated and the results so slow in coming.

We have talked and corresponded with the principals of a variety of institutions and programs in several countries about the ambiguities and disturbances of establishing a favorable climate. We have chosen two descriptions to reproduce here at some length. One, in Box 10.2, is from the principal of a well-known experimental school in a developing country. The second, in Box 10.3, is from K. A. Rice, who directs an annual leadership training program organized jointly by the University of Leicester and the Tavistock Institute of Human Relations in London. They all write of the trainers' drawn-out insistence on seeing the principal both as *The* authority and as *No* authority, as being too close to the participants and also too distant from them. In short, at the outset of major institutional development the trainers feel thoroughly insecure, quite at sea. The principals for their part see the trainers as "listless" on important questions, "as if neither the questions nor the answers mattered much." The trainers seem personally involved only in discussions

Box 10.2

A SCHOOL PRINCIPAL AT WORK IN A
DEVELOPING COUNTRY

How does one get people to link their hands together in joint effort? Why do teachers in some groups seem so insensitive to the problems of the young? What is it in me that seems to block the perception in others? I suppose the order of my question should be revised, but I ask them this way.

From what I gather from my staff, I constantly confuse issues that others seem to see clearly in black and white terms until I enter the scene. I can live with error but my colleagues can't live comfortably with error in me.

As one of them stated it, "I hated you that time I knew I was right and you were wrong." Another put it, "Why aren't you consistent? You make a decision and later change it." When I replied, "I thought the new facts we gathered were sufficient cause," the answer was, "When there were already so many variables that made the decision difficult, you doubled the difficulties many times over when you changed it." "Sometimes you are like a general in the army fraternizing with us, the unlisted men, and sometime you are just the General."

The teachers in one school feel I am too close to the children and *"know too much* about individual children to be an impartial observer of their (the teachers) work"! They see me either as The Authority or as No Authority. This is my constant dilemma.

There are two schools, with about the same enrollment in each. One school moves along with children, with a minimum of acute behavior problems. Children and teachers alike radiate a happiness and a quality of reaching out toward others which is noticeable enough to be mentioned even by strangers entering the gate. The other school, with a much better physical plant and facilities, is full of problems, yet I can't spot *why* this difference should exist. I can list a number of possibilities, such as space which limits the number of face-to-face contacts in day-to-day situations, the difference in social class and the pressure on a rising middle class. But why these situations give rise to the particular problems and what can be done about it requires more provisions and not less concern! But free teachers are less active in the interests of children.

I use the word *awareness* often in discussion with the teachers, yet they seem resistant. I admit to being more aware of child needs than teacher needs and I suppose I'm impatient to get at crucial conditions affecting the *child*. I think about the teacher and try to, I suppose, manipulate her into doing that which I see as needing to be done. But if the teachers in school A can do it—why don't the teachers in B?

Box 10.2 (Continued)

I feel the heaviness of so much I don't like to see and so little of what I want to see at B. Yet, as teacher personalities, as managers in the classrooms, as subject matter specialists, they are an exceptionally well-selected group.

In a New Education that can help children to go forward on their own, teachers too have to move forward on their own. What training can help do this? Teachers need help to gain insight into the significance of the process by which a child comes into an active awareness of the world around him. But how does a teacher achieve this awareness? Can teachers identify their own "intentions" with respect to their work? Can they see the necessity for total effort yet accommodate wide difference among themselves? Can they accept me in my role as a co-worker without damage to their own security on the job, or do I need a "strong" administrative assistant to hold the teachers in line while I play among the variables!

Considering the problem of staff turnover, of the effects of rapid expansion and the mixing of untrained, newly trained, and overtrained on the job, the difficulties arising out of missed cues in communication among such groups, and from and to me, are very painful. Perhaps, I'm just assuming too many roles at one time to deal effectively with any one of them. What kind of training do I need to serve in the process now called in-service training? How can I handle the details of a school day that often get mixed into the training process to mould the "goals" we find so annoyingly elusive—now you see them, now you don't?

SOURCE: Private communication.

of administrative questions that directly affect them: hours of work, salaries and benefits, physical amenities.

Another principal considered discontinuing professional meetings because "only I and a very few others wanted them." He kept them going because of two slender possibilities. One possibility was that the listlessness of the trainers might be expressing some accumulated resentment against earlier authority figures. By their listlessness they were able to deny the principal something he obviously wanted. If the trainers had such resentment to express, he concluded, it better come out in the open, if necessary through this listlessness and denial. The second possibility was that the trainers found the changes the principal proposed so unsettling that they needed to hang on to concrete, measurable, short-term issues, mainly to steady themselves. Issues at hand for this purpose tended to be administrative. This possibility looked the more plausible whenever trainers toyed eagerly with simple solutions to delicate problems, as if almost *any* solution was preferable to continued worrying.

Box 10.3

A PROGRAM DIRECTOR AT WORK

K. A. RICE

Though I was appointed director by my colleagues who have formed the conference staff, and though I continue to hold office only with their sanction, I have directed in my own way; and as director I have been in a privileged position when decisions about design and method have had to be made. My colleagues have not always agreed either with my approach to, or with my actions in, the conferences. But they have not disagreed so much as to make our disagreements intolerable or their support impossible. They have influenced not only conference design but also my own conduct in more ways than I can make explicit or even know about. We still disagree on some points of theory and on more of practice. At this stage of our understanding of problems of interpersonal and intergroup relations, I believe it to be right and healthy that we should continue to differ, provided we can also continue to use our differences constructively.

This is not therefore an agreed account, and I have to accept responsibility for it. I am nevertheless writing it now because developments are continually taking place, and if we wait until we are all agreed about what we are doing and how we are trying to do it, I doubt if an account will ever be written.

[In a later passage he poses the problem of separating fantasy from reality and notes the illusion that administrative questions can be at all clearly separated from professional ones.]

When I am involved I have to ask whether my own anxiety about my performance is making me even more obstinate than usual. How far is the difficulty due to my capacity for blackmailing my colleagues by threats to resign the role of director? How far am I using in an inappropriate way the authority delegated to me? How far is the quarrel due to the intransigence of the colleagues with whom I am in dispute? Is the disagreement based on genuine technical differences or does it arise mainly from different views of the conference and its events? These questions are not peculiar to conference direction; they are inherent in any discussion about policy in any group that is responsible for leading and managing. What is important for a staff group running a conference that is itself about leadership and management is that the group's attention to its own difficulties should sufficiently differentiate fantasy and reality for the result, as it affects the members, to enhance learning opportunities.

One of the difficulties of separating reality from fantasy is the toleration of uncertainty of outcome demanded of the staff. In a staff meeting, anyone who expresses a point of view with sufficient strength, or seems sure in his prediction, tends to wield more influence than either the point

Box 10.3 (Continued)

of view or the prediction sometimes deserves. One consequence is that when I exercise decisively the authority delegated to me, I can sometimes do so with more power than I was intended to have. The very demonstration of power makes it more difficult for others effectively to oppose the decision. In addition, because of the need to make drastic economies in the time (and money) spent in preconference planning, almost all administrative decisions have been left to the conference secretary and myself. But "administrative" decisions, particularly those that have to do with what is sent out to inquirers and to members, are frequently found, like administrative decisions elsewhere, to have modified or even predetermined the policy they were intended only to implement. In solving some problems we have now to beware that our solutions do not serve to suppress other problems that need equal attention.

[Yet, even with all the meticulous training and years of experience Rice and his colleagues have had consistently in this orientation, Rice is still conscious of his colleagues' need to hide things from him and propitiate him with token gifts.]

It appears to be assumed that though the director need not be told anything important, he should be told all that is unimportant. He needs, in other words, to be treated with respect and consideration, and a way of doing this is to propitiate him with token gifts. Behind the respect and consideration, however, is the hope that providing him with useless information may keep him from finding out anything useful, and hence make it easier to discredit him. The major communications to management are inferential; they have to be deduced not from what is said, but largely from what is not said.

SOURCE: K. A. Rice, *Training for Leadership* (London: Tavistock Publications, Ltd., 1965), pp. 3–4, 150–52, 109.

They showed undiscriminating eagerness to accept a "solution" proposed by the principal, even when he put forward only a suggestion or an idea. This principal concluded that if he could only keep going steadily in the same direction for a while, the anxieties and resentments would indeed get expressed and exhausted, and the trainers would then be ready to join him in a basically different kind of relationship. But he was unsure whether the next stage could start without more support than he had from the general environment, in particular without more institutional control over some key areas which now required decisions by his board of directors.

Several principals mentioned "very disquieting" declines in the motivation for work and the efficiency of many trainers during the early stages of major changes. For instance, joint responsibility initially seems to mean no one's responsibility. As a result, participants receive less supervision and help from trainers than before. They raise the question, to themselves really, of how far they can get ahead of their colleagues. A principal's personal commitment to effecting significant change can itself become a block to change if it makes him impatient for visible progress and intolerant of other people.

The innovating principals seem weary and a little discouraged. To the outsider, though, they are clearly quite far along in the process of change. For one thing, the trainers have become free to express some of their resentments directly. There is far more openness, more frankness than usual. The principals themselves talk of proceeding by agreement to differ. "We still disagree on some points of theory and on more of practice; [that is] right and healthy provided we can also continue to use our differences constructively."

The fullest picture we have of a principal and the group of trainers engaged in close collaborative work is in Lynton's *The Tide of Learning, The Aloka Experience.* The extracts from it that follow this chapter as a reading deal particularly with faculty meetings. Just the statistics reveal something of the great amount of work involved in establishing and maintaining collaboration. During the week preceding the start of a program, there were daily long meetings. During the first four weeks of the course, faculty meetings were still almost daily, declining to meetings every other day during the remaining eight weeks of the program. On an average a meeting lasted an hour and a quarter, substantially lengthening an already long working day. The meetings were tape recorded. By way of content, analysis reveals that fully three quarters of the time of meetings during the initial four weeks was taken up by reporting on individual participants and building up a picture of each. That done, the preoccupations shifted to how to deal with the most active and also with the silent participants; how to accept the hostility that came as the relationships between trainers and participants changed; how to adjust the program to take account of needs that were becoming clear only now in the later stages; and finally what the principal and the trainers were learning that would be of use in future programs.

What comes through the statements and descriptions of all the innovating principals is not a particular outcome labeled success opposed to something labeled failure, but the difficulties and excitements of professional people together getting more and more involved in their work and improving its quality. They do not leave things alone. They worry them and churn them up until they promise further improvement. There is a continuous endeavor toward greater effectiveness, a need to concern oneself with better and better questions. This atmosphere of the institution, of the principal, trainers, and administrators, all struggling to learn, is not lost on the participants. In fact, it may be the most important and pervasive communication of them all: that the process of learning is continuous and that it engages everyone, certainly the principal and the trainers. It is this that puts the institution really on the road to development.

CRISES, DILEMMAS, AND RESOLUTIONS IN INSTITUTIONAL DEVELOPMENT

From our work in new institutions and from watching sister institutions start and grow we have become conscious of important similarities in the "life cycles" of all institutions—to transpose the term Erik Erikson uses for an individual. Rough though the analogy may be, even a brief systematic description of the uniformities may interest those charged with setting up new institutions, as well as innovating principals who are attempting to move existing institutions toward greater maturity.

The uniformities are systematically set out in Exhibit 10.2. They are ordered into three concepts. One is the crisis; not in the sense of an emergency, but of a constellation of forces internal and external that insistently pose a dilemma—the second concept. The dilemma is not a problem to be solved, once and for all; the constellation of forces does not dissolve. The alternatives it offers are tempting but a false choice. What the dilemma demands is resolution—the third concept: resolution sufficiently deep to embrace both. Working out such a resolution calls, in the first place, for quiet pause from day-to-day activities, a disengagement for reflection, a turning inward. For this disengagement Erikson uses the word "moratorium." The moratorium is not itself the resolution but sets up a condition for discovering it.

The crises occur in a certain predictable order: We have called them birth, identity, growth, maturity, development. Each has characteristic patterns and issues. They overlap, and occasionally there may be a regression, but the sequence broadly stands. Only after the current dilemma is resolved and the crisis passed is the institution ready for the next phase of its development. This phase in turn will shape towards a

Exhibit 10.2

CRISES IN THE LIFE OF AN INSTITUTION

Crisis	Characteristic Features	Dilemma	Resolution
1. Birth	A few individuals full of of ideas and zest. Frenzied activity. Attention oriented outward—power points, sister institutions, customers.	When should the institution be born and how large? Planning for every contingency or have a crash program?	Strong continuing leadership.
2. Identity a) Seeking identity	Search for main focus or foci. Conflict and uncertainty. Internal competition for attention.	Perfection of one thing or value on all comers?	Clearly explicit long-range objectives as a priority system for decision making.
b) Seeking acceptance	Search for relationships with existing systems. Interorganizational jealousies. Attention outward.	Stress likeness and conformity or stress novelty and differences?	Moratorium to establish standards, largely in isolation.
c) Seeking balance	One or two activities have made a quick start, threaten to dwarf or belittle others. Jealousies within.	Curb fast starters or let them run loose?	Focus on lagging functions to encourage their momentum.
3. Growth	Great demands for services, mostly short-term. Temptation to take on too much load. Meeting demands increases demands.	Consolidate and develop slowly or expand in all promising directions?	Moratorium to reexamine objectives and priorities. Publicize long-range plans.
4. Maturity	Success revives interorganizational jealousies, even threatens sponsors. Attacks on autonomy and independence.	Forego identity and submit or revolt and break away?	Develop interdependent relationships focused on tasks.
5. Development	Self-satisfaction. Temptation to rest on laurels. Reluctance to work out new ideas.	Fossilize or break up into progressive and conservative, young and old?	Check objectives against changing situation, rejuvenate institution, build in indices of relevance.

crisis. Characteristically unresolved, any crisis persists and prevents further development. So every phase holds the seeds of institutional death. "Doom" would be a better word: growth stifled, an atmosphere of death. The institution may continue to exist; institutions usually do. But it is at a halt.

THE INSTITUTION AS AN AGENT FOR GENERAL DEVELOPMENT

Studies tell us very little as yet either about the amount of general support that an institution requires to allow, sustain, or promote a major innovation in its development, or how strong and active an institution has to be in order to affect its environment directly. Certainly all the people at the institution—the principal, trainers, administrators, and staff of all kinds—no less than the participants, are children of the surrounding society and the prevailing traditions. They bring "the outside" in. In reverse, through the outgoing participants and the direct contacts it has with their work organizations, the institution conveys to the society around what is going on by way of change within. The further ripples of this two-way influence include everyone's family and friends and their myriad contacts in turn with others.

The general conceptual picture of the relationship between the institution and the world outside is therefore clear: It is that of any subsystem within the larger systems to which it belongs, the immediate one and those beyond. What studies of innovation still have to clarify are the operational demands of this relationship, the sequences, weights, and priorities involved. Meanwhile we will use whatever general indications are available.

The overriding consideration is simply that the relationship between the innovating institution and its surroundings matters and is most worthy of attention. We have already seen how training departments and staff colleges that form part of a work organization may not be allowed to develop in significant directions if top management is preoccupied with early "concrete" results or fearful of possible disturbances to production and services "caused" by the training wing. A similar possibility exists where the institution is autonomous but so small and weak that its efforts are swamped by traditional influences. Any changes within its walls may then be offset by forces outside. We do not know what is "so small" or "so weak," but we do know many institutions that struggle valiantly but vainly in this constraint. Often it is only the principal's determination that prevents the institution from sliding back into the undifferentiated, thoroughly human trend to randomness.

If institutional development can be so smothered by general forces, the answer may be institutional autonomy and independent strength, both. Many new institutions in India have been set up as autonomous bodies. Actually they face the same danger, only indirectly. For autonomy and strength are not synonymous. The autonomous institution normally starts with more and better national contacts than local ones. But because its independence often spells separateness, it has additional difficulties in developing more and stronger local links. Without these it is deprived of the opportunity of acting effectively as an agent for accelerated development right outside its walls. Traditional forces in the locality may not be able to swamp the institution, because it is too strong. The dangers of ineffectiveness lurk beyond the locality. Over a wider area, a state, a region, the whole country, the institution's contacts may be too scattered to affect general development. It is the scattered participants and their scattered organizations who are then in danger of being swamped by the enveloping traditions in their various localities and organizations. It is a matter for anxiety that national institutions in India that draw participants from so many places often have only a few or none from the localities in which they themselves are situated.

Effective contact between the institution and its environment raises questions of structure, of what makes for strength in the institution and the environment, and of the kinds of relationships that might be effectively built. As to structure, the historical development of professional bodies may suggest ways of combining optimum autonomy for effecting change with local relationships for influence. Universities in many countries consist of autonomous "schools"—of medicine, architecture, public administration, and so on. They profit from sharing skills and facilities. But they profit most from sharing an atmosphere in which learning is the primary task. And many have local roots. Whatever the formal relationship, studies show that close contact between institutions in the same locality goes hand in hand with sustaining and spreading development in general. Geographical proximity—clustering of institutions—is the most obvious condition for local contact and collaboration.

In studying the diffusion of new teaching materials, Matthew Miles reports that clustering of institutions was the dominant condition for quick diffusion. Four out of five early users were geographically close to other users. Those who were cut off from other users either tended to give up the innovation or to stimulate colleagues to use the new materials also and so acquired other users. Most commonly the materials were used in such tightly knit groups and in clusters of institutions. That the institutions were of different kinds was not important, only that they were geographically close. What happened, apparently, was that principals and trainers decided to go in for the change after actually seeing it in operation in a nearby institution. On seeing it they reached the decision to change. It was only after they had reached the decision to use the materials that they tried to develop the necessary skills and material resources. Direct observation or firsthand reports tipped the balance.[5]

Institutions cluster automatically in large towns. It seems important to encourage similar clustering in smaller towns, for example, market towns in rural areas. The wisdom of this is confirmed by another observation: that innovation feeds on other innovations, no matter what the subject or field; that there is a kind of atmosphere of development. People get used to development and to seeing institutions develop. Development creates the climate for further development. In this way, development can become a self-perpetuating process, just as stagnation can.

We have already noted that institutional development depends, in the first place, on having at the head a principal who is eager for change and has the skill to create a favorable climate for it, and, in the second place, on having trainers with wide professional interests and contacts. To complete the prognosis for development, we need to add financing. Just as most innovative farmers operate larger farms and have higher incomes and savings than other farmers, and as most innovative doctors have richer patients, and innovative companies have larger operations, so also most innovative training institutions serve organizations and localities with higher levels of income and expenditure.[6] The process is an interlocking one. Development often starts with an institution that has some extra resources. Foundation grants can play a key role in priming the pump. Once development gets under way, it becomes easier to raise funds independently.

The localities in which innovating institutions prosper are also characterised by certain strengths. The institution's objectives are widely known and understood in them and expectations of the institution's contribution to the locality are high. Understanding and expectations of this sort are associated usually with education, socio-economic class, and the distribution of political power but they are also open to deliberate influence by the institution.

An institutional service to the locality may be an excellent first step towards developing a sound local base for training. A small factory that trainers help to run well, a new community health service that is both an additional facility and also one that is clearly more effective than others run on "normal" lines, a modern farm operated on land and with

---

[5] Miles, *op cit.,* pp. 262–65.

[6] Miles, *op. cit.,* p. 314.

physical resources also available to local farmers—these are examples of effective services. They mark the institution's goodwill and interest in the locality. They show what training can produce by way of actual results. They make the point that effective training develops in participants new attitudes, knowledge, understanding and skills that can transform other resources, whatever they are, into contributing streams to development.

Reading 10.1

BUILDING TRAINERS INTO A TEAM*

R. P. Lynton

In the field, the discussion room, and the numerous informal contacts with the members, the actions of faculty members were rooted in their individual experiences prior to coming to Aloka, in the kinds of people they each were, and also in the close contact they had with one another both before and throughout the course. It was common for two faculty members to be at the same session and to use the break-time and after class for checking with one another how it was going. They used to go in and out of each other's living quarters, sharing ideas, talking of some experience they had just had, expressing the feelings they had controlled during the contact with the members, exchanging written assignments, and enjoying the close personal relationship. Traditions grew up according to which faculty members congregated in the office or had tea together regularly, without necessarily anything specific to talk about. So with their very different backgrounds and varied professional training, and their different styles of teaching, they yet achieved a consistency in their orientation and in the kinds of cues they use and their reactions to them.

Their consistency cut across the faculty assignments to different parts of the programme. All faculty members taught some case sessions, and several took turns with the work programme and field visits. But for the most personal discussions, those in which members reviewed their own experience, the same faculty member stayed with a group. That was one important division which faculty meetings needed to bridge. A second

---

* From R. P. Lynton, *The Tide of Learning, The Aloka Experience* (London: Routledge & Kegan Paul, 1960), pp. 182–95.

division existed between those faculty members who lived very closely with the members, sharing a cottage and meals, and those who lived in separate cottages with their families. This division was not just one of convenience. The faculty members who lived most closely with the members did not lead the most personal, and possibly threatening, group discussions and deliberately stayed out of situations which might have inhibited their developing and maintaining close informal relations with the individual members. For the members they were the faculty members who could most readily be approached with questions, problems, and any kind of personal help. For the faculty as a whole they were often best able to assess the impact of a session and to check how individual members were getting on.

Usually those faculty who lived most closely with the members were junior faculty, people who had been outstanding members of Aloka courses and who had been brought back to develop further their considerable promise as trainers. Thus their age and recent experience as well as their living arrangements and professional assignments put them nearer to the members.

In some ways the junior faculty were in positions of particular stress, since they were closer to the members but not of them, and at the same time members of the faculty but apprentice members, so to speak. One of the things we have learned is the value of bringing junior faculty in pairs, just as the members were chosen in pairs, in order to give them a colleague with whom to share continuously their questions, their anxieties, and their moments of triumph.

The scheduled meetings of the whole faculty put some certainty into the picture of spontaneous consultation and exchange. They ensured that enough time was indeed set aside for discussing everything necessary, for the timetable of a residential course tends to be overful and overlong. Two and a half hours of classroom work per day was usual for a faculty member, twice that not uncommon. Preparation, commenting on written assignments, correspondence, their part in the arrangements for field visits and speakers' evenings, and individual conferences with members demanded varying amounts of additional time. And then there was the almost continual informal contact with members, including taking part in games and socials. Without scheduled faculty meetings some points would perhaps not have received consideration, particularly such longer term matters as training design. The meetings were useful also to ensure that all faculty members were familiar with what had been of significance in the sessions, not merely the two or three who were present at the sessions or checked with one another on the spur of the moment. Without this, the unity of the learning process would have been endangered and the faculty members' own learning reduced.

The certainty that there would be the opportunity to discuss a point at the scheduled meeting also protected faculty members from each other! The call could wait, the exciting cue of someone learning, the good idea for next week, the report of the session, the check on the written assignment—many of these could wait a few hours till the meeting. If there had been no meeting, faculty members would have interrupted one another even more than kindred spirits naturally do and cut up everybody's day into little bits until nobody could have called any part of it his own.

There were six faculty meetings in the days just before that course began and forty-two more during the three months, lasting an average of one hour and a quarter each. Half the meetings took place in the first four weeks, when meetings were daily with only very few exceptions and each lasted longer than the average. During the second four weeks there were twelve meetings; during the last four weeks, nine.

Though they were scheduled in advance and all four faculty members were expected to take part, the meetings were quite informal. They usually took place in the evening over after-dinner coffee in the director's cottage. They had no set agenda. Faculty members spoke about what was important to them from the day's work and for looking ahead. This chapter will, in fact, not do justice to the free association which thinking together led to, now in one direction, now in another. Grouping certain kinds of data together makes the process seem more systematic than it was. The atmosphere of free talking and listening, some of it in disappointment, some in joy, much of it in fun, and all in close and growing fellowship, that was of its essence. Here was the professional base of operations; the emotional base, too, where faculty members found support and encouragement, tried out first thoughts, and relaxed. And from which they emerged refreshed and reassured.

Building Up a Picture of Members

The characteristic start of a faculty meeting during the course was a general question from the director, such as, 'Well, we have many things to discuss. Any particular wish for a start?' or to one of the faculty, 'You look as if you want to start. How did it go?' This usually led into a piece of summary reporting of some significant happening.

Of particular importance at this level of discussion was the sharing of the cues by which to assess a member's and the group's development, and the results of attempting to help them along. Such as assessment was always difficult, but even more so in an international group.

Fully three quarters of the time of faculty meetings during the first four weeks was taken up by reporting on individual members in the course and building up a picture of each. The data for this understanding came from the whole range of training and living arrangments: where he chose to sit in the discussion room or at meals, how he walked, whom he teamed up with in dishwashing, what appeared from written assignments or a personal conversation, the manner of his working with agricultural tools, what his late-coming might mean; and so on. It seemed that once the faculty had agreed on the overall programme of the course (and that had been accomplished before the members arrived) they were content to respond to the group as they saw fit at the moment and to focus their attention almost exclusively on the development of individuals. This stage of faculty meetings was not over until the picture of each member in the course had been checked and confirmed against his behaviour in many situations.

There was some mention of each member in every faculty meeting during the first week, even if it was only a check on whether the faculty had noticed anything at all revealing about him to add to the picture. On an average, 80% of the members were talked about during any of the first month's meetings.

The silent members were by their inaction more difficult to understand. Their silence could mean so many things. Understanding them rested largely on indications from their behaviour in their rooms, at games and meals, and at other occasions of informal contact. The faculty member who lived with the members and was close to them had most to contribute there.

When the silent members began to speak in class, it was an event worth reporting in faculty meetings. Often when the first member of the 'silent block' started to speak, he was quickly followed by some of the others. Often the slowness of a session when the usual talkers were unprepared, sulking, or silently consolidating their gains from the previous sessions allowed or impelled the more silent members to come forward.

Accepting Hostility

Increasingly the attention of the faculty rested on a few active people. The volunteer leaders attracted attention not only by their being active and dominating, and productive of things to report at faculty meetings, but also because the faculty had continuously to consider what to do in relation to them. Presently, concern with the talkers assumed very great prominence in the faculty meetings.

The faculty expected that members would feel hostile, at least initially, and welcomed the expression of hostility as a sign of development. To review one's established attitudes and habits is not easy or comfortable; unscheduled, quiet self-examination which is not recorded is even less comfortable than the group discussions which are the data here. These negative feelings must come out if positive ones are to emerge. If the hostility can be expressed to the faculty, who can be seen as having initiated this painful process, it is better than that it be directed at secondary targets, such as other members. The hostile feelings need not go on for so long nor be expressed so crudely as they were in the course from which the recordings for this chapter are taken. But they are essentially the same in every course.

What did the faculty members do with this hostility? Listened to it, in the first place, and encouraged its expression in and out of the scheduled programme. Shared their own feelings about it with the other faculty members, as at the faculty meetings and even more in informal contacts among themselves. And finally, they used the indications to adjust the programme and design the course to fit as closely as possible the needs of the particular people in it.

Adjusting the Programme

The basic constituents of the Aloka course are pretty well fixed. The mixture is what changes with every group and from day to day. What to do is really less of a question than whether to do it now. Is this the moment for a statement? Was this interpretation premature? Is it too early for the written autobiographies? Would a review session help? Is this the time to go easy or to take a risk? These are the unspoken questions the faculty have in their contacts with members in and out of the discussion room. In terms of charting the course they come up again and again at faculty meetings.

The fact that the same ingredients recur in course after course obscures the fact that they may be introduced or their timing determined for very different reasons. For instance, in most of the courses the group is subdivided for the first hour of case discussion. These sub-groups are instituted at some point within the first four weeks but for a variety of reasons. In some courses, they are introduced in response to the faculty's estimate that the members are ready to begin leading groups themselves. In some, the faculty regard them more as an opportunity for the timid members to participate in discussion in a more intimate group, often without the presence of a faculty member. In the course from whose faculty meetings these recordings are taken, the small groups had a particular importance. The faculty hoped in part to double the chance for the silent members to talk and the pressure on them to do so. They wanted not only to break Du's monopoly of the class discussions but to give the other members a chance to interact and to put forward their ideas for consideration. At the same time this would give the faculty a basis for a better understanding of them.

In most courses such division is done wholly by the members and reviewed and possibly changed by them on a suitable occasion later in the course, when the division fits into a clearly emerging pattern of relationships. The same procedure was initially followed in this course. The more silent members took this opportunity to assort themselves in resistance to Du. This expression, in their own passive way, encouraged them to develop independently of him. In a move to support this fragile new growth, it seemed desirable to rethink the structure of the sub-groups.

> FA: I had an idea that maybe for a few preparatory sessions we should see that Ne and Du are in the same group so that they compete with one another and not with the more submissive ones. I will take the silent group with the idea that, since I generally teach the big group too, they would come into it with some confidence that things they've tested out will still hold good. Then may be they'll be braver about getting their comments in before the discussion has taken some other turn and they're already behind.

Before the meeting was over, the plan was further modified to divide the group not into two parts but into smaller units of three or four members each. After considerable deliberation the faculty themselves made the division in the hope of ensuring a change in the pattern of the group as they understood it. Their attempt was to put into the same small group those who were about equally vocal and also at somewhat the same stage of understanding. The junior faculty member, who was presumably the least threatening, then sat with the members who found it most difficult to talk in class; the director worked with the most dominant; and the others sorted themselves out in between. After several sessions like that, the faculty began to rotate among the groups.

Several days later, Fa commented on the signs of a split between Du and Ne, and Du's efforts to re-establish himself as the leader.

> FA: I thought at first that Ne used to feel very guilty talking when Du was silent. I'd like to look at those interaction charts that we kept, but I have the impression that Ne never talked first on a point, he took his departure from

something that Du said, often with a formal acknowledgement, and occasionally took it further. But if he took it too far, then Du would do something to disrupt, and one of his favourite tricks was something he tried today: passing notes. For a school teacher, Du is a great old note-passer, and what he tries to do is to pass notes through Ne, whenever Ne is on a point that's too far from the point Du tried to make.

FI: His notes seem to have had no effect today, I thought.

FA: No. I don't know whether the effect is wearing off, or whether Ne was feeling his independence.

FE: I think a part of it was that Ne was in a different preparatory group—and that Ne thought he had it.

FA: I thought he was very hesitant at first about talking at all. Then he warmed up through a series of 'M-hmm's' when other people talked to the point where he was just about carrying it.

FE: Well, there wasn't the usual communication with Du. Usually, well, there has been no situation like this before where they have been separated and allowed to develop independently.

FI: That in itself resulted from the separation in the preparatory groups. . . .

The faculty meetings were full of this kind of spontaneous reviewing of the programme: a suggestion for this, adjustment there, a thought filed for future reference, a prediction on how something would work out. The concern which underlay these detailed considerations and action questions was with fitting all the pieces together into a unified experience for the members. The whole programme was to convey the stimulation and reflection conducive to learning. It was one, though it had many pieces. The faculty was concerned to provide a learning experience not only in the formal training programme; the same consideration also guided the location of Aloka and the design of the physical arrangements, the way linen was given out, the relations between members and the permanent house staff, the facilities available for recreation, the setting for informal contact. As the members were at work with themselves, as they changed in bursts, or slowly, painfully, intrigued individually by this or by that—the unity yet had to be maintained. Its communication was to 'go on learning. There is no escape from that. It is wherever you look, all around you and most of all inside you.' In this shifting and changing it was the faculty's business to maintain this unity, this balance, this totality.

Worrisome concern may seem from these recordings to have set the tone of the faculty meetings. To some extent it was so, particularly in this course. But the impression is due more to their deliberate choice of what to talk about at the meetings, and this emphasis has not been adjusted here. Elation and statements of something having gone well do not occupy much time. But they are very real and important and provide the refreshment with which the faculty members turn back to the problems which must occupy their attention.

General Reflections

What also stands out clearly from the recordings is the apparently limitless capacity the faculty members had to be intrigued in their work and to learn much from it that was relevant to future courses and to larger issues.

Informally and unpredictably, the faculty meetings ranged over what was immediate to what was distant, what was personal to one member in the course to what threw light on the kind of community he came from, what had happened that day in the discussion to the personal basis within himself from which the faculty member responded. In these meetings the faculty members stretched and exercised their capacities, explored and examined their own limits and practiced their ability to work as equals, as cooperative people, as people able and inclined to reflect and to learn from their experience. Essentially they could only communicate to the members the value of care by themselves caring, of cooperation by themselves cooperating, of learning and developing oneself by themselves learning and developing as persons. In the faculty meetings the faculty members had the same unified experience that they sought to provide for the members in the course.

Reading 10.2

ORGANIZATIONAL HEALTH OF A TRAINING INSTITUTION*

Matthew B. Miles

Organizational health can be seen as a set of fairly durable *second-order* system properties, which tend to transcend short-run effectiveness. A healthy organization in this sense not only survives in its environ-

---

Abridged from Matthew B. Miles, "Planned Change and Organizational Health: Figure and Ground," in R. O. Carlson *et al., Change Processes in the Public Schools* (Eugene, Ore.: Center for the Advanced Study of Educational Administration, 1965), pp. 11–36. The paper was originally written to refer to *any* organization. It has been abridged and slightly adapted to be clearly relevant to the special case of "training institutions."

ment but continues to cope adequately over the long haul and continuously develops and extends its surviving and coping abilities. Short-run operations on any particular day may be effective or ineffective, but continued survival, adequate coping, and growth are taking place.

A *steadily* ineffective organization would presumably not be healthy; on balance, "health" implies a summation of effective short-run coping. But notice that an organization *may* cope effectively in the short run (as for example by a speed-up or a harsh cost-cutting drive), but at the cost of longer run variables, such as those noted below. The classic example, of course, is an efficiency drive which cuts short-run costs and results in long-run labor dissatisfaction and high turnover.

To illustrate in more detail what is meant by "second-order property," here is a list of 10 dimensions of organizational health that seem plausible to me. Many of them are drawn by heuristic analogy from the behavior of persons or small groups; this does *not* mean, of course, that organizations necessarily are precisely homologous to persons or groups—only that thinking in this way may get us somewhere on what, it must be admitted, is a very complex problem indeed.

The first three dimensions are relatively "tasky," in that they deal with organizational goals, the transmission of messages, and the way in which decisions are made.

1. *Goal focus.* In a healthy organization, the goal (or more usually goals) of the system would be reasonably clear to the system members, and reasonably well accepted by them.[1] This clarity and acceptance, however, should be seen as a necessary but insufficient condition for organizational health. The goals must also be *achievable* with existing or available resources and be *appropriate*—more or less congruent with the demands of the environment. The last feature may be most critical.

2. *Communication adequacy.* Since organizations are not simultaneous face-to-face systems like small groups, the movement of information within them becomes crucial. This dimension of organizational health implies that there is relatively distortion-free communication

---

[1] Note that the question of actual goal achievement as such is here conceived of as separate, analytically speaking, from the question of organizational health. Argyris has suggested that organizational effectiveness, a concept resembling the health notion, resides in the organization's ability to (1) achieve goals, (2) maintain itself internally, (3) engage in adaptation processes with the environment—and to accomplish these three "core activities" at a constant or increasing level of effectiveness, given the same or decreasing increments in energy input (Chris Argyris, *Integrating the Individual and the Organization* [New York: John Wiley & Sons, Inc., 1964], p. 123). This three-way scheme is also used in the present discussion.

"vertically," "horizontally," and across the boundary of the system to and from the surrounding environment. That is, information travels reasonably well—just as the healthy person "knows himself" with a minimum level of repression, distortion, etc. In the healthy organization, there is good and prompt sensing of internal strains; there are enough data about problems of the system to ensure that a good diagnosis of system difficulties can be made. People have the information they need, and have gotten it without exerting undue efforts, such as moseying up to the superintendent's secretary, reading the local newspaper, or calling excessive numbers of special meetings.

3. *Optimal power equalization.* In a healthy organization the distribution of influence is relatively equitable. Subordinates (if there is a formal authority chart) can influence upward, and even more important, they perceive that their boss can do likewise with *his* boss. In such an organization, intergroup struggles for power would not be bitter, though intergroup conflict (as in every human system known to man) would undoubtedly be present. The basic stance of persons in such an organization, as they look up, sideways and down, is that of collaboration rather than explicit or implicit coercion. The units of the organization (persons in roles, work groups, etc.) would stand in an interdependent relationship to each other, with rather less emphasis on the ability of a "master" part to control the entire operation. The exertion of influence in a healthy organization would presumably rest on the competence of the influencer vis-à-vis the issue at hand, his stake in the outcome, and the amount of knowledge or data he has—rather than on his organizational position, personal charisma, or other factors with little direct relevance to the problem at hand.

These then are three "task-centered" dimensions of organizational health. A second group of three dimensions deals essentially with the internal state of the system, and its inhabitants' "maintenance" needs. These are resource utilization, cohesiveness, and morale.

4. *Resource utilization.* We say of a healthy person, that he is "working up to his potential." At the organization level, "health" would imply that the system's inputs, particularly the personnel, are used effectively. The overall coordination is such that people are neither overloaded nor idling. There is a minimal sense of strain, generally speaking (in the sense that trying to do something with a weak or inappropriate structure puts strain on that structure). In the healthy organization, people may be working very hard indeed, but they feel that they are not working against themselves or against the organization. The fit between people's own dispositions and the role demands of

the system is good. Beyond this, people feel reasonably "self actualized": they not only "feel good" in their jobs, but they have a genuine sense of learning, growing, and developing as persons in the process of making their organizational contribution.

5. *Cohesiveness.* We think of a healthy person as one who has a clear sense of identity; he knows who he is, underneath all the specific goals he sets for himself. Beyond this, he *likes himself;* his stance toward life does not require self-derogation, even when there are aspects of his behavior which are unlovely or ineffective. By analogy at the organization level, system health would imply that the organization knows "who it is." Its members feel attracted to membership in the organization. They want to stay with it, be influenced by it, and exert their own influence in the collaborative style suggested above.

6. *Morale.* The history of this concept in the social-psychological literature is so appalling that I hesitate to introduce it at all. The implied notion is one of well-being or satisfaction. Satisfaction is not enough for health, of course; a person may report feelings of well-being and satisfaction in his life, while successfully denying deep-lying hostilities, anxieties, and conflicts. Yet it still seems useful to evoke, at the organization level, the idea of morale: a summated set of individual sentiments, centering around feelings of well-being, satisfaction, and pleasure, as opposed to feelings of discomfort, unwished-for strain and dissatisfaction. In an *un*healthy system, life might be perceived rosily as "good," or as unabashedly bad; in a healthy organization it is hard to entertain the idea that the dominant personal response of organization members would be anything else than one of well-being.

Finally, there are four more dimensions of organizational health, which deal with growth and changefulness: the notions of innovativeness, autonomy, adaptation vis-à-vis the environment, and problem-solving adequacy.

7. *Innovativeness.* A healthy system would tend to invent new procedures, move toward new goals, produce new kinds of products, diversify itself, and become more rather than less differentiated over time. In a sense, such a system could be set to grow, develop, and change, rather than remaining routinized, and standard.

8. *Autonomy.* The healthy person acts "from his own center outward." Seen in a training or therapy group, for example, such a person appears nearly free of the need to submit dependently to authority figures *and* from the need to rebel and destroy symbolic fathers of any kind. A healthy organization, similarly, would not respond passively to

demands from the outside, feeling itself the tool of the environment, and it would not respond destructively or rebelliously to perceived demands either. It would tend to have a kind of independence from the environment, in the same sense that the healthy person, while he has transactions with others, does not treat their responses as *determinative* of his own behavior.

9. *Adaptation.*   The notions of autonomy and innovativeness are both connected with the idea that a healthy person, group, or organization is in realistic, effective contact with the surroundings. When environmental demands and organization resources do not match, a problem-solving, restructuring approach evolves in which *both* the environment and the organization become different in some respect. More adequate, continued coping of the organization, as a result of changes in the local system, the relevant portions of the environment, or more usually both, occurs. And such a system has sufficient stability and stress tolerance to manage the difficulties which occur during the adaptation process. Perhaps inherent in this notion is that the system's ability to bring about corrective change in itself is faster than the change cycle in the surrounding environment. Explanations for the disappearance of dinosaurs vary, but it is quite clear that in some way this criterion was not met.

10. *Problem-solving adequacy.*   Finally, any healthy organism— even one as theoretically impervious to fallibility as a computer— *always* has problems, strains, difficulties, and instances of ineffective coping. The issue is not the presence or absence of problems, therefore, but the *manner* in which the person, group, or organization copes with problems. Argyris[2] has suggested that in an effective system, problems are solved with minimal energy; they stay solved; and the problem-solving mechanisms used are not weakened, but maintained or strengthened. An adequate organization, then, has well-developed structures and procedures for sensing the existence of problems, for inventing possible solutions, for deciding on the solutions, for implementing them, and for evaluating their effectiveness. Such an organization would conceive of its own operations (whether directed outward to goal achievement, inward to maintenance, or inward-outward to problems of adaptation) as being *controllable.* We would see active coping with problems, rather than passive withdrawing, compulsive responses, scapegoating, or denial.

---

[2] Argyris, *op. cit.*

The Special Case of Educational Organizations

These dimensions can presumably be applied to any type of organization. Much of the theory and empirical data on which they are based was generated in industrial organizations where "organization improvement" programs have become more and more widespread in the last few years. But emphasis on the commonality of all types of organizations has tended to obscure the fact that educational systems have special properties which condition the propositions of organizational theory in reasonably predictable ways. What, then, are some of these properties?

1. *Goal ambiguity.* For many different reasons, it has seemed difficult to specify the output of educational organizations very precisely. Some of this is realistic: change in human beings is going on, with presumably cumulative effects over a long period of time. But part of this output measurement difficulty also seems to be a form of organizational defense or protection against criticism from the surrounding environment.

Whatever the reasons, supposed "unmeasureability" of organizational output (hence, of the effectiveness of particular role occupants) seems a fairly durable feature of educational organizations as we know them today.

This ambiguity and pseudo consensus around output measurement encourages the institutionalization and ossification of teaching procedures. If it cannot really be determined whether one course of action leads to more output than another, then why stop lecturing? There is a further consequence (stemming particularly from the unacknowledged but powerful custodial function of the school): rigid time and personnel allocations.

2. *Input variability.* Another, possibly unique, property of educational organizations is a very wide variation in input from the environment, particularly in relation to participants and personnel. The range of intellectual ability, interpersonal skill, and knowledge of subject matter among teachers is probably at least as great as that among pupils. This variability causes considerable stress in educational organizations and develops the need to provide teaching personnel with methods and procedures which are (in effect) teacherproof.

3. *Role performance invisibility.* Classrooms are in effect the production departments of the educational enterprise; in them trainers

work. Yet, this role performance is relatively invisible to status equals or superiors. Learners can observe, usually very acutely, the quality of a teacher's execution of his role, but they are not allowed to comment on this, and have few, if any, sanctions to bring to bear. Thus, rewards in the teaching profession seem relatively detached from others' estimates of one's performance; the average teacher gains most satisfaction from intrinsic properties of the role behavior involved. Teaching thus becomes a craft-like occupation, rather than a profession, and substitute criteria for teaching effectiveness, such as "interest of the kids," begin to appear and are used vigorously. Perhaps this is what teachers mean when they say it is not difficult to know when they are doing a good job.

4. *Low interdependence.* A further characteristic of educational organizations, when compared with thing-producing systems, seems to be a relatively low interdependence of parts. Teacher A's failure to teach anything to the participants affects the job-relevant behavior of Teacher B very little—except in a rather diffuse, blaming sense.

This low interdependence has several consequences. First, it tends to reinforce the pyramidal "man-to-man" style of supervision which Likert[3] and others have shown to be inimical to organizational effectiveness.

The reported stresses and strains in most accounts of team teaching—an attempt to increase interdependence in educational organizations—are mute testimony to the strength with which "separatist" norms have become institutionalized.

High interdependence is not without its difficulties, of course. The classical division of industrial organizations into specialized departments tends to promote hostility, competitiveness, and disjunction between the authority system and other aspects of the organization such as communication patterns, friendship relationships, and work flow. An alternative organization model has been suggested, involving the existence of "product division," each of which contains in it all the specialties necessary to undertake an operation such as buying materials for, producing, and marketing a washing machine. Schools are organized in a product division manner, in effect. But the suggestion—this is crucial—depends on the existence of simple, rapidly available output measures, so that the performance of a product division can be monitored. As we have seen, the absence of such measures—and more fundamentally, the belief that

---

[3] Rensis Likert, *New Patterns of Management* (New York: McGraw-Hill Book Co., 1961).

they can never be produced—is a serious barrier to the effectiveness of educational organizations.

5. *Vulnerability.* Educational institutions are subject to control, criticism, and a wide variety of "legitimate" demands from the surrounding environment: everyone is a stockholder. To the system inhabitants, the organizational skin seems extremely thin. Many kinds of ingenious defenses are adopted to solve this problem. This state of affairs represents a serious failure of adaptation skills of organizations and tends to reduce autonomy sharply.

6. *Lay-professional control problems.* Many educational institutions are governed by laymen. Even where the board is "well trained" and leaves the execution of policy to the administration, notice that the question of *educational policy* determination still remains a moot one.

And there are internal lay-professional problems as well. In many respects, the administrator may find himself far behind the capabilities of particular trainers (in terms of expert knowledge)—and he is in this sense a layman as well. The problems of organizations with high proportions of professionals have been studied vigorously (for example, hospitals and research organizations); I only wish to indicate here that the fruits of such study so far have found little application in educational institutions.

7. *Low technological investment.* Lastly, it seems very clear that the amount of technology per worker in institutions is relatively low. From 60% to 90% of an educational institution's budget ordinarily goes to salary, with a fraction for equipment and materials. Even if we count buildings as "technological investment," the picture is rather different from that in most industries. This has consequences: social transactions, rather than sociotechnical transactions, come to be the major mode of organizational production. Because of this, it is possible that education has never made it out of the folk culture stage. And we are back once again to goal ambiguity and its problems.

These, then, strike me as special strains, ways in which educational organizations as such depart from the generalized model of organizational health outlined earlier. In sum, I would suggest that, in terms of the dimensions above, the major difficulties to be expected would center around goal focus (as a consequence of goal ambiguity); difficulties in communication adequacy and power equalization stemming from low interdependence; and perhaps most centrally, failures in innovativeness autonomy adaptation, and problem-solving adequacy, because of vulnerability and lay-professional conflict.

The Induction of Organizational Health

By now a fair amount of experience exists, drawn from the interesting blend of consultation and research in which an increasing number of behavioral scientists now find themeslves involved, primarily with industrial organizations. These methods can perhaps most usefully be considered as *interventions* in the ongoing life of a system; this term implies an action which interferes with or reorients processes—either pathological or normal—ordinarily occurring in the system. A trainer's intervention in a participant's problem solving serves to reorient his thinking; perhaps more importantly, it can aid him to mobilize his own energies more effectively. Thus the usual aim of an intervention is to start internal change processes going in the system at hand, rather than only causing an immediate change. Below are described six interventions aimed at improving organization health.

1. *Team training.* In this approach, the members of an intact work group meet for a period of several days away from their offices, with consultant help. They examine their own effectiveness as a problem-solving team, the role of each member in the group and how it affects the group and the person himself, and the operations of the group in relation to its organizational environment. This problem solving may be based on fairly careful prior data collection from individuals as to their views on the current problems of the system; these data are summarized and form the beginning of the group's agenda. Occasionally, exercises and theoretical material on group and organization functioning may be supplied by the outside consultant.

Under these circumstances, the members of the group usually improve in their abilities to express feelings directly, and to listen to—and understand—each other. Communication adequacy is thus considerably increased. The members also deal with internal conflicts in the team, and learn to solve problems more effectively as a unit, thus presumably increasing their ability to meet the demands placed upon them by other parts of the system. Over a period of time, beginning with the top decision-making group of the system, this intervention may be repeated with other groups as well. Industrial programs of this sort have been described by Argyris[4] and Blake and Mouton.[5]

---

[4] Chris Argyris, *Interpersonal Competence and Organizational Effectiveness* (Homewood, Ill.: Dorsey Press, 1962).

[5] Robert Blake and Jane S. Mouton, *The Managerial Grid* (Houston, Texas: Gulf Publishing Co., 1966).

2. *Survey feedback.* In this approach, data bearing on attitudes, opinions, and beliefs of members of a system are collected via a questionnaire. An external researcher summarizes the data for the organization as a whole and for each of a number of relevant work groups. Each work group, under the guidance of its own superior, and perhaps with consultant help, examines its own summarized data, in comparison with those for the organization as a whole. The group makes plans for change stemming from these discussions and carries them out. The focus of this intervention is on many or all of the work groups within a total setting. The aim is to free up communication, leading to goal clarification and problem-solving work. The relative objectification involved in looking at data helps to reduce feelings of being misunderstood and isolated, and makes problems more susceptible to solution, rather than retaining them as a focus for blaming, scapegoating, griping, and so on. For an account of survey feedback procedure, see Mann;[6] Gage[7] has tried a similar approach effectively with student-to-teacher feedback and is now studying teacher-to-principal feedback.

3. *Role workshop.* Sometimes called the "horizontal slice" meeting, this intervention involves all the people in a particular role (for example, *elementary* principal). They fill out research instruments dealing with role expectations which various others hold for them, the fit between their own wishes and these expectations, their actual role performance, etc. These data are summarized, and form the vehicle for a series of activities (discussion, role practice, decision-making exercises, problem solving, and so on) at a workshop attended by all the people in the role. The main focus here is on role clarity, effectiveness, and improved fit between the person and the role. By sharing common role problems, people occupying the role may develop alternative solutions which result in better performance of that role and more "self-actualized" operation in general.

4. *"Target setting" and supporting activities.* In this approach, periodic meetings are held between a superior and each of his subordinates, separately. In an institution this might involve a principal and his trainers. The work of each subordinate is reviewed in relation to organizational and personal goals, and the superior and subordinate agree collaboratively on new targets for the subordinate's work and personal

---

[6] F. C. Mann, "Studying and Creating Change," in W. G. Bennis, K. D. Benne, and R. Chin, *The Planning of Change: Readings in the Applied Behavioral Sciences* (New York: Holt, Rinehart & Winston, Inc., 1961), pp. 605–15.

[7] N. L., Gage, "A Method for 'Improving' Teacher Behavior," *Journal of Teacher Education,* Vol. XIV, No. 3 (1963), pp. 261–66.

development. These "targets" are in turn reviewed after some work time (usually six months or so) has elapsed. During that period, other activities such as role meetings, consultation, self-operated data collection, academic courses, and workshops, may be engaged in by the subordinate to develop needed skills and understandings as he works toward the collaboratively set goals. The focus of attention here is the working relationship between superior and subordinate, and the degree to which they are together able to help the subordinate grow and develop on the job. Improved trust, feelings of support, better and more satisfying role performance, and more open communication usually result. Zander[8] has reviewed thoroughly the problems and values of performance appraisal, including commentary on the target-setting approach.

5. *Organizational diagnosis and problem-solving.* This intervention involves a residential meeting of members of an intact work group, usually at the top of the organization (or in small organizations, up to size 40–50, the entire work force). They meet for several days to identify problems facing the system, and the reasons for the existence of these; to invent possible solutions; to decide on needed system changes; and to plan implementation of these through regular channels and newly constructed ones. The procedure differs from team training as described above in that relatively less attention is given to team relationships and interpersonal effectiveness as such and more to system problems in the large. The main focus of attention is on the organization and its current functioning. The improvement of problem-solving activity and communication adequacy are typical results. For an account of two such meetings conducted with an industrial organization, see Zand, Miles, and Lytle.[9]

6. *Organizational experiments.* In this approach, a major organizational variable of interest is changed *directly,* by agreement of the responsible administrators and needed implementation efforts. One such approach is described vividly by Morse and Riemer.[10] In several divisions of a large organization, the level of decision making was moved radically downward, thus giving more autonomy to subordinates; in

---

[8] A. Zander (ed.), *Performance Appraisals: Effects on Employees and Their Performance* (Ann Arbor, Mich.: Foundation for Research on Human Behavior, 1963).

[9] D. Zand, M. G. Miles, and W. O. Lytle, Jr., "Organizational Improvement through Use of a Temporary Problem-Solving System," in D. E. Zand and P. C. Buchanan (eds.), *Organization Development: Theory and Practice* (forthcoming).

[10] N. Morse and E. Reimer, "The Experimental Change of a Major Organizational Variable," *Journal of Abnormal Social Psychology,* Vol. LXII (1956), pp. 120–29.

several other divisions the level of decision making was moved up; and in several divisions no change was made. Such an approach requires the careful collection of pre-post data, and the use of control groups in order to test the consequences of the change. The halo of "experiment" is an aid to acceptance, since the arrangement is seen as not only temporary, but scientific, and responsibly managed. Such an approach ordinarily includes a feedback stage, in which the results are examined carefully and implications for the continuing functioning of the organization drawn.

These then are six possible approaches to the induction of organizational health. Certain common threads appear to flow through all of them.

1. *Self-study.*   These approaches reject the "technocratic" change model involving the recommendations of a detached expert, and actively involve the system itself in what might be called organizational introspection. The same holds true for approaches involving group self-study for various teams in the organization, and personal introspection and reexamination by role occupants.

In common with the action research movement in education, these approaches also carry the assumption that an operant stance on the part of the organization is both theoretically and practically preferable to the problems involved in dependence on outsiders for system change.

2. *Relational emphasis.*   These approaches do not conceive of the organization as a collection of jobs with isolated persons in them, but as a network of groups and role relationships; it is the functioning of these groups and relationships, as such, which requires examination and self-operated, experimental alteration. The aim is not to ferret out and change the "attitude" of old-fogy Principal A, but to focus on the relationships and group settings in which Principal A's attitudes are evoked.

3. *Increased data flow.*   These approaches all involve the heightening or intensification of communication, especially vertically, but also diagonally and horizontally. New feedback loops are often built in to the existing system. The use of status-equalizing devices such as intensive residential meetings also encourages fuller and freer flow of information through channels which may have been blocked or have always carried distorted messages.

4. *Norms as a change target.*   By focusing on groups and relationships, and increasing data flow, these approaches have the effect of altering existing norms which regulate interpersonal transactions in the organization. If, for example, a work group where the norms are "play

it close to the vest, and don't disagree with the boss" engages in a team training session, it is quite likely—since all group members have participated in the experience—that norms such as "be open about your feelings whether or not they tally with the boss's wishes" will develop. These approaches thus have a strong culture-changing component, based on intensive, data-based interaction with others.

5. *Temporary-system approach.* But norm changing is by definition very difficult under the usual pressures of day-to-day operation in the organization. "Business as usual" has to prevail. Most of the interventions described involve the use of residential meetings, which constitute a detached, "cultural island" approach to organizational introspection and self-correction. They are in effect temporary systems, where new norms can develop, and where, given the suspension of the usual pressures, meaningful changes can be made in the structure and functioning of the permanent system.

6. *Expert facilitation.* All of these interventions also include the presence of a semidetached consultant figure, whose main functions are to facilitate, provoke, and support the efforts of the system to understand itself, free up communication, and engage in more adequate problem-solving behavior. The outsider role, however, is seen as impermanent; it is only associated with the system during the actual period of the intervention itself. If the intervention is successful, the organization itself continues the self-corrective processes which have been begun by the intervention.

Whether or not these interventions, drawn from work with thing-producing organizations, can be used plausibly with people-processing organizations such as schools is an interesting question, in any case.

It might be useful to point out in conclusion that the position taken in this paper is *not* that an organization must necessarily be brought to a state of perfect health before it can engage in any meaningful short-run innovative projects at all. Rather we feel it is quite likely that the very act of carrying out small-scale projects in planned change can undoubtedly strengthen the health of an educational organization—but only if *direct attention is paid concurrently to the state of the organization.* The basic innovative project, we believe, must be one of organization development itself.

Chapter 11

Action Research for the Trainer

Some Questions for Trainers to Study

Some Steps for Action

Figure

Readings

Research to Promote Training

ʕʕʕʕʕʕʕʕʕʕʕʕʕʕʕʕʕʕʕʕʕʕʕʕʕʕʕʕʕʕʕʕʕ

"Perfect as is the wing of a bird, it never could raise the bird up without resting on air. Facts are the air of a scientist. Without them you never can fly. . . .

"But learning, experimenting, observing, try not to stay on the surface of the facts. Do not become the archivists of facts. Try to penetrate to the secret of their occurrence, persistently search for the laws which govern them.

—*Pavlov's Bequest to the Academic Youth
of Soviet Russia,* February 27, 1936

TRAINING FOR DEVELOPMENT has been addressed primarily to the practicing trainer. He is engaged in the challenging task of increasing the effectiveness of organizations through developing the people working in them. A practitioner, yes, but not thereby an amateur. On the contrary, our theme throughout has been that training is a profession with goals and methods—and ethics—that can be stated and generally deserve recognition and respect.

We have supported the theme on two pillars. One pillar is our experience of developing, administering, and conducting a variety of training programs, and the experiences of others. From this have come the illustrations and examples to make the theme come alive with the kind of signs that practitioners recognize as their language. But the second pillar is important, too, and deserves particular attention because it tends to be neglected, even in this age of science. This pillar is research and onward study. From research in training and education, and the wider field of the social sciences, have come the concepts and theories, the framework, for ordering the myriad experiences and making them serve a general purpose. Research, too, is essential to a profession, the part that goads continuous improvements in practice, such as high professional standards demand.

If trainers in the time-honored tradition of practitioners impatiently brush aside the idea that research deserves their attention, indeed, as we will urge, that they themselves carry out this research, research workers are in part to blame. All too often research connotes the esoteric and impractical. This is not what we mean. By research, we mean, in the first place, a wish for improvement followed by action. But this action, second, is not off the cuff or based only on a hunch or on intuition. Intuition has its place: at the creative moment where research has as yet nothing to say, yet action has to be taken into the unknown. It is a moving frontier, the frontier of knowledge that we want trainers to engage themselves to push back, further and further. Research is systematic action to enhance knowledge and understanding. Its essence is not that it be abstract and erudite but that it be systematic and planned. We would like to end this book on the note of improving training continuously through research.

The formulations we have presented in this book are valid, at best, for now. If they inspired training generally, it would surely be more effective and economical than it is. But beyond that, there is always more to know to improve training strategies and methods, and more to understand about how training plays its part in general designs for development.

Maybe research will look more practical if we consider several levels short of high-level abstractions, rigorous hypotheses, and statistical models. These can be left to the specialist, though even these are safe with him only if the questions which he addresses are rooted deep down in practice. At the other, most practical, end of the range is the research into individual experience that we usually call reflection. What happened then? Why? How shall I try to do better next time? What indicators are there by which I can assess my progress? These are questions for this level of "research." As we saw earlier, reflection like this makes the difference between a passing event and an experience. And practitioners are quite right: we learn only from experience.

The next level of research looks for data beyond an immediate experience to the experiences also of other people and similar experiences in the past. It seeks to generalize more widely, notes uniformities. It tends beyond individual learning towards checking and sharing with others.

The third level of research starts with extracting from these more or less tentative uniformities some experiments which they suggest. Nothing very rigorous yet, perhaps, but essentially akin to testing a hypothesis: What will happen if in that situation, I do *x?* I rather think the result will be *y.* I will try it and see.

ACTION-RESEARCH FOR THE TRAINER

Improvement comes out of a concerted effort to face squarely the questions needing to be answered, to search systematically for answers to such questions, to test the answers rigorously, and to accept the tested solutions for action as the best now available, and as a basis for further search if necessary. This approach requires a new kind of discipline on the part of the trainer, one to use side by side with his intuition guided by experience. It is the discipline of action research, research to improve action.

Action research is a way of approaching problems or questions. Four beliefs underlie action research:

1. Solutions of problems are more effective and enduring when they come out of systematic search for them rather than from the dictates of authorities or the practitioner's intuition alone.
2. Research done by practitioners themselves on problems they face contributes more to the solution of these problems than does research done by others.
3. Research consists in analyzing problems, searching for solutions, and testing and evaluating solutions. It consists of skills which can be learned and developed by every practitioner. Research is not the prerogative of an expert.
4. Development of people's capacities, for example, through training, is basic to improvement in practices.

Action research is the scientific way of problem solving and involves the same steps: identification and focusing of the problem, diagnosis for probable causes, selection of one or a few causal relationships for the formulation of hypotheses, formulation of an action hypothesis which can be tested, designing an action plan based on the hypothesis, evaluation of the action, and generalization or formulation of further questions. It grows into a feedback system for the practicing trainer. Starting on a minimal basis of self-motivation to improve by searching for answers to a question, skills in problem analysis, and a favorable organizational climate, trainers engaged in action research find these prerequisites growing stronger in the process.

Trainers who lack the essential minimum research skills will find that acquiring them involves more diligence than difficulty. The readings following this chapter further describe action research and outline a short training program for developing the necessary skills.

The complete feedback model of action research is shown in Figure 11.1.

Figure 11.1

FEEDBACK MODEL OF ACTION RESEARCH

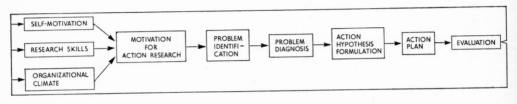

SOME QUESTIONS FOR TRAINERS TO STUDY

Below is a short list of questions that seem to us to call for research by trainers, and lend themselves to action research. They are illustrative only; many more could be listed. They are ordered in the sequence of the book and so allow us to walk over the same ground again—with questions.

GENERAL

1. What are the different uses of the word training? What are the implications of each for (*a*) training practice, and (*b*) organizational development?
2. How can the costs of training be calculated accurately? Direct and indirect cost? Cost per session? Above all, cost of what result?
3. When is an organization ready for training? What are the characteristics of a client system likely to benefit most from training?
4. What happens to the participant during the training? What is a useful model of a participant learning? For example:

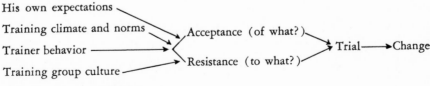

THE PRETRAINING PHASE

1. What are the ratios of people benefiting and not benefiting from training? It seems in general about ⅓ do not benefit at all, about ⅓ benefit much, about ⅓ benefit to a limited extent. How are these ratios in fact operating?
2. What are useful indicators of individual readiness for training? Which kind of training, when, and under what conditions? Do people ready for

training have distinct clusters of personality characteristics? Expectations? Motivation? How can we measure these? How can we spot such people?

3. What are useful indicators of individual "unreadiness" for training?
4. How might trainers deal with those who are in the category of "not likely to benefit"? Any special pretraining work? Special work with them during the training period?
5. What can be done to "prepare" (pretraining work) participants for a training program? Feedback on behavior? Pretraining laboratories? Shifting responsibility for selection to participant, i.e., voluntary versus nominated participation?
6. What is the role of the participant's organization in pretraining work? Does the role vary according to the type of organization?

TRAINING STRATEGIES

1. Which strategies can be effectively combined? For what purposes? With what stresses?
2. What are the lead times for introducing specific strategies? What is the minimum concentration of skilled trainers, etc. for changes in strategy?

ESTABLISHING TRAINING NEEDS

1. What methods are most effective for working out specifications for which jobs?
2. How can training needs for an organizational change be assessed? By what methods, and how can we evaluate their effectiveness?

TRAINING METHODS

1. Different methods and their effectiveness: Under what conditions are particular methods effective?
2. What training sequences are most effective for what purpose?
3. Research questions in each method: For example, what are the purposes and places of field experiences in training? Is field training effective when it is concentrated? Or phased? When?

DEVELOPING THE PROGRAM

1. Program mix: which sequences are most effective? Blocks? Parallel series?
2. How much flexibility is required in different programs? How can it be provided effectively and efficiently?
3. How can outside part-time resources be integrated in the program?

TRAINING GROUP

1. Group composition: Within what ranges of age and experience can participants be effectively combined for training? For what purposes? What methods?
2. What are the cycles or phases in the development of a training group? How can the maturity of the training group be measured? How enabled to develop at certain stages?

THE TRAINER

1. What values in the trainer contribute to what kinds of behavior in the participants?
2. What are the different roles of a trainer? What are the role congruencies? Role conflicts?
3. What different systems of expectations is a trainer expected to meet and how can he be helped to integrate these into his perception of his own role?
4. How are role conflicts resolved? Adequate and inadequate coping mechanisms for the resulting stress?

THE POSTTRAINING PHASE

1. How can the participant be helped to avoid or offset losses in transferring new learnings from the training to the work situation?
2. How can the training institution assess more accurately the effects of training on (*a*) the participant and his growth, (*b*) the use of new knowledge by the organization, (*c*) the range and speed of changes of various kinds?
3. What are effective roles that the training institution can play to support changes produced by training in different kinds of organizations?
4. What are the various methods and their comparative effectiveness of involving the organization in posttraining work?

THE TRAINING INSTITUTION

1. What are effective role mixes for trainers and how can the institution organize itself for their systematic performance?
2. What are effective specializations within the training institution? For example, administration and training? Training and services?
3. What contributes a favorable climate for change in an institution? What are the advance indications of climatic change?
4. What are the phases in the life of an institution? The crises? Dilemmas? How are these generally resolved? Effective and ineffective behavior? by whom?
5. What are effective ways of building and maintaining morale in training institutions?
6. What are effective institutional supports for action research? How can they be built into (*a*) new (*b*) existing situations?

SOME STEPS FOR ACTION

Let us say that a trainer has chosen a question for action research. The next step is to keep on working, open-eyed and attentive to detail, and to record data about problematical experiences in meticulous detail: quantitative facts (for example, how many participants borrowed books from the evening library), and also qualitative facts (for example, about human relationships and feelings; sequences and other linkages of facts; records of meetings, dialogues; anything, in short, that may throw light on the problem in hand). As he begins to record experiences in detail, the trainer will notice his world enlarge, as if the courtesy of his attention brought to life many aspects of the problem which had not existed for him before. He will also feel his capacities for observing, listening, and recording expand with practice, and along with them, his sense of being more fully alive. A generally questioning attitude develops and may become a general trait of his, and a whole lot of things will become interesting all around.

The trainer will need this curiosity to strengthen him for the rigor and discipline and, be it said, often troublesome routine of collecting data of sufficient quality, quantity, regularity, and duration to light up the problem. This is the second step. Sound evidence is needed at all steps of problem solving, right from the step of problem identification. Indeed, with awesome regularity important known problems of long standing are redefined in the light of evidence accumulated for problem identification. Then, at every stage, evidence is needed to evaluate the effectiveness of an action, even if it be the action of collecting more data. General impressions by themselves are not reliable enough for detailed action, certainly not for significant evaluation.

One series of steps then takes the trainer toward collecting adequate data for analysis and understanding. Another series takes him toward increasingly close relationships with his colleagues, and also beyond the institution. Action research ideas, designs, the formulation of hypotheses and methods, all profit from frank examination with colleagues. More basically, many problems that call for action research extend beyond the preview and competence of a single trainer. Our list has numerous examples of this general trend. Worthwhile research results and processes, finally, should be shared.

The institution's primary contribution to action research is a favorable climate. The crucial evidence for the existence of this climate is the allocation in plans and budgets of regular and substantial time on research by trainers. Additional resources are secondary and often minor, and can never take the place of professional time. Further evidence of the climate is the respect and advancement offered to trainers who keep on improving themselves and their training practice through research.

All through this book we have seen the effective trainer as the kind of person he wants the participant to become. His engagement in action research is one more aspect of this theme. He, too, the trainer, must be involved in a permanent process of learning, of *becoming*. So he becomes part—and a changing, growing part—of the life he studies and influences.

Reading 11.1

THE PROCESS OF ACTION RESEARCH*

Udai Pareek and Adarsh Khanna

Action research is an attempt to help the practitioners develop scientific ways of thinking and acting and to seek actions that will result in the improvement of practices.

The main purpose of research is to discover facts that bear upon a problem and to find answers to one or more aspects of the problem in the light of the facts discovered. Research falls on a continuum of human thinking involving the processes of problem solving. Research can be viewed as an attempt to make human thinking on problem solving more objective, more scientific, and more systematic. Assuming such a continuum, the question is where research begins, and on what basis a particular study can be distinguished as a research study from a common-sense approach to problem solving. Research has now acquired a definite connotation. Even if we adopt the various processes involved in problem solving and arrive at correct solutions of the problems, we cannot claim to be doing research. The practical answer to the question where action research begins and at what point of continuum it can be demarcated from common-sense thinking on problem solving can be given in terms of awareness of the processes involved on the part of the researchers. If the various processes are consciously used and perfected for the solution of a particular problem, we can say that research is being undertaken; but if the various processes are being used unknowingly and the person is not aware of them, we cannot say that he is doing research. This is a practical answer to a rather fruitless point of discussion and does not in any sense minimize the value of attempts made at problem solving by persons without being aware of the processes involved. Such attempts may be highly valuable and useful. But to

---

* Abridged and adapted from Udai Pareek and Adarsh Khanna, "Action Research in Education," *Shiksha*, Vol. XIV (July 1961), pp. 131–55.

avoid confusion, the term research should be used only for the efforts which are made consciously by the individuals concerned.

The procedure of action research is developed mainly with a view to helping in finding out solutions for some problems and in evaluating the effectiveness of those solutions. Various steps are involved in the process of problem solving, which is the basic process in research. The same steps are involved in action research also. These steps should lead steadily to the solution of the problem and should help the practitioner in assessing the progress on the action to be undertaken.

The various steps in the process of action research may, for convenience, be stated as follows:

1. Dissatisfaction with the present state of affairs.
2. Identification of a problem area.
3. Identification of specific difficulty to be eliminated.
4. Formulation and imaginative testing of a hypothesis.
5. Choice of a hypothesis.
6. Design of action for testing the hypothesis.
7. Evaluation of effects.
8. Generalization.

Need for Change

It is necessary that the practitioner feels an urgent need for change in his practice. He should be dissatisfied with the existing practices. The attitude of complacency comes in the way of research.

Problem Selection

When the practitioners are dissatisfied about their current practices, they will see a need for change. This leads to the selection of a problem area. They could be helped to identify the problem area. This requires training. While identifying a problem area, diagnosis has to be made of the various difficulties facing them. Several ways can be adopted in helping the identification of the problem area. Sometimes individual conferences may be necessary, and sometimes group meetings are needed. It is always useful to identify a problem area in terms of difficulties rather than in terms of goals, because awareness of difficulties is often sharper than awareness of goals.

After the broad problem area has been identified, there is need to sharpen and focus the problem. Global problems cannot be attacked easily. It is necessary to break the broad problem into specific problems that can be taken up for research. For this purpose various criteria may be used, for example, the problem should be real and not imaginary, be important to the practitioner, be simple and well defined, be concerned with the practitioner, and require simple tools for its solution.

It is necessary to analyze the problem carefully in order to focus on it and sharpen it. For this purpose preliminary evidence may have to be collected about the existence of the problem. Sometimes the evidence collected reveals the problem in quite a different way. Continuous questioning regarding the various aspects of the problem may be useful. The problem should be discussed in causative terms. A number of causes for a particular difficulty may be thought about and taken down. The problem when focused upon should be precise; it should be neither too broad nor too narrow. If it is too broad, a good research design cannot be prepared; if it is too narrow, research becomes spurious. The pinpointing or bringing the problem into focus is not easy, as accepted patterns of thinking get in the way of correct analysis of the problem. The only useful way of analysis is continuous questioning and fact gathering.

Search for Hypotheses

When a problem is pinpointed and brought into focus, a number of possible solutions emerge in the mind. It is useful to think of various hypotheses in this way. When a number of hypotheses are framed, it is necessary to weigh them, to see their pros and cons. A preliminary investigation and collection of evidence may sometimes be needed for the imaginary testing of the hypotheses. The various resources available should be fully utilized for this purpose. If research consultants or advisers are easily available, they may be consulted at this stage.

Choice of a Hypothesis

After the imaginary testing of the hypotheses, only one hypothesis or a few hypotheses are selected so that they can be tested through the research design easily. Here, also, a number of criteria may be considered and evolved. It may, for example, be necessary to see that the hypothesis chosen is important enough, is easy to implement, is simple, takes into account the resources available, does not conflict with the established patterns of organizational norms, does not involve much expenditure, does not interfere with the routine activities of the practitioners much, and is concrete and precise.

Design of Action

Once the most promising hypothesis has been selected, the details of testing the hypothesis in terms of research and action program may be formulated. Sometimes a difficulty arises because we want to solve problems in the simplest way and we do not want to take up research seriously. It is necessary to work out details of the design of action, in defined steps with time targets, if possible. While working out such details, various important elements have to be controlled. Various new techniques will have to be used, and it would, therefore, be necessary to provide training to the participants in the use of such new methods. Importance of human relations cannot be overstressed in this connection. From time to time expert consultation may be needed for making simple research methods and statistical techniques comprehensible to the practitioners.

Evaluation

Evaluation is an important aspect, since it shows to what extent the research plan has been successful. It is necessary to use simple methods to measure change. The main aim of action research program is to make a change in the current practices. It is necessary to find out how far this change has been in the desired direction.

Generalizations

It is quite natural that the results achieved in a particular research program are generalized. We tend to think about similar problems in the same way. The question of generalization in action research is an intricate question. Generalization for a practitioner may imply that he would apply the results achieved in a particular research program with some confidence to his future work. Three kinds of generalizations have been distinguished: generalization about a single individual, about characteristics of a group of individuals, and about administrative and instructional procedures. These are differentiated by the referent for the generalization—an individual, a group of individuals, or an administrative practice. It has been suggested that generalizations are made at two major levels—generalization as to the event and the possibility of its occurrence, and generalization as to the degree of relationship that exists between any two or more factors and variables. The first is roughly the concept of reliability and the second roughly the concept of causation. Generalizations in a simple way may be taken to mean generalizations applicable to the future groups with whom the practitioner works.

Reading 11.2

WORKSHOP FOR ACTION RESEARCH TRAINERS*

Stephen M. Corey and Udai Pareek

This short paper is addressed to those trainers who want to provide a certain kind of in-service training for educational practitioners. The kind of training we have in mind is to facilitate experimentation or research that is undertaken by individuals in order to improve their own professional practices. The training design we advocate for this purpose is the workshop. Whatever specific proposals we make are meant to be suggestive only, for one of the main advantages of the workshop is that participants in it are continuously involved in planning and implementing their own learning activities.

What Is Action Research?

Speaking very generally, there are two somewhat contrasting ways of trying to bring about improvements in school practices. One way involves having the expert, usually a superior, diagnose what is being done, decide what improvements are needed, tell the school practitioner what he must do, and then supervise him closely to see that he does it. The second way involves encouraging schoolteachers and administrators to take time to study their own problems and to experiment with more promising practices, materials, and methods. When such study and experimentation are relatively disciplined and obective and scientific, the school person who is trying to improve himself is engaging in action research. He is conducting research, in other words, to improve his own actions.

---

* Adapted from Stephen M. Corey and Udai Pareek, "The In-Service Training Action Research Workshop," *Journal of Education and Psychology* (1967, in press). Much of the contents of the paper are borrowed from Stephen M. Corey and Udai Pareek, "Planning an Action Research Workshop" (mimeographed; New Delhi: TCM Office, American Embassy, 1961).

Who Should Come to an Action Research Workshop?

We have the population of educational practitioners in our mind—teachers, administrators, supervisors—who volunteer to participate. Before doing so they must have the workshop's purposes and methods explained to them carefully. The workshop will be appreciably less effective if its members are deputed. We are assuming furthermore that each person volunteering to be a participant in the workshop will already have developed sufficient dissatisfaction with his own professional practices to want to work to improve them. In other words, he is aware of some teaching or administrative or supervisory difficulty that is interfering with his effectiveness and he is motivated to do something about it.

What Are the Major Purposes of the Action Research Workshop?

The workshop we have in mind and are describing has two central purposes. The first is to help the participants get experimentation under way in their own institutions—experimentation intended to make them more effective professional workers. For this experimentation to be more than trial and error; it must be subjected to some discipline. Learning how to be disciplined and objective and pay continuous attention to facts and evidence is the first task worked on in the workshop. The second function is to begin to teach the sensitivities, concepts, and skills that are required for successful small-group work. Most of the difficulties in an institution cannot be coped with successfully unless several of the persons involved in the difficulty work together cooperatively. If these cooperative efforts are to be maximally successful, the people engaged in them must be able to work *productively* in small, face-to-face, task-oriented groups.

What Preparations Should Precede the Workshop?

Such a workshop assumes that a great deal of planning and work have been done before the participants arrive. On the basis of their expressed interest, resulting from studying a carefully prepared memorandum describing the intended workshop, no more than 20 participants have been invited to attend. It is well to ask them to submit in advance the particular difficulty they plan to work on. This assures some preliminary thinking. Plans for convening the workshop on the campus of a well-known training institution or a college or a university, under the general direction and chairmanship of someone who deals with problems of institutional change, must be completed. Facilities for the workshop, including a rather large classroom for general sessions and several places where small groups can work, as well as mimeographing and typing facilities, must be arranged for. It is well to have available a small library of references. There should be at least one consultant available full time—a person who is thoroughly familiar with action research procedures and problems. Members of the college or university teacher training faculty should be available on a part-time and "when needed" basis. The best possible living arrangements should be provided.

What Is the Role of an Action Research Consultant?

Every action research training workshop should have, as we have already stated, one full-time resource person who has had experience working with educational practitioners who want to undertake experimentation to improve their own practices. Generally, it is this consultant who will prepare the materials needed for the workshops, deliver the lecturettes, and arrange for the demonstrations and other training activities. This consultant will also be available for conferences with the participants regarding the problems they are facing as they plan their own action research projects. Members of the college or university faculty who are available for consultation should probably be expected to spend one or two hours each day conferring with the participants. They might benefit, too, from attendance at the general sessions of the workshop where action research procedures and small group work are talked about and demonstrated.

What Will Be the Variety of Workshop Activities?

One central intention of the workshop must be to demonstrate the benefits of action research in the operations of the workshop itself. The workshop small-group procedures must also demonstrate the best of such procedures. The very complexity of what it is the workshop is trying to accomplish should lead to wide variety of activities. Some of the more important of these activities are named and briefly explained below:

General Sessions.   General sessions are meetings of the entire workshop personnel, including the consultants. The main activity in most general sessions will be a lecturette-cum-discussion or a lecturette-cum-demonstration. During any single general session an attempt is made (*a*) to provide theory or conceptualization, (*b*) to demonstrate the application of the theory to practice, (*c*) to involve the participants in a discussion of what they have heard and seen, and (*d*) to provide an opportunity to raise questions with the consultants.

Small-Group Work. The total workshop group will frequently be divided into small groups for discussion or other purposes. It is almost always advantageous to keep these working groups small. One of the best arrangements to get serious work done is in groups of three (the triad). Part of the workshop will involve training the triads in order to improve the quality of the help each can give to and receive from the other two members.

Commitment Reports. It is usually desirable to conclude the workshop by having each participant describe to the others the experimentation he will engage in when he returns to his job. These reports not only enable all workshop participants to know what the others are planning to do. They also constitute something of a public pledge to do it which greatly increases the likelihood that the things learned at the workshop each day are evaluated.

Evaluation. In an effective workshop each day's activities are evaluated, and an attempt is made to modify the next day's activities in light of these evaluation data. This is best done by using, at the end of each day, some kind of simple "postmeeting evaluation" form or questionnaire which makes it easy for each participant to report the way he feels about the things that have been done during the day.

Follow-up. Specific and definite arrangements to follow up on the effects of the workshop as they extend into the future are always desirable. In other words, whoever is responsible for planning and staging the workshop makes a strenuous effort to be sure that what the participants plan to do is done. In this connection he attempts to provide continuing help to the participants as they try to get their experimentation under way. It is much easier to plan under the stimulus of the workshop environment than it is to carry the plans out when the workshop is over and the participants have returned to their "back-home" working situations.

Practice Laboratory. The most effective in-service workshops provide participants with numerous opportunities to practice the skills they will need to make their experimentation successful. Arrangements are made actually to construct instruments for procurring evidence. Complicated human relation situations are "role-played" so as to get the feel of dealing with them. Instructional materials that are integral to the experimentation are prepared. The workshop, in other words, is much more than "talking about" experimentation.

What Might a Five-Day Action Research Workshop Schedule Look Like?

On the basis of their experience in several in-service training action research workshops the authors are suggesting below one pattern of activities for five consecutive daily sessions. Numerous modifications would, of course, be made in these suggestions in the case of any specific workshop. Many of these modifications would result from involving the participants in the planning of the session by session activities.

	9–12 Morning	*2–4 Afternoon*
First day	1. Opening ceremonies (brief) 2. Self-introductions giving name and position, nature of work "back home," expectations from the workshop 3. Clarification of workshop purposes 4. Lecturette-demonstration "Ways of Improving School Practices"	1. Lecturette "Action Research to Improve School Practices" 2. Small-group discussions 3. Panel interrogates lecturer 4. Statement of problems to be worked on and formation of small working groups 5. Lecturette "Giving and Receiving Help" 6. Election of a steering committee
Second day	1. Lecturette "Defining the Problem" 2. Demonstration of conference to "Help Define the Problem" 3. Lecturette "Criteria for Choosing a Focus for Experimentation" 4. Small-group work on problem definition and analysis 5. General session to give further consideration to major problems met in attempts to define focus	1. Lecturette "Getting Evidence of Change" 2. Small-group discussion of lecturette with spokesmen interrogating lecturer 3. Practice laboratory to prepare evidence—getting instruments 4. Small-group work on problem diagnosis 5. Reporting general session
Third day	1. Lecturette "The Action Hypothesis" 2. Demonstration of help giving in hypothesis 3. Lecturette "Criteria the Hypothesis Must Meet" 4. Small-group planning action researches	1. Lecturette "Measuring Attitudes" 2. Practice session: constructing an attitude scale 3. Discussion in general session of problems faced in attitude assessment
Fourth day	1. Lecturette "Measuring Overt Behavior" 2. Demonstration-cum-practice regarding measuring 3. Small-group work	1. Lecturette "Designing the Experiment" 2. Individual work putting plans in final form
Fifth day	1. Each participant presents his research plan and gets comments from other members of the workshop.	1. Overall workshop evaluation 2. Arrangements for follow up 3. Closing ceremonies

Index

Index

A

Academic strategy, 41
Action
  force as means of, 11–13
  knowledge in relation to, 5–7
  learning in relation to, 8–10
  training as means of, 11–13
Action-program strategy, 44, 45
Action research
  beliefs underlying, 385
  defined, 385, 390, 394
  design of action, 393
  evaluation, 393
  feedback model of, 386
  generalizations, 393, 394
  hypotheses, study of, 392
  hypothesis, choice of, 392
  levels of, 384, 385
  need for, 383, 384
  need for change, 391
  problem selection, 391, 392
  procedure in undertaking, 390, 391
  purpose of, 390
  questions calling for, 386–88
  steps in process of, 391
  steps taken by trainer in, 388–90
  workshop for trainers, 394
    activities of, 396, 397
    consultant's role, 396
    participation in, 395
    preparations preceding, 395, 396
    purposes of, 395
    schedule for five days of, 398
Activity strategy
  assumptions underlying, 43
  concept of, 42, 43
  pitfalls of, 43, 44
  updating of, 44
Alter ego, use of, 150, 151
Anxieties, 57
Assumptions underlying training, 4 ff.
  action in relation to knowledge, 5–7
  action in relation to learning, 8–10
  action through training or force, 11–13
  experience, 6, 7
  knowledge and action, 5–7
  learning, 7–10
  new concepts, 6

Assumptions underlying training—*Cont.*
  prevailing concepts, 6
  skill and experience, 7
Audience role playing, 151, 152

B

Behavior, development of norms or standards of, 231–33
Bell System study, 168
Benne, Kenneth, 299
Blue Monday, 110
Boredom, 134
Brainstorming, 136
Business games, 123–25; *see also* Role playing

C

Case method
  advantages of, 164
  degrees of identification, 164–66
  difficulty in preparation for, 130
  dramatized, 152
  fields used in, 165
  incident process, 128, 129
  instructor's task in, 167
  limitations in use of, 129, 130
  outline specifications of, 131
  preference for, 166
  purposes of, 128, 164
  selection of cases, guidance in, 166, 167
  trainer's role in, 129
  vicarious experiences, 128
  weakness of, 165
Change agent
  ambiguous, 294
  competence of, 295
  insecure, 294
  marginal, 293, 294
  professional, 293
  risky, 294
  role of, 293, 294
Change-inducing temporary system, 38, 39
Checklist for determining training needs, 86
Classroom
  conflict in, 252
    cultural values, 252
    personality, 252–55
    role expectations, 252, 253
  leadership in changing behavior, 254

401

*This book has been set in 12 point Garamond
No. 3, leaded 1 point, and 10 point Garamond
No. 3, leaded 2 points. Part numbers are in 30
point Garamond Bold with 66 point Weiss
Series I figures, and chapter numbers in 18 point
Garamond Bold. Part titles and chapter titles are
in 24 point Garamond Bold.*